## Weight
### Conversion Table

| Kilograms | Pounds |
|---|---|
| 0—7 kg | 0—16 lbs |
| 6—9.5 kg | 14—21 lbs |
| 9—12.5 kg | 20—28 lbs |
| 11.5—15 kg | 26—33 lbs |
| 14—18 kg | 31—40 lbs |
| 16.5—21.5 kg | 37—48 lbs |
| 20—24.5 kg | 45—55 lbs |
| 23—29 kg | 52—64 lbs |
| 28—36 kg | 62—80 lbs |
| 34—43 kg | 75—95 lbs |

## Clothing Size
### Conversion Chart

| Japanese size | Height in inches |
|---|---|
| 60 cm | 0–26″ |
| 70 cm | 26–30″ |
| 80 cm | 30–34″ |
| 90 cm | 34–38″ |
| 100 cm | 38–42″ |
| 110 cm | 42–46″ |
| 120 cm | 46–50″ |
| 130 cm | 50–53″ |
| 140 cm | 53–57″ |
| 150 cm | 57–61″ |

## Washing Instructions

| Symbol | Description |
|---|---|
| | Gentle wring or spin dry |
| 弱 40℃ | Machine washable (max. water temperature shown) |
| エンソ サラシ | Can use bleach |
| | Drip dry in the shade |
| | Use press cloth between iron and fabric |
| ドライ | Dry clean only |
| 手洗イ 30℃ | Hand washable (max. water temperature shown) |
| 高 | Iron (with high temperature) |
| 中 | Iron (with medium temperature) |
| 低 | Iron (with low temperature) |
| X | "X" over any symbol means that it should not be done |

# Japan for Kids

# Japan for Kids:
## The Ultimate Guide for Parents and Their Children

Diane Wiltshire
Jeanne Huey

KODANSHA INTERNATIONAL
Tokyo • New York • London

Note to the Reader

This edition of *Japan for Kids* has been completely revised. Thousand of changes were made to the existing material and a substantial amount of new material was added. Every attempt has been made by the authors and publisher to secure the latest details, but due to the sheer volume of information contained in these pages and the ever-changing dynamics of Tokyo, Japan, and the Internet, some facts may have changed yet again. Any comments or updates can be sent to the authors in care of the publisher or directly to Diane Wiltshire at 🖳 <Japan4kids@aol.com>, and will be added to subsequent printings.

Interior art by Akio Harada
Jacket art by Renee Naomi Lancet, age 5; rear end papers, age 14

Distributed in the United States by Kodansha America, Inc., 575 Lexington Avenue, New York, N.Y. 10022, and in the United Kingdom and continental Europe by Kodansha Europe Ltd., 95 Aldwych, London WC2B 4JF. Published by Kodansha International Ltd., 17–14 Otowa 1-chome, Bunkyo-ku, Tokyo 112–8652, and Kodansha America, Inc.

First edition, 1992
Second edition, 2000

01 02 03 04   10 9 8 7 6 5 4 3 2
ISBN 4–7700–2351–0

**Library of Congress Cataloging-in-Publication Data**

Wiltshire, Diane
   Japan for kids : the ultimate guide for parents and their children /
   Diane Wiltshire Kanagawa and Jeanne Huey Erickson.–1st ed.
   Diane Wiltshire and Jeanne M. Huey.–revised ed.

   Includes index.
   1. Child rearing–Japan.   2. Mothers–Travel–Japan.
   3. Children–Japan.   4. Americans–Japan.   5. Europeans
   –Japan.   I. Erickson, Jeanne Huey, 1962–      II. Title.
HQ769.K29   1992 (rev. 2000)                    92–978
649'.1'0952–dc20                                CIP

*www.thejapanpage.com*

# CONTENTS

*Foreword*   Dr. Ryoko Dozono • **7**

*Introduction* • **8**

*Acknowledgments* • **10**

1  Getting Out and About • **11**

2  Shopping around Town • **35**

3  Equipping the Kids • **83**

4  Books, Toys, and Libraries • **97**

5  Parks, Playgrounds, and Gardens • **125**

6  Amusement Parks, Aquariums, and Zoos • **157**

7  Museums, Sports, Activities, and Classes • **179**

8  Celebrating in Japan • **233**

9  Having a Baby in Japan • **259**

10  Kids' Health • **293**

11  Educating the Kids • **315**

12  The Care and Nurturing of Parents • **347**

13  Bicultural Parenting Resources • **371**

14  Tips for Residents-to-Be • **379**

*Index* • **393**

# FOREWORD

## RYOKO DOZONO, M.D., PH.D.

When I first heard that Diane and Jeanne were writing a parents' guide to Japan, I was elated. As a mother of young children myself, I knew that I could look forward to some pertinent and practical help on all aspects of parenting.

As a gynecologist catering largely to the foreign community, I realized how valuable a book like this would be to English-speaking residents of Japan. Everyday I encounter parents who are desperate for information and advice on a variety of topics. "Where can I find extra-large maternity clothes?" "Which international preschool would be best for my child?" "Do you know a magician for my son's birthday party?" One can find this information in Japan but it is time-consuming to track down. The life of a parent is busy enough, especially for those residing in a foreign country. A manual with all of these tips and inside scoops is much needed.

I was impressed with the authors' dedication to this projects. Over two years were spent exploring parks and zoos, schools and toy stores, and checking out numerous tips from other parents. Jeanne and Diane jokingly remarked that their market research for this book took place every day of their lives as the parents of five young children between them.

During the writing of the book, I marveled at their creativity and their enthusiasm, but especially at their attitude toward Japan. Always looking at the positive aspect of every situation, they remind many of us of what a wonderful place Japan is to live with young children. The cultural gap of East and West is bridged by *Japan for Kids*. As I read through the original drafts of this book, I realized that this was a definitive source book for all parents, whatever their nationality. Nowhere else is there such a comprehensive listing on such a wide range of subjects geared to make parenting in Japan easier and more enjoyable. What fun it is to view parenting in Japan through the eyes of these two energetic American mother.

# INTRODUCTION

A re the characters on "Sesame Street" more familiar to you than many of your relatives? Do your wildest fantasies involve an uninterrupted night's sleep? Does the rattle in your glove compartment turn out to be Crayons and Cheerios? If you answered yes to any of the above, then perhaps you live in a home with children. So do we. Our combined experiences as parents in Japan run the gamut from childbirth in a Japanese hospital to finding the right elementary school for a six-year-old. This is a book of information we have gathered in the process. Sometimes we learned the hard way—have you ever paid U.S.$65 for a child's haircut?! Sometimes new friends shared their secrets.

There is no doubt that life with young children can be challenging, if not overwhelming at times. A posting or long vacation to a foreign land such as Japan can send even the most experienced parent into a panic. In this book, you will find innovative ideas and suggestions for dealing with everything from the high cost of living to the language barrier. We have found that a little advance planning can make all the difference. Whether you are preparing for a new baby in the family or your initial move to Japan, knowing what to bring or where to buy it here can make adjusting to your new life-style infinitely easier.

After a combined total of thirteen years in this country and five children of various ages between us, we feel qualified to say that Japan is a terrific place to raise children. The Japanese have a special place in their hearts for children, and this is reflected in their cultural traditions as well as in their tolerance for the typical two-year-old.

We hope that *Japan for Kids* will give you the courage and confidence to enjoy life with your children in this wonderful country. We urge you to take advantage of the exciting possibilities awaiting you. After you survive the initial adjustment period, you will find your family's life forever enriched by the time spent in Japan.

## NOTE TO THE NEW EDITION

Updating this book was a labor of love that lasted far beyond our time in Japan. We never imagined how much work it would be to completely revise *Japan for Kids*, and we never could have undertaken such a huge project without the help of many friends who volunteered their time, contributed information, and kept our spirits up as we revised and rewrote over a three-year period.

In the eight years since *Japan for Kids* was first published, our own children have grown and changed, enabling us to expand the focus of the book to serve a wider range of needs and interests. New information on dental health, the Japanese school lunch (*obento*), and houseguest etiquette was added based on readers' feedback over the years. Besides the ups and downs of the Japanese economy, the biggest changes in the book were due to the popular acceptance of the Internet. Having access to the World Wide Web has made traveling or moving to a foreign country much less isolating and intimidating. Through the Internet you can find out all about Japan well in advance, and after you are resettled you'll be able to stay in touch with friends and family back home through e-mail. Wherever possible, we tried to list websites that would be useful to families. Besides the numerous Internet addresses in this edition, we have also listed some of the more valuable websites in the endpapers at the back of the book.

We hope the tone of *Japan for Kids* is still friendly and easy to read, and in spite of the hard work, we feel that revising it was a worthwhile endeavor. Throughout the process, our goal remained the same as always: to make life just a little easier for international families visiting or living in Japan.

### KEY FOR *JAPAN FOR KIDS*

☎ = Telephone     🖷 = Facsimile     🖳 = Website or e-mail
🚇 = Nearest station(s) and rail line(s)     🕘 = Hours

# ACKNOWLEDGMENTS

This book is dedicated to our daddies, who always encouraged us to look farther than our own backyards: R. Curtis Huey (in memoriam 1931–88) and William A. Wiltshire.

We would like to thank the following people for their advice, time, and support:

| | | |
|---|---|---|
| Dr. Ryoko Dozono | Stephanie Cook | Pam Noda |
| Dr. Gabriel Symonds | Kathy Yamane | Beverly Huey |
| Louise Shimizu | Mary Noguchi | Ann B. Wiltshire |
| Etsuko Sekine | Kay Ueno | Sabine Schmid |
| Mercy Wijesiri | Noriko Faust | Rial Ellsworth |
| Kumiko Nishimura | Sumiko Kataoka | Jean Pearce |
| Cecile Click | Barry Lancet | Judith Ravin |
| Janet Ohuchi | Hilary Sagar | Peter Booth |
| Beckie Johnson | Michiko Uchiyama | Minato Ward Office |
| Mary Nino | Kazuko Matsuzaki | Members of AFWJ |

Mike and Ray at the McComb Post Office
Members and friends of Tokyo Union Church

For their invaluable assistance with this new edition, we are indebted to Patrick Newell and the following parents at Tokyo International School: Ayumi Temlock, Kris Koelling, Cindy Powell, Laura Cohen, Diane Turner, Maria Murphy, and Aileen Emerling.

A number of others lent their time, energy, and assistance, including Dolores McMullen, Hilary Kitasei, Carla Lev, Elena de Karplus, Cornelia Kurz, Richard Santos, Mike and Kaori Kanagawa, Kirsten Sansom, and Amy Jorrisch.

Special thanks and appreciation go to our children, Kennedy and Kane Kanagawa, Jessica Santos, and Michelena, Nathan, and Gabriella Erickson.

# 1

# Getting
## out
## and about

Japan is a land of contrasts, from sleepy hillside villages to the sprawling concrete expanses of the major cities. It is a country that offers an endless variety of things to do and interesting places to visit and, at first sight, a veritable nest of routes and transport systems which can make getting out and about a frustrating and time-consuming ordeal. A language problem and a couple of screaming kids do not make your task any easier. However, with a little planning and flexibility, it is possible to run errands, do the shopping, and visit friends without taking all day or spending a fortune on cab fares. How you choose to travel to any one place may differ from day to day, depending on the traffic, weather, time, and budget considerations, not to mention your energy level. With these factors in mind, take time to consider your options carefully.

If you walk to the train with the baby in the stroller, you then have to carry the stroller and your child up and down the stairs in the train stations. Should you drive to the department store on a Saturday to pick up an item if you have to sit in your car for forty-five minutes waiting for a space in the parking garage? If you take the bus, you could be home by the time you get the car parked. Being well prepared and knowing your options—a bus route near your home, a good corner to catch a cab, the back-street shortcuts—will prove invaluable.

## THINGS TO TAKE ALONG

Never leave home without a few of the necessities your small children might need. Diapers, wipes, zip-lock bags, and a change of clothes are standard fare for diaper bags worldwide. In Japan, however, you need to add a few items to the list that you may not usually carry. For example, small packs of tissue are a must as many public toilets do not provide toilet paper or paper towels.

In the summer heat and humidity, you will see many Japanese carrying a handkerchief (*hankachii*) to wipe their brow. A *hankachii* is great in the summer, particularly those made of absorbent gauze and toweling. They can be used year-round for cleaning up hands and faces after eating or washing while on the move. Kid-size handkerchiefs, decorated with cartoon characters, are available in addition to designer versions for Mom and Dad.

For cold weather, the Japanese have a wonderful "hot pack" for warming the kid's hands and bodies. Called *tsukaisute kairo*, these packs are handy for outdoor activities. They are sold in packages of ten or so and range from the size of a child's hand to the size of an adult's hand. They can be found in most drugstores, where they are prominently displayed during the winter months. To activate the packs, take them out of the plastic and rub them between your hands. After about five minutes, they will be warm and can then be tucked into coat pockets or under clothing, or held in the hand. They will stay warm for four to twelve hours and are especially useful when traveling outdoors in winter or for trips to the zoo or amusement park. Do not get caught, as we once did, watching the afternoon parade at Tokyo Disneyland while our hands froze because we had underestimated the cold. All the Japanese children sitting on the curb had these little hot packs; we finally had to buy gloves for our children at ¥2,000 a pair!

## FOOD FOR ON THE GO

A few snacks can go a long way toward keeping the kids happy while traveling. Although the Japanese consider it impolite to eat in the train, bus, or taxi, young children are usually exceptions. If you find yourself in a tight spot and need to give the children a little something to keep them going, try to snack as neatly as possible and always clean up your mess, even if it is just a few crumbs. Older children should sit on a bench at a bus stop or on the train platform for snacking. On the Shinkansen (Japan's super-express railway line) or other long-distance trains, eating is acceptable and tables are provided.

For travel or school meals, Japanese children pack their lunch or snacks in a small box. Lacking the handle by which Western lunch boxes are carried, these containers are carried in drawstring bags or wrapped in square cloths and carried by the knot. This portable meal is called an *obento*, and it is a custom that has been practiced for centuries by the Japanese. Special *obento* equipment is available that includes matching carrying bags or cloths, matching *obento* boxes, pint-size thermos flasks and mugs, and matching cutlery and chopstick sets. Some thermoses even come with a pop-up straw. Children get thirsty in the strangest of places, and a small thermos of water tucked in the diaper bag can come in handy when on the road.

To go with the *obento* boxes there are matching *oshibori* sets. These are small washcloths that fit in a plastic cylinder or zippered bag. When you leave the house in the morning, dampen the washcloth, close it in the cylinder or bag and it will stay wet all day long for cleaning up after play or meals. Just do not forget to wash it, or you will find a moldy *oshibori* on your next outing.

Some of the best-quality *obento* boxes for children are found at the Sanrio shops in department stores (see chapter 2). Sanrio is a large company that manufactures children's goods featuring cartoon characters, such as Hello Kitty and the Runabouts, in an amazing array of designs from stuffed animals to stickers to underwear to *obento* boxes. You will be surprised what the kids will eat when the food is appealingly arranged in one of these boxes!

Filling the *obento* box can be fun for everyone. Besides the usual nutritious snacks such as crackers and peanut butter, cheese cubes, and apple slices, there is a whole new snack world to explore in the Japanese supermarket.

*Osembei* are Japanese rice crackers, and they come in every shape, flavor, and size imaginable. Most grocery stores have an entire aisle filled with different kinds of rice crackers, from festive, seasonal crackers to the standard peanut or *nori* (seaweed) mixture. Most kids enjoy these snacks, which are also sold in individually wrapped packages.

Those parents who like to sneak nutrition into their children's snacks should try a small, round cracker called a *tamago boru* (literally, "egg ball"). This popular snack is full of calcium and dissolves in the mouth, making it suitable even for babies. *Tamago boru* come in large bags filled with single-serving packs decorated with bright cartoons. Most stores also carry large bags of alphabet or animal crackers that are low in sugar and inexpensive.

Besides *osembei*, you might want to introduce your child to "good-for-you" Japanese treats such as dried seaweed, or *nori* strips.

These come in individual packs, just right for slipping into your bag. Be aware, however, that the *nori* sometimes sticks to the teeth or the roof of the mouth. One of our toddlers was stared at because the bits of *nori* stuck to his teeth made them look black. Another interesting snack choice is strips of dried squid (*saki ika*). Many children love the salty flavor and chewy texture. For an unusual taste sensation, try the strips of squid with cheese sandwiched in between.

In the refrigerated section of your supermarket, you will find small cartons of juice, milk, and yogurt. They range in size from tiny (three swallows) to the average drink-box size (200 ml). To identify the contents, it is usually safe to look for a picture of a fruit on the carton or to judge by the color of the carton—red for apple, orange for orange, and so on. Many of these drink cartons are decorated with cartoon characters that appeal to children. When looking for milk, if you can find a carton with a picture of a cow—take it, it is most likely what you want. The brown-colored cartons usually contain chocolate or coffee drink variations. Plastic bottles of *yakuruto,* a sweet yogurt-based drink popular with children, are also sold.

In addition to food, a small surprise or wrapped package to open en route can go a long way toward keeping the kids occupied on public transportation or while you maneuver through rush-hour traffic. We fill our purses and glove compartments with hand-size pinball games, sticker books, finger puppets, and small pencil and crayon sets. For distracting the kids during a long trip, some good children's cassette tapes and books are helpful. If you want these in your native tongue at a reasonable price, bring them with you or order from home (see the Mail-Order Books and Toys from Abroad section in chapter 4).

## TRANSPORTATION

Before discussing the specifics of traveling around Japan, there are a few general guidelines for safety that the foreigner should be aware of.

First, never leave your house without identification of some sort. By law, you should have your alien registration card (or passport if you are not a resident) with you at all times.

Second, your children should also have some form of identification on them, especially for day trips or visits to crowded places. Chances are that your child would have no way to communicate with the authorities if he or she were separated from you. We put our *meishi* (name card) in our older children's pockets and pin a plastic laminated card on the baby's back. In Japan, small school children often wear plastic badges with I.D. information slipped in. These can be bought at stationery or school supply stores. In the U.S., the Beverly Hills Collar Company makes quality steel bracelets for kids. Contact them at ☎ 800–891–2663 or 🖳 <www.kids-id.com>.

Third, when traveling away from home, always carry a copy of your insurance card and a reasonable amount of cash—¥20,000 or so—in case emergency medical care is needed. If you have Japanese National Health Insurance or company insurance, the hospital will want your policy number; if you have private insurance, you will have to pay cash for treatment.

### RIDING THE RAILS

The quickest way to travel around the cities is by train and subway. Most children find the ride exciting, and you will not need to do too much in the way of distracting them. Besides being quick, the trains are clean, safe, and on time. You will see Japanese schoolchildren as young as six and seven riding the train alone. Throughout Japan, public transportation (subways and buses) is free for children up to the age of six, and children from age six to twelve ride for half fare.

Certain times of the day should be avoided when traveling with small children on the train. There really are men whose job it is to stand and shove passengers onto the train before the doors close! Needless to say, a child could be injured or at least seriously frightened in the crush. On the train, no allowances are made for a little person to breathe or see out the window. When caught in this situation with a three-year-old, one friend lifted his child up and held her over his head for the duration of the ride. It worked, but we do not recommend it for daily travel. The exact time of this rush is different for each train station and line and is one of those things that you have to learn from experience.

A good train map including JR, subways, and private lines will be a lifesaver, but the best way to learn to ride with ease is to do it often. During non-rush-hour times, the other passengers will smile and coo at your young children. If you have a stroller or a sleeping child, often someone will offer you their seat or help in some way. A complete stranger once took a friend's heavy stroller and bags all the way up three flights of station stairs so that she could carry her tired and grumpy two-year-old.

You can buy a train or subway pass (*teiki*) at most stations. Passes are sold for one route only, so unless you ride a regular route often, they may not be worth buying. One way to avoid the crush at the ticket machines is to buy *kaisuken*—books of eleven tickets for the price of ten.

A couple of things to remember: The "silver seats" at one end of the train car are reserved for elderly or handicapped passengers. If your children want to kneel on a seat to look out the window, make sure they slip their shoes off and place them on the floor with the toes pointing out, as Japanese children do. Also, be careful when boarding the train as the gap between the train and the platform can be dangerously wide at times.

### LONGER TRAIN TRIPS

For information on all JR services, including the Shinkansen, you can call Infoline Service in English at ☎ (03) 3423–0111, Monday through Friday (except holidays) from 10:00 A.M. to 6:00 P.M. You can get transportation as well as tourist information in English through the toll-free Travel Phone, which operates from 9:00 A.M. to 5:00 P.M. at ☎ 0120–444–800.

Reservations cannot be made through Infoline Service or the Travel Phone. To reserve seats on the Shinkansen or any other long-distance train, such as a resort-bound train, you will need to call a travel agent or go to a major train station, depending on the line and your plans.

In general, reserved seats are not available on local trains, though some trains have a first-class car, called a Green Car, where seats can be reserved. Seats on resort trains must be reserved, and the fare often includes the bus ride from the station to the resort.

The Shinkansen is an experience that should not be missed while in Japan. From the age of six, children must have their own seat, and they travel at half fare in economy and reserved seats until age twelve. If you have a child under six, you may buy a children's ticket or hold the child in your lap. If you happen to be traveling during an off time, say, the middle of the week or midday, there will often be empty seats nearby that your small child can occupy if you did not reserve one.

Besides nonreserved and reserved seating (both of which are

available in smoking and nonsmoking cars), each Shinkansen has a first-class car, the Green Car, where each person, including small children, must have their own seat and pay full fare. There are also four types of private compartments available. Not all types may be available on every train; it depends on where and when you are traveling. These compartments are nice if you are traveling with children, and, as in first class, every person in the compartment pays full fare.

The ride on the Shinkansen is smooth, and the cars are clean, spacious, and quiet. Bathrooms are plentiful, trays unfold in front of each seat to hold snacks or coloring books, and shades pull down to keep the sun out of sleepy eyes. Children can be made quite comfortable, especially if they have their own seat.

### BY BUS

The bus can come in handy after a long day out with the kids, especially if there is a stop near your house. As with a cab, the bus can be a great help for that 10-minute walk from the station with the kids. Also, bus routes cover many places that the subway lines do not, so on special outings the bus may be your only alternative. Buses run as efficiently as they can considering they have to maneuver through traffic.

If you have your stroller with you, a balancing act worthy of a juggler is required to manhandle stroller and baby onto the bus and to hold them both while riding. You must take the baby out of the stroller to board the bus and so a stroller that folds up easily with one hand is useful. The rush-hour crowd on the bus can be a crush, so use your judgment when riding with children.

Japan has many bus companies, many of which are privately owned. If you want to ride the bus regularly on a particular route, you will need to find the end of the line for that bus (either end; usually a train or subway station) and go there. That is where you will find an office with a map (*chizu*) of the route and regular passes for sale.

### CATCHING A CAB

Taxi cabs are the most expensive way to travel within a Japanese city; the meter just keeps ticking while you keep sitting. Cabs are best when you have a short distance to go—time it so you can get out just before the meter turns past the first fare—or when you encounter adverse circumstances: you are caught in the rain without an umbrella, you bought too much, or the kids will not walk another step.

Japan's cabs are probably the cleanest and safest in the world. The drivers take pride in their cars, which you are expected to respect as you would your own, maybe even more. Some rules for riding a cab are "understood." First, the back door on the left side of the cab pops open automatically, so keep children away from the door's range, and do not try to open it yourself. Second, you will notice that there are white covers on the seats and that many drivers wear white gloves. This is a clean car. Do not let your child walk across the seat or put his feet on it in any way; if necessary, slip his shoes off upon entering the car. Place the stroller with its dirty wheels on the floor of the car. Be courteous and friendly to the driver, and he will do his best to get you where you need to go.

When giving directions to a driver, there are a few Japanese words that everyone should know. If the place you are going to is not well known and you do not have a map, give him the name of an obvious landmark nearby. Once you have the driver going in the right direction, you can tell him where to turn or go straight. A bit more vocabulary would come in handy, but if you are desperate, use these words:

Right: *migi*
Left: *hidari*
Straight: *massugu*
Stop here: *tomatte kudasai* ("Stop" and "O.K." also work well.)

For those who frequently take cabs or who are sometimes caught without any money, cab tickets are available in Tokyo. No more madly counting your change to see if you can afford to ride all of the way home. The cab coupons are available at Takashimaya or Mitsukoshi department stores, in Tokyo, or the Daimaru Department Store next to Tokyo Station. These coupons are available in various amounts and can be used for any cab company.

### DRIVING A CAR

If you are a foreigner and drive a car in Japan, congratulations. You have entered a new phase of tolerance testing. You probably know that driving on the freeway with a screaming child in the back seat can be hair-raising. Just wait until you are creeping three kilometers per hour in traffic with a screaming child in the back seat and no discernible street signs in sight! It is not always that bad, but making adequate preparations beforehand will save you a headache or two.

You may be able to drive for a limited amount of time with a license from your home country or an International Driver's License. If you are a resident of Japan, however, you should have a Japanese license. If you do not speak Japanese, you may want to take a Japanese-speaking person with you to the licensing bureau, although the English forms are quite easy to fill out. If you do not have a license from your home country, you must take the same driver's test as the Japanese. The test is available in English, but it is very extensive and attendance at a driving school is required to pass. The cost for the driving school is exorbitant, so it is really not worth the time and expense involved. If possible, try and get your driver's license before you leave your home country. To apply for a Japanese license, you will need your passport, alien registration card, one photo (2.4 cm by 3 cm), and a valid license from your home country. It is important to note that you must have at least three months experience in your home country before you can apply for a Japanese license. To find the licensing bureau nearest you, call the Samezu Unten Menkyo Shikenjo (in Japanese) in Tokyo at ☎ (03) 3474–1374, or write to 1–12–5 Higashi Oi, Shinagawa-ku, Tokyo.

In Japan, all passengers must wear seat belts "while riding in a car furnished with seat belts." The safest place for children to ride is in the back seat, and if they are young, they should be in a special infant or toddler car seat. Many good brands of car seats are available in department and children's stores (see chapters 2 and 3). See-through shades for car windows are a must for protecting children's eyes and can be ordered through the Safety Superstore listed in chapter 3.

Before you drive, it is important to get the English-language book *Rules of the Road*. Published by the Japan Automobile Federation (JAF), it can be purchased for a small fee. JAF is an organization similar to the American Automobile Association (AAA) in the United States. For a nominal yearly fee, it provides a number of helpful services, should anything happen to your car while on the road. JAF's Tokyo branch is at 3–11–6 Otsuka, Bunkyo-ku, Tokyo, ☎ (03) 5976–9777. Another branch is located at 2–4–5 Azabudai, Minato-ku, ☎ (03) 3578–1471. Offices are also located throughout Japan and can be reached in the following cities at these numbers: Yokohama, ☎ (045) 485–1222; Osaka, ☎ (06) 6543–5811; Kobe, ☎ (078) 871–7561; and Kyoto, ☎ (075) 682–6000. For road service, call ☎ #8139 to connect you to the nearest JAF road service center. Be sure to press the pound sign first.

As you may have noticed, most cities in Japan were not laid out "as the crow flies." There is not much modern logic in the layout of the streets; there is no street numbering system and only the major streets have names. As a result, your road map will become your best friend. Try to find one in English that has street names, block numbers, and as much detail as possible. Since you will be using the map often (even taxi drivers use maps to find their way around Tokyo) buy some clear adhesive film and cover both sides of the map. This way it can be easily rolled up and will not disintegrate or get mutilated in the glove compartment. For Tokyo residents, one good choice is *Tokyo City Atlas: A Bilingual Guide* (Kodansha International, 1998), which is a city map in book form (see chapter 14).

Getting lost from time to time while driving is a natural state of affairs in Japan. New arrivals are often told that the average time spent finding one's way after getting lost is one hour. When you have to travel to a new location for an important appointment, consider taking a practice run the day before, if possible. You'll find there are not too many cars on the road before 7:00 A.M., so use the time to practice learning shortcuts and back streets. Shortly after moving here, one friend got so tired of driving around trying to find his way home that he gave up, hailed a cab, gave the cabbie his *meishi* and money for the fare, and then followed the taxi home in his own car.

### BIKING IT

Throughout Japan, parents and their children run errands, buy groceries, and go on outings—all by bicycle, and often on the same bicycle. One of the most amazing sights for newcomers to Japan is the petite Japanese mother riding her bike with a child on the front and a child on the back. Most lightweight touring bikes cannot carry the load, but the bikes sold in Japan are made specifically for this kind of travel. The child bike seats available here allow a child to ride in the front (great for balance and control of the child) or on the back of the bike. These seats do not have the high back for support found on the seats in the United States. For those molded seats with chest straps or for cartoon character seats, such as Cookie Monster, you will have to order from overseas or bring one with you. See the Safety Zone in chapter 3 to order these seats from the United States.

If you want to ride a bike in Japan, you can get some pretty good deals here. You can buy a new bike from your neighborhood bike shop or a used one through the newspaper or bulletin boards where foreigners sell used items. (See publications listed in chapter 12.)

After you buy your bike, you are required to register it in order to park it in any of the bike parking areas and to protect your loss in case it is stolen. To register your bike, take it to the local *koban*, or police box. The police will check it to see that it meets safety regulations (i.e., brakes in good condition, adequate light for riding at night) and then put a sticker on it to show that it has been registered. At the same time, it is a good idea to have them put your name, address, and phone number on the bike in Japanese. Also be sure to write down your registration number at home as you will need it if the bike is lost or stolen. If you buy a bike here, the shop that sold it will register it for you. If you do buy your bike from a local shop, chances are that they will take a personal interest in your bike's maintenance and up-keep. One friend who rides her bike everywhere says that each time she rides by the shop where she bought her bike, they run out and stop her so that they can check the tires!

We have not found any hard and fast rules as to where or how you can park your bike. Every once in a while, the neighborhood police will round up all bikes that are questionably parked. Friends who ride often say this occurs every three or four months. If your bike is not where you left it, go to the nearest *koban* to report that it is missing. Most large train stations have a bike lot nearby. Department stores usually have lots around to the side or at the back. If someone does not like where you have parked, they will let you know. However, when in doubt, park with others—sometimes there is safety in numbers.

It is a good idea to lock your bike when you leave it for any length of time. Despite the relative safety of Japan, bikes are stolen, and foreign bikes may be more likely to be taken. A strong chain or bar lock is best. Most Japanese bikes have a wheel lock that allows you to lock one wheel with the turn of a key. Even though you may keep one key permanently in the lock, do not lose the other one. A friend had a prankster remove his key once, leaving him with a locked wheel.

Most cyclists in Japan do not wear helmets, nor do their children. This does not mean that biking is less dangerous in Japan than anywhere else. Cyclists, especially young children, should always wear a helmet. Bike helmets are available in some stores, but for the most part they are made of styrofoam and are not as advanced as the molded plastic type readily found in the United States. If you have difficulty finding a safe, top-quality helmet, you will have to order from overseas or contact one of the following outlets in Japan. The demand for these helmets up to this point has been low, so many stores do not stock them.

The sturdy Bell brand of bike helmets is one of the best in the United States, and there is a distributor in Tokyo. Intertec does not handle any retail business, but it will direct you to the nearest supplier of Bell bike helmets in your area. Contact Intertec at 4–10–3 Hamadayama, Suginami-ku, Tokyo, ☎ (03) 5377–1444, 📠 (03) 5377–1441. Another good brand of helmet, O.G.K., can be purchased from the Osaka Grip Mfg. Co., Ltd. For the retailer nearest you, write to 2–1–3 Nishinomachi, Mikuriya, Higashiosaka-shi, Osaka-fu, or call ☎ (06) 6783–5906.

Check out the Daiei chain of stores (see chapter 2) for a selection of all bike supplies, including helmets. In Tokyo, the USA Mountain Bike Shop Nukaya, in Meguro, also carries children's bike helmets. It is located at 1–26–10 Kami Meguro, Meguro-ku, ☎ (03) 5721–3760, 📠 (03) 5721–3761.

There are two bike accessories popular in Japan that we have found to be especially helpful in the cold weather. "Handle warmers" are mitts that attach to the bike handles, eliminating the need for gloves on a cold or windy day. Another must for cycling in windy weather is a bike windshield. This clear plastic shield, which fits on the front of the bicycle, protects a child sitting on a front bike seat from the cold wind.

For the most part, bicycles travel on the sidewalk. This is safer for the cyclist, but not as fast as riding on the open road in a bike lane. The sidewalks are crowded, and you must stop and start a lot. This is one reason why women here ride ladies' bikes and not the men's type with a crossbar. It is illegal to ride a bike on which you cannot touch the ground with your toes when mounted (this is one of the things that the police check when registering your bike).

On a road without sidewalks, bikes also travel inside the guardrail or white line. This is where pedestrians walk, too, and if there are many poles and people on the road, you will be doing a lot of starting and stopping here as well. A word of advice from one experienced biker is to practice measuring how long it takes you to meet an approaching object. When pedestrians are approaching and there is a pole in the way, you need to be able to judge when to slow down, ring your bell, stop, or get off your bike.

For information about rules for cyclists, see the same JAF publication, *Rules of the Road*, as mentioned in the section on driving.

See chapter 5 for recreational cycling facilities in Tokyo.

## WALKING

One of the nicest things about living in Japan is the chance you have to walk to stores, to parks, or to just stroll in the sunshine. Japan is full of people walking; and in the cities there are side streets and paths just for pedestrians and bikes. The rule at crosswalks is that, if a pedestrian puts out his hand to signal he wants to cross, cars are to stop. This practice is not foolproof, but it gives you some idea of the respect traditionally granted to pedestrians by most drivers.

Major streets usually have ample sidewalks, and those that do not will have a white painted line or a guardrail. One of the main things to watch for when walking, especially with children, is bicycles. They often approach at a brisk speed, so it is best to hold your child's hand on the sidewalk.

The easiest way to walk any distance with small children is with a good stroller (see chapter 3). You will not see many Japanese children over the age of two or three in a stroller, but we never let that stop us from putting our older preschoolers in a stroller whenever they were tired. No complaints about heat, sore feet, or whatever, and they can snack or just enjoy the sights as you go along. One word about sore feet: avoid them by wearing comfortable walking shoes. A good pair of walking or running shoes (preferably from another country for size and economic reasons) are a valuable investment for you and your children.

For a leisurely walk to the park or corner store, there are small trikes and pedal cars that a three- or four-year-old can ride while you walk. A special feature of some of these trikes and cars is a steering handle that allows Mom or Dad to push from behind as the child rides (see chapter 3).

## AIRPLANE TRIPS

Even if you view long airplane trips with thrill rather than trepidation, you will probably feel daunted by the prospect of flying for hours and hours with an infant or young child. Throughout the years, we have survived long plane rides with and without spouses, with newborns, and with two-year-olds. We hope some of our experiences will make your own travel a little less harried.

As soon as you know your travel date, reserve your seat on the plane. When traveling with children, most people feel that the best seats on the plane are either in front of the bulkhead or on a row near the front of the middle section. If possible, request that your travel agent book you on a flight that is not too full.

We also highly recommend flying an airline that has individual video screens in front of each seat. This allows for endless hours of video games and parent's choice of movies. Children of all ages can entertain themselves for hours this way, a big plus on a long flight.

Due to new regulations, some airlines require infants and young children to be strapped into safety seats for the duration of the flight. Other airlines still provide a bassinet for infants that attaches to the wall in front of the bulkhead seat. The size of the bassinet will depend on the airline you are flying with; some bassinets are padded and large enough for a six-month-old, while others are little more than cardboard boxes that can barely hold a six-week-old. An infant can also spend some time in a front carrier, which frees Mom or Dad's hands to read or eat a meal. Although it is more expensive, as you are paying for an extra seat on the plane, the safest option is to travel with an infant car seat.

Toddlers and older children will probably prefer the middle rows where the armrests can be raised. They are not removable in most bulkhead seats, which makes it impossible for a child to lie across any empty seats. In case there is no extra room for your children to stretch out and sleep, we suggest packing inflatable neck rests for everyone.

We have a few friends who give their children a mild over-the-counter sedative, such as Dramamine or Benadryl, before boarding. Both of these medications combat air sickness and may cause drowsiness. The only drawback is that the medicine may also have the opposite effect. You should ask your pediatrician for advice if you are thinking about using such drugs.

When traveling with more than one young child, you will need a sturdy, lightweight stroller that folds up easily. Also, for an infant, a front or back carrier is a must if you are traveling alone. We pile as many bags as possible on the stroller, sometimes even strapping the carry-on luggage in the seat. Whenever our preschooler feels like riding, he sits on top of the heap. Of course, this system is a problem when going through security clearance. Their rules require you to empty the stroller, which means you have to unload all the bags and then put them back on again.

If your stroller is a narrow model that will fit down the aisle of the plane, go ahead and push it right onto the plane and to your seat. Some parents prefer to board with the kids when the preboarding message is announced. This enables you to get settled without blocking the aisles, and you can claim overhead storage space and blankets and pillows. The drawback of early boarding is extra time you then have to spend on the plane.

In our carry-on bags we pack a change of clothes for everyone—even Mom—in case of air sickness or spills. Cups with lids and straws or spouts are a must when traveling with small children. Put any drinks that they serve on the plane into these cups to minimize spills. For cleanups, it is helpful to have a wet washcloth or two in a zip-lock bag. In separate plastic bags, put diaper-changing supplies and a mini first-aid kit containing acetaminophen, Band-Aids, and lots of tissues. A small spray can of mineral water is soothing for dry faces and is a quick way to clean sticky hands. There are also some new antibacterial wipes on the market that come in handy for wiping off the toilet seat or children's hands before they eat. It is also good to take disposable bibs, or clothespins to make bibs out of a napkin, as well as slipper socks for everyone to wear during the flight.

Apart from carry-on luggage and all of the essentials that make a trip go smoother, we recommend a system that has saved our sanity many times. If your children are old enough, let them each carry a backpack full of small games and toys. You can also give each of them their own bag filled with gaily-wrapped surprises and treats that can be opened at intervals during the trip. Even the best-behaved children will become bored and restless on a long plane ride, so it is better to have too many surprises than not enough. Remember, the plane could always be delayed, and once you arrive at your destination you still have to go through immigration, wait for luggage, go through customs, and, if you are coming into Japan through Narita, you will most likely have to ride in a bus or taxi for an hour or more to reach your home.

When you are ready to pack the goodies to keep the kids busy, remember that they do not have to be expensive items. Be on the lookout for small toys, stickers, markers, and pads, and stock up when you find them. Sometimes we even use old toys that our children have not played with for a while. Wrap them all in gift paper before the flight, and you have instant "presents." Wrapping is not necessary, but for very young children it does add to the excitement.

If you have a nursing infant with you, you can rest assured in the knowledge that breastfeeding often during the long flight will be the most comforting thing for your baby. For infants, sucking is the best way to relieve ear pain due to changes in cabin air pressure. Remember to drink plenty of fluids and to wear comfortable clothes that allow for discreet breastfeeding. You may want to book a window seat for extra privacy.

If you have a child in diapers, make sure that you take plenty with you. Airlines often stock diapers, but you should not count on their supply. Although we are proponents of cloth diapers, disposables are invaluable when traveling long distances. For easy changes, dress children who are still in diapers in clothes that unsnap at the crotch. Soft, comfortable clothes are important for everyone, and we usually dress our children in sweat suits with T-shirts underneath to accommodate temperature changes.

No matter how your child is dressed, changing diapers is a bit of a hassle on an airplane. Some airlines have installed changing tables in the bathrooms, while other airlines still leave you to change the baby on the toilet lid. It is wise to bring a plastic pad for diaper changes; and if you have a row of seats to yourself and need to change a wet diaper, just do so on the seat. Passengers in the bulkhead seats can try using the floor space. Bring small plastic bags for soiled diapers, or use the airsick bags in the seat pockets. Be sure to ask the flight attendant where you should dispose of them.

You may want to bring a portable potty seat for young children. The company Children-On-The-Go makes an incredibly small folding seat that slips into a plastic case for easy storage. See the One Step Ahead catalog in chapter 3 for this product.

For older children it is a good idea to take along a small thermos of water for each child. The best kind are the ones with the pop-up straw that even the youngest child can operate without spilling. Sucking on the straw can help relieve ear-aches from pressure changes, and the water helps to ward off dehydration. In addition to water, you may also want to pack small cartons of fruit juice and some favorite snacks, such as Cheerios, apple slices, and peanut butter crackers. For picky eaters, it helps to have sandwiches and snacks that can be eaten in place of airline food. On flights to and from Japan, you can often order an *obento* meal, or you can ask for the special kids' meal. Both of these consist of foods that kids usually like, and they are most often served cold. This means that you can conveniently save part of the meal for the child to eat later if he is sleeping or not hungry when the meal is served.

Last but not least, jet lag is an inevitable part of international flights. There are many books, diet plans, and remedies on the market to combat jet lag, but for young children the only strategy we have found that works is patience. Let them sleep when they are tired and eat when they are hungry, and eventually everyone will be back on schedule. (For more information about jet lag and how it affects your children, see the Visiting Japan section in this chapter.)

## Now That You Are International

Traveling abroad can be a great adventure for the entire family. It is nice to keep a record of trips for children, and one way to do this is to have a travel book for each child. The Sanrio shops (see chapters 2 and 4) have cute "travel" books, or you could purchase a plain autograph book at a stationery store. On the airplane, ask a flight attendant, or perhaps the pilot if he is available, to sign the child's book. Having a memento of a flight is an educational way to remember different routes and destinations.

A helpful book for families on the go is the Family Travel Guides Catalogue. Published by Carousel Press, this catalog offers a thorough selection of English-language books about worldwide travel with children of all ages. The catalog also carries games, atlases, and activities geared toward the traveling family. To get a copy, write to Family Travel Guides Catalog, P.O. Box 6061, Albany, California 94706, USA, or visit ⌨ <www.familytravelguides.com>.

Also for traveling families, a company called Rascals in Paradise offers a variety of trips and tour packages with both U.S. and international destinations for parents and children. For a brochure, write to them at 650 Fifth Street #505, San Francisco, California 94107, USA, call ☎ (415) 978–9800, or visit ⌨ <www.rascalsinparadise.com>. You may want to take advantage of a personal shopping service set up especially for families living overseas. If you would rather not burden friends or relatives with requests for care packages, you can rely on this service to shop for you and ship just about anything anywhere. A ten percent fee is charged. The minimum order is $10.00. Contact Shop America, 25 McLean Dr., Sudbury, Massachusetts 01776, USA; ☎ (508) 443–7751, 🖶 (508) 443–7752, 🖳 <shopamer@ma.ultranet.com>.

Families living abroad might want to consider some of the home exchange programs that cater to families traveling and vacationing abroad. For those with young children, staying in someone's home can be less stressful and less expensive than an extended stay in a hotel. The following programs offer your family a chance to exchange friendship and culture with families all over the world.

### International Home Exchange Service
Intervac U.S., P.O. Box 590504, San Francisco, California 94159, USA
☎ (415) 435–3497    🖶 (415) 386–6853    🖳 www.intervac.com
Intervac U.S., the world's largest home-exchange network, has served the worldwide traveler for over forty years. Their Exchange Book, issued three times a year, lists over eleven thousand exchange opportunities in more than fifty countries. Subscribers are free to contact any party listed to arrange for a mutually agreeable house or apartment swap.

### Servas International
Regenburgsgade 11, Aarhus C, DK–8000, Denmark
☎ (45) 86–190319    🖳 servas@aol.com
Servas is an international cooperative system of travelers and volunteer hosts that was established to help build world peace, goodwill, and understanding by providing opportunities for contacts between persons of different cultures and backgrounds. Hosts (mostly individuals and families plus some community groups) provide information about themselves for listing in a national host directory. Approved Servas travelers choose the hosts they wish to contact about possible visits (usually for two nights) to share life in the hosts' homes and communities. Servas charges travelers a small fee. No money changes hands between travelers and hosts. Servas is a nonprofit, interracial, and interfaith organization with consultative status as a nongovernmental organization in the United Nations. For more information or to join, call Kozo Ikeyama at ☎ (077) 579–2253 or Kunio Tanaka at ☎ (03) 3721–1507. You can also contact the Servas Japan coordinator at 3–13–15 Denenchofu, Ota-ku, Tokyo, or write to the headquarters in Denmark.

## VISITING JAPAN (OR HOW TO AVOID BEING THE HOUSEGUEST FROM HELL)

Almost from the moment we moved to Tokyo, our family had a steady stream of houseguests, all of whom had somehow obtained my phone number: my college roommate and her kids, a former boss, my mother's bridge club, relatives I didn't even know I had. Everyone took the opportunity to visit Japan and stay for free with me and my family.

Because Tokyo is so expensive, many of these people could not have afforded the trip otherwise, so I didn't mind offering our guest room. Besides, I have visited friends all over the world with my own brood and can appreciate the convenience of this hospitality.

The following etiquette tips are almost guaranteed to keep you and your little darlings from being labeled "the houseguests from hell" during your visit to Japan. (On the other hand, if you are planning to host any parents and children in your own home in Japan, you may want to send your visitors these suggestions in advance. Or, for a subtler touch, try placing them in the guest bathroom. The tips of course, not the guests!)

To prepare for the plane ride to Japan, you may want to review the travel advice in this chapter. Once you've survived the flight across umpteen time zones, you will be faced with jet lag, a malady which tends to zap your energy and make your children cranky and unpredictable during the first few days. You may find that everyone is wide awake the first night and absolutely wiped out the next day. As it is very difficult to keep young children quiet during these middle-of-the-night wakeful spells, you may want to bring an entertaining video or two from home.

Also, bring a few favorite foods from home that kids can munch on whenever hunger strikes; their appetites will be as erratic as their sleep schedules for a while. Some suggestions are cereal in resealable plastic bags, a large jar of peanut butter and some crackers and, for yourself, your own coffee. (Your kid's favorite cereal is probably not available in Japan, and peanut butter and coffee tend to be expensive.)

If you've been up all night, you might as well take the whole gang out for a walk just before dawn. It's always invigorating to watch the sun rise, and exposure to the light will help your body clock adjust more quickly. This is also a good time to get acclimated to your host's neighborhood, checking out any nearby convenience stores, parks, and so forth.

Before you venture off on your own, make sure to get a brief orientation course from your host, ideally as soon as you arrive. You will need some basic information in order for your family to function as independently as possible during your stay. Some helpful items to request are a map to your host's home with the address in English and Japanese; the telephone number; and locations of the nearest bank, supermarket, park, subway or train station, and police box.

During your orientation, it is helpful to look at a map of Tokyo or to ask your host to draw a rough sketch of the area. If you didn't bring a guidebook with you, ask to borrow one from your host. You can pick up a free map from any of the major hotels or one of the Tourist Information Centers, located in Tokyo, Chiba (New Tokyo International Airport), Kyoto, and Osaka (Kansai International Airport). See listings at the end of this chapter.

Teletourist, ☎ (03) 3201–2911, is a useful phone number for twenty-four-hour taped information in English. The other information that you should get as soon as possible from your host has to do with the operating of household appliances. You'll notice that the labels and directions for the telephone, microwave, VCR, rice cooker, and just about every major appliance are most likely in Japanese. It can get a bit tedious for your host to explain time after time how to use these things, so try to get it straight the first night. As your brain will probably feel like cotton, take notes if necessary.

If you find yourself faced with a Japanese-style bathroom, there are a few special rules that apply. If the toilet is recessed (rather than above ground), remember to squat over it (rather than sit on it), facing the pipes. The kids may need some assistance until they get the hang of it. However, most Japanese homes today have Western-style toilets, many with high-tech, computerized systems that are more confusing than their old-fashioned counterparts. Heated toilet seats are also quite common. By all means get the operating instructions for the toilet from your host.

When using a Japanese-style bath, or *ofuro*, the main point to remember is: no soap in the bath! The proper procedure is to scrub yourself clean outside the tub, rinse off, and then soak in the bath. As the bath water tends to be quite hot, carefully check the temperature before taking the plunge. Children need plenty of supervision around a Japanese-style bath!

Ask your host questions about the household rules. Many homes in Japan, even Western-style ones, have entrances where your shoes should be taken off and left neatly on the floor before entering the rest of the house. If your host prefers that you take off your shoes, try to help your children remember this. It takes some getting used to! You may be offered slippers to wear inside the house. Place them neatly back in the entrance each time you go out.

Other rules involve the disposal of garbage. Recycling is mandatory in Tokyo, therefore your host will probably have separate bins for burnable and unburnable garbage. There may be additional bins for newspapers and magazines, so be sure that you are clear about what goes where.

Regarding the telephone, use it sparingly as even local charges are quite high in Japan. Above all, be certain that friends and family back home are aware of the time difference.

I suggest that you fine-tune your antennae to what bothers your host. As space is often much more limited in homes in Japan, try to keep all your possessions confined to one room, or even a corner of one room. Don't allow the kids to take food or drink into other parts of the house.

Try not to depend too much on your host for getting around or even for meals, unless offered. And make an effort to replenish some of the basic food supplies such as milk or bread. Markets are located everywhere. If there is anything you can do to make your host's life a little easier during your visit, then do it! If time allows, you could offer to baby-sit, cook dinner, help with homework, or even work on their computer if that's your thing.

For families who have a bed-wetter in their midst (there are lots out there, but no one talks about it!), overnight travel can be tricky. I recommend traveling with a lightweight, wide piece of plastic, which can be draped over the mattress. If you have room in your suitcase, you may want to bring a supply of disposable diapers or, for the older child, disposable pants (the Good Nites brand fits up to sixty-five pounds). You may still have to wash sheets in the morning, so it is a good idea to brief your host confidentially on the situation.

All in all, if you and your family have the opportunity to be house guests in Japan, consider yourselves lucky indeed. You will save a tremendous amount of money by not paying for a hotel or eating out for every meal. For inexpensive meals, check out the local noodle shops. If the kids are having cuisine culture shock, take them to any of the fast-food restaurants such as McDonald's or Kentucky Fried Chicken (KFC) for a taste of home. You can even order pizza from Domino's in Japan!

Besides the money saved, another bonus of being a house guest is the chance to spend big chunks of time with your children, checking out their manners and social skills. Your whole family can work together to be considerate of your host, from making the beds to washing the dishes. These experiences will go a long way in teaching your kids how to be well-brought-up, exemplary guests!

One more bit of advice: As Tokyo is so expensive, you are not expected to treat your host family to a dinner out during your stay. (For house guests visiting the United States, this is considered a nice gesture.) However, a small inexpensive gift of something that they can't get in Japan would go over well. Consider asking ahead of time what they would like you to bring.

When traveling to Japan, pack as light as possible. Not only is it a pain to maneuver heavy bags through Narita Airport (no skycaps to assist you), but also, getting the bags out of the bus, into a smallish taxi, and then into your friend's home is an extra burden. If you take the trains, you will have endless flights of stairs to contend with. Consider packing a collapsible duffel bag if you plan to buy lots of souvenirs.

Last, but not least, it is worth mentioning the obvious courtesies since looking after children in a foreign setting can be an all-consuming task. When departing from your host's home, leave your room as clean as possible. Allow a little extra time to gather up sheets and towels for washing; empty wastebaskets, and perhaps leave a brief note or small gift. As soon as you arrive home, a thank-you note to your host will be much appreciated. Who knows? You may even be invited back next year!

## TOURIST INFORMATION

### Tourist Information Center (Tokyo)

Tokyo International Forum, B1F, 3–5–1 Marunouchi, Chiyoda-ku, Tokyo
☎ (03) 3201–3331    東京都千代田区丸の内 3–5–1 東京国際フォーラム B1F
🚇 Yurakucho Station, JR Yamanote, Yurakucho lines; Tokyo Station, JR Yamanote and various lines
🕐 9:00 A.M. to 5:00 P.M. Monday through Friday. 9:00 A.M. to noon on Saturday. Closed on Sundays and holidays.

### Tourist Information Center (Narita Airport, Chiba)

Passenger Terminal 2, 1F, New Tokyo International Airport (Narita), Chiba
☎ (0476) 34–6251　千葉県新東京国際空港（成田）パッセンジャーターミナル2 1F
🕐 9:00 A.M. to 8:00 P.M. daily.

### Tourist Information Center (Kyoto)

Kyoto Tower Bldg., 1F, Shichijo Karasuma Sagaru, Shimogyo-ku, Kyoto

☎ (075) 371–5649　京都府京都市下京区七条烏丸下ル　京都タワービル 1F
🚃 Kyoto Station, various lines
🕐 9:00 A.M. to 5:00 P.M. Monday through Friday. 9:00 A.M. to 12:00 P.M. on Saturday. Closed on Sundays and holidays.

### Kansai Tourist Information Center (Kansai Airport, Osaka)

Passenger Terminal Building, 1F, Kansai International Airport, Osaka
☎ (0724) 56–6025　大阪府関西国際空港パッセンジャーターミナルビル 1F
🕐 9:00 A.M. to 9:00 P.M. daily.

### Japan Travel Updates

🖵 www.jnto.go.jp

Provides useful travel information on Japan.

## VAN TAXIS FOR SHORT TRIPS WITH LUGGAGE

Universal Taxi is a van taxi service that is perfect for families. Our typical load of kids and luggage heading to Narita (via the nearest limosine bus service) never did fit into one taxi so we'd end up taking two. Now that Universal Taxi's vans are available, we just call to reserve one and all pile in with room to spare. And the prices are the same as a regular taxi! Do call in advance as these vans are becoming quite popular. They're also available for charter. Call ☎ (03) 3790–0117 or fax 🖨 (03) 3790–0110.

# a
# Shopping
# around
# Town

The service lavished upon the customer in Japan can make shopping a heady experience for even the most jaded shopper. From the moment you enter the store and encounter the ranks of bowing salespeople chorusing "*irasshaimase*" (welcome), your wish is their command, right down to the intricate wrapping of even the smallest package. In Japan, the customer is king, and this can mean a lot to busy parents shopping with active children.

## DEPARTMENT STORES

You and your entire family could spend several days comfortably ensconced in any of Japan's state-of-the-art department stores. There is nothing like these stores anywhere else in the world. Some of them have better facilities for children than others, but all of them are fun and easy to visit with the kids. Our listings cover stores and floors of particular interest to parents and young children. Renovations are continually taking place in the major stores, so there is usually something new and exciting to discover each time you visit. Each store has a different personality, but you will be happy to know that almost all of them have that wonderful Japanese invention, the Baby Room. Forget the times you had to pretend to try on clothes in department stores just so you could breastfeed your baby in privacy. Never again will you experience the hassle of finding a place to change a dirty diaper in the middle of a mall. We thought we had found paradise the first time we stumbled upon the rows of clean changing tables, vending machines dispensing diapers, Gerber juice, hot water for mixing formula, and private booths with comfortable chairs for mothers to feed their babies. And there's more! These department stores provide an infinite number of services for parents and children. Whether it's an electric breast pump you want to rent or a beloved toy that needs repair, the department store is a good place to look for help. If you have a lot of shopping to do, consider using the babysitting service available at some of the major stores. You must call ahead for reservations, but it is worth looking into. All department stores are open on Saturdays and Sundays and closed one day during the week, except during the summer and year-end gift-giveng seasons. It can make you crazy trying to remember which day which branch of which store is closed, so keep a record in your wallet.

Upon entering a department store, ask at the information counter for an English information brochure, which is available at some of the larger stores. Also check to see if there are any special sales that day. In many department stores, the next to the top floor is the bargain space, and we have run into great sales on everything from used kimonos to children's potties. Fortunately, all department stores accept major credit cards; many stores also offer their own credit card to customers. You can pick up an application form for store credit cards at the general information desk or at the foreign customers' service desk if they have one. If you didn't bring your stroller, ask at the information counter for one of their complimentary "baby cars." The supply is limited; on crowded weekends it's best to bring your own.

On the children's floor, inquire about a membership club for kids. Registration is usually free and will entitle you to invitations to special sales as well as other bonuses throughout the year. Even if there isn't a children's club, ask to be put on the mailing list for the sales of children's clothing that are held several times a year. If you find a brand of clothing that you especially like, try to get on that particular mailing list as well. We have a few favorite designers whose clothes are so expensive that we can only afford to buy them at sale prices. Most designers of children's clothing have sales at the end of each season. It is easier to get on these lists if you are a regular customer, but each designer has his or her own policy about these invitations—don't be afraid to ask at the counter.

A word about children's fashions in Japan. Japanese designers are noted for their originality and the quality of their adult clothes; the same holds true for their trendy and colorful collections of children's wear. Many of the designer names you will see on children's clothing are those of Japanese designers. Some are world-famous designers of adult clothes who sell a line of children's wear in Japan; others are imported from Paris, London, or Milan. Wherever they are from, you can be sure that children's wear purchased in Japan will be the best in design and quality. Almost all of the clothes that you buy here will be sized according to the Japanese system. Refer to the chart below for translating Japanese sizes into Western sizes.

| Japanese size | Height in inches | Weight in kilograms and pounds | |
|---|---|---|---|
| 60 cm | 0–26" | 0–7 kg | 0–16 lbs |
| 70 cm | 26–30" | 6–9.5 kg | 14–21 lbs |
| 80 cm | 30–34" | 9–12.5 kg | 20–28 lbs |
| 90 cm | 34–38" | 11.5–15 kg | 26–33 lbs |
| 100 cm | 38–42" | 14–18 kg | 31–40 lbs |
| 110 cm | 42–46" | 16.5–21.5 kg | 37–48 lbs |
| 120 cm | 46–50" | 20–24.5 kg | 45–55 lbs |
| 130 cm | 50–53" | 23–29 kg | 52–64 lbs |
| 140 cm | 53–57" | 28–36 kg | 62–80 lbs |
| 150 cm | 57–61" | 34–43 kg | 75–95 lbs |

Many stores offer a free delivery service, although, depending on where you live and the time of year, it may take a few days. If you need an item repaired that was purchased at the store, there is usually only a small fee, if any. We had a Combi stroller repaired for ¥450 once. Even though we had not purchased it at the store that repaired it, they accommodated us because they carry that brand.

When you get hungry, don't forget the restaurant floor that can be found in most stores. There is often a children's restaurant on the children's floor, so be sure to look around there first if you have the kids with you. Even at the adult restaurants, kiddie meals, complete with kid-size utensils and a treat, are usually available. The food sections in the basement are the perfect place to pick up dinner on your way home. The deli selections are terrific—everything from fried chicken to won ton soup—plus the prices are often reduced at the end of the day.

Department store pet shops are always fun for the kids to visit. Some stores have puppies and kittens in addition to the usual assortment of birds, turtles, and fish. A few places have rooftop play areas, and many have beer gardens on the roof in the warmer months.

While in Japan, try to visit a few, if not all, of the major department stores. Don't forget to take visiting friends and relatives on a grand tour from basement to rooftop, for a unique Japanese experience. We're sure they'll agree that there is nothing like it back home!

Check the listings below to find out what special features each store offers. A detailed description is given of a number of department stores that have a lot to offer children. Although only the main branch of a particular department store is described here, the image of the store and the types of services available at other branches are similar despite the different location.

## Isetan Department Store

3–14–1 Shinjuku (Foreign Customer Service Counter, 7F), Shinjuku-ku, Tokyo
☎ (03) 3225–2514 (Foreign Customer Service)　東京都新宿区新宿 3–14–1
🚆 Shinjuku Station (east exit), JR Yamanote and various lines; Shinjuku 3-chome Station, Marunouchi, Toei Shinjuku lines
🕐 10:00 A.M. to 7:30 P.M. Closed some Wednesdays.

Isetan spares no expense when it comes to appearance or customer satisfaction and service. From the foreign customer club ("I" Club), to the sports club, to the travel agency, this company's aim is to become involved in all aspects of its customers' lives. If you are a foreigner, free membership to the "I" Club will enable you to receive information on sales and events. Information is mailed out in English each month. Contact the Foreign Customer Service Counter. Other perks include two hours of free parking at the store and complimentary tickets to their Museum of Art. Isetan has branch stores in Kichijoji, Tachikawa, Fuchu, Sagamihara (Kanagawa), Matsudo (Chiba), Urawa (Saitama), Niigata, Shizuoka, and Kyoto.

Isetan in Shinjuku is hard to miss. If you take the train, go out the east exit of JR Shinjuku Station and turn right. If you drive, it is easy to find on Meiji Dori. The store boasts one thousand parking places in its two garages.

### Maternity/Newborn

The sixth floor of the Isetan store in Shinjuku houses maternity, newborn, and children's wear. A checklist is available—in English at the Foreign Customer Service Counter—that covers all the items mothers may need for a newborn. Maternity fashions are by Onward, Wacoal, Blanc d'oeuf, and many more Japanese designers. Both manual and electric breast pumps are sold.

### Facilities for Babies

On the seventh floor near Eat Paradise is a bathroom with a private toilet and sink large enough for a mother, toddler, and newborn to share. On the sixth floor, there is a bathroom made especially for children, with small-scale sinks and toilets. The Newborn Baby Corner is a quiet, spacious area that has baby beds, comfortable chairs, and a nursing room. There are vending machines for disposable diapers, juice, and baby food.

### Kids' Fashion and Toys

For kids, the sixth floor is a haven of toys and fun. Parents will find all their favorite children's brands here in abundance. There is a large Sanrio shop and, on this floor, Isetan holds its toy hospital. Call the Foreign Customer Service Desk to confirm repair days, which are usually on the first and third Sunday of every month. Repair periods range from the same day to two to three weeks. During long holidays such as spring vacation, Golden Week, and summer vacation, the store holds toy fairs and special events for kids and parents at the sales corner on the fifth floor and on the roof. Check their newsletter for information.

### Play Areas

Children will enjoy visiting the pet store on the roof. On the sixth floor and throughout the store, there are videos for kids to watch while you shop. Of course, in the toy department there are enough toys on display to entertain the kids for an hour or more.

### What's to Eat?

There is a wide choice of food available on the seventh floor, and restaurant Petit Monde has a special children's menu. From pasta to sushi, fancy to family, you will find something to suit your taste here. For a quick snack, don't forget the food samples in the basement.

## Matsuya Department Store

3–6–1 Ginza, Chuo-ku, Tokyo   東京都中央区銀座 3–6–1
☎ (03) 3567–1211
🚇 Ginza Station (A12 exit), Ginza, Marunouchi, Hibiya lines
🕐 10:30 A.M. to 7:30 P.M. Sunday to Tuesday. 10:30 A.M. to 8:00 P.M. Wednesday to Saturday. Closed some Tuesdays.

If you are shopping in Ginza, head to Matsuya for the best facilities in the area for babies and children. Matsuya has a young and trendy image, and the store has kept up with the competition with its recent renovations. Although it is not as large as some of the other stores, it is extremely well organized. For information in English, call the International Information Section at ☎ (03) 3248–8318.

Matsuya has two stores in Tokyo: in Ginza and Asakusa. To get to Matsuya in Ginza, take the A12 (Matsuya) exit at Ginza Station. If you drive, there is garage parking at Matsuya, or meter spaces are often available on nearby streets.

### Maternity/Newborn

On the sixth floor near the Baby Room is the newborn gift area. This section contains a lovely selection of infant wear and special gifts. Maternity wear is also in this area, with brand names such as Wacoal and Comme Ca Du Mode.

### Facilities for Babies

The Baby Room on the sixth floor has clean, padded changing tables. There are vending machines here for juice and milk. A private booth with stools, but no comfortable chairs, is available for nursing mothers.

### Kids' Fashion and Toys

The emphasis at Matsuya is on trendiness with creations by Japanese designers at the forefront, though the stock and focus changes periodically. The boutiques are arranged in an orderly fashion, not too far from the toy section, so you can let the kids play but still keep an eye on them as you browse.

Big discount sales and semi-bargain sales are held twice a year. Apply for invitations on the sixth floor. Matsuya does not have a babysitting service or a children's club, but every year during the summer vacation they do stage a model train show, which is a fun outing for the kids.

### Play Areas

In one corner, near the children's clothing section, is a play area full of wooden blocks and some climbing equipment. Small stools for parents surround the area, which is a great place to turn the kids loose for a while. Just remember to take their shoes off before they enter the play area.

The rooftop level houses a pet shop and Playland, which is open every day from 10:30 A.M. to 7:00 P.M., except in rainy weather. There are a dozen or so ¥100 rides here, in addition to an outdoor cafe and snack bar. There is a covered area with numerous video games that is open even on rainy days.

### What's to Eat?

If the kids start whining for a snack, you can buy a pack of cheese sticks at the Sanrio shop on the sixth floor. For meals, try the restaurants on B2 and the eighth floor. Don't forget the snack bar on the rooftop in nice weather.

## Mitsukoshi Department Store

1–4–1 Muromachi, Nihombashi, Chuo-ku, Tokyo　東京都中央区日本橋室町 1–4–1
☎ (03) 3241–3311
🚇 Mitsukoshi-mae Station, Ginza, Hanzomon lines
🕐 10:00 A.M. to 7:00 P.M. Closed some Mondays.

We usually take visitors to the Nihombashi main branch of Mitsukoshi for the ultimate Japanese welcoming act. At 10:00 A.M., when the store opens, you will hear music played on a huge pipe organ in the middle of the store. This serenade is accompanied by hundreds of employees lined up at the entrance, bowing a welcome to every customer who enters. The performance only lasts a few minutes so be sure to arrive early.

Mitsukoshi prides itself on its well-qualified staff. Nutritionists are on hand to give advice in the baby goods department, shoes fitters sell children's shoes, and toy consultants handle the toys. The concept is meant to ensure safety, high quality, and luxury in all of their products. Mitsukoshi has always had a more elite image than other stores, and one of the most obvious differences is their tendency to carry more formal, traditional clothing, especially in the children's wear department. This is where you can find an Eton suit for your four-year-old son's preschool graduation.

The Mitsukoshi store in Ginza is smaller than their flagship store, but it has a Sanrio shop and a nice selection of children's clothes and toys.

There are six branches in the greater Tokyo area, located in Nihombashi, Shinjuku, Ginza, Ikebukuro, Ebisu, Yokohama, and Chiba. Other branches are in Osaka, Osaka Hirakata, Hiroshima, and Kobe.

The Nihombashi store is easy to find. At Mitsukoshi-mae Station there is a subway-level entrance into the store, and if you exit onto the street, the store is directly in front of you.

### Maternity/Newborn

Mitsukoshi carries standard infant wear and gifts for new babies. Maternity wear is by Mitsukoshi Original and Sara, to name a few. Free seminars on pregnancy and delivery are given several times a year at the baby consultation room on the fourth floor.

### Facilities for Babies

The Baby Room on the fourth floor is equipped with changing tables, a baby swing, and two private rooms with comfortable chairs for breast-feeding mothers.

### Kids' Fashion and Toys

The clothing department on the fourth floor is quite spacious. The entire floor was renovated in 1990 to reflect Mitsukoshi's new concept in children's fashion. The main theme of the children's floor is "noble European style creating an elegant children's world." The tendency is toward fancy, formal clothes for children, with European designer names being the most prominent. Here is the largest selection in town of suits for little boys, in sizes as small as eighteen months. Party dresses, coats, and fancy shoes are available in all sizes for girls. The toy section is spread over a large area, with a small space set aside for children to play with new products and display toys. Kids can also try out the tricycles and pedal cars. You'll find American brands of imported toys and a good selection of Japanese toys, puzzles, and games.

Special sales are held three or four times a year, and customers are notified by mail. To put your name on the mailing list, call the store or ask at the information counter. Special children's fairs are held on holidays such as Children's Day, Mothers' Day, Christmas, and so on.

### Play Areas

If the kids get restless in the afternoon, take them down to the ground floor for an organ concert, which are held daily at noon and 3:00 P.M. Sometimes, special concerts are held at noon as well. You will find seats for about one hundred people at the foot of the giant cloisonne statue in the center of the store. The organist performs from his perch several floors above.

### What's to Eat?

Coffee shops are located on almost every floor. There is a tea room in the basement and restaurants on the fourth and seventh floors.

## Seibu Department Store

21–1 Udagawacho, Shibuya-ku, Tokyo    東京都渋谷区宇田川町 21–1
☎ (03) 3462–0111
🚇 Shibuya Station, JR Yamanote and various lines
🕐 10:00 A.M. to 8:00 P.M. daily, 10:00 A.M. to 9:00 P.M. on Friday. Closed some Wednesdays.

There are three Seibu department stores in Tokyo, located in Ikebukuro, Yurakucho, and Shibuya. Serving the greater Tokyo area are the stores in Funabashi and Kawasaki. In Osaka, there is a branch in Takatsuki, and there are approximately twenty-four branches throughout the rest of Japan. All Seibu branches have a bright, informal atmosphere particularly suited to the modern mother and her offspring. A good idea is to check out the members' clubs in the children's section of Seibu stores.

Car parking is available in three locations near the store, though these lots are often crowded. We sometimes find parking on the street nearby, or take the train or bus to Shibuya Station and walk 5 minutes to the store.

### Maternity/Newborn

On the sixth floor of their Building B (B-*kan*) in Shibuya, Seibu offers many special services for pregnant women. The "Club on Baby" is open to expectant mothers and mothers with children under two years of age.

### Facilities for Babies

Near the maternity clothes is the Baby Room, with changing tables, a padded sofa, and a private breastfeeding booth. There is also hot water, a washstand, scales, and vending machines with juice, diapers, and so on. A uniformed clerk is usually on duty if you need help.

### Kids' Fashion and Toys

The children's clothing department on the sixth floor is clean, sleek, and well designed. Infant wear and baby gifts are displayed in clearly designated areas. Clothing for children is spread out over a vast area, with separate boutiques for each designer. A wide variety of styles is represented, from trendy to frilly.

On the same floor, next to children's clothes, is the toy section. The usual sample toys are here, as well as children's videos to keep the kids entertained.

Special sales are held in spring, summer, and autumn that offer big discounts on baby and children's wear, in addition to toys. To be included on the invitation list, inquire at the children's department.

### What's to Eat?

Restaurants are located on the eighth floor of Building A (A-*kan*).

## Sogo Department Store

2–18–1 Takashima, Nishi-ku, Yokohama-shi, Kanagawa
☎ (045) 465–2111　神奈川県横浜市西区高島 2–18–1
🚇 Yokohama Station (east exit), JR Tokaido and various lines
🕐 10:00 A.M. to 7:30 P.M. Closed some Tuesdays.

The Sogo Department Store in Yokohama is one of the largest department stores in all of Japan. It is a great place for kids and parents at any time, but the rooftop playground and snack bar make it especially nice on sunny days.

There are eleven Sogo stores around Japan, including locations in Saitama (Omiya, Kawaguchi), Chiba, and Kobe. Sogo in Yokohama is only a few minutes' walk from the east exit of Yokohama Station. There is parking for fifteen hundred cars.

### Maternity/Newborn

Pregnant women and mothers with babies up to three years of age can join the Sogo Baby Circle. If you join, you will receive invitations to various events, opportunities for medical consultations, a present when your baby is born, discounts on baby snacks, and much more. For more information, contact the Baby Salon on the eighth floor. A variety of maternity wear is available at Sogo. Some of the more popular brands are Comme Ca Du Mode and Wacoal. You can also purchase or rent breast pumps.

### Facilities for Babies

In the Baby Salon, on the eighth floor, there are fifteen changing tables, hot water for mixing formula, juice machines, and a nursing room with comfortable chairs for mothers. Changing facilities are also provided in the rest rooms on other floors. Babysitting is available for two- and three-year-olds. The parent is given a beeper to wear while shopping in case he or she is needed.

### Kids' Fashion and Toys

Clothes and toys for children of all ages are on the eighth floor. Every popular brand of clothing is here in all sizes from newborns to teens. As in most department stores in Japan, the toy displays allow you and your children to experiment with new products. This is the easiest way we know to keep the kids happy while you shop! There is a Sanrio shop on this floor as well.

### Play Areas

Besides the toy department on the eighth floor, there is a rooftop play area with wooden climbing structures and a snack bar. These facilities close at 5:00 P.M., although the department store is open until 7:30 P.M.

### What's to Eat?

When you get hungry, you can choose from any of the twenty-four coffee shops located throughout the store. The largest selection of restaurants is on the tenth floor. On the B2 level you will find the food hall.

## Takashimaya Department Store

2–4–1 Nihombashi, Chuo-ku, Tokyo　東京都中央区日本橋 2–4–1
☎ (03) 3211–4111
🚇 Nihombashi Station, Ginza, Tozai, Toei Asakusa lines
🕐 10:00 A.M. to 7:00 P.M. (6:30 P.M. on weekends and holidays). Closed some Wednesdays.

Takashimaya in Nihombashi has recently revamped its children's areas on the fifth floor, and the result is increased convenience and fun for parents and kids. We have always liked this department store, whose image is a little more elegant and cosmopolitan than some of the others.

Takashimaya has large branch stores in Nihombashi, Setagaya (see Tamagawa Takashimaya Shopping Center in this chapter), Shinjuku, and Tachikawa. They also have stores in Osaka, Kyoto, Sakai, and Wakayama.

The Nihombashi store is easy to get to by subway. At Nihombashi Station simply follow the arrows to the exit into Takashimaya's basement. There is plenty of parking available if you drive.

### Maternity/Newborn

The Baby Corner is full of wonderful goodies for new babies. There is a wide variety of baby gifts and infant wear, including our favorite collection of Western-style christening gowns. The area has obviously been designed with pregnant women in mind. Comfortable chairs and small tables are scattered around the spacious room, which is separated from the rest of the children's floor. Clerks in neat uniforms are helpful and knowledgeable.

The maternity-wear section is adjacent to the Baby Corner. Here you will find all manner of undergarments in addition to breast pumps. The selection of maternity clothing by such designers as Pierre Cardin is fashionable, though like most Japanese maternity clothes, the styles tend to be a bit on the cutesy side.

### Facilities for Babies

The Baby Room has plenty of cots for naps or diaper changes. There is a feeding room with comfortable chairs and space for about five nursing mothers. One unique feature of this store is Baby Snack, a snack bar in the middle of the fifth floor. Even though there are only a few tables, it is a well-designed area, with highchairs and Mom-size chairs as well. Uniformed waitresses are on hand to heat jars of baby food, which are sold there. You may also purchase yogurt, milk, and juice, all in baby-size containers. A small basin is conveniently located for quick cleanups. This little restaurant can be crowded on weekends, but we have never had to wait very long for a place. (Note: Baby Snack closes at 4:00 P.M.)

There is a "tutor room," on the fifth floor, where two babysitters will watch your children while you shop. This service operates on a membership system, and appointments are necessary. Each Saturday, a counseling session on child care is available free of charge for Star Circle members (see below). An appointment is necessary for this service.

### Kids' Fashion and Toys

Takashimaya carries many lines of European, American, and Japanese children's clothes. You won't find many bargains here unless you stumble upon a sale, but the selection is one of the best. The Disney store on the eighth floor has videos, toys, clothing, and other character goods.

Star Circle is a children's membership club at Takashimaya. There is no charge to join, but registration is necessary. Birthday parties for children who are members are held once a month. Special discount sales for children's clothing and toys are held three to four times a year for Star Circle members. Regular discount sales take place on the eighth floor in January, March, June, and October of each year.

### Play Areas

Takashimaya boasts a small rooftop play area and another small area in the toy department on the fifth floor. Interactive areas allow children to rest and play with new toys. You will be amazed at the variety of activities available for all ages within this limited space.

### What's to Eat?

If you are an infant, you will dine in style at Baby Snack, a snack bar on the fifth floor. Otherwise, you will have to visit Takashimaya's only restaurant, down in the B2 level. It is spacious, with highchairs and a decent menu for kids, but it is dreadfully crowded at mealtimes. We have always faced a long wait, which is a miserable experience with hungry kids. For a change of scenery, try taking the kids down to the food counters in the basement, where there is usually a selection of food samples from which to choose. Some of the delicacies are rather exotic, but you may be surprised at what your kids will try in these basement food halls. Our pickiest eater decided that he liked mushrooms after trying them sautéed in butter and soy sauce in a department store basement.

## Tokyu Department Store

2–24–1 Dogenzaka, Shibuya-ku, Tokyo　東京都渋谷区道玄坂 2–24–1
☎ (03) 3477–3111
🚇 Shibuya Station, JR Yamanote and various lines
🕙 10:00 A.M. to 7:00 P.M. Main store closed on some Tuesdays, Toyoko store closed on Thursdays.

Tokyu Department Store in Shibuya is known for its sales and bargains. The store has two buildings in Shibuya, one conveniently located in Shibuya Station (called the Toyoko store) and the main store, which is located next to the Bunkamura complex in Shibuya. Both stores offer a wide selection of goods, and a shuttle bus runs every fifteen minutes between the two. Information in English is available on the first floor of the main store. Tokyu has branches in Kichijoji, Machida, and Tama Plaza.

### Maternity/Newborn

Maternity wear and children's goods are available on the seventh floor of the main store and the sixth floor of the Toyoko store. Brand names for maternity wear include Wacoal (especially good for undergarments and nightwear) and Hiroko Koshino. Breast pumps are available by special order. The main store has a gift counter for help with the selection and delivery of gifts for newborns.

### Facilities for Babies

Adjacent to the maternity wear departments in both stores is a Baby Room. Here there are cribs for changing diapers, hot water for mixing formula, and vending machines for juice.

### Kids' Fashion and Toys

The main store in Shibuya has perhaps the largest variety of children's brand-name clothes in Tokyo. The Toyoko store has less variety, but is well known for its sales and bargain bins. You can join the Familiar Group of Friends Club and Miki House Club and receive a newsletter with advance notice of sales. Members receive birthday cards for their children and invitations to special sales. Both stores have display toys set up for children to play with and the usual brands of toys for sale.

### Play Areas

There is a pet store on the rooftop level of the main store. Although within the stores there are no real play areas for children apart from the toy departments, the main store is adjacent to Bunkamura, a large cultural center that has theaters, a museum, gallery space, and two cinemas. There is also an art gallery on the eighth floor of the main store. For restless children, many of these spaces can provide a welcome diversion from continual shopping.

### What's to Eat?

The eighth floor of the main store houses fresh food, delicatessens, and restaurants. There are casual coffee shops as well as fancier restaurants here. At the Toyoko store, a food fair is located in the basement.

## Hankyu Department Store

8–7 Kakutacho, Kita-ku, Osaka-shi, Osaka-fu　大阪府大阪市北区角田町 8–7
☎ (06) 6361–1381
🚃 JR Osaka Station, JR Tokaido and various lines
🕐 10:00 A.M. to 8:00 P.M. Closed on some Tuesdays.

This department store aims to make customer service and satisfaction its number-one goal. Most of the store's branches are conveniently located near railway stations, and they boast spacious floors arranged so as to make shopping a pleasant experience. As with most major department stores in Japan, Hankyu prides itself on keeping abreast of all of the latest in fashion and style.

Hankyu has two branch stores in Tokyo, at Yurakucho and Sukiya-bashi. In Osaka, there is another store at Senri, and the Hyogo-ken stores are in Takarazaka, Kawanishi, and Kobe. There is also a branch in Kyoto at Shijo-kawaramachi.

The Osaka store is just a few minutes' walk from Osaka Station. There are no parking facilities, so you will need to find street or nearby lot parking.

### Maternity/Newborn

On the fourth floor of the Osaka store is the Baby World Corner. Here you will find many international brands of baby and maternity products. Among the maternity wear brand names are Comme Ca du Mode, Canlemon, and Wacoal. Special sales are featured in this department periodically as well as a class, called Mainichi Baby Sodan, which offers advice to new mothers, Wednesday through Saturday from 1:30 P.M. to 4:00 P.M. (arrive by 3:30).

### Facilities for Babies

In the Baby Room, there is a nursing room with changing tables and other amenities for baby. The nursing room is closed on Tuesdays and Sundays.

### Kids' Fashion and Toys

Also on the fourth floor is an exciting array of children's toys and fashions for all ages. You will find a Sanrio shop on this floor as well.

### What's to Eat?

Restaurants are located on the eighth floor.


## SHOPPING DISTRICTS

At first glance, shopping in Tokyo may appear to be expensive and exhausting. There are certain shopping districts and specialty stores, however, that are well worth a visit because of their low prices and/or selection of merchandise. The following shopping areas have been chosen because they are easy to navigate and they have the most to offer families with children.

### Azabu Juban

Azabu Juban Station, Oedo and Nanboku lines

The Azabu Juban shopping street is in one of the oldest neighborhoods in central Tokyo. Here you will find an interesting selection of stores selling everything from umbrellas to handmade Japanese rice crackers (*osembei*).

The main shopping street, about a 10-minute walk from Roppongi Station, runs parallel (one block from Roppongi) to the busy street coming from Shiba Park to Roppongi Tunnel via Ichinohashi. You can start with the Wendy's hamburger restaurant at the east end or the Sweden Center at the west end and take a leisurely stroll through several blocks. There are a number of good places to feed the kids along the way. The Chinese restaurant Toho Hanten is very accommodating to parents and young children. Our favorite restaurant is Sarashina, located on a corner near the Juban post office. This traditional Japanese *soba* (noodle) shop has been in business at the same spot for two hundred years. If you have young children, ask for a table on the tatami. Our kids always enjoy a simple bowl of *tempura soba* (noodles with two pieces of fried shrimp) or *tori soba* (noodles with pieces of chicken). Just remember to clean up any mess before you leave. It is amazing how many strands of noodles can end up on the tatami when dining with kids!

Eating aside, there are many stores worth visiting in Azabu Juban. Our first stop is always the Kobayashi toy store on the corner, which carries a nice assortment of toys, including traditional Japanese ones that you do not often see in department stores. If you turn left here, walk one block, and turn right, you will be across the street from Blue and White, a special gift shop full of unusual things. Sometimes you will find children's clothes made out of traditional and not-so-traditional *yukata* (a cotton kimono) fabric, in addition to T-shirts and stuffed toys.

Next door to Blue and White is the Daimaru Peacock supermarket. The second floor has bargains in household products and Japanese dishes as well as inexpensive gifts and toys.

If you go back to the covered main Azabu Juban shopping street, you will find several other stores that kids like to browse in. A Sanrio shop is located down the street from Kobayashi toys, and there is also a shop selling fish and aquariums. We like to stop for a snack at the outdoor *yakitori* (chicken kebab) stands and the *osembei* shops, where you can watch rice crackers being made the old-fashioned way—by hand.

In the summertime, Windsor Coffee Shop on the corner becomes an outdoor cafe and sells refreshing *kakigori* (shaved ice, flavored with fruit syrup), a real treat for the kids when the weather is hot. In August and early autumn, the annual Juban festivals are fun for the entire family (see chapter 8 under Japanese Holidays). If you live in the neighborhood, you might want to try the famous hot springs bath, which is located at the west end of the shopping street.

### Ebisu Garden Place

Ebisu Station, JR Yamanote, Hibiya lines

In 1994, this spacious (twenty-acre), modern complex was created on the site of the former Sapporo Beer brewery. With the elegant Westin Hotel on one side and Mitsukoshi Department Store on the other, the open space of Ebisu Garden Place has a distinctly European atmosphere.

Besides strolling around amid the greenery and fountains, families can enjoy viewing outdoor sculptures, visiting an indoor art gallery, taking in a movie, or touring the Beer Museum.

One of the most dramatic views of Tokyo can be found on the thirty-ninth floor of the Ebisu Garden Place Tower. You'll want to check out the small shops, bakeries, and restaurants scattered throughout the square. The outdoor beer garden and Grand Beer Hall (with five hundred seats) is a favorite with dads. Children love to watch the performance of the tiny marionettes at Marionette Clock Square, at noon, 3:00 P.M. and 6:00 P.M. daily. At night, the whole place comes alive with twinkling lights. There are frequent concerts and other entertainment in the central-stage area.

## Harajuku—Omotesando

🚇 Omotesando Station, Hanzomon, Ginza, Chiyoda lines; Meiji Jingu-mae Station, Chiyoda Line; Harajuku Station, JR Yamanote Line

Although these two districts are not famous for their children's shops, no discussion on shopping in Tokyo would be complete without a description of sophisticated Omotesando and funky Harajuku. For strolling and window-shopping, the wide Omotesando boulevard cannot be beat. This is where the exclusive boutiques and street-side cafes are—the places to see and be seen.

Don't forget to show the kids the revolving steel sculpture on top of the Hanae Mori Building. At the corner of this building, turn left to find Crayon House (see chapter 4 for details).

Continuing down the tree-lined boulevard, you will come upon a traditional piece of Japanese architecture painted bright orange. This is the Oriental Bazaar, our favorite place in town for gifts and trinkets. It basically caters to tourists, but the prices are cheaper than in other similar stores. It is convenient one-stop shopping for all your gift needs, from kimonos and cotton *yukata* to Japanese dolls and paper fans.

When you are ready for some food, Omotesando has all the fast-food outlets you could possibly want: Shakey's Pizza (a few stores down from the Oriental Bazaar) and, across the street, Wendy's, Haagen Dazs, and McDonald's. On Omotesando near the Meiji Shrine end, there are several family-style restaurants. The only problem we have had in this area is finding a convenient place to change a diaper.

After lunch, don't forget to hit the toy stores. Kiddyland, Tokyo's most exciting toy store, is near the junction with Meiji Dori, and just around the corner is a Bornelund shop (see chapter 4 for details on both stores). On either side of Kiddyland are trendy outdoor cafes. We like to take a break and people-watch here. The kids can join you for a soda, or they can play in the street-turned-playground next door. This blocked-off street has swings, slides, and sandboxes stretched out over five or six blocks, running alongside the building that houses Shakey's Pizza. Directly across Omotesando, this playground continues for a few more blocks.

At the intersection of Meiji Dori and Omotesando, look for the neon Chicago sign (it's two stores up the street from the landmark shop, Condomania!). Chicago, a basement-level shop, is basically a used clothing store, but what outrageous stuff you'll find! Everything from ball gowns to football jackets plus a fabulous collection of used kimono all await you here at reasonable prices. A good place to outfit your growing teenager, or for funky additions to your younger ones' dress-up box.

Parallel to Omotesando, from Meiji Dori to Harajuku Station, is the Harajuku shopping district, where Japanese teenagers and young adults flock each weekend. Sunday is the day to cut loose in Harajuku, and they come from far and wide to parade around in punk regalia and far-out hairdos. To work your way down to the Harajuku shopping street, look first for the LaForet building, which you can see from the intersection of Meiji Dori and Omotesando. This building houses boutiques full of trendy fashions for adults, but a couple of buildings down is a LaForet building exclusively for children. Dear Kids LaForet opened in the spring of 1990 and contains four floors of children's designer clothes and toys. From Ralph Lauren to Sonya Rykiel Enfant to Shirley Temple to the children's art showroom on the top floor, this building is a child's paradise. Most of the stores are clothing stores, but they all have clever displays and gimmicks to attract the children's attention while you shop. The top floor houses a play room called "D" Kids Studio and a children's restaurant, which is also available for birthday parties.

Back on Meiji Dori, get ready to turn left onto Takeshita Dori. At the corner you'll see Cafe Crepes, a little pink house serving mouth-watering take-out dessert crepes. As you turn the corner you'll find Burger King, and next door to that is Miki House, four floors of chic children's clothes. From here to Harajuku Station are trendy little stores, too numerous to count, with imported, vintage, classic, punk, and fashionable clothes for hip people of all ages. Many of the clothes in these stores are sized for Japanese teens and look rather small to us. If you have a twelve- or thirteen-year-old who wants to add some spice to his or her wardrobe, this is the place to shop. The prices are very reasonable compared with the department stores; here you get the feeling you have made a major find.

As you continue toward Harajuku Station, the shops full of trinkets, stuffed animals, goodies to eat, and more just spill out onto the street.

The atmosphere in this part of Harajuku is always alive and jumping. You may want to calm the kids down by taking a stroll through Meiji Shrine afterward. You can see the entrance to the shrine just behind Harajuku Station.

One warning about shopping on Takeshita Dori with children: It is always crowded, but especially so on Sundays. Since this is a narrow street, be careful to get out of the way when cars try to make their way through the chaos. Just past Harajuku Station, look for the grand curved roof of the National Olympic Stadium, where sports fairs or exhibitions are often held on weekends.

### Jiyugaoka
Jiyugaoka Station, Tokyu Toyoko Line

Jiyugaoka is a pleasant, compact shopping district that has a different feel from many of the shopping areas we have visited in Japan. Instead of the usual Japanese coffee shops and shoe stores, there is Laura Ashley, "American country," and health food. There are many cafes and restaurants where you can sip cappuccino while you listen to classical music. If you want to window-shop without the crowds, this is the place to go.

Take the train to Jiyugaoka Station and you are at a great place to start your trek. If you drive, follow Meiji Dori to Jiyu Dori and turn down it toward the station. There is parking on the streets or in paid lots in this ten- to fifteen-block area.

If you start at the station, turn to the right in the direction of the Jiyugaoka Department Store (this actually looks more like a flea market!). Here, there are a number of independently owned shops on the street level that have toys and clothes for children. Walk all the way up to the XAX sports club (look for the Jiyugaoka Juko Service and enter across the street), and you'll find the Laura Ashley store, plus a cluster of stationery and kitchenware stores.

Next to XAX is the Children's Museum, which is not a museum at all but three floors of fine children's shops. In this building are housed ab's d' absorba, Mini-batsu, bebe, and Granpapa stores, to name a few. Often there is a candy and popcorn vendor in front of the building, and there is a large *gelato* shop across the street.

If you continue down the street past the Children's Museum, you will come to a large Anna Miller's restaurant. If the kids are hungry, Anna Miller's has a children's menu and some of the best pies in town.

On the same street as Anna Miller's is a boutique with exquisite baby and children's clothes, just before the large pachinko parlor. If you turn left here and head back toward the station, you will find more small shops full of interesting things. On this street is a fabric store called Pico that carries a good selection of children's and interior print fabric. There are two other Pico stores in the area, so ask for a map if you want to look for more fabric.

On the same street as Pico's but heading away from the station, you'll find Jumpin' Kiki, an American country-style children's clothing store. (They even sell red metal wagons.) On the corner is Tutto Chico, a posh Italian boutique, which carries two floors of gift items for newborns and also those stylish Italian strollers. Make a left here and you'll see Pier 1 Imports (three floors) and ABC Sports Mart, which has a large selection of children's sneakers. Next is Palms Resale and Import Shop, where you'll find good quality new and used items for children. Their mail-order catalog lists Little Tykes products.

Wind your way back to the station and, just before you get there, keep your senses alert for the sight and aroma of Mont Blanc bakery. They have all kinds of delicious goodies and, should you need a cake made in a special shape or design, Mont Blanc can do it for you.

If upon your arrival in Jiyugaoka you take the main exit (facing the Jiyugaoka Department Store), turn right and go under the tracks. Turn right at the next intersection (facing Wendy's), and you'll see a Gap store, with its charming selection of both kids' and adult clothing. Just before the Gap is a Thom McAn store with a great selection of children's shoes. There is also a country-style children's shop on this street called Enough. On the side street from Thom McAn, American Market Place carries Hawaii Crazy Shirts in kid's sizes. Turning left at the Gap will bring you to Home Cake, a shop with all sorts of Wilton cake–decorating pans, decorations, and other supplies.

If you turn right at the Gap, you'll find L. L. Bean (children's department on the second floor). Two stores away is the Nature Company (great birthday gifts) with a good selection of books in English.

### Kichijoji
Kichijoji Station, JR Chuo and Keio Inokashira lines

Just 20 minutes from Shinjuku Station on the JR Chuo Line is a haven of bargain shopping for the entire family. Often referred to as Sun Road and Diamond City, the streets just across from Kichijoji Station are stuffed full of shops, both large and small, that offer great selection and even better prices.

If you take the central exit from Kichijoji Station, you will see a Mitsubishi Bank and a sign over the street next to it that says Sun Road. Head down this road and don't look back. Narrow pedestrian streets branch off this main street and continue for a couple of blocks to the next wide road that has a large Tokyu Department Store. Some of the streets are covered, others are out in the open, but they are all full of shops and restaurants. There are also many major banks in this area in case you run out of cash.

Both Isetan and Tokyu department stores have branches here. The stores are large and spacious and have a wonderful feeling of calm that you don't always find in the downtown branches. Isetan has children's clothes and toys on the fifth floor. Here, too, is Zusso, a great place for haircuts. Children can sit in fire trucks and watch videos as they get their hair cut. The big attraction on this floor is Dr. Kids Town, made to resemble "Main Street USA." The play area is loads of fun and there are tables where kids can sit and try out new toys. The B1 level has the usual food fair, and there is plenty of parking in the basement.

In the Tokyu Department Store, the sixth floor is for children. There is a huge Disney store in one corner, as well as a larger selection of clothes and toys. On the roof there is a spacious outdoor playground with the usual ¥100 rides, a pet shop, and video games in a covered area. There is also food in the basement and two levels of parking below that.

For shopping on the street level, check out Rogers and Marble. Both are down the side street that turns off Sun Road to the left before McDonald's. Rogers is a large discount shop with everything from pet supplies, to overcoats, to sporting goods. We have heard that everything in the store is marked down fifty percent or more from the usual retail price. Across the street is Marble, a children's shop with cute and affordable clothes in a wide variety of styles. In the station, near the central exit, is Lonlon Department Store. Check out their Ultraman Shop on the second floor. While you're in the area, be sure to check out the Grab Bag, a resale shop for children's clothing and toys. Run by American Ellen Motohashi, the Grab Bag has some terrific bargains. There is also story time in English, 11:00 A.M. on Tuesdays and Thursdays, at 1–34–11 Hommachi, Motohashi Building, 2F; ☎ (0422) 21–7057.

If you still have energy after shopping on Sun Road (or if you need to take a break), take the kids to 0123 Kichijoji. A 15-minute stroll from Sun Road, this is a haven for both parents and young children. In the garden are log houses, sand boxes, and baby swimming pools (great in summer). Inside, there is a play kitchen, dress-up area, piano, lovely wooden toys, and sponges for building. You'll find everything you need for babies (a nursing room, changing tables, and minikitchen), but bring snacks as there is no restaurant. Address: 2–29–12 Kichijoji Higashi Machi, Musashino-shi, Tokyo; ☎ (0422) 20–3210. Open 9:00 A.M. to 4:00 P.M.; closed on Sundays, Mondays, and holidays except for Children's Day (May 5).

No matter what street you end up on, you will come across small fabric and hobby shops, stationery and toy stores, electronic goods outlets, and numerous shoe stores (this is a great place to buy kids' sandals). Time for lunch? The bakeries, ice cream shops, take-home Japanese food, and popular fast-food stores will guarantee that no one in the family goes hungry for very long.

### Musashi Koyama Shopping Area
4–4–1 Ebara, Shinagawa-ku, Tokyo    東京都品川区荏原 4–4–1
🚃 Musashi Koyama Station, Tokyu Mekama Line

By car, the shops are only about a 10-minute drive from Gotanda Station, and you can usually find a parking space on a street nearby. If you're going by train, take the Mekama Line out of Meguro Station to Musashi Koyama Station. Most of the stores in the area are open every day except Tuesday from 11:00 A.M. to 7:00 P.M.

We love Musashi Koyama. Actually, we lived in Tokyo for years without knowing about this traditional Japanese shopping mecca, but now we go there as often as possible to make up for lost time. An enticing arcade offers over five hundred stores with bargains galore. You will find everything from futons to fur coats as you stroll down the long thoroughfare. For children, check out the cheap diapers, cute dishes, and discounted designer duds.

If you take the train to Musashi Koyama Station, look for the clock as you exit. Then head for the lane of stores that begins with a jewelry shop on the right-hand side. Just down that lane, look for Pocket Town 321, a women's clothing shop, and you'll be in our favorite arcade. Your best bet is to start at this end and stroll all the way down just to see the plethora of shops. Tokiwa Drugstore (they have cheap Pampers) marks the end of this arcade.

The great thing about shopping at Musashi Koyama is how much fun it is for the kids. Each time they start to get restless, don't worry as you will soon come across another toy store or Sanrio shop to explore. We warn you, however, that you will spend more time than you ever imagined browsing through the mall. It is a good idea to make it a full day's outing, especially on your first trip. Also, although many stores take credit cards, most of the smaller ones do not, so bring along plenty of cash.

We always get so preoccupied with the children's clothing bargains in this area that we forget to shop for women's and men's clothes. If you do take the time to look for adult fashions, you will find a stylish selection at very reasonable prices. Another good buy is bedding. Check out Bena for futons, blankets, and other bedding in all price ranges. Two interior shops, Interior Station Hoshinoya and Matsumura Interior, have some of the cheapest prices in town for window treatments, carpets, and household and bathroom goods. Several of the furniture shops carry inexpensive bookshelves and desks—items sometimes difficult to find in Tokyo.

Shinryudo and Total Fashion Seikado have casual clothes for kids in popular styles at bargain prices. Across from these shops is a large Sanrio store, look for the giant Hello Kitty popcorn machine in the mall, and remember this Sanrio store for holiday goodies around Halloween, Christmas, and Valentine's Day.

Next to Sanrio is Azuki, a tiny shop that makes delicious cream-filled (or, if you prefer, red-bean-filled) pastries. The warm cakes are especially yummy on a cold day. Directly across from Azuki, you will see Tenyodo, another good shop for bargains in sleepwear, *asobigi* (playsuits for the park), and maternity clothes. Nearby is Tamuraya Kimono, where we buy inexpensive festival costumes for the kids. They also have a good selection of *hanten*, those padded coats that Japanese children wear instead of bathrobes.

In this same area, you will find the DoBe toy store, which is full of fun stuff for all ages. Look for the big red trolley at the entrance. Across the way are a couple of shops that carry children's designer clothes, such a NAF NAF, Miki House, and Mou Jon Jon. These stores usually have sale bins out front.

A few steps more and you are at McDonald's. This is one of the McDonald's in Tokyo that has a birthday room. The space (for a maximum of ten kids) can be reserved by calling ☎ (03) 3781–3417. The only charge is for what the kids eat, plus the birthday cake. There are several other restaurants in the area, including a fast-food sushi shop where sushi is served on a revolving belt.

If you are looking for baby clothes, don't miss the store with a picture of Dumbo on the sign out front. They carry cute baby and children's clothes and shoes. Throughout the mall, shoes are a prominent item. From kids' rainboots to "squeaky shoes" (sandals and shoes with a squeak in the heel), you will find everything you need in the shoe line here.

While at the mall, you may want to take advantage of the low prices of groceries at the Hankyu Koei store (especially if you go by car). Look for the store's red canopy near the Funland video games and the Chaplin key shop.

## Osaki New City

1–6–4 Osaki, Shinagawa-ku, Tokyo　東京都品川区大崎 1–6–4
☎ (03) 3490–2283
🚃 Osaki Station, JR Yamanote Line

Opened in the 1980s in Shinagawa, this gleaming white structure is a great place to shop for the whole family. Osaki New City is open every day from 10:00 A.M. to 7:30 P.M. and is conveniently located at Osaki Station. The station exit leads directly to the third-floor level, and car parking is available underground. On the third floor are some fast-food eateries and also a lovely outdoor water fountain and square where the kids can run around on a nice day.

Take the elevator to the second floor and step out into a consumer's paradise with a giant shopping center called My Place on one side and a large supermarket on the other. My Place carries everything a family needs, from toys to chinaware. Complimentary strollers are available for the little ones, and the store accepts all major credit cards. Its selection of children's bikes and bike accessories, such as carriers and helmets, is especially good. You'll also find a terrific toy department with plenty of display items to keep the kids busy while you shop. Also on this floor you'll find a Sanrio shop, McDonald's restaurant, a shoe store, and a bookstore.

In the children's clothing section, there are many inexpensive brands in addition to designer duds by Mou Jon Jon and Mickey Mouse. Be sure to check out the sales, as there are bargains throughout the store. In particular, the *obento* boxes and thermoses in the kitchen and houseware department are very reasonably priced.

## Shimokitazawa
 Shimokitazawa Station, Odakyu, Inokashira lines

Shimokitazawa is an area in Setagaya that is famous for its large variety of restaurants and side streets crammed with shops. For adults, the bars and restaurants that line each alleyway are fun to explore in the evening. For parents shopping for the kids, two budget department stores and a plethora of small neighborhood shops offer bargains galore. The shops are conveniently located near Shimokitazawa Station; using either the north or south exit will put you in the heart of the main shopping area. If you drive, you can try to park as close to the station as possible, although many of the streets are narrow alleyways, and parking is limited. Most of the small stores do not open until 11:00 A.M., but there is usually enough happening at 10:00 A.M. to keep you busy for the first hour.

Start at the south exit for the largest concentration of shops. Just outside the station are the inevitable fast-food restaurants, as well as some fine bakeries. Each street is lined with small shops and restaurants, just waiting to be explored. If you walk down the street with the Shopping Center sign over it, you will come to Big Ben, the building that has the Rock 'n' Roll Diner in it. This restaurant is a great place to take the entire family for a fun evening of music and American food. If you head back to the station and continue around the corner to the left (as you face the station), you will see the Chujitsuya supermarket/department store, which has three floors of food, clothes, and household goods. On the third floor there are sale bins and toys.

To get to the other side of the tracks, go back to the station and cross over to the north exit. Just outside is the four-story Daimaru Peacock store. This large branch has groceries, children's and adults' clothing, and household goods at reduced prices. Across the street from Peacock there is a nice fabric store and more small alleyways and side streets to wander down.

## Tamagawa Takashimaya Shopping Center
3–17–1 Tamagawa, Setagaya-ku, Tokyo　東京都世田谷区玉川 3–17–1
☎ (03) 3709–2222 (shops) and (03) 3709–3111 (Takashimaya Department Store)
 Futako Tamagawa-en Station, Denentoshi, Oimachi, Shin Tamagawa lines

When we start to long for our modern shopping malls back home, this is where we go. The Takashimaya mall, as we call it, is one of Japan's most modern and spacious indoor shopping centers. It is easy to get to, just off route 246 and across the street from the Futako Tamagawa-en

Station. There is plenty of covered parking at the mall, and most stores are open daily from 10:00 A.M. to 9:00 P.M. The Takashimaya Department Store is open from 10:00 A.M. to 7:00 P.M. and closed on some Wednesdays.

Anchored at one end by a large Takashimaya Department Store, the mall comprises four buildings, all connected by glassed-over walkways. This mall underwent complete renovation in 1989, and the result is an interior that is a gleaming, highly polished, art deco statement of shopping in style. Whether you are shopping for something in particular at one of the mall's many specialty shops or just need to get out of the house with the kids, the wide marble hallways and stunning displays are a nice change of pace to shopping downtown. And best of all, everything is indoors, making the mall a great place to escape to in rainy weather.

There is an information desk on the first floor with leaflets and information in English. On the second floor in the main building is a corridor a little off the beaten track (just past Laura Ashley) with huge, padded wicker chairs that is the perfect resting place for new or expectant mothers and tired shoppers. Throughout the buildings, you will find chairs and tables, drinking fountains, and spacious bathrooms that nicely accommodate parents with children.

Some of our favorite downtown stores have branches, but the great thing is that here they are all together in one easy location. For imported decorations and goodies for the holidays, try the large Sony Plaza store in the south building on the basement level. Up on the third floor in the same building is a branch of Ginza's Itoya stationery store that always has an abundant supply of greeting cards and small gifts. Also on the third floor is Hobbyra Hobbyre (look under Hobbies in the mall directory), a fabric and yarn store that is full of hard-to-find one hundred percent cotton calico imported from the United States.

In the main building, check out Laura Ashley for women's clothes and interior fabrics, and the many designer boutiques from Ginza. There is a fancy fabric store here called Maruchu that stocks fabric from Yves St. Laurent and other major names. For the flavor of the Southwestern United States, go to Uhn Good. It is a large store with imported dried flowers, pottery, and throw rugs.

The basement level is dedicated to food, and it is almost impossible to leave here hungry. Besides the department store's usual Food City, there are restaurants to suit every taste and budget. If you cannot find what you want here, go to the sixth floor of the south building, where there is another group of restaurants.

## MYCAL Hommoku

19–1 Hommokuhara, Naka-ku, Yokohama-shi, Kanagawa
☎ (045) 624–2121　神奈川県横浜市中区本牧原 19–1
🚆 Negishi Station, JR Negishi Line; Sakuragicho Station, JR Negishi, Tokyu Toyoko lines
🕐 10:00 A.M. to 8:30 P.M. daily (stores); 11:00 A.M. to midnight daily (restaurants); 10:00 A.M. to 11:00 P.M. daily (sports facilities).

The MYCAL shopping plaza in Yokohama consists of seven fun-filled buildings of shopping and eating enjoyment. This new concept in Japanese shopping malls takes its cue from the sunny southern California life-style. The design is fresh and colorful, and in these buildings you can do your banking, shop for groceries, mail a package, visit the beauty salon, and see a movie—all without moving the car once! If you want to get out of the rat race of Japan for an afternoon, this is the place to go.

The names of the buildings reflect the trendy, informal outlook of the designers with their wacky use of English to describe what can be found inside. For example, block number one, "The Section For Young Urbanites And Their Families," is a five-story building containing children's fashions and toys, men's and ladies' apparel, and food. The first floor of this building has food and household goods, but the highlight of the building has to be the Fisherman's Wharf on this floor where you'll find yourself surrounded by huge fish tanks full of seafood. Lobsters, octopus, and many kinds of fish are here for you to choose from; you can take them home to cook yourself, or eat them there at the restaurant. They even have refrigerated coin-lockers for you to leave your purchases in while you complete your shopping. On the third floor of this building is a food-fair section where you can choose from a variety of food and eat it at the tables provided. There is something for everyone here!

Another building, entitled "A Section Suggesting A Pleasant Atmosphere," not only sells home accessories and furnishings, but also offers an exterior/interior design consulting service. "A Section Featuring A Range Of Services For The Community" has parking for over four hundred cars and real estate, banking, and postal services. "The International Section, Filled With The Sights And Sounds Of Other Countries" houses sports clubs, cinemas, international fashions, and restaurants featuring international cuisine. Throughout the buildings, there are clean, pleasant rest rooms, many with changing tables for infants and chairs where you could breastfeed a baby.

From Negishi Station, take any bus from platform 1 to Wadaya-maguchi. From Sakuragi-cho Station, take bus #8, #58, or #125 from platform 2, #108 from platform 3, or #99 from platform 8. Parking is available in almost all the buildings, with more than one thousand parking spaces in total.

## SPECIALITY AND DISCOUNT STORES

Throughout Japan, there are a number of chain stores that parents should know about. Some of these are discount stores that offer quality merchandise at discount prices. Others are specialty shops that market hard-to-find items. Here are brief descriptions of a few of these stores.

### Daiei

4–1–1 Himonya, Meguro-ku, Tokyo　東京都目黒区碑文谷 4–1–1
☎ (03) 3710–1111
🚂 Toritsu Daigaku Station, Tokyu Toyoko Line
🕐 10:00 A.M. to 8:00 P.M.

Daiei has 311 discount-style department stores in Japan. The company's head office can give you information about stores in your area if you cannot locate one. Their phone number is ☎ (03) 3433–3211.

The Himonya Daiei store on Meguro Dori is a great one-stop shopping center and is representative of what you will find in the larger Daiei stores. To get there by car, drive down Meguro Dori toward Jiyugaoka. After you pass Denny's restaurant on your left, look for the red-orange half-moon logo on the white, ten-story Daiei building, also on the left. Parking is available in two large lots behind the store or on the side streets. On foot, the store is 15 minutes from Toritsu Daigaku Station.

The supermarket on the first floor has great prices on a wide selection of food, and throughout the store you will find bargains on everything from fabric to stereos.

In the children's clothing department, you can purchase good-quality styles at reasonable prices. Rain gear, backpacks, and lunch box supplies are all excellent buys here. For the best deals on the children's floor, check out the bargain bin of clothes in a corner of the store. If you are a seamstress, the fabric here is cheap, cheap, cheap.

Two of the nicest things about Daiei are the many restaurants throughout the store and the ¥100 rides on the landings between floors. The grocery store on the first floor has a wide selection of take-out food, perfect for a picnic in nearby Himonya Park (see chapter 5).

Daiei sells their own brand of certain products, such as diapers. For newborns, who don't need extremely thick diapers, a case of Daiei diapers is the best deal in town. The price is a fraction of what you would pay elsewhere, and the plastic on the outside of the pants is nice and soft. In fact, parents-to-be would do well to go on a pre-natal shopping spree at Daiei. On the children's floors in Daiei you will find everything from Nuk pacifiers to strollers and car seats.

If you live near a Daiei store, you will save a bundle by shopping regularly for their low-priced groceries and household goods. For those a bit father away, it is still worth your time to make the trip to Daiei once a month or so. In the Himonya store, there is only one elevator, plus a central escalator, so this is not a great place for a stroller. We use the stairs for speed and to reach the rides.

## Tokyu Hands

12–18 Udagawa-cho, Shibuya-ku, Tokyo　東京都渋谷区宇田川町 12–18
☎ (03) 5489–5111
🚃 Shibuya Station, JR Yamanote and various lines
🕐 10:00 A.M. to 8:00 P.M. Closed the second and third Monday of each month.

Tokyu Hands branches are located in Shibuya, Ikebukuro, Shinjuku, Futako Tamagawa, Machida, Yokohama, and Fujisawa. There are also stores in Osaka (Esaka, Shinsaibashi), Kobe (Sannomiya branch), Nagoya-ANNEX, Hiroshima, and Sapporo. The main store, in Shibuya, is located behind Seibu Department Store. Look for the large sign across from Hachiko Square in the heart of Shibuya.

Tokyu Hands is a one-stop hobby, fix-it, and do-it-yourself shop —a rarity in Japan. The large stores contain supplies for every craft and home-improvement project you can think of. Fabric, paper supplies, lumber, paint, silk flower, gardening tools and plants—they are all here. The large Shibuya store also has a coffee shop where you can get ice cream and sandwiches, although the multiple half floors aren't exactly stroller-friendly. The Shinjuku Tokyu Hands in the Times Square shopping complex is much easier to navigate.

The larger branches have customer service counters where you may be able to get help in English. Tokyu Hands can also arrange for an independent painter, builder, or other contract workers to do work for you. They can make custom windows or kitchen counters, paint your house, or wallpaper your bedroom.

Even though there is nothing specifically for children at Tokyu Hands, parents with children will find the store invaluable both because there are so many items in one place and because the store can order or custom-make anything you need. We have gone to Tokyu Hands for shelving for the kids' rooms, fabric for Halloween costumes, plastic trash cans for storing toys, wallpaper paste for putting up a border in a child's room, custom blinds, and even artificial turf for the garage when we held a child's party there.

### Seibu Loft
See chapter 8.

### Office Depot
•Ginza Branch: 1–2–3 Ginza, Chuo-ku, Tokyo　東京都中央区銀座 1–2–3
　☎ (03) 5524–1211
•Gotanda Branch: TOC, 1F, 7–22–17 Nishi Gotanda, Shinagawa-ku, Tokyo
東京都品川区西五反田 7–22–17　TOC 1F
　☎ (03) 3494–5555　0120–778–700 (catalog shopping, 8:00 A.M. to 6:00 P.M.)
　🕐 8:00 A.M. to 8:00 P.M. Monday through Friday, 9:00 A.M. to 8:00 P.M.
Saturday, 10:00 A.M. to 6:00 P.M. Sundays and holidays.

The world's largest office-products retailer opened in Japan in 1997. The Gotanda store is twenty-one hundred square meters and stocks over ten thousand products at discount prices. Definitely the place for all computer and office needs, but also check out the desks, lamps and other student-related furniture, as well as school supplies. You can request special items from the store's catalog and utilize its printing and copying services. Other branches opened to date are located Nishi Shinjuku, Shibuya, Ichigaya, and Shimbashi.

### Kinko's
☎ 0120–001–966 (toll-free)

This office service center has opened in Japan and, while not exactly a specialty shop, it is convenient to have twenty-four-hour access to printing and copying services as well as office supplies.

### ¥100 Shops
Thousands of these little shops sprang up in Japan after the bubble burst. Here you can find everything from kitchen utensils and toiletries to toys and beer, all for the low price of ¥100. Our kids love these

shops, and you can definitely find some bargains. Just be aware that many ¥100 shops have short-term leases—some move in and out of a neighborhood in a matter of weeks. Look for the ubiquitous "¥100" or "100円" signs.

## SPECIALTY SHOPPING DISTRICTS IN TOKYO

The four shopping districts described below have long been shopping havens for residents and tourists alike. They are not usually advertised as places for children's items, but we have found a surprising amount of gadgets, party supplies, and household goods that parents of young children could use. When visiting any of these three districts, you can either drive and park on the streets, or take the train or bus to the station of the same name. The shops and bargains you have heard so much about are in the stores in the backstreets just out of the station. If you want to explore, you can strike out on your own and check out the entire area, but we have always found more than enough things to buy within a few steps of the station exit.

### Akihabara

 Akihabara Station, JR Yamanote, JR Keihin Tohoku, JR Sobu, Hibiya lines

This shopping district, well known for its huge selection of electronic and computer goods, has a surprising amount of things that parents and children can use. For low prices on humidifiers, electric heaters and fans, heated carpets, and hand-held vacuums, go to Akihabara. Should you want to buy something with adjustable voltage to take to another country when you leave Japan, go to one of the tax-free or export shops—usually identified by the international flags outside the shop.

Besides electronic goods, there are many small shops with interesting items on the busy streets here. On the way to our car from a large export shop one day, we passed a book and record store, a shop full of Sesame Street character goods, and a vendor selling miniature sponge lobsters that grow to life-size when you place them in water. You never know what you will find on the side streets of Akihabara, so take plenty of cash.

### Asakusabashi

 Asakusabashi Station, JR Sobu, Toei Asakusa lines

Asakusabashi is best known for its paper products, and rightly so. You will never have seen so many varieties of paper, nor so many shops devoted to selling it. *Washi* paper is available here all year round. If you are looking for holiday goods, you can usually shop a month or two in advance. For Christmas you can shop from October. Artificial trees and garlands, ribbons, bells, lights, and all other Christmas decorations imaginable can be found here.

Asakusabashi is also known for its craft stores, particularly those which sell kits and materials for making Japanese dolls. In this area there are also stores that sell kimono and *obi* fabric off the bolt—great for covering tea boxes and making other Japanese crafts.

We have found Asakusabashi to be a gold mine of trinkets and small gifts for children, as well as a good place to find costume and party supplies. Some stores in the Asakusabashi area are wholesale outlets, but we have never had any problem buying from them.

### Kappabashi

🚇 Tawaramachi Station, Ginza Line

Kappabashi is a wholesale district for restaurant and kitchen supplies west of Tawaramachi Station between Asakusa and Ueno. Paper products such as plates and cups are also a good deal here. Often stores will sell you only a large quantity of a certain item, whether it be china cups or paper napkins. This area is also the place to buy the infamous plastic food that is used as samples in so many restaurants in Japan. This artificial food is more expensive than most people think, but for the right person it makes a great gift.

### Naka Okachimachi

🚇 Naka Okachimachi Station, Hibiya Line

Every now and then, we head to Naka Okachimachi for the super discount stores located there. If you get off at Exit 3, you will be at the intersection of Kasuga Dori and Showa Dori in Taito-ku, about 30 minutes from Roppongi. The tall gold building looming overhead is called There, and inside are nine floors of just about anything you'd ever need at rock-bottom prices. On our last visit we bought a stylish vest for ¥1,800, a lamp for the children's room for ¥1,500 and a box of Teddy Grahams cookies for ¥100.

Next door to the gold building you will see two purple buildings, part of the Takeya super discount stores. There and Takeya have similar merchandise, but the children's toy selection at Takeya is the cheapest merchandise we have found. Excellent quality toys such as Legos, Barbies, remote-control Shinkansens, and puzzles are offered at forty to seventy percent discounts. A one-thousand-piece puzzle of Mt. Fuji was priced at ¥1,500; recently we saw the same one at Tokyu Hands for ¥2,500. Toiletries, stationery supplies, and auto equipment are also excellent buys at both stores. Fax prices start at ¥29,000 and Sony Walkmans are available from ¥2,900.

If you turn left at the corner of the second purple building, you'll see yet another purple building. Ask here for directions to the bicycle and stroller shop, which has been relocated. This branch of Takeya has the cheapest bike and baby gear in town. The Takeya stores, ☎ (03) 3835–7777, are open every day from 9:00 A.M. to 8:00 P.M., except for the second and third Wednesdays of the month.

## CLOTHING SPECIALTY STORES

### Familiar

• Ginza branch: New Melsa, B1, 5–7–10 Ginza, Chuo-ku, Tokyo
☎ (03) 3574–7111　東京都中央区銀座 5–7–10　ニューメルサ B1
🚇 Ginza Station (Matsuzakaya Department Store exit), Ginza, Hibiya, Marunouchi lines
🕐 11:00 A.M. to 8:00 P.M.

• Minato-ku branch: Hiroo Garden, 1F, 4–1–29 Minami Azabu, Minato-ku, Tokyo
☎ (03) 3441–0345　東京都港区南麻布 4–1–29　広尾ガーデン1F
🚇 Hiroo Station, Hibiya Line

Familiar produces a line of children's clothing in Japan. Familiar products are sold in most department stores, and there are many Familiar stores throughout Japan. Their flagship store is in Ginza, and here you will find fine-quality clothing for infants and children. There is also a small restaurant overlooking Ginza that serves sandwiches and cake, a playroom, and a Baby Room for changing diapers or feeding baby.

In addition to its own line, Familiar carries a fine selection of classic clothes with other brand names. It also stocks a wide variety of imported shoes. Familiar's clothes are on the expensive side, but the quality is excellent. For beautiful infant knitwear, it is one of our favorite stores. Familiar's seasonal sales let you enjoy substantial discounts on Japanese designer clothes. At the store, you will receive a member's card that is stamped after each purchase, entitling you to a discount when the card is full.

Besides Familiar's numerous smaller stores and boutiques in department stores, there is a large store in the Kobe Motomachi area.

## Gap

3–37–1 Shinjuku, Shinjuku-ku, Tokyo　東京都新宿区新宿 3–37–1
☎ (03) 5360–7800
🚃 Shinjuku Station, JR Yamanote and various lines
🕐 11:00 A.M. to 9:00 P.M. daily.

Opened in 1998, the new Flags shopping complex in Shinjuku houses Gap, Oshman Sports, and a huge Tower Records. Call the above number for its other store locations.

## Land's End

Call ☎ 0120–554–774 for a catalog.

## Laura Ashley

6–10–12 Ginza, Chuo-ku, Tokyo　東京都中央区銀座 6–10–12
☎ (03) 3571–5011
🚃 Ginza Station (Matsuzakaya Department Store exit), Ginza, Hibiya, Marunouchi lines
🕐 10:30 A.M. to 8:00 P.M.

Laura Ashley is known for her classic British clothes for women and children. The stores also have design books, interior accessories, and upholstery fabric.

There are numerous Laura Ashley shops in greater Tokyo, including those in Ginza, Aoyama, and Jiyugaoka. Nagoya and Hiroshima have large stores, and there are Laura Ashley boutiques in the Kintetsu Abeno and Kawanishi Hankyu department stores—both in Osaka—and in the Sogo Department Store in Kobe.

## L. L. Bean

1–16–6, Minami Machi, Kichijoji, Musashino-shi, Tokyo
☎ (042) 271–1100　東京都武蔵野市吉祥寺南町 1–16–6

The twenty-one retail stores in Japan offer the same high-quality wear that has made L. L. Bean a household name. Call the above number for the location of the nearest store.

## Talbot's Japan

5–5–7 Ginza, Chuo-ku, Tokyo　東京都中央区銀座 5–5–7
☎ (03) 3571–2922

There are shops in Yotsuya, Ikebukuro, Shinagawa, Jiyugaoka, and Akabane.

# DIANE GOES BARGAIN HUNTING

When it comes to buying clothes, Tokyo can be a bit pricey if you don't know where to shop. Many expats try to avoid the problem by stocking up on clothing for the whole family on annual visits to their home countries. Others plan shopping sprees in Seoul or Hong Kong, well known for their clothing bargains. However, if you find yourself in need of a new outfit, there are resale shops in Tokyo that offer surprising savings.

Each season, I regularly visit several boutiques to sell outdated or outgrown styles and to add a few new items to my wardrobe. Most stores accept used clothes in good condition on consignment, paying sixty percent to you and keeping forty percent of the profit upon sale.

My favorite store is Florence, ☎ (03) 3407–0318, located at 5–49–8 Jingu-mae, just off Aoyama Dori. Coming from Shibuya, pass Children's Castle and turn left at the corner of Citibank. Florence is a 2-minute walk from here, on the right side of the street, next to a china shop. Their store accepts select women's clothes, shoes, and accessories for resale. When dropping off your clothes, Florence requests that you bring in a maximum of five items per week. The shop will price the items for you, and you may pick up your profit after one month. Bank transfer payment is also available.

I have found numerous bargains here over the years, such as a peach cashmere scarf for ¥800 and a linen summer suit for ¥4,000. All the employees are friendly and helpful; if you need to communicate in English, ask for Chieko. Florence is open from 11:00 A.M. to 6:00 P.M. The store is closed Sundays, Wednesdays and holidays.

Another popular resale shop features two convenient locations. Vintage Clothes 0324 can be found on the second floor of a red-brick building at 6–3–15 Minami Aoyama, just off Kotto Dori, on the street leading to Aoyama Cemetery; ☎ (03) 3486–1535. The store is open daily.

Vintage Clothes accepts seasonal clothing and accessories on consignment, with the seller receiving sixty percent. Their hours of operation are 11:00 A.M. to 6:00 P.M. Cut-rate designer clothing is also in stock at times. Unfortunately, English is not spoken at the store, so you may want to bring a Japanese friend along.

For years, I had heard about the great bargains to be found at the Salvation Army's weekly bazaar of used goods in their warehouse near Nakano. I finally made the trek and it was well worth the effort. I bought a Balans chair, like new, for my computer for only ¥2,000, along with a collapsible wooden *kotatsu* table for ¥4,000. The best deals were on furnishings, such as bookshelves, desks, and baby equipment, including high chairs, car seats, and backpack carriers.

The bazaar is held every Saturday from 9:00 A.M. to 1:00 P.M. at 2–21–2 Wada, Suginami-ku; ☎ (03) 3384–9114. If you plan to haul your purchases away, you can usually bargain for a further discount. Otherwise, the Salvation Army will deliver. The nearest subway is Nakano Fujimicho on the Marunouchi Line; it is a 10-minute walk from the station.

By car, take the Shuto Expressway. Get off at Shinjuku, and go straight until the road runs into Ome Kaido. Turn left here. After you pass Higashi Koenji Station, turn left at the Kannana Intersection. A little farther down the road, past a gas station, you will see a large temple on your left in the distance. Turn left towards the temple, go to the third traffic light, and turn left at Wada 1-chome. Go three blocks and take another left. Look for the bazaar in a white building on your right. The Japanese name is Kyuseigun Danshi Shakai Hoshi Center.

For those of you who want to furnish your home with Japanese accents and accessories but can't afford the prices at antique shops, the shrine sales are your best bet. Togo Jinja (shrine) in Harajuku is a favorite of our whole family. While I am on the lookout for interior furnishings, such as bamboo shades, *shoji* screen frames, old chests, and coffee tables, the kids look for special bargains, too. My children have purchased autographed baseballs, dress-up clothes for the costume box, and vintage toys. The shrine sale is open from 7:00 A.M. to about 3 or 4:00 P.M. on the first, fourth, and fifth Sundays of the month, but canceled in case of rain. The nearest station is Harajuku on the JR Yamanote Line or Meiji-Jingu-mae on the Chiyoda Line. By car for Shibuya, go north on Meiji Dori past the Omotesando intersection. Look for the shrine on your left. Check the English-language newspapers and periodicals for other shrine sales.

I am often amazed at what is thrown away in Japan. Keep your eyes open for treasures that your Japanese neighbors may discard. A few years ago I found a beautiful old *tansu* chest that had been put out on the street for a garbage pickup. Other finds include ikebana containers and baskets.

Another source for bargains is the Tokyo American Club's annual garage sale usually held in the spring. Vendors in the Zodiac Sale must be TAC members, but the sale itself is open to the public. There is usually a huge selection of children's toys, clothes, and books, in addition to nearly new housewares, adult clothing, and other items. The American Club is located just behind the Russian Embassy at 2–1–2 Azabudai, Minato-ku; ☎ (03) 3583–8381. The parking lot is open to members only. The nearest subway stop is Kamiyacho on the Hibiya Line.

## CLOTHES AS A HOME BUSINESS

Some Tokyo residents sell imported clothes from the United States and Great Britain as a home business. Ownership changes every few years owing to the mobility of foreign residents, but if you ask around at the international schools or at functions with foreign mothers, you will be able to find out who is selling what this year. These clothes are sold at private sales and at the international bazaars in Tokyo.

## RENTAL CLOTHES AND SERVICES

The Japanese often go to rental shops for a special party dress or for formal attire. Now that concept has expanded to include children's clothes. Throughout Japan, rental children's ceremonial kimono and Western-style formal wear are available through the stores and catalogs for baby equipment mentioned in chapter 3. In Tokyo, we recommend the following stores.

### Allegretto

4–15–6 Minami Azabu, Minato-ku, Tokyo    東京都港区南麻布 4–15–6
☎ (03) 3280–3789
🚇 Hiroo Station, Hibiya Line
🕐 11:00 A.M. to 6:00 P.M. Closed on Tuesdays.

Here, you will find a selection of lovely dresses for girls and a few suits for boys available for rent. Most of the clothes are from the United States or Italy, but there is an especially pretty line of dresses designed by the owner. Suits are available from age two to preteen. Patent leather shoes or traditional loafers can also be rented.

### Ark

1–21–7 Ebisu Nishi, Shibuya-ku, Tokyo    東京都渋谷区恵比寿西 1–21–7
☎ (03) 3476–4141
🚇 Ebisu Station, JR Yamanote, Hibiya lines
🕐 11:00 A.M. to 8:00 P.M. daily.

Formal clothing for women, men, and children.

### Renrie

Kobari Bldg., 3F, 4–11–30 Nishi Azabu, Minato-ku, Tokyo
東京都港区西麻布 4–11–30  小針ビル 3F
☎ (03) 3400–8799, toll-free 0120–22–8799
🚇 Roppongi Station, Hibiya Line
🕐 12:00 A.M. to 8:00 P.M. Closed on Sundays and holidays.

Specialty shop renting kimono, *furisode*, and *hakama*. Kimono available for ¥9,000 and up for two nights. The shop is a 10-minute walk from the station.

### Taisei Ishou

1–11–11 Higashi Nakanobu, Shinagawa-ku, Tokyo
☎ (03) 3786–4781　東京都品川区東中延 1–11–11
🚉 Ebara Nakanobu Station, Tokyu Ikegami Line; Nakanobu Station, Tokyu Oimachi Line
🕐 10:00 A.M. to 6:00 P.M. Closed on Tuesdays.

Rental service for kimono, wedding and party dresses. The perfect place for festive Japanese kimono in children's sizes. Your teenage daughter can check out the party clothes.

### United Rent All

2–17–1 Meguro Honcho, Meguro-ku, Tokyo　東京都目黒区目黒本町 2–17–1
☎ (03) 3794–3431
🚉 Gakugei Daigaku Station, Tokyu Toyoko Line
🕐 9:00 A.M. to 7:00 P.M. daily.

Party supplies, ski wear, and video cameras are just a few of the items you may find more practical and less expensive to rent rather than buy in Japan. At Japan's premiere rental company, you can choose from more than one thousand items in stock. Shops are located in Meguro-ku (a 15-minute walk from the station), Koto-ku, Nerima-ku, and Kita-ku.

## RESALE OUTLETS

We have unearthed a few select shops that sell used children's clothes and other items. Until recently, Japanese did not like the idea of purchasing stranger's discarded items. However, the idea is catching on, especially when the used items are well preserved. If you want to sell or buy children's clothing or toys, look for a recycle shop in your area and go in and see what they have. Even if they do not have any children's clothes in stock, they may be willing to sell yours on commission.

### BX Plaza Suginami

1–17–17 Shoan, Suginami-ku, Tokyo　東京都杉並区松庵 1–17–17
☎ (03) 3333–3773
🚉 Mitaka-dai Station, Keio Inokashira Line
🕐 10:30 A.M. to 6:00 P.M. Closed the second Thursday each month.

This is a different kind of consignment shop in that it allows you to exchange your goods for other items. Their selection includes children's clothing and toys. A membership card entitles you to a twenty percent discount on purchases.

### Fukushi Center

1–12–20 Oogi, Adachi-ku, Tokyo    東京都足立区扇 1–12–20
 ☎ (03) 3896–1536
📍 Nippori Station, JR Yamanote, Joban, Keisei lines

The Fukushi Center has large sales four or five times a year. You can obtain a schedule by calling the center. To get there, take a bus from JR Nippori Station for Adachi Ryutsu Center and get off at the Oogi Ohashi Kitazume stop.

### Garage Shop Nakanishi

3–19–3 Tamagawa, Setagaya-ku, Tokyo    東京都世田谷区玉川 3–19–3
☎ (03) 3708–3930
📍 Futako Tamagawa-en Station, Tokyu Shin Tamagawa, Oimachi lines
🕐 10:30 A.M. to 6:00 P.M. daily.

This resale shop sells and accepts baby furniture in addition to children's clothes and toys. The shop's commission is only twenty-five percent.

### Grab Bag

Motohashi Building, 2F, 1–34–11 Kichijoji Hommachi, Musashino-shi, Tokyo
☎ (0422) 21–7057    東京都武蔵野市吉祥寺本町 1–34–11　本橋ビル2F
📍 Kichijoji Station, JR Chuo, Keio Inokashira lines
🕐 10:30 A.M. to 5:30 P.M. Closed on Mondays and holidays.

Opened by American Ellen Motohashi, Grab Bag specializes in European and American children's clothing, toys, and books in English. Slightly used items are accepted for consignment. The owner invites children to join her for story time on Tuesday and Thursday mornings at 11:00 A.M.

### Kaiten Mokuba

2–27–21 Naka Ochiai, Shinjuku-ku, Tokyo    東京都新宿区中落合 2–27–21
☎ (03) 3954–0559
📍 Shimo Ochiai Station, Seibu Shinjuku Line
🕐 10:00 A.M. to 6:00 P.M. Closed on Sundays and holidays.

This recycle shop's large selection of women's and children's clothes is sold at extremely competitive prices.

### Kids Freak

Subaru Bldg., 4F, 6–2–2 Minami Karasuyama, Setagaya-ku, Tokyo
☎ (03) 3308–9864    東京都世田谷区南烏山 6–2–2　スバルビル 4F

**￦** Chitose Karasuyama Station, Keio Line
🕐 11:00 A.M. to 5:00 P.M. Closed Saturdays, Sundays, and holidays.

Mostly clothing, some of it name brand, for children up to age ten. The store also carries a few kimono for resale, usually in the smaller sizes.

### Ninjin

1–31–5 Asagaya Kita, Suginami-ku, Tokyo　東京都杉並区阿佐ヶ谷北 1–31–5
☎ (03) 3310–1739
**￦** Asagaya Station, JR Chuo Line (call for directions from Asagaya Station)
🕐 11:00 A.M. to 4:00 P.M. Monday through Saturday. Closed on holidays.

This recycle shop is completely devoted to children's goods. Here you can find not only clothes but also secondhand books and toys at very reasonable prices. English spoken.

### Recycle Shop Koko

Green Heim, 1F, 3–29–8 Nakanoshima, Tama-ku, Kawasaki-shi, Kanagawa
☎ (044) 911–5526　神奈川県川崎市多摩区中之島 3–29–8　グリーンハイム1F
**￦** Nakanoshima Station, JR Nambu Line
🕐 11:00 A.M. to 5:00 P.M. Closed Wednesdays, the second and fourth Sunday each month, and holidays.

You'll find all kinds of children's wear on consignment, from ¥100 T-shirts to festive kimono and dolls for Girl's Day.

## SEW IT YOURSELF

Another alternative to outfitting the kids without busting the budget is to sew their clothes yourself. For those of you who enjoy sewing, either for your children or yourself, Japan has some terrific fabric shops. "Do-it-yourself" may not appear to be as popular here as in some other countries, but there are large numbers of people who sew for home decorating, for their children, or simply for their own enjoyment.

As a foreigner, you might consider purchasing some items in your home country to save time and money. We would suggest buying patterns, notions, and perhaps a basic supply of fabrics in colors that you use often. It is also helpful to subscribe to a sewing magazine that can supply you with the newest fashions in patterns from your home country. Most of the sewing supplies you will need can be found here, but some specialty items are difficult to locate. For example, we have yet to find a store that carries fine-quality cotton batiste for smocking little-girls' dresses. Also, the selection of Swiss eyelet, in either trim or fabric, is limited and expensive.

Conversely, there are some things that you will find in abundance in Japan that may be hard to find elsewhere. You will see a wide selection of children's fabrics and prints for clothes or decorating in almost every store. Among our favorite fabrics in Japan is the one hundred percent cotton stretch fabric that is available in a wide variety of colors and patterns.

The listing below contains a few select fabric stores in Tokyo. Most department stores have a small section of notions and fabric. Tokyu Hands has a whole floor full of sewing and knitting supplies in their store in Shibuya, and other locations have sewing supplies also. Throughout Japan, there are large craft stores that have floors and floors of buttons, lace, ribbon, and notions galore. You will also come across small neighborhood fabric stores that will have bolts of fabric but no notions. Whether you are an avid seamstress or just a fabric fanatic, you will enjoy browsing through the stores listed here.

## Blue and White

2–9–2 Azabu Juban, Minato-ku, Tokyo　東京都港区麻布十番 2–9–2
☎ (03) 3451–0537
🚇 Roppongi Station, Hibiya Line
🕐 10:00 A.M. to 6:00 P.M. Monday through Saturday and 11:00 A.M. to 6:00 P.M. on Sundays. Closed on holidays.

A unique source for gift items, this store stocks an original selection of *yukata* fabric. All designs are made especially for Blue and White, and each motif is based on a traditional source. The *yukata* fabric is available in shades of blue and white, red and white, or pink and white.

## Fabrications

Crossroad Bldg., 1F, 1–29–1 Shoto, Shibuya-ku, Tokyo
☎ (03) 3462–0233　東京都渋谷区松濤 1–29–1　クロスロードビル 1F
🚇 Shibuya Station, JR Yamanote and various lines
🕐 11:00 A.M. to 8:00 P.M. Closed on Tuesday.

This store has a wide selection of interior and children's fabrics. They also offer classes and demonstrations on sewing for the home, and anything that they do not have in stock they will order. The store is conveniently located just past the main Tokyu Department Store and across from Bunkamura.

## Horiuchi

2–25–6 Dogenzaka, Shibuya-ku, Tokyo　東京都渋谷区道玄坂 2–25–6
☎ (03) 3496–5411
🚇 Shibuya Station, JR Yamanote and various lines

⏱ 9:00 A.M. to 6:00 P.M. Closed on Sundays and holidays and the third Saturday each month.

This little shop is a great place to find notions, lining fabrics, interfacings, and knitting supplies. The store is across the street from the main Tokyu Department Store.

### Laura Ashley

For locations, see the Clothing Specialty Stores section of this chapter.

Most Laura Ashley outlets carry a small stock of upholstery and interior fabric. Should you want some design that they do not stock, they will try to find it for you in another of their stores in Japan. If they have to order it from England, there is a 5-meter minimum order. All branches can supply you with a catalog and fabric swatches for the entire Laura Ashley line. For top-quality British fabric and design, Laura Ashley is the place to go.

### Okadaya

3–23–17 Shinjuku, Shinjuku-ku, Tokyo　東京都新宿区新宿 3–23–17
☎ (03) 3352–5411
🚇 Shinjuku Station (east exit), JR Yamanote and various lines
⏱ 10:00 A.M. to 8:30 P.M. Closed every third Sunday from January to October.

Paradise for any seamstress is to be found at Okadaya. A number of stores are grouped together near Shinjuku Station, and the easiest store to find is across the street from the east exit. Each floor of the four locations carries a different item—one floor for ribbon, one floor for buttons, one floor for lace, and so on. This store is also a good place to find better fabrics as well as lace for evening wear and wedding dresses.

### Pico

See the listing for Jiyugaoka in the Shopping Districts section of this chapter.

### Shibuya Marunan

2–5–1 Dogenzaka, Shibuya-ku, Tokyo　東京都渋谷区道玄坂 2–5–1
☎ (03) 3461–2325
🚇 Shibuya Station, JR Yamanote and various lines
⏱ 10:00 A.M. 8:30 P.M. daily.

This store is easy to get to, is open late, and has a fabric stock representative of what you can expect to find in most stores in Japan. At first glance, the store seems tiny, but there are several floors to explore. Notions are also sold. Shibuya Marunan is across from the cylindrical 109 Building in the heart of Shibuya. Look for the bolts of sale fabric stacked outside the store as you walk from the station to the 109 Building.

## Takatomi Elegance

1–10–13 Bakuro-cho, Nihombashi, Chuo-ku, Tokyo
☎ (03) 3663–3151　東京都中央区日本橋馬喰町 1–10–13
 Bakurocho Station, JR Sobu, Toei Shinjuku lines
🕐 10:00 A.M. to 6:00 P.M. Monday through Saturday, 10:00 A.M. to 5:00 P.M. Sundays and holidays. Closed the first and third Sunday each month.

This fabulous chain store specializes in fine fabrics. Branch stores are in Tokyo at Yurakucho, Kanda, Kitasenju, Omori, Ikebukuro, Meguro, Shinjuku and, in Kanagawa-ken, at Yokohama and Atsugi. There are also a chain of apparel stores by the same name. At the main branch you will find everything from imported British woolens to Chinese silks to sequined velvets; this store has the best quality and most expensive fabric available for sewing one-of-a-kind garments. Even if you settle for something out of the bargain bin—as we usually do—a trip to Takatomi is a must for fine-fabric lovers.

## Tamagawa Takashimaya Shopping Center

At this mall, you will find many stores carrying imported and designer fabric. For a more detailed description, see the listing under Shopping Districts earlier in this chapter.

## TOA Textile World

1–19–3 Jinnan, Shibuya-ku, Tokyo　東京都渋谷区神南 1–19–3
☎ (03) 3463–3351
🚉 Shibuya Station, JR Yamanote and various lines
🕐 10:00 A.M. to 8:00 P.M. daily.

## Yuzawaya

8–23–5 Nishi Kamata, Ota-ku, Tokyo　東京都大田区西蒲田 8–23–5
☎ (03) 3734–4141, (0422) 79–4141 (Kichijoji branch)
🚉 Kamata Station, JR Keihin Tohoku, Tokyu Mekama, Tokyu Ikegami lines
🕐 10:00 A.M. to 8:00 P.M. daily.

Yuzawaya is more than a store, it is a way of life. Actually it is a complex of ten stores conveniently located near the south exit of Kamata Station. Taking the correct exit will save time. Do not walk down the long corridors of the station to the main exit. Instead, take one of the exits close to the ticket booth (these have no name or number, so ask).

From there it is a 5-minute walk straight down the street to the nearest store. At Yuzawaya you'll find not only clothing and interior fabric at bargain prices, but also the materials for making any kind of craft imaginable: stained glass, leather crafts, Japanese dolls, needlepoint, artificial flowers, kilns, more than twenty-eight hundred kinds of yarn . . . need we say more? Get there at 10:00 A.M. and stay all day.

## CHILDREN'S CLOTHES—MAIL ORDER FROM ABROAD

Global people and their global children need the first genuinely global way to shop: the Internet. As much as we love pouring over piles of catalogs and following the time-honored method of sticking Post-its on every page that includes an item that we can't live without, there is nothing quite like the thrill of the one-click checkout, with the e-mail confirmation that comes almost before you turn your computer off. If you have a short-napper in the house, the Internet is the way to shop. Even during a fifteen-minute respite, you can go online, locate birthday gifts, baby gates, and all-natural cotton diaper covers, and still have a minute to rest before duty calls.

You really have two choices when Internet shopping. The easy way is to go to one of the large retail chains that ship worldwide and sell almost everything under the sun. Some of our favorites for families with children are ⌨ <www.Americasbaby.com>, <www.KBKids. com>, <www.BabyCenter.com>. If you are more adventurous, try a search engine like Yahoo, Excite, or Lycos, and scour the world for the rare and unusual items. Whatever your route to the Internet, this is where the goods are, and most websites offer a page that allows you to request a catalog for those long browsing sessions that we like so much. Be sure to check the shipping rate when shopping on the Internet, because not all sites will be able to give you the final cost of shipping to Japan.

We have used the following catalogs and have found the quality of their products and the reliability of their service to be excellent. Not only are the prices reasonable, but often the styles are a refreshing change from what you will find in Japan. Even though the companies listed are all in the United States, you will find a wide selection of clothing from around the world. Cotton clothes from Sweden, *très* chic designs from France, and matching brother-and-sister outfits are just a few of the items these catalogs feature.

### After the Stork/Playclothes

- P.O. Box 44321, Rio Rancho, New Mexico 87174, USA
  ☎ (505) 867-7168    🖷 (505) 867-7101    💻 www.afterthestork.com
- PLAYCLOTHES: ☎ (505) 867-7176    🖷 (505) 867-7101

Children's sizes six months to fourteen, and some adult sizes as well. This company offers a wide variety of styles from sporty playclothes to frilly dresses for babies and sophisticated outfits for pre-teens. There is also a good variety of hundred-percent cotton playwear for all sizes.

### Biobottoms

617 C 2nd Street, Petaluma, California 94952, USA
🖷 (540) 670-2121    💻 www.biobottoms.com

Children's sizes from newborn to fourteen. Good-quality cotton clothes and infant wear. Fashionable designs that are practical and durable.

### Children's Wear Digest

3607 Mayland Court, Richmond, Virginia 23233, USA
☎ (540) 345-7640    🖷 (540) 345-6546    💻 www.cwdkids.com

Children's sizes from twelve months to sixteen. Sturdy, U.S. brand-name apparel for children. Great selection of Oshkosh overalls, jeans, and swimsuits. Also, costumes for Halloween in the fall catalog.

### Eastbay

427 Third Street, Wausau, Wisconsin 54403, USA
☎ (715) 848-9588    💻 www.eastbay.com

This is a sportswear clothing company and the top supplier in our households of sports jerseys, team uniforms, and even bats, balls, and shoes. Goods from every professional and college team in the United States are represented here, as well as major brand sports shoes. Call the number above and ask for an international order form along with you catalog. Sizes—youth through adult.

### Hanna Andersson

- 1010 N.W. Flanders, Portland, Oregon 97209, USA
  ☎ (503) 242-0920    🖷 (503) 222-0544
- Tokyo: Hanna Andersson Service Center
  ☎ (03) 5354-7888    🖷 (03) 5354-7857

Children's sizes, from newborn to teens, as well as adult sizes. Top-quality one hundred percent cotton clothing made in Sweden for the entire family. Practical and whimsical designs, beautiful colors, and lasting construction—any kid would be lucky to wear Hannas. To meet the growing demand for these fabulous clothes in Japan, Hanna has opened a Tokyo Service Center, from which you can order by fax or phone. The service center offers inventory information and detailed assistance for sizing. Call to request a catalog. In exchange for the required $5 cost of the catalog, you will receive a $10.00 discount coupon to use on any order within six months. Help is available over the phone in both English and Japanese. Hanna also accepts JCB credit cards.

## Lands' End

1 Lands' End Lane, Dodgeville, Wisconsin 53595, USA
☎ (608) 935–6170   🖷 (608) 935–4000   💻 www.landsend.com

Lands' End offers fabulous quality and service at reasonable prices. Outerwear, cotton separates, sturdy playwear, sportswear, and shoes —their children's catalog has it all. From size six months to twenty. Also available is the general catalog for adult sizes and specialty catalogs for men, women, and the home. Lands' End is a cut above in customer service, with a generous return and replacement policy, and helpful and courteous sales people.

## L. L. Bean

☎ (207) 552–6878, 800–441–4913   🖷 (207) 552–4080
💻 www.llbean.com

The best of the Northeast brought directly to your door. The children's catalog contains rugged sports and outdoor wear for children sizes six months to twenty. Khakis, swimsuits, outdoor wear, and footwear are the mainstays of L. L. Bean. Don't forget to ask for their adult, home, and travel catalogs as well.

## Storybook Heirlooms

333 Hatch Drive, Foster City, California 94404, USA
☎ (415) 525–2179   🖷 (0066) 3380–0094 (toll-free fax from Japan)
💻 www.storybookheirlooms.com

Children's sizes twelve months to sixteen. Fabulous, fairy-tale clothes for kids and mothers. Many matching outfits. This clothing company offers a catalog just for Japan. The catalog costs $5 and can be requested by phone or fax. If you want the U.S. version of the catalog, ask for the domestic version, otherwise ask for the Japanese version. Most of the clothing descriptions in the Japanese version are in English, but the order form is in Japanese. The catalogs contain primarily the same items.

## The Wooden Soldier

P.O. Box 800, North Conway, New Hampshire 03860, USA
☎ (603) 356–7041    🖷 (603) 356–3530

Children's sizes from three months to sixteen. Exquisite selection of dressy clothing for infants, teens, and moms too. Brother-and-sister outfits and other matching sets for the family. Frilly and unique clothes.

# 3

# Equipping

# the

# kids

THERE ARE ALSO CHILD-SIZED "FUTONS".

## BABY NEEDS

Japan is full of wonderful things to buy for babies, from high-tech strollers to traditional futon. Many affordable and high-quality products are sold here. Even though many well-known products from other countries have not been available up to now, with the internationalization of Japan, baby products and accessories from the United States and Europe are showing up in the stores more frequently. If you decide to buy or rent these items here, you will find that outfitting baby in Japan can be as easy and as fun as it would be back home.

If you will be living in Japan for only a short time, you should consider renting baby equipment from any of the numerous companies that provide baby goods. Most publish catalogs with a wide range of products from maternity clothes to cribs. The bulk of their stock is for rent, but some of the merchandise is for sale. See the section in this chapter on baby equipment catalogs in Japan for further information.

Tiny babies do not need a large crib for the first few months, thus in Japan "Moses baskets" are popular for newborns instead of a traditional bassinet. There are also child-size futons that the baby can sleep on next to your bed. These are especially convenient if you use a futon yourself. Both are portable and inexpensive options for baby's first months.

When you are ready to buy a full-size crib, you will find many styles available. We would suggest shipping one if you have the option, as Western full-size cribs are rather expensive in Japan. For a good selection of cribs, try the Nursery Collection by Grandoir. This company imports some very special baby furniture from France, Italy, and the United States, in addition to carrying lovely cribs, baby baskets, and chests of drawers.

One of the best products we've found that is ideal for baby at home or while traveling is the Arm's Reach Bedside Co-Sleeper, which attaches to the side of almost any bed. This places baby close to Mom for comfort or nursing at night, and the whole sleeper folds up into a portable carrying case. The award-winning design is popular with several of our friends who travel frequently with their infants. Contact Arms Reach Concepts at 5699 Kanan Road, Suite 330, Agoura Hills, California 91301–3358, USA, ☎ 800–954–9353, 🖷 (818) 991–5999, 🖳 <www.armsreach.com>.

Baby baths or bath seats are useful to have, and you can find some original models in Japan. One that we like by Combi has a tilted bouncy seat that you strap the child into and then place in the bathtub.  Large plastic tubs, good for bathing babies on the counter or floor, are also available. For toilet training, there are plenty of cute potties for sale; one company's combination stepstool and toilet seat is a popular choice.

Baby walkers are also easy to find here, but we think the playpens are too expensive. The battery-operated swings that our children loved as infants are also pricey. Similar swings are available, but they are not as sturdy as the newest models from the United States.

Highchairs in Japan come in all shapes and sizes. Models that become a regular child's chair when baby has outgrown it and chairs at floor-level for tatami rooms are both available.

The Japanese use frontpacks and backpacks to carry babies, but the soft-straps model is more common. Metal-frame backpacks and baby slings, which are harder to find, can be mail ordered from the overseas catalogs listed in this chapter.

Some of the best strollers in the world can be found in Japan. Combi and Aprica are two of the most famous brands, and both are available in a variety of styles. Depending on your needs, you may want a large model that converts from a pram style to a regular stroller, or just a lightweight umbrella stroller. Some families buy one of each, but you will be surprised at the cost of the top-of-the-line designs. As one new dad complained, "My kid's new stroller cost as much as my first car!" A popular option is to buy a medium-size stroller that is lightweight and folds down easily for travel but which also has storage under the seat and hooks on the handles for bags.

Car seats are an essential item if you plan on driving with baby. If you are using a regular-size child's car seat for a newborn, try to get one of those newborn headrests to fit inside the car seat, or make your own by rolling up a soft towel or blanket and placing it around the top of baby's head as a cushion.

When buying a regular-size car seat, be sure to get one that your child will not outgrow too soon. Combi and Aprica both make good car seats, but we found Guardian's seat the roomiest for our kids to use up to about age four. Car seats are now required by law, but unfortunately the prices are rather high. You can always watch the notice boards at grocery stores and look around the rummage sales at local churches. Make sure the model is recent (made within the last three to four years) to be assured of maximum safety. You also may want to buy a car seat that has been approved by the airlines if you plan on flying with baby.

## BABY EQUIPMENT STORES

Department stores in Japan (see chapter 2) carry a vast assortment of baby products. The shopping districts mentioned in the same chapter are a good source of bargains for baby merchandise. The following stores have a particularly good selection of goods to meet your baby's every possible need.

### Akachan Hompo

• Head office: 3–3–21 Minami Hommachi, Chuo-ku, Osaka-shi, Osaka
☎ (06) 6251–0625　大阪府大阪市中央区南本町 3–3–21

• Nihombashi branch: 7–18 Yokoyama-cho, Nihombashi, Chuo-ku, Tokyo
☎ (03) 3662–7651　東京都中央区日本橋横山町 7–18
🚇 Bakurocho Station, JR Sobu Line; Bakuro Yokoyama Station, Toei Shinjuku Line
🕒 9:00 A.M. to 5:30 P.M.

If you are outfitting baby on a budget, you will want to head straight for Akachan Hompo. Besides baby equipment, Akachan Hompo's more than thirty stores sell children's clothing and toys, maternity clothes and accessories, and gift items. To shop at the stores and take advantage of the wholesale prices, you must become a member by paying ¥2,000. The first time you go, ask at the checkout counter for a membership form. Members receive a card that must be shown each time you shop. You will also receive advance information on sales and special events at the stores. Other stores in the Kanto area are Gotanda and Nakanobu (Shinagawa-ku), Funado (Itabashi-ku), Higashi Hokima (Adachi-ku), Tanashi-shi, Omiya (Saitama-ken), Yokohama and Ebina

(Kanagawa-ken), Kashiwa and Yachiyo (Chiba-ken). Other branches are located in Sapporo, Sendai, Aomori, Nagoya, Shin Osaka and Izumi (Osaka), Kyoto, Takamatsu, Iizuka and Hakata (Fukuoka-ken).

## Grandoir Nursery Furniture

Head office: 19 Aza Nagakute Yokomichi, Nagakute-cho, Aichi-gun, Aichi
☎ (0561) 62–4063   🖷 (0561) 62–9496   愛知県愛知郡長久手町字長久手横道 19
🕐 9:00 A.M. to 6:00 P.M. Closed weekends and holidays.

The Grandoir line of nursery furniture is sold at select locations in Japan. Call the head office to request a catalog from which you can order by phone. You can also buy Grandoir furniture at the major department stores.

## Wise Mammy

Shima Building, 2F, 2–14 Yotsuya, Shinjuku-ku, Tokyo
☎ (03) 3359–6301   東京都新宿区四谷 2–14   嶋ビル2F
🕐 11:00 A.M. to 6:00 P.M. Closed Sundays and holidays.

This lovely store carries European designer layettes and name-brand clothing (sizes are for babies up to about nine months). Check out the exquisite nursery furniture.

# BABY EQUIPMENT CATALOGS (IN JAPAN)

## King Baby Co.

• Head office: 2–2–7 Sembanishi, Mino-shi, Osaka   大阪府箕面市船場西 2–2–7
  ☎ (0727) 29–6666   🖷 (0727) 29–9204   🖳 www.kingbaby.co.jp
• Tokyo branch: 1–6–2 Ningyo-cho, Nihombashi, Chuo-ku, Tokyo
  ☎ (03) 3667–4361   🖷 (03) 3667–4364   東京都中央区日本橋人形町 1–6–2

The King Baby Co. has a catalog with a large selection of baby products and accepts both mail and phone orders. Of special interest are their good-quality cloth diapers and diaper covers, as well as maternity underwear and cotton baby clothes. Call or write for a catalog.

## Marie Foret

Maternity Division: 7–22–17 Nishi Gotanda, Shinagawa-ku, Tokyo
東京都品川区西五反田 7–22–17
☎ (03) 3494–3377   toll-free 0120–003–377   🖷 (03) 3494–2578

This is a catalog of maternity and baby wear and accessories. You can order by phone, postcard, or fax. Items are delivered within two to three days, and payment is due within two weeks after receipt of the merchandise.

## Paren Co.

Ichikura Bldg., 2–2–4 Kanaya-cho, Chuo-ku, Osaka-shi, Osaka
大阪府大阪市中央区鎗屋町 2–2–4　イチクラビル
☎ toll-free 0120–067–858 (9:00 A.M. to 9:00 P.M.)

This company's catalog carries a big selection of all the goods necessary for equipping baby in style. Call or write to request a catalog.

# BABY EQUIPMENT CATALOGS (FROM ABROAD)

### Hand in Hand

891 Main Street, Oxford, Maine 04270, USA
☎ (207) 539–8305　🖷 (207) 539–2935

A good selection of baby products, bath toys, books, videos, toys, and clothing in sizes two to six is available from this catalog.

### One Step Ahead

P.O. Box 517, Lake Bluff, Illinois 60044, USA
☎ (847) 615–2110　🖷 (847) 615–7234　🖥 www.onestepahead.com

This is the most comprehensive catalog for new parents and babies that we have ever seen. Convenient products, educational toys, bedding, and travel and safety items are all included. If you only order one catalog, make it this one!

### Safety Superstore

🖷 (905) 761–6857　🖥 <www.safetysuperstore.com>, <BabyProofingPlus.com>

Here, you will find 450 products online! Download, print, and fax back their baby/child-proofing checklist and they will reply with the cost and location of the items you should have. Everything you need for safety in the home and travel.

### The Safety Zone

Hanover, Pennsylvania 17333, USA
☎ (717) 633–3370　🖷 (717) 633–3222

This company's catalog offers all the items you could possibly want for keeping the home safe for you and your children. Along with a wide variety of baby-proofing devices and car seats, you can order gadgets such as safety lights, electric roach traps, battery chargers, and water filters, to name a few.

### Tot Tenders

P.O. Box 998, Poway, California 92074, USA
☎ (619) 679–2104, 800–634–6870   🖳 www.babycarriers.com

A six-position baby carrier is available from Tot Tenders that allows a baby to be carried in six different positions, including facing outward. It also secures a baby in a grocery cart or adult chair. This company makes the only twin baby carrier we know of, and one for triplets as well. It also has products for toddlers with attention deficit disorder.

## BABY EQUIPMENT RENTAL OUTLETS

These rental outlets have baby equipment and supplies for rent and/or sale. Many of them also carry a selection of children's party clothes, ceremonial kimono, and maternity clothes. Call them and they will send you a catalog from which you can order.

GREATER TOKYO AREA

### Aiiku Baby
☎ Tokyo branch: (03) 3935–3111   Yokohama branch: (045) 472–8191

### Aioi Baby
☎ toll-free 0120–101–456

### Baby Lease
☎ toll-free 0120–158–181

### Hoxon Baby
☎ toll-free 0120–240–800

### Sanai Baby Lease
1–7–7 Inukura, Miyamae-ku, Kawasaki-shi, Kanagawa
☎ (044) 977–7933   神奈川県川崎市宮前区犬蔵 1–7–7

This company has outlets in Tokyo ☎ (03) 3366–4450, Yokohama ☎ (045) 311–9895, Tama ☎ (0423) 75–9333, and Sagamihara ☎ (0427) 47–5911.

### United Rent All
See chapter 2, Rental Clothes and Services.

**Baby Futabado**

☎ (075) 623–1717

This company will deliver in Kyoto, Osaka, and Shiga.

**Osaka Baby Center**

☎ toll-free 0120–123–747　🖷 toll-free 0120–744–447

They will deliver in the Osaka area.

**Petite Angel Yamasaki**

☎ In Okayama: (086) 222–4081

## DIAPERS AND ACCESSORIES

Diapers are of course a necessity when outfitting any baby, and a variety of diapers are available in Japan. Disposable diapers have become more popular in recent years, with many good-quality brands now on the market. There are also many diaper services that make using cloth diapers easy and affordable. In Japan, nonbreathable plastic pants to put on over cotton diapers have been consigned to history. Instead, you will find "waterproof" cotton diaper covers, and the most wonderful wool and Goretex diaper covers. All of these covers close with Velcro at the front, so no pins are necessary.

We prefer the U.S. brands of baby wipes to the Japanese, but the only way to get them is through the Foreign Buyers Club (see chapter 10). The Japanese brands are expensive and flimsy—you need four or five for each diaper change. One suggestion is to buy Japanese-brand wipes when they are on sale and to use washcloths at home to save money.

## DIAPER SERVICES

Some diaper services deliver cloth diapers, while others deliver both cloth and disposable diapers. If you use cloth diapers, you will need a large diaper bucket to store them in between pickup dates. Cloth diapers may come in two varieties—Western or Japanese. You may or may not be given a choice. What they call a Western-style diaper is most likely made of all-cotton—like a cotton dish towel, that can be folded into many sizes and styles. The Japanese-style diaper is usually made out of a cotton gauze-type fabric.

The following diaper services provide cloth diapers for rent only.

GREATER TOKYO AREA

### Hemmy Diaper Service

3–38–3 Ebisu, Shibuya-ku, Tokyo    東京都渋谷区恵比寿 3–38–3
☎ (03) 3444–4491 (closed Saturday and Sunday)

This company delivers both cloth and disposable diapers to hospitals and homes in central Tokyo once a week. English spoken.

### Seigyokusha

264 Ichinotsubo, Nakahara-ku, Kawasaki-shi, Kanagawa
神奈川県川崎市中原区市ノ坪 264
☎ (03) 3700–5157, (03) 3467–7404, (03) 3682–1901 (Japanese only)

Deliverys of both cloth and disposable diapers throughout Tokyo twice a week.

### Tokyo Diapers

3–22–11 Shinjuku, Katsushika-ku, Tokyo    東京都葛飾区新宿 3–22–11
☎ (03) 3607–5231 (Japanese only)

Tokyo Diapers delivers within Tokyo once a week. They will provide both cloth and disposable diapers.

## DECORATING THE KID'S ROOM

Decorating and organizing your child's room can be a challenge whether you live in a spacious house or a tiny apartment. No matter where you live, you will want your child's room to be fun yet functional. Many convenient accessories and products for decorating can be bought in Japan. Check the TownPage telephone directory for listing of furniture shops; you'll also find a large number of furniture lease companies with attractive Western-style furnishings for the home. For hard-to-find products from overseas, read through the mail-order section at the end of this chapter.

The biggest problem facing most of us in Japan is lack of space, and we have a few suggestions on how to make the best of what you have. The world's greatest collection of storage containers is available here in a variety of colors, sizes, and shapes. Bright-colored plastic baskets and bins are just the thing for keeping kids' clutter organized, and we use them to store everything from Legos to bath toys. Look for them in local houseware and hardware stores.

Closet space can be doubled with the use of extenders made just for this purpose. The wire rods hook onto the clothes bar and hang down below, so another bar can then be extended between them on a lower level. Not only do you have twice the space with this system, but even the youngest child can reach his clothes. Extenders are sometimes available from overseas catalogs, but the same effect can be achieved with a homemade version. Take a bamboo pole and two pieces of wire or strong string. Tie the bar to the wire, trapeze-style, and suspend it from the original clothes bar at the right height for your child.

You should utilize every inch of storage space in your child's room. We found that a vinyl hanging shoe rack hung low on the back of the door was just the place to store mittens and other small items that are easily lost in drawers. Of course, it is always a good idea to have hooks that the kids can reach in the bedroom and bathroom, for hanging up towels, clothes, backpacks, and what-not. If you like personalized coat racks, you can either make them yourself with a board, some paint, and markers, or order them from one of the catalogs listed in this chapter. Other hand-painted personalized items that kids love, such as wooden stools, rocking chairs, and nameplates, are not readily available in Japan but may be ordered from abroad.

Even if your child's room is the size of your closet back home, a color-coordinated look can enliven the space considerably. Most landlords in Japan will not allow you to put up wallpaper, but there are some alternatives. Try to coordinate the fabric on the curtains and beds, using a theme or character that appeals to your child. A variety of styles, from Barney to ballerinas, can be ordered from catalogs such as J. C. Penny or Sears and Roebuck. You can purchase some adorable children's fabrics in Japan (see chapter 2), but unless you can sew, the cost of having anything custom made is quite expensive.

Another way to liven up the walls is to tape or tack up a matching wallpaper border. You can put it just below the ceiling level or at chair-back height. Posters and prints are also easy ways to decorate without spending too much time or money. Since children grow quickly and their tastes change, there is no need to have the posters framed. Just tack them securely to the wall with two-sided tape or thumb tacks.

For a wide selection of wallpaper borders and posters, it is best to order from overseas. The selection in Japan is limited (mostly Disney characters), and prices are high. Maps are a must for any family with children, and world and other maps are available—in Japanese, of course. Maps in English can be found at the major English-language bookstores (see chapter 4).

We suggest that you bring all the bedding that you will need when you move to Japan. From crib sheets to king-size beds, the size and selection in Japan is quite limited. Bassinet sheets are almost impossible to find. For options on sleeping arrangements for baby, see the introduction to this chapter. For toddlers and older children, duvets are a good choice. Kids can easily make their own beds using the duvet instead of a top sheet and blanket. The mail-order section of this chapter lists discount outlets for down comforters and bedding.

For a new baby, there are several essentials that make a lovely nursery. If you choose a crib, do not forget bumper pads, crib skirt, or canopy to complete the look. If you order items from overseas, make sure you allow enough time for delivery by sea mail to save money. In addition to crib fabric, a companion fabric that can be used for window treatments or a chair cushion and pillows is a good choice. If you are lucky enough to have a large shipment coming to Japan, make sure to include a comfortable rocking chair, as your only chance to find one here may be from a friend, through the want ads, or at international bazaars and flea markets. Also important to have is a changing table, a playpen, and a state-of-the-art highchair. An area rug in the same colors as the nursery is a nice addition that you can take with you when you move.

In Tokyo, during most months of the year morning sunlight will stream in through your windows bright and early. If you hope your child will sleep past sunrise, you will need some form of window treatment to block out the sunlight. Blackout fabric, sold at custom drapery shops and some fabric stores, can be made into curtains or shades to fit behind your decorative window treatment. Another alternative is to use inexpensive miniblinds and top them off with a whimsical valance. You can make simple swags and bows and staple them up around the window. If you do not sew, just drape the fabric and staple at will. Full custom-made curtains for a child's room are not worth the price you have to pay here.

When buying overseas, remember that standard-size curtains often will not fit Japanese-size windows. If you want to order curtains that match your bedding but you are not sure of the fit, either order two sets and sew them together or buy an extra set of sheets to make your own window treatments. Extra sheets also come in handy for pillows, cushions, and even covering a headboard.

Other suggested items to order from overseas or to bring with you include baby monitors, night lights and baby lamps, and mobiles for hanging above a crib.

If your only option is to use Japanese products for your child's nursery or playroom, be sure to go to a discount shop first to see what they have. If you are looking for Western-size cribs and foreign baby equipment, place a want ad on a public bulletin board or in the English-language newspapers and magazines.

Perhaps you would like a Japanese theme for your child's room. Try some of the delightful patterns of *yukata* fabric for throw pillows and window treatments. One friend incorporated her collection of small, pastel-colored fans into a window treatment in her daughter's room by attaching them to a bamboo screen. For a boy's room, try hanging the brightly-colored Boys' Day carp streamers or paper kites from the ceiling or walls. These same carp streamers can be stuffed for an unusual bed pillow. A collection of traditional Japanese wooden toys make an attractive bookshelf arrangement. Many products made from *washi* paper are suitable for decorating a child's room: mobiles, storage boxes, wastebaskets, picture frames, and more can all be used in decorative ways. Brightly-colored Noh masks are also fun for kids to collect and display on a bedroom wall. Japanese tea boxes, which come in many sizes, can be covered in colorful fabric and used as toy or clothes storage boxes.

## RESOURCES IN JAPAN

### Murray and Doug (formerly Textile Iida)

1–25–11 Higashi, Shibuya-ku, Tokyo　東京都渋谷区東 1–25–11
☎ (03) 5468–5001　🖷 (03) 5468–5075　🖳 trading@textileiida.co.jp

The fabric design house of Textile Iida has expanded into a new shop, Murray and Doug. In addition to a showroom full of exquisite imported fabrics, you'll find the "Speedy" line of accessories and fabric for children, as well as gifts for the home. Murray and Doug/Textile Iida is also a reputable source for sewing and upholstery work.

## Pier 1

Aoyama Bell Commons, 2–14–6 Kita Aoyama, Minato-ku, Tokyo
☎ (03) 3475–8020　東京都港区北青山 2–14–6　青山ベルコモンズ

A large selection of furniture, much of which is suitable for a child's room. A variety of items in wicker and pine, inexpensive throw rugs, and many accessories make this shop worth a visit. Prices, though not exorbitant, are not as low as in the United States. Tokyo branches can be found in Meguro, Jiyugaoka, Kunitachi, and Tama Center. In the Kansai area there are shops in Omeda (Osaka) and Roko Island (Kobe).

## *MAIL-ORDER FROM ABROAD*

The following companies have everything for decorating your child's room, from posters and wall hangings to rocking chairs, all of which you can order by mail. For more room accessories, look at the mail-order catalogs listed in chapter 4.

### American Library Association

ALA Graphics, 50 E. Huron St., Chicago, Illinois 60611, USA
☎ (312) 944–6780

Posters from your favorite books, such as *Curious George* and *The Cat in the Hat*. These inexpensive posters are aimed at promoting reading and library use.

### Art.com

For art on the internet visit ⌨ <Art.com>. This is the website for any poster you ever imagined. Decorate your child's room with reprints of the masters' classics or their favorite cartoon and movie characters. Visit the online framing gallery to mat and frame, or have the print delivered rolled for your own framing.

### Child Graphics Press

P.O. Box 7771, Hilton Head Island, South Carolina 29938, USA
☎ (803) 689–3030　🖶 (803) 671–4665

Creative art posters from many favorite fairy tales.

### The Company Store

500 Company Store Road, La Crosse, Wisconsin 54601, USA
☎ (608) 785–1400　⌨ www.thecompanystore.com

A fine collection of goose- and duck-down bedding, including cotton crib sheets, dust ruffles, and bumper pads. Also available from the catalog are one-hundred-percent merino wool stroller throws, car seat covers, and playpen and crib mattress pads. They also sell beds, futons, air mattresses, and roll-aways, as well as a line of window treatments and closet accessories. The quality is unbeatable and they are continually adding to their home furnishings section.

### Fun Furniture

8451 Beverly Blvd., Los Angeles, California 90048, USA
☎ (213) 655–2711

This is the most innovative idea in children's furniture that we have ever seen. Fun Furniture creates unique, architect-designed chairs, headboards, shelves, lamps, etc., in a variety of tantalizing colors. The furniture is either plastic-laminated or hand-painted, and the designs consist of castles, animals, and other whimsical motifs. The company will pack and crate the furniture and also help you arrange for overseas shipping. They do not publish a catalog, but you should call if you are looking for custom children's furniture.

### The Peaceable Kingdom

2980 College Ave., Suite 2, Berkeley, California 94705, USA
☎ (510) 644–9801    🖷 (510) 644–9805

Posters of Peter Rabbit, Babar, Curious George, and many other characters from children's classics are to be found in this catalog. Maurice Sendak's *Where the Wild Things Are* is available, along with a special poster he created for the International Year of the Child.

### Rand McNally and Co.

P.O. Box 1697, Skokie, Illinois 60076–9871, USA
☎ (847) 673–9100

This is the place for globes, maps, and atlases for the home and office.

4

Books, & toys, and Libraries

THANK YOU, DAO.

Just when you think your children have more than enough books, toys, and games, you find that the little rascals have grown out of them. Children advance in reading, toys break or become otherwise obsolete, and games are no longer a challenge. Children move on to new interests and activities. We have accepted the fact that our house is nothing more than a revolving door through which an unlimited number of books, toys, and games will pass as the children grow up.

Living in Japan is a mixed blessing in the endless cycle of book, toy, and game acquisitions. There is no question that some of the most intriguing toys are made here, and those that are not manufactured here are imported. Books and games in English are another story. Compared to other items for children, only a handful of these are available in Japan. We have found mail-order sources from abroad to fill the gap, however, and so our children's libraries continue to grow. Public libraries serve the same purpose in Japan as anywhere else, allowing children to borrow a book, enjoy it, and return it. Depending on where you live, public libraries can be a practical asset or a once-in-a-while outing.

## BOOKS AND MAGAZINES

We know of a few special children's books available about Japan and its people that are good for entertaining and educating children about the Japanese way of life. *Sayonara, Mrs. Kackleman,* by Maria Kalman (Viking Penguin, 1989), is the most adorable, hysterically funny book we have ever seen about Japan. It is written from a child's point of view about a visit to Japan, and the whimsical pictures make the book a delight. The book can usually be found in the children's book section of Maruzen bookstore. Another book you may want to look for is *How My Parents Learned to Eat*, by Ina Friedman (Houghton Mifflin Co., 1984). This lighthearted tale takes place in Japan and is interesting for children age four and up.

For a fun, musical introduction to the Japanese language for children, we recommend the book and cassette series *Teach Me Japanese*, by Judy Mahoney. *Teach Me More Japanese* is now available, as well. To order this fun and educational series, write to Teach Me Japanese, 10500 Bren Road East, Minneapolis, Minnesota 55343, USA; ☎ 800–456–4654 or (612) 933–8086.

For grades K-3, the World Neighbor Series produces an excellent book on Japan. Full of crafts, maps, facts, and music, it lists additional video and reading suggestions. (The Sesame Street video, *Big Bird Goes to Japan*, is a great introduction to Japan for young kids.) To order the World Neighbor Series, contact Creative Teaching Press, Cypress, California 90630, USA.

See also recommended websites in chapters 12, 13, and 14.

There is a series of coloring books about Japan called *American-Japanese Coloring and Talking Books*, illustrated by N. Sugimura (Charles E. Tuttle Co., 1952). Each book in the ten-volume series focuses on a subject of interest to children, such as fairy tale characters, animals, or holidays. It then compares the Japanese version of the subject with the American version using easy story lines and fun-to-color pictures. They make great gifts! A hardcover book that contains twenty of Japan's best-loved children's tales called *Japanese Children's Favorite Stories*, edited by Florence Sakade (Charles E. Tuttle Co., 1953), is also available. Any of these books make a treasured addition to anyone's collection.

## BOOKSTORES

### Crayon House

3–8–15 Kita Aoyama, Minato-ku, Tokyo　東京都港区北青山 3–8–15
☎ (03) 3406–6492
🚇 Omotesando Station (A1 exit), Ginza, Chiyoda, Hanzomon lines

This bookstore makes for a great outing with the kids. Not only do they have a fabulous selection of hardback and paperback children's books in English, French, German, and Japanese, but they have a nice family restaurant in the basement. From the menu to the kiddie seats to the staff that "ooh and ah" over your children, a visit to this restaurant is a treat for everyone. Go to the second floor for stationery goods and calendars with all of the popular storybook themes (Babar, Winnie the Pooh, etc.) plus a great selection of imported wooden toys.

Crayon House also has a baby-sitting service; call ahead in Japanese to make a reservation. To get there, take the subway to Omotesando Station and go out the Hanae Mori exit (A1). Crayon House is located one block behind the Hanae Mori Building. The store is open daily from 11:00 A.M. to 7:00 P.M., and the restaurant is open from 11:00 A.M. to 10:00 P.M.

## FBC Bookstore

The FBC Bookstore (part of the Foreign Buyers Club family of wholesale foreign goods) continues to offer everything from bestsellers to Disney videos through their mail-order business. You can contact them at ☎ (078) 857–9001, ☏ (078) 857–9005, or ⌨ <www.fbcusa.com> for a free catalog.

## Fiona

Solofiole, 5–41–5 Okusawa, Setagaya-ku, Tokyo
☎ (03) 3721–8186　東京都世田谷区奥沢 5–41–5　ソロフィオーレ
🚈 Jiyugaoka Station, Tokyu Toyoko Line
🕐 11:00 A.M. to 8:00 P.M.

Tokyo has quite a few excellent bookstores for English-language books, some of which specialize in children's reading material. Such is the case with Fiona, at Jiyugaoka. Advertised as having the largest selection of children's books in English in the city, Fiona also stocks video tapes, CD-ROMs, games, and educational material.

## Good Day Books

Asahi Building, 3F, 1–11–2 Ebisu, Shibuya-ku, Tokyo
☎ (03) 5421–0957　☏ (03) 5421–0958　東京都渋谷区恵比寿 1–11–2　朝日ビル 3F
🚈 Ebisu Station, JR Yamanote, JR Saikyo, Hibiya lines
🕐 11:00 A.M. to 8:00 P.M. Monday through Saturday and holidays, 11:00 A.M. to 6:00 P.M. on Sunday. Closed on Tuesdays.

If you want to find excellent bargains on used books, try Good Day Books, located in Ebisu. This shop carries a varied selection of new books as well, but the deals on used books are hard to resist. Spend a morning cleaning out bookshelves with the kids and then bring your stash to Good Day Books. The credit vouchers you are given for the books they accept enable you to get any used book free, or fifty percent off new books. All of your old books will be considered for trade with the exception of hardback novels and damaged or out-of-date books. They will also order new books for you at a fair exchange rate. Your order will arrive in a few short weeks. Call for book-exchanging hours.

## Jena Co.

5–6–1 Ginza, Chuo-ku, Tokyo   東京都中央区銀座 5–6–1
☎ (03) 3571–2980
🚇 Ginza Station (B5 exit), Ginza, Hibiya, Marunouchi lines
🕐 11:00 A.M. to 8:00 P.M. Monday through Saturday, from noon to 7:00 P.M. on Sunday.

This three-story bookstore has a small selection of foreign books and magazines on the third floor. The children's selection consists mostly of hardbacks in English, ranging from board books for infants to the classics for three- to twelve-year-olds.

Jena is just outside the B5 exit. If you are walking from the center of Ginza, take the road with the Wako Building and the round Sanae Building for two short blocks. Jena is on the same side as the Sanae Building.

## Kinokuniya Bookstore

5–24–2 Sendagaya, Shibuya-ku, Tokyo   東京都渋谷区千駄ヶ谷 5–24–2
☎ (03) 5361–3301
🚇 Shinjuku Station (south exit), JR Yamanote and various lines
🕐 10:00 A.M. to 8:00 P.M. daily.

The main English-language bookstore is in Shinjuku's Times Square, with foreign books on the times square floor. The children's selection is diverse, although small. Most of the books are top-quality hardbacks from the United States, Canada, and Great Britain. There are a few books in German and French. We were pleased to find a selection of children's Bible story books (not easy to find in Japan), as well as books about traditions and holidays from many countries around the world.

Another central Tokyo branch with foreign books is in Tokyu Plaza in Shibuya. Branches outside Tokyo include Kami Ooka (Yokohama), Nagoya, Osaka (Umeda store), Kobe, Hiroshima, Fukuoka, and Kumamoto. These stores carry only a small selection of books in English, but they will order specific titles from the main store in Shinjuku for you.

## Little America Bookstore

3–6–21 Ozasa, Chuo-ku, Fukuoka-shi, Fukuoka　福岡県福岡市中央区小笹 3–6–21
☎ (092) 521–8826　🖷 (092) 521–2288

This bookstore has everything you need to learn to speak, read, or write English; indeed, the store was originally opened to provide supplies for teachers of English as a second language. The result is a store with fun and educational games, tapes, and workbooks. The store has many hard-to-find items in English, such as maps, learning posters, card and board games, and flash cards. For the price of a stamp, they will send you a catalog from which you can order by mail.

## Mandarake

Shibuya Beam Bldg., 31–2 Udagawa-cho, Shibuya-ku, Tokyo
☎ (03) 3477–0777　東京都渋谷区宇田川町 31–2　渋谷ビームビル
🕐 12:00 P.M. to 8:00 P.M. daily.

We don't know whether to include this place under books or toys because it has both. Mandarake is actually a comic book "den," a sprawling cavern, four floors underground, filled with every Japanese comic (no porn was apparent), and many English comics, too. Besides the comics, you can choose from a huge selection of related action figures. The staff are walking around dressed as comic-book characters and occasionally burst into a spontaneous performance. Look for the fun house–type entrance across from McDonald's near Tokyu Hands.

## Maruzen

2–3–10 Nihombashi, Chuo-ku, Tokyo　東京都中央区日本橋 2–3–10
☎ (03) 3272–7211
🚇 Nihombashi Station, Tozai, Ginza, Toei Asakusa lines

This is by far the best general bookstore in Tokyo for children's books in English. Located on the fourth floor is the children's section where you will find an exquisite collection of books in English and other languages. They have Caldecott medal winners, classics, and our favorite Elsa Beskow books. You can browse for hours among the selection, but don't forget to check out the maps, language tapes, and videos. For parenting or health books, go to the second floor, where most of the English books for adults are stocked.

The bookstore is directly across from Takashimaya Department Store. A subway exit leads right into the basement level of Maruzen. Hours are Monday through Saturday, 10:00 A.M. to 7:00 P.M. The Ochanomizu branch in Tokyo also carries a large selection of books in English. The Osaka branches are at Shinsaibashi and Temma; the Kobe branch is at Motomachi.

## National Azabu Bookstore

4–5–2 Minami Azabu, Minato-ku, Tokyo　東京都港区南麻布 4–5–2
☎ (03) 3442–3505
🚇 Hiroo Station, Hibiya Line

Although it is called a bookstore, this is more like a stationery store. There is a good selection of greeting and holiday cards, wrapping paper, paper products for parties, small gift items, and foreign and local magazines for all ages. The books consist mostly of best-selling paperbacks and books about Japan but the store also stocks a few children's story books and some activity-type books for preschoolers.

Located above the National Azabu Supermarket, across from Arisu-gawa Park, the bookstore is open daily from 9:30 A.M. to 7:00 P.M.

## Paperweight Kids Books

Kitamura, 60-Kan, 201, 5–16–1 Hiroo, Shibuya-ku, Tokyo
東京都渋谷区広尾 5–16–1 キタムラ60館
☎ (03) 3498–5260　🖨 (03) 5420–1504　💻 www.kidsbks.co.jp
🚇 Hiroo Station, Hibiya Line

Initially started as a mail-order book company, Paperweight Kids Books has expanded to a cozy retail bookstore in Shibuya. In addition to a delightful selection of children's books, it also carries educational material such as the School Zone series. Hours of operation are 11:00 A.M. to 7:00 P.M. Monday through Saturday, including holidays, and 11:00 A.M. to 6:00 P.M. on Sundays. Closed the first and third Monday of each month.

## Tower Records

1–22–14 Jimnan, Shibuya-ku, Tokyo　東京都渋谷区神南 1–22–14
☎ (03) 3496–3661
🚇 Shibuya Station, JR Yamanote and various lines
🕐 10:00 A.M. to 10:00 P.M. daily.

Tower Records's store in Shibuya offers the ultimate browsing experience on a sweltering summer day. The store has an international plethora of books, magazines, CDs, videos, all at very reasonable prices. Up on the seventh floor, you can spend the whole day in the cool oasis of the imported book and magazine section.

In addition to Shibuya, Tower Records now has locations in Shinjuku, Ikebukuro, Hachioji, Yokohama, Kawasaki, Sagamino, Chiba, and Minami Koshigaya, although not every branch has English books and magazines. A mega Tower Records is located in the new Flags shopping complex next to the east-south exit of Shinjuku Station at 3–37–1 Shinjuku, Shinjuku-ku; ☎ (03) 5360–7811. It is open from 11:00 A.M. to 11:00 P.M. daily.

## Tuttle Bookshop

1–3 Jimbo-cho, Kanda, Chiyoda-ku, Tokyo    東京都千代田区神田神保町 1–3
☎ (03) 3291–7071
🚇 Jimbo-cho Station, Hanzomon, Toei Mita, Toei Shinjuku lines

Here you will find an excellent selection of books from a variety of publishers. Among their selection for children are pop-up books, coloring books, audiocassette and book sets, paint-with-water books, and almost anything else a child could want in a book. Our favorite coloring book series, *American-Japanese Coloring and Talking Books*, are usually available at this store, although sometimes they have to be ordered.

The store is a 10-minute walk from Jimbocho Station. It is open Monday through Saturday from 10:30 A.M. to 6:30 P.M., but closed on Sundays. The Osaka branch is in the Wako Bldg., 2–7 Showa-cho, Suita-shi, Osaka-fu; ☎ (06) 6382–5020.

## *BOOKSTORES ONLINE*

### Amazon.com

🖥 www.amazon.com

The pioneer in online book selling and much, much more. You'll find books, videos, toys, and, with its zShop tie-ins, almost anything you need. Their discounts are deep and they ship overseas. If you order several books at a time, you can easily undercut many of the booksellers in Japan.

### Barnes and Noble

🖥 www.barnesandnoble.com

One of America's biggest bookstore chains is now on line, giving Amazon some competition. Barnes and Noble has a huge selection of books, magazines, videos, tapes, software, and so on.

### Skysoft

☎ (03) 5204–6551    🖨 (03) 5204–6553    🖥 www.sky.co.jp

Skysoft, a Japan-based service, accepts orders on its website and can deliver titles within two weeks. There is no shipping charge or handling cost as long as you pick up your order at any of the 185 Bunkyodo locations. Choose from two million titles, including music scores.

## OTHER SOURCES

Throughout the year, there are many opportunities to purchase books at the fairs and bazaars held by the international schools, churches, and private clubs around Tokyo. The books at these sales are sometimes provided by individuals who sell books as a home business. Sometimes these sources provide mail-order catalogs.

### La Leche League International

La Leche League (LLL) of Japan stocks copies of several English-language books that are unavailable in bookstores in Japan. The LLL manual, *The Womanly Art of Breastfeeding*, is always available in English and Japanese, and their cookbook, *Whole Foods for the Whole Family*, is very popular. They also sell books by Dr. William Sears, such as *Nighttime Parenting*, in addition to books on pregnancy, childbirth, and breastfeeding by other authors. Contact an LLL leader in your area if you are interested in purchasing books or borrowing from their library.

For more information, see the LLL listing in chapter 9.

## BOOK-OF-THE-MONTH CLUBS

Book-of-the-month clubs in the United States, Canada, and Great Britain sell books to members at reduced prices. Books range from the classics to early readers to special-interest books, depending on the club. Unfortunately, because of prohibitive shipping costs these clubs generally will not mail to individuals in Japan. There is one book club in Great Britain, however, that will mail to groups, such as schools, play groups, and reading circles. It seems that shipping large quantities is profitable for them, and as the books are priced twenty-five to forty percent lower than in Tokyo bookstores, it is also worth it for you.

Again, we stress that this club is not intended for individual families but for groups. This means that if you can get six to ten families together for a reading circle, you can make use of this club! For more information, write to Baker Books Puffin Book Club, Manfield Park, Cranleigh Surrey, GU6 8NU, England. Alternatively, call ☎ (1483) 26–7888 or ☎ (1483) 26–7409.

# MAGAZINES FOR KIDS ONLY

Imagine the joy your child would experience at receiving his own magazine in the mail each month. Just as we hunger for new and up-to-date resources to feed our interests, so do our children. This list of magazines from the United States and Canada contains periodicals for children from two to fifteen years. The magazines are full of informative, educational, and insightful articles, stories, and projects, and most are advertisement-free. Payment must be made in U.S. dollars or by VISA or MasterCard unless otherwise noted. Write or call for subscription information, or search for an online website.

### ChickaDEE Magazine

179 John Street, Suite 500, Toronto, Ontario M5T 3G5, Canada
💻 www.owl.on.ca/chick/csub.html

For four- to nine-year-olds. This magazine contains articles, arts activities, and stories that aim to interest young children in the world around them in an entertaining and lively way.

### Disney Magazine

P.O. Box 37263, Boone, Iowa 50037, USA
💻 disney.go.com/DisneyMagazine/

Here it is. The kids' magazine by Disney that is full of their favorite Disney characters and stories. Fun for all ages.

### The Dolphin Log

The Cousteau Society, 8440 Santa Monica Blvd., Los Angeles, California 90069, USA
☎ (757) 523–9335    🖷 (757) 523–2747    💻 www.dolphin.org

For seven- to fifteen-year-olds. This is an educational publication for children that covers marine biology, ecology, natural history, and other water-related topics. No credit cards accepted.

### Faces

30 Grove St., Peterborough, New Hampshire 03458, USA
☎ (603) 924–7209    🖷 (603) 924–7380

For eight- to fourteen-year-olds. A fun, informative magazine on world cultures and history. Each issue focuses on a single subject or culture.

### Highlights for Children

2300 West Fifth Avenue, P.O. Box 269, Columbus, Ohio 43216–0269, USA
☎ (614) 486–0695    🖷 (614) 876–8564

For two- to twelve-year-olds. Full of entertaining stories, games, and puzzles, this magazines is one of the longest running and most popular magazines for children in the United States. The majority of the materials is geared for eight- to twelve-years-olds to read to themselves and two- to seven-year-olds to listen to. There are special pages of interest for each age group so you can save the back issues and read them again as your child grows order. Also request their product catalog, which is full of fun and educational toys.

### Kids City

P.O. Box 51277, Boulder, Colorado 80321–1277, USA

For six- to ten-year-olds. Published by the same publisher as *Sesame Street Magazine*, this periodical is full of humor, stories, and activities. No credit cards accepted.

### National Geographic World

National Geographic Society, 17th and M Streets N.W., Washington, DC 20036, USA

☎ (202) 857–7000    🖷 (301) 921–1347

🖥 www.nationalgeographic.org/world/index.html

For eight- to thirteen-year-olds. This is a highly visual magazine with factual stories about animals, geography, sports, and outdoor adventure.

### Nickelodeon Magazine

P.O. Box 37214, Boone, Iowa 50037, USA

The popular children's television network publishes this magazine that is full of interviews, fun facts, and articles about the kids' favorite stars, sports celebrities, movies, and TV shows.

### Ranger Rick

National Wildlife Foundation, 8925 Leesburg Pike, Vienna, Virginia 22184, USA

🖥 www.nwf.org/nwf/rrick

For six- to twelve-year-olds. From the same publishers as *Your Big Backyard*, this magazine is geared toward an older audience.

### Sesame Street Magazine

P.O. Box 52000, Boulder, Colorado 80321–2000, USA

For two- to six-year-olds. All of the favorite Sesame Street characters are here! This publication, put out ten times a year by the people who bring us TV's "Sesame Street," is informative, educational, and—most of all—fun. Each issue contains games, projects, and stories to entertain your child for hours. An extra bonus is the accompanying Parent's

Guide. The magazine is worth subscribing to just to get this guide full of parenting tips and stories. Published by the Children's Television Workshop. No credit cards accepted.

### Stone Soup

Children's Art Foundation, Box 83, Santa Cruz, California 95063, USA
☎ (408) 426–5557   🖷 (408) 426–1161   🖳 www.stonesoup.com

For four- to thirteen-year-olds. *Stone Soup* is a bimonthly literary magazine of writing and art, including fiction, poetry, book reviews, and artwork by kids through age thirteen.

### Stork, Turtle, Humpty Dumpty, Children's Playmate, Jack and Jill, Child Life, Children's Digest, and U.S. Kids

Children's Better Health Institute, 1100 Waterway Blvd., Box 567, Indianapolis, Indiana 46206, USA
☎ (317) 636–8881   🖷 (317) 684–8094   🖳 www.cbhi.org/magazines.htm

For two- to fifteen-year-olds. These magazines are all published by the Children's Better Health Institute in the United States. Each magazine is geared for a slightly different age group, but all combine fun with learning in eight issues per year. Illustrated stories, poems, puzzles, games, and songs help children learn about health, nutrition, hygiene, exercise, and safety.

### 3–2–1-Contact

P.O. Box 51277, Boulder, Colorado 80321, USA

For eight- to fourteen-year-olds. A third magazine published by the Children's Television Workshop, this one is in the same exciting yet educational style as their TV show of the same name.

### Your Big Backyard

National Wildlife Foundation, 8925 Leesburg Pike, Vienna, Virginia 22184, USA
🖳 www.nwf.org/nwf/ybby/index.html

For three- to five-years-olds. This is a wildlife magazine emphasizing ecology and conservation in an entertaining way for children. It offers nature lore and activities in addition to stories.

### Zoobooks

P.O. Box 85384, San Diego, California 92186, USA
☎ (619) 745–2809   🖳 www.zoobooks.com

For all ages. A real treat for the whole family, these magazine-type books come every six weeks or so—there are ten per year. Each issue focuses on a different animal, exploring its prehistoric ancestors, describing its anatomy, and illustrating where the different varieties of the species can now be found. Young children will enjoy the full-page illustrations and pictures. Older children can use them as reference books for school projects or for learning about a favorite animal.

## TOYS AND GIFTS

Although you may miss the bargain toy stores back home, you can find a wide variety of affordable children's toys here in Japan. In order to give you an idea of what is available, we have highlighted some of our favorite purchases over the years. Some of these items are so unique that you will want your kids to have one as a memento of their stay in Japan. Others are the perfect gift to send back home without spending a fortune.

For those of you with very young children, the selection of riding and push toys here is unbeatable. The cars, trucks, and animals come in all colors and designs, with a sturdy bar across the back for your child to hang onto as he learns to walk. Pick one with all the extras, such as a telephone, beeping horn, and hidden compartments. Your children will spend hours scooting around on these, and they're quite reasonably priced in Japan. For a bit more money, you can purchase a wooden version of this toy. One of our children was given a beautiful Japanese hand-crafted wooden train push toy, which we consider a family heirloom!

Many toys made in Japan are designed with the parent in mind. This is especially true of the tricycles that come with a steering stick in the back for parents to guide their child along the road. No more stiff backs from pushing little ones whose feet do not touch the pedals. These trikes even have footrests and a safety bar around the seat that can be removed as the child grows.

Pedal cars are another excellent toy. The cars are quite small, so a large three-year-old might not fit, but they are safe for even a one-year-old. Pedal cars come in every model imaginable, from Mercedes to Volkswagens, police cars to fire engines. They can be found at department stores and toy stores for around ¥15,000 or less.

Sesame Street, Disney, Winnie the Pooh, and other cartoon toys and accessories are very popular in Japan, but many of the products are different from those sold overseas. We have found some inexpensive gifts which appear quite "Japanese," such as *obento* boxes and *oshibori* containers decorated with various themes or characters.

Several companies make the Velcro-and-plastic food sets that children of all ages enjoy. Children love to "slice" the food with the plastic knife and then put it all back together again. There are vegetable sets, fruit sets, sandwich sets, and more. When we send these overseas, we always buy the sushi set as a unique gift from Japan. Sanrio shops carry a mind-boggling assortment of Japanese character items that make great gifts. In addition to *obento* boxes, you may choose from travel toothbrush sets, Band-aids, towels, or thermoses, all designed with character or color-coordinated themes. The best thermos design is the kind with the straw that pops up when the lid is snapped open. It is leak-proof and easy to use when traveling. Our friends back home always ask for more of these when we return there on vacation.

Everyone knows Hello Kitty, but don't forget the other characters, such as The Runabouts and Little Twin Stars. Rice bowls, fork and spoon sets, and chopsticks are all available with these characters on them. We have started a collection of different pieces for several of our friend's children; additions over the years are easy and affordable.

We have had our best luck finding unusual toys in small neighborhood toy or stationery stores. Japanese paper balls, miniature pen sets, and sticker packs are all very lightweight to mail as gifts. Japanese bath toys can be found just about anywhere. Many of the toys in the smaller shops are seasonal, so keep your eyes open year-round for the best bargains.

Every summer we buy "squeaky shoes" for our kids to wear to the pool. These sandals are brightly colored and emit a loud squeak with every step. They are available only in sizes up to about age three, but they are a big hit with that crowd. We give them as gifts along with Japanese summer pajamas or T-shirts.

Gifts that educate a child about Japan are always appreciated. We often give the plastic money sets that include yen coins, bills, and a small abacus. These are cheap and can be found in any small toy store or festival booth during the summer and fall.

Japan has many traditional toys to offer. Spinning tops, kites, dolls, and other toys made of bamboo and wood are a special part of Japan that your child should experience. For the New Year, buy a *hagoita* for the whole family to enjoy. This is a wooden paddle, often elaborately decorated, that is used to bat a tiny shuttlecock in a game similar to badminton. Other traditional toys are made from *washi* paper and can be used as decorations in a child's room. In Tokyo, these can also be purchased at a shop in Roppongi called Washikobo (see the Traditional Japanese Toys section of this chapter). Origami is fun for all ages, and sets of fancy paper with instruction books in English are available in toy and book stores. There are exquisite dolls available in Japan but they are rather expensive. For little girls, it is perhaps safer to buy the soft dolls in kimono with the pretty plastic faces that look like porcelain. They are less destructible than the fancier dolls, and cheaper. Another option is the *kokeshi* doll. These hand-painted wooden figures are often inexpensive, and the different types are fun to collect.

Of course, the electric gadgets and robot toys available in Japan are ideal for older children. The electronic pet, Tamagotchi, originated in Japan, and has spawned dozens of cute cousins since its debut in the mid-1990s. Akihabara (see chapter 2) is famous for the wide variety and the latest designs in home video games, portable Game Boys, Tamagotchi, and so on. Check your local toy stores for discount prices on used Nintendo game cartridges. Some shops sell them for as cheap as ¥500 each (they run from ¥3,000 to ¥7,000 new). An inflatable robot that we mailed home one Christmas was a big hit, and our own children are fascinated by the robot toys that can be transformed into vehicles. You'll soon find out that something called Print Club is all the rage with kids in Japan. These photo booths, found in department stores, video arcades, and malls, will snap a series of mini-photo stickers, adding silly backgrounds, headgear or hairstyles to your picture. The Pokémon card game is another fad from Japan that has caught on internationally. Most cards sold here are in Japanese, although Kiddyland sells card sets in English as well. The character-related items, starring cuddly Pikachu, are popular with all ages. The wave of new fads in Japan is constant, and long after Pokémon and Print Club have faded, there will be intriguing new ones that will keep your kids enthralled for hours. Just keep your eyes and ears open.

## TOYS IN DEPARTMENT STORES

As you can imagine, the toy selection at major department stores is extensive. There is always a new gadget or gizmo on display, and you can find a large selection of Japanese toys in addition to imported ones from Fisher Price and Playskool. All major department stores display sample toys to keep the kids busy while you shop—a real advantage for parents. Department stores are forever changing their floor layout and their merchandise in an effort to stay ahead of the competition. Generally, however, all department stores carry the same products. (See chapter 2 for detailed descriptions of each department store.)

## TOY STORES

### Bornelund

- Hara Bldg., 1F, 6–10–9 Jingu-mae, Shibuya-ku, Tokyo
  ☎ (03) 5485–3430　東京都渋谷区神宮前 6–10–9　原ビル 1F
  🚉 Meiji Jingu-mae Station, Chiyoda Line; Harajuku Station, JR Yamanote Line
  🕐 11:00 A.M. to 7:30 P.M. daily.
- Osaka branch: Crest Shinsaibashi 1F, 4–12–9 Chuo-ku, Osaka-shi, Osaka
  大阪府大阪市中央区4–12–9　クレスト心斎橋 1F

Also located in some department stores, Bornelund is a toy manufacturer from Denmark. The store carries educational toys and games, as well as baby rattles, beautiful German dolls, and a very expensive line of clothing from the Netherlands. To get there from either station, walk four blocks from the Meiji and Omotesando intersection toward Shibuya Station.

### Hakuhinkan Toy Park

8–8–1 Ginza, Chuo-ku, Tokyo　東京都中央区銀座 8–8–1
☎ (03) 3571–8008
🚉 Ginza Station, Ginza, Hibiya, Marunouchi lines
🕐 11:00 A.M. to 8:00 P.M. daily (toy store), 11:30 A.M. to 10:00 P.M. (restaurant floors).

This spacious store has a different atmosphere from many other toy stores—it is almost luxurious. A wide, carpeted, spiral stairway leads from each of the four floors to the next (there is also an elevator), and soothing music plays over loudspeakers. The toys are not crammed together but neatly displayed on large shelves. The mood is very relaxed—except on weekends when the store gets crowded. Adult toys and games—fancy remote-control cars, golf putting kits, stationery goods, and video games—are on the first two floors. The third and fourth floors have a wide selection of Japanese and imported toys. Character toys, electronic games, beautiful Japanese dolls, and a toy hospital are all to be found here.

To get a bite to eat, try the coffee shop in the basement or the sandwich shop on the second floor. For more serious eating, the fifth and sixth floors house French, pasta, steak, and Japanese restaurants.

Concerts and other shows are held at the eighth-floor theater. For information, ask at the ticket counter on the first floor.

To get there, go out the A5 exit. This will put you in the heart of Ginza. Walking away from the main intersection, you will find Hakuhinkan at the end of the street—past Matsuzakaya Department Store, Familiar, Wendy's, and McDonald's—just before the Shuto Expressway.

## Kiddyland

6–1–9 Jingu-mae, Shibuya-ku, Tokyo　東京都渋谷区神宮前 6–1–9
☎ (03) 3409–3431
🚈 Meiji Jingu-mae Station, Chiyoda Line; Harajuku Station, JR Yamanote Line
🕙 10:00 A.M. to 8:00 P.M. Closed every third Tuesday.

This is probably the best single toy store in Tokyo, but do not try to navigate it with the little ones on a weekend. The crowds are horrendous and the layout, even though there are six floors, is cramped and confusing. We also try to avoid Kiddyland on weekday afternoons, when hordes of giggly adolescents clog every aisle. When we do make the trip, however, we always find an abundance of toys for all ages and plenty of new items. Throughout the store, there are enough displays to keep the kids busy while you look around. There is only one small elevator, so you may end up taking the stairs. This is difficult with a stroller, so plan your strategy before leaving home. Despite the inconvenience, Kiddyland is the ideal toy store according to just about every kid we know. The store is near the intersection of Meiji Dori and Omotesando.

## Niki Tiki Toy Shop

• Daikanyama branch: Park Side Village, 9–8 Sarugaku-cho, Shibuya-ku, Tokyo
  ☎ (03) 3770–4686　東京都渋谷区猿楽町 9–8 パークサイドビレッジ
  🚈 Daikanyama Station, Tokyu Toyoko Line
  🕙 10:00 A.M. to 6:00 P.M. Closed on Wednesdays.

• Kichijoji branch: 2–28–3 Kichijoji Hommachi, Musashino-shi, Tokyo
  ☎ (0422) 21–3137　東京都武蔵野市吉祥寺本町 2–28–3
  🚈 Kichijoji Station, JR Chuo, Keio Inokashira lines
  🕙 10:00 A.M. to 7:00 P.M. Closed on Thursdays.

• Shibuya branch: Hiroo Plaza, 2F, 5–6–6 Hiroo, Shibuya-ku, Tokyo
  ☎ (03) 3449–3469　東京都渋谷区広尾 5–6–6 広尾プラザ 2F
  🚈 Hiroo Station, Hibiya Line
  🕙 10:30 A.M. to 8:00 P.M. daily (7:30 P.M. in winter).

Niki Tiki Toy Shop has one of the most extensive collections in town of wooden toys, games, and ornaments from Sweden and Germany. They also have collector-quality dolls and a good selection of Ravensburger puzzles and games. Most of their hand-painted Christmas ornaments and decorations are on display year-round. The first store is located one block from the main Daikanyama shopping street, just past the NTT B Building. The Kichijoji store is down the side street to the right of the main entrance to Tokyu Department Store.

### Toys R' Us

Sun Street, 6–31–1 Kameido, Koto-ku, Tokyo
☎ (03) 3638–1511　東京都江東区亀戸 6–31–1 サンストリート内
🚉 Kameido Station, JR Sobu Line

After the Japanese government revised the Large-Scale Retail Store Law, the world's largest retail toy chain, Toys R' Us, opened a store in Ibaraki-ken in December 1991. The chain sells eighteen thousand children's items, including toys, clothing, and nursery goods, of which about twenty percent is imported. Toys R' Us now operates ninety-one stores throughout Japan, with several in the greater Tokyo area.

For more information, contact the head office at Solid Square West Tower, 580 Horikawa-cho, Saiwai-ku, Kawasaki-shi, Kanagawa; call ☎ (044) 549–9111 or visit them online at 🖥 <www.toysrus.co.jp>.

## *TRADITIONAL JAPANESE TOYS*

### Bingoya

10–6 Wakamatsu-cho, Shinjuku-ku, Tokyo　東京都新宿区若松町 10–6
☎ (03) 3202–8778
🚉 Waseda Station, Tozai Line; Akebonobashi Station, Toei Shinjuku Line
🕐 10:00 A.M. to 7:00 P.M. Closed on Mondays.

Bingoya is Japanese folk-craft shop in the finest tradition. Pottery, handwoven fabric, paper products, carved wood, and, best of all, traditional kids' toys from all over Japan fill this five-story shop. The basement is stuffed full of *kokeshi* dolls from almost every prefecture in Japan, each in the area's own traditional style. There are also huge paper kites in the shape of warriors, fish, and other traditional Japanese symbols. The papier-mâché figurines come in animal shapes representing the years of the zodiac in addition to sumo wrestlers and kimono-clad women. Any of these crafts is suitable for collecting or for decorating a child's room. We were also delighted to find many hand-painted wooden pull-toys at Bingoya. These are similar in style to the wooden toys of West Germany, but they have a Japanese look to them and are reasonably priced. Don't forget to explore the other floors for gifts for the whole family. The hand-blown glass, handmade pottery, and baskets are of the finest quality and are one-of-a-kind, something you don't often find in department stores these days.

Bingoya is a 15-minute walk from Akebonobashi Station or Waseda Station. To get there by car, drive down Meiji Dori heading north through Shinjuku, turn right at Shokuan Dori, the second major intersection past Isetan Department Store, and follow the street for about five minutes. Bingoya is on the left-hand side of the street; you will pass a Benton grocery store on the way. By bus from Shinjuku Station's west exit, catch #76 (for Akihabara or Iidabashi) or #74 (for Tokyo Joshi Idai). Get off at the eighth stop, Kawada-cho, which is just past the store.

### Edo-Tokyo Museum Shop

Edo-Tokyo Museum, 1F, 1–4–1 Yokoami, Sumida-ku, Tokyo
☎ (03) 3626–9974　東京都墨田区横網 1–4–1　江戸東京博物館 1F
🚈 Ryogoku Station, JR Sobu Line
🕐 10:00 A.M. to 6:00 P.M. Tuesday, Wednesday, Saturday and Sunday; 10:00 A.M. to 8:00 P.M. Thursday and Friday; closed Mondays.

This museum shop carries traditional games, kites, crafts, and toys, all from the Edo era (1600–1868). These unique items are well-made reproductions not found in other toy stores. There is also a display of antique dolls and musical instruments.

### Washikobo

1–8–10 Nishi Azabu, Minato-ku, Tokyo　東京都港区西麻布 1–8–10
☎ (03) 3405–1841
🚈 Roppongi Station, Hibiya Line
🕐 10:00 A.M. to 6:00 P.M. Closed on Sundays and holidays.

In addition to all the toys and accessories made out of *washi* (Japanese paper) that you could ever wish for, Washikobo has a large selection of other Japanese traditional toys. Washikobo is conveniently located a few minutes walk from Roppongi Crossing.

## OTHER SOURCES

### Educational Toy Library

9–2 Hachiyama-cho, Shibuya-ku, Tokyo　東京都渋谷区鉢山町 9–2
🚈 Shibuya Station, JR Yamanote and various lines

This is not really a toy store, nor a library in the traditional sense, but rather a toy-borrowing center. Located at the Tokyo Baptist Church on Kyu Yamanote Dori in Shibuya, the toy library is run by the Tokyo International Learning Community (TILC; see chapter 11). The library has a wide variety of educational toys for all ages. Of special interest is the selection of therapeutic toys for handicapped children.

For more information, call TILC at ☎ (03) 3224–6946 (afternoons only).

### Japanese National Council of Toy Libraries

Kawamura Bldg., 7F, 2–6–7 Komagata, Taito-ku, Tokyo
☎ (03) 3845–8994    🖷 (03) 3845–2203    東京都台東区駒形 2–6–7 河村ビル 7F

These toy libraries, although established for the mentally and physically disabled, are open to all children. You can request a list of over four hundred locations throughout Japan. Toys can be checked out or played with at the location.

### Omocha Bijutsukan (Toy Museum)

2–12–10 Arai, Nakano-ku, Tokyo    東京都中野区新井 2–12–10
☎ (03) 3387–5461
🚃 Nakano Station (north exit), JR Chuo, Tozai lines; Arai Yakushi-mae Station, Seibu Shinjuku Line
🕐 10:30 A.M. to 4:30 P.M. Closed on Fridays.

More than just a museum, this three-story building with showroom and play space aims to introduce children to toys from all over the world. Children and parents are welcome to join groups to learn how to make toys from recycled goods. Toys may also be borrowed every Saturday free of charge for two weeks. Admission is ¥500 (over three years old).

## Toy Hospitals

### Isetan Department Store Toy Hospital

3–14–1 Shinjuku, Shinjuku-ku, Tokyo    東京都新宿区新宿 3–14–1
☎ (03) 3352–1141

On the first and third Sundays of the month, a toy doctor visits the store to repair broken toys. Look for this toy repair service on the sixth floor in the toy section.

### Meguro-ku Shohisha Center Toy Hospital

2–4–36 Meguro, Meguro-ku, Tokyo    東京都目黒区目黒 2–4–36 区民センター内
☎ (03) 3711–1121
🚃 Meguro Station, JR Yamanote, Tokyu Mekama lines
🕐 1:00 P.M. to 3:00 P.M. Sundays only. Closed every third Sunday.

This consumer center, run by the metropolitan government on the fourth floor of the Meguro Kumin Center, will repair dolls, electrical toys, picture books, even antique wind-up toys—and all free.

### Shohisha Center

Oi 1-chome Kyodo Bldg., 1–14–1 Oi, 1F, Oi, Shinagawa-ku, Tokyo
☎ (03) 5718–7181　東京都品川区大井 1–14–1　大井1丁目共同ビル 1F

Run by the Shinagawa Ward Office. Volunteers repair broken toys on Saturdays from 1:00 to 3:30 P.M. Repairs are free.

## MAIL-ORDER BOOKS AND TOYS FROM ABROAD

The book, cassette, video, and toy catalogs listed below offer a variety of products from around the world.

### The American Girls Collection/The Pleasant Company

8400 Fairway Place, Middleton, Wisconsin, 53562–0192, USA
☎ (608) 831–5210　🖶 (608) 828–4790　🖳 www.americangirl.com

The Pleasant Company has created the most wonderful line of dolls and accessories we have ever seen. These dolls are placed in various periods of American history and are accompanied by a set of books that tell of their adventures. The books, appropriate for age five to twelve and even older, are well-written and historically accurate. The dolls and period accessories are collector quality, but suitable for all ages. The baby doll collection is wonderful for a first doll or for an older sibling when there is a new baby in the family.

### Animal Town

P.O. Box 485, Healdsburg, California 95448, USA
☎ (805) 682–7343

Animal Town specializes in children's tapes, books, and puzzles with animal and environmental themes. They also have a good selection of noncompetitive and nature-oriented games for children and adults.

### Anthroposophic Press

3390 Route 9, Hudson, New York 12534, USA
☎ (518) 851–2054　🖶 (518) 851–2047

This catalog contains many educational and spiritual books for adults, but its selection of children's books is interesting and unique. Many beautifully illustrated fantasy books are available, and it also carries a comprehensive list of printed lectures and books by Rudolf Steiner, founder of Waldorf education, in addition to other books about early childhood education and parenting.

## Aristoplay

P.O. Box 7028, Ann Arbor, Michigan 48107, USA
☎ (313) 995–4353    🖷 (313) 995–4611

This catalog contains a choice selection of educational and cooperative games for adults and children over the age of four. The games are based on such themes as pollution, great composers, and geography, our favorite being Friends Around the World, a game of world peace. This catalog is a must for international families.

## Back to Basics Toys

31333 Agoura Road, Westlake Village, California 91361, USA
☎ (818) 865–8301    🖷 (818) 865–9771    🖳 www.backtobasicstoys.com

This catalog offers the best quality and selection we have seen of wonderful toys, games, play furniture, and instruments. Many of the items are suitable for use in a preschool or kindergarten. Table-top sports games, building blocks, doll houses, and teepees—this catalog has it all.

## Books of Wonder

16th West 18th Street, New York, New York 10011, USA
☎ (212) 989–3270    🖷 (212) 645–3038    🖳 www.booksofwonder.com

This large New York City bookstore sends out fabulous catalogs containing virtually every children's book you have ever heard of. A monthly newsletter, Books of Wonder News, is available at no charge. They have several different catalogs, one of which is devoted only to signed editions of children's books. Searching for hard-to-find books is one of their specialties.

## A Child's Collection

151 Avenue of the Americas, New York, New York 10013, USA
☎ (212) 691–7266    🖷 (212) 691–9154

This catalog has a lovely selection of books for children from newborns to twelve-year-olds and up, including award winners and new authors.

## Chinaberry Book Service

2830 Via Orange Way, Suite B, Spring Valley, California 91978, USA
☎ (619) 670–5200    🖷 (619) 670–5203

Chinaberry offers a wide range from picture books for toddlers to safety books for preschoolers, to adventure and fiction for the advanced reader. Many of the classic storybooks for children are available here in updated, beautifully illustrated editions. There are also many parenting books available, as well as craft and family project books, videos and cassette tapes. The company also provides a book-fair packet for school fund raisers.

## A Gentle Wind

P.O. Box 3103, Albany, New York 12203, USA
☎ (518) 436–0391

This catalog has cassettes of traditional songs as well as new music and recorded stories for all ages. The independent children's recording label, A Gentle Wind, has won numerous awards for its music.

## Hearth Song

P.O. Box 1773, Peoria, Illinois 61656, USA

A truly exquisite catalog containing unusual and creative toys, books, and games. Many are made exclusively for Hearth Song from natural fibers and wood. This catalog also includes many old-fashioned and country craft projects for older children and adults.

## Metropolitan Museum of Art Children's Catalog

Special Service Office, Middle Village, New York 11381, USA
☎ (718) 326–7050

This well-known museum publishes a separate children's catalog, which is full of beautifully illustrated books and fine toys and games. Some of these items are designed exclusively for the Metropolitan Museum of Art, such as a song book illustrated with artwork from the museum.

## Music for Little People

Box 1460 Redway, California 95560, USA
☎ (707) 923–3991

A beautiful catalog filled with music cassettes, music videos, and musical instruments for you and your children. You will find more than just the ordinary selections of children's tapes here. There is every kind of music imaginable—from Afro-Cuban to Indian to jazz.

## Pied Piper

2922 North 35th Ave., Drawer 11408, Phoenix, Arizona 85061–1408, USA
☎ (602) 272–1853

The Gifted Children's Catalog, available from Pied Piper, contains a fine selection of children's toys, games, books, and project kits from around the world. All of the products emphasize the educational aspects of fun.

### Spoken Arts

8 Lawn Avenue, New Rochelle, New York 10802, USA
☎ (914) 633–4516

This company offers recordings of stories, poems, and speeches. Children's classics, such as *Peter Rabbit*, are available as well as fairy tales. For older children, try Aesop's fables or Mark Twain's yarns. Recordings are available in several different languages, and there are also tapes for adults.

### Toys to Grow On

P.O. Box 17, Long Beach, California 90801, USA
☎ (310) 603–8890   📠 (310) 537–5403

This catalog for educational and imaginative play offers a vast selection of toys and school materials for all ages.

## PUBLIC LIBRARIES

Public libraries abound in Japan—there are over 260 libraries owned and operated by the Tokyo Metropolitan Government alone. You have access to all of them just by working, studying, or living in Japan. Each ward or city has a number of libraries under its care, and your local ward or city office is the first place to look for information regarding the one nearest you. Some areas that have more foreign residents (e.g., Minato-ku) will have better selections of books in English. Remember that you are able to register at and use any of public libraries, not just the ones in your particular ward or city.

Children's books in English are popular, and most libraries will have a fairly large selection of them. Adult books are another matter; the number of good books in English will vary from library to library. CDs and videos are also available for checkout. Ward- and city-operated libraries are great places to go on a rainy day, as most of them offer story time, children's movies (often from the United States), and other activities for kids. To register at the library, you will need your Alien Registration Card or some other proof that you live, work, or study in Japan. If you do not speak Japanese, you might consider taking along someone who does so that the rules and regulations of the library can be explained to you.

## PRIVATE LIBRARIES

As a foreigner living in Japan, you may also have access to private libraries that serve the foreign community. Contact your local embassy or consulate for more information. Also, many private clubs have libraries that are available to members.

Below is a short list of libraries containing reference books and information in English that adults may find helpful while living in Japan.

### Australian-Japan Foundation Library

2–1–14 Mita, Minato-ku, Tokyo　東京都港区三田 2–1–14
☎ (03) 5232–4005
🚇 Mita Station, Toei Mita, Toei Asakusa lines
🕐 10:00 A.M. to 5:30 P.M., Monday to Friday. Closed weekends and holidays.

This library stocks around one hundred children's books in English. Up to three books may be checked out for a period of two weeks.

### Suidobata Toshokan

2–16–14 Suido, Bunkyo-ku, Tokyo　東京都文京区水道 2–16–14
☎ (03) 3945–1621
🚇 Edogawabashi Station (exit 4), Yurakucho Line

This library has a collection of two thousand picture books and English-language books for children, and more than five hundred titles in other languages. The entire first floor houses the children's collection (adults books are on the second floor). A large collection of Japanese picture books is also available. The staff is extremely helpful (several speak English), and there are plenty of places to sit down and read with the children. To get there, cross the highway and continue straight across the Furukawabashi Bridge. Go another block to Makiishi Dori and turn right at the Kuritsu Gochu-mae Intersection, which has a signal. Walk 5 minutes and look for the library on your right.

### Tokyo Baptist Church Library

Over seven thousand English-language books are available to the public at no charge. Membership in the church is not required, just simply fill out a card with basic information and you can check out as many books as you wish for a two-week period. The cozy space offers comfortable armchairs to relax in while you read; there is also a special children's corner with a nice variety of reading material for all ages.

The address for Tokyo Baptist Church is 9–2 Hachiyama-cho, in

Shibuya-ku. Located on Kyu Yamate Dori, the church is about a 5-minute walk from Daikanyama Station, on the Toyoko Line. The lending library is open Tuesday to Thursday from 9:00 A.M. to 5:00 P.M. For more information call ☎ (03) 3461–8425.

## LOCAL LIBRARIES

Several of the local libraries in the Tokyo area carry a limited selection of English-language books. You may want to call your ward office to see which library has the largest collection. Shibuya and Hibiya both carry English-language children's books in their main libraries.

### British Council Library

1–2 Kagurazaka, Shinjuku-ku, Tokyo　東京都新宿区神楽坂 1–2
☎ (03) 3235–8031
🚇 Iidabashi Station, JR Sobu, Tozai, Yurakucho, Namboku lines
🕐 10:00 A.M. to 8:00 P.M. Monday to Friday. Closed weekends and on both Japanese and British holidays.

Open to any resident of Japan, this library lends books and videos for a ¥4,000 annual fee. It has a good selection of children's books and books on Japan, as well as English literature.

### Japan Foundation Library

Ark Mori Bldg., West Wing, 20F, 1–12–32 Akasaka, Minato-ku, Tokyo
☎ (03) 5562–3527　東京都港区赤坂 1–12–32　アーク森ビル西館 20F
🚇 Tameike San-o Station, Namboku, Ginza lines
🕐 10:00 A.M. to 5:00 P.M., Monday through Friday. Closed weekends, holidays, and the final Monday of each month.

This library is a fabulous source of information on Japan and things Japanese. All you need to do is apply for a free member's card. The library is a 3-minute walk from the Hotel New Otani.

### Metropolitan Hibiya Library

1–4 Hibiya Koen, Chiyoda-ku, Tokyo　東京都千代田区日比谷公園 1–4
☎ (03) 3502–0101
🚇 Hibiya Station, Hibiya, Chiyoda, Toei Mita lines
🕐 10:00 A.M. to 8:00 P.M. Monday through Friday; 10:00 A.M. to 5:00 P.M. Saturday, Sunday and holidays.

There is a special children's section open every day except Sunday. With your Alien Registration Card you can check out five books for two weeks.

## Shibuya-ku Chuo Library

1–5–34 Jingu-mae, Shibuya-ku, Tokyo　東京都渋谷区神宮前 1–5–34
☎ (03) 3403–2591
🚇 Meiji Jingu-mae Station, Chiyoda Line; Harajuku Station, JR Yamanote Line
🕐 9:00 A.M. to 7:00 P.M. Tuesday through Saturday, 9:00 A.M. to 5:00 P.M. Sunday, closed on Mondays.

Bring your Alien Registration Card and you may check out up to five books for a period of two weeks.

## Tokyo Metropolitan Central Library

5–7–13 Minami Azabu, Minato-ku, Tokyo　東京都港区南麻布 5–7–13
☎ (03) 3442–8451
🚇 Hiroo Station, Hibiya Line
🕐 9:30 A.M. to 8:00 P.M. Tuesday through Friday, 1:00 P.M. to 8:00 P.M. Monday, 9:30 A.M. to 5:00 P.M. on weekends and national holidays. Closed the first Thursday, third Sunday, and twenty-fifth day of each month.

Located in Arisugawa Park, this is the central library of the metropolitan government library system—over one million books are here! They also have many periodicals, videotapes, films, newspapers, and music tapes and records which unfortunately cannot be taken out. You must be over sixteen years of age to use this library.

## World Magazine Gallery

The Magazine House Co., 1F, 3–13–10 Ginza, Chuo-ku, Tokyo
☎ (03) 3545–7227　東京都中央区銀座 3–13–10　マガジンハウス1F
🚇 Higashi Ginza Station, Hibiya, Toei Asakusa lines
🕐 11:00 A.M. to 7:00 P.M. Monday through Friday.

Well, it's not really a library, but we can't subscribe to all the magazines we love, so we read them here. You will find approximately nine hundred periodicals in over fifty languages here. It is fun to see articles on fashions, food, and sports from around the world but leave the kids at home unless you are a fast reader. Magazines cannot be bought or checked out.

# 5
# Parks, Playgrounds, and Gardens

There is no question that much of Japan is crowded, especially the cities. While living here, you may miss your suburban backyard, but there is probably a nice neighborhood park within walking distance of your residence. Many of these neighborhood parks are now being designed with small children in mind, and we have listed some from the twenty-three wards in Tokyo. In addition to small parks, you will also find many large ones with vast areas of open space. Some parks are more enjoyable than others for young children. This selection of parks, playgrounds, and gardens should provide the most fun for children under six with a minimum of hassle for everyone involved.

## NEIGHBORHOOD PARKS

In each ward, there are many parks (*koen*) or playgrounds with facilities ranging from simple swings to giant slides and sandboxes. An excellent way for your child to make friends in the neighborhood—and for you to meet some of the parents—is to visit the park. During the week, many mothers bring their children to the park at the same time every day. If your schedule is flexible, you might try going at different times to meet a variety of children. Perhaps you will find a particular group whose company you enjoy enough to meet regularly. In any case, there are a few basic rules you should learn to make you feel more comfortable and to fit in at the playground in Japan.

You will notice that other mothers readily offer your child a snack —often candy—so you might want to bring along something to share with other children who may be at the park. Besides bringing healthy snacks, it is a good idea to bring your *oshibori* with you, as playgrounds are usually dirty. Almost all neighborhood parks have water fountains, rest rooms (don't forget to bring tissues), and even clocks, but, unfortunately, no grass. If you bring sandbox toys, label them so you know which are yours, and prepare your child to be ready to share with other children because they (or their parents) will almost always offer to share toys with him.

There are a few important words that should be part of your playground vocabulary. You will often hear mothers saying "*abunai yo*!" and "*ki o tsukete*!" *Abunai yo* means "Look out—that's dangerous," and *ki o tsukete* means "Be careful." You might also find that your child picks up the word "*dame*" rather quickly. This is what other children will say to him if he knocks down their sandcastle. *Dame* means "Stop it!" in a very firm manner. It's a good idea to learn early on how to say thank you (*arigato*) and excuse me (*sumimasen* or *gomen nasai*), since they are frequently used playground words as well.

If you have ever lamented the difficulties involved in chasing a crawling baby around a dirty playground, or worse, not taken your infant to the playground for fear of him getting dirty, then you'll be delighted to hear about the Japanese *asobigi*. This baggy coverall is made with elastic at the wrists and ankles and pulls over whatever baby is wearing. Your inquisitive baby or toddler can then be free to explore without ruining a full set of clothes with the infamous "Tokyo dirt." When it's time to leave the park, just give the hands a good wash, pull off the *asobigi*, and you've got a clean baby once again. These suits come in all colors and sizes, with lightweight cotton fabric for summer and sturdier denims and corduroys for cold weather. Look for them in any department store or neighborhood clothing store.

A new concept in neighborhood playgrounds is a "*shinsui* park." *Shinsui* means literally "to be friendly with water." A *shinsui* park is one with plenty of water attractions that provide children with a chance to get used to water by playing in it. These parks are often found within a larger park or playground, and most of them have a shallow wading pool and educational water toys and games in a small playground area. These spaces attract parents and kids year-round and are especially refreshing during the oppressive summer heat.

The neighborhood parks that we have listed are popular with families and have something special just for children. These parks are listed according to wards and cover greater Tokyo from north to south.

## ADACHI-KU

### Higashi Ayase Koen

3–4 Higashi Ayase, Adachi-ku, Tokyo　東京都足立区東綾瀬 3–4
☎ (03) 3605–0005
AREA: 15.6 ha
🚃 Ayase Station, JR Joban, Chiyoda lines

This is a relatively new park in a nice residential area, made mostly to house sport facilities and for strolling or jogging.

### Minumadai Shinsui Koen

4–5 Toneri, Adachi-ku, Tokyo　東京都足立区舎人 4–5
☎ (03) 3855–6523
AREA: 1,720 meters long
🚃 Takenozuka Station, Tobu Isezaki Line

This popular "friendly with water" park has lots of free play space for kids.

## ARAKAWA-KU

### Arakawa Yuen (Arakawa Amusement Park)

6–35–11 Nishiogu, Arakawa-ku, Tokyo　東京都荒川区西尾久 6–35–11
☎ (03) 3893–6003
AREA: 0.4 ha
🚃 Arakawa Yuen-mae Station, Toden Arakawa Line

This park has a children's playground, a small petting zoo, and a "water-play" area.

### Nippori Minami Koen

5–19–1 Higashi Nippori, Arakawa-ku, Tokyo　東京都荒川区東日暮里 5–19–1
☎ (03) 3802–3111 (ward office)
AREA: 3,500 sq. meters
🚃 Nippori Station, JR Yamanote Line

This park features an attractive playground for children.

## BUNKYO-KU

### Hongo Kyusuijo Koen

2–7 Hongo, Bunkyo-ku, Tokyo　東京都文京区本郷 2–7
☎ (03) 3816–1517
AREA: 7,271 sq. meters

🚇 Suidobashi Station, JR Sobu, Toei Mita lines

Here you can enjoy a Japanese-style garden, a rose garden with forty-eight varieties, and a children's playground.

### Kyoiku no Mori Koen

3–29 Otsuka, Bunkyo-ku, Tokyo　東京都文京区大塚 3–29
☎ (03) 3944–6342
Area: 2.1 ha
🚇 Myogadani Station, Marunouchi Line

This park has an open area for children and a nice playground with lots of trees.

CHIYODA-KU

### Shimizudani Koen

1 Kioi-cho, Chiyoda-ku, Tokyo　東京都千代田区紀尾井町 1番地
☎ (03) 3264–0151 (ward office)
Area: 1 ha
🚇 Akasaka Mitsuke Station, Ginza, Marunouchi lines; Nagatacho Station, Hanzomon, Yurakucho lines

This is a small park with a few swings located across from the New Otani Hotel, 8 minutes from Akasaka Mitsuke Station.

CHUO-KU

### Tepozu Jido Koen

1–5–1 Minato, Chuo-ku, Tokyo　東京都中央区湊 1–5–1
☎ (03) 3543–0211 (ward office)
Area: 2,900 sq. meters
🚇 Hatchobori Station, JR Keiyo, Hibiya lines

Here there is a shallow wading pool, sandbox, swings, and slides.

### Tsukishima Daichi Jido Koen

4–2–1 Tsukishima, Chuo-ku, Tokyo　東京都中央区月島 4–2–1
☎ (03) 3543–0211 (ward office)
Area: 3,700 sq. meters
🚇 Tsukishima Station, Yurakucho Line

A great place for the kids to burn off some energy on the swings, slides, balancing bar, and wooden climbing equipment. There is also a sandbox.

### Kasai Rinkai Koen

6–2–1 Rinkai-cho, Edogawa-ku, Tokyo　東京都江戸川区臨海町 6–2–1
☎ (03) 5696–1331
📻 Kasai Rinkai Koen Station, JR Keiyo Line; ferry from Hinode Pier near
JR Hamamatsu-cho Station

Opened in 1989, this park includes two man-made beaches for sun-
bathing and picnicking. Don't miss the large aquarium (see chapter 6).

### Komatsugawa Sakaigawa Shinsui Park

Hon-Isshiki 1-chome~Chuo 4-chome and Matsushima 1-chome, Edogawa-ku,
Tokyo　東京都江戸川区本一色 1丁目~中央4丁目、松島1丁目
☎ (03) 3652–1151 (ward office)
AREA: 3.2 kilometers long
📻 Shin Koiwa Station (south exit), JR Sobu Line

This is a large "friendly with water" park with many flowering plants,
set along a river. To get there, take bus #21 or #22 from the south exit
of Shin Koiwa Station.

ITABASHI-KU

### Akatsuka Koen

3–1 Takashimadaira, Itabashi-ku, Tokyo　東京都板橋区高島平 3–1
☎ (03) 3938–5715
AREA: 22.9 ha
📻 Takashimadaira Station, Toei Mita Line

This park has many sports facilities and is good for walking. A 10-
minute walk from Takashimadaira Station.

### Nishidai Koen

1–23–1 Nishidai, Itabashi-ku, Tokyo　東京都板橋区西台 1–23–1
☎ (03) 3964–1111 (ward office), (03) 3579–2525 (park section)
AREA: 0.6 ha
📻 Nishidai Station, Toei Mita Line; Tobu Nerima or Kami Itabashi Station,
Tobu Tojo Line

Popular with children, this park has an athletic park, forest, and a small
stream.

### Ukima Koen

2–15–1 Funado, Itabashi-ku, Tokyo　東京都板橋区船渡 2–15–1
☎ (03) 3969–9168

Area: 11.6 ha

🚉 Ukima Funado Station, JR Saikyo Line

There are good picnic areas and some scenic lakes in this park.

---

## KATSUSHIKA-KU

### Mizumoto Koen

3–2 Mizumoto Koen, Katsushika-ku, Tokyo　東京都葛飾区水元公園 3–2
☎ (03) 3607–8321
Area: 61.4 ha
🚉 Kanamachi Station, JR Joban, Keisei lines

Opened in June 1989, this man-made beach is fabulous for children. The large, open areas of sandy beach are ideal for playing, fishing, and water sports. From the south exit of Kanamachi Station take a Keisei bus leaving from #2 bus stop and get off at the Mizumoto Koen-mae stop.

### Shinkoiwa Koen

1–1–3 Nishi Shin Koiwa, Katsushika-ku, Tokyo　東京都葛飾区西新小岩 1–1–3
☎ (03) 3696–9512
Area: 4.7 ha
🚉 Shin Koiwa Station, JR Sobu Line

This general-purpose park, with sections for water, family, and sports play, is a 5-minute walk from Shin Koiwa Station.

---

## KITA-KU

### Asukayama Koen

1–1–3 Oji, Kita-ku, Tokyo　東京都北区王子 1–1–3
☎ (03) 3910–8882
Area: 6.1 ha
🚉 Oji Station, JR Keihin Tohoku, Namboku lines

Asukayama Koen is famous for its cherry blossom trees, which were planted in the Edo period (1600–1868). There is also a large water fountain, a steam locomotive, and a rotating observatory.

### Nanushi Waterfalls Gardens

1–15–25 Kishimachi, Kita-ku, Tokyo　東京都北区岸町 1–15–25
☎ (03) 3908–1111 (ward office, parks division)
🚉 Oji Station, JR Keihin Tohoku, Namboku lines
🕐 9:00 A.M. to 5:00 P.M. daily (until 6:00 P.M. from July 15 to September 15).

These are beautifully landscaped gardens boasting four waterfalls.

During summer months, children are allowed to play in the pond and to take home as pets any tiny goldfish they can catch.

### Kameido Chuo Koen

9–37–28 Kameido, Koto-ku, Tokyo　東京都江東区亀戸 9–37–28
☎ (03) 3636–2558
AREA: 10.2 ha
🚇 Kameido Station, JR Sobu Line

Check out the children's playground with a wooden swing bridge and other playground equipment. There is also a rest house in the center of the park.

### Sendaihorikawa Koen

1, 4, 5 chome Minamisuna, 6, 7 chome Kitasuna, Koto-ku, Tokyo
☎ (03) 3647–9111 (ward office)　東京都江東区南砂 1, 4, 5丁目　北砂 6, 7丁目
AREA: 10.4 ha
🚇 Toyocho or Minami Sunamachi Station, Tozai Line; Ojima Station, Toei Shinjuku Line

There is not only a "friendly with water park" but also a cherry tree boulevard, cycling road, open square, and pond for fishing. The park is a 10-minute walk from either station.

### Yumenoshima Koen

Yumenoshima, Koto-ku, Tokyo　東京都江東区夢の島
☎ (03) 3521–8273
AREA: 40.8 ha
🚇 Shin Kiba Station, JR Keiyo, Yurakucho lines

This park, built on reclaimed land, has a large playground, coliseum, and baseball stadium. Also here is the Yumenoshima Tropical Botanical Garden ☎ (03) 3522–0281 with over 4,300 trees of 127 different species under one glass dome. The garden is open Tuesday through Sunday, 9:30 A.M. to 4:00 P.M. Closed Mondays. Admission is ¥250 for adults; no charge for children under twelve and adults over sixty-five.

### Komaba Koen

4–3–55 Komaba, Meguro-ku, Tokyo　東京都目黒区駒場 4–3–55
☎ (03) 3467–3419

AREA: 4.0 ha

🚆 Komaba Todai-mae Station, Inokashira Line; Shibuya Station, JR Yamanote and various lines

Once a private garden, this is now a quiet place for a walk or picnic. There is a small play area for children, and lovely grounds. The park is a short cab ride from Shibuya Station.

### Saigoyama Park

2–10 Aobadai, Meguro-ku, Tokyo　東京都目黒区青葉台 2–10
☎ (03) 3715–1111 (ward office)
🚆 Daikanyama Station, Tokyu Toyoko Line

This park boasts a beautiful man-made waterfall for kids to play in and lots of grass. No playground equipment.

---

MINATO-KU

### Shizen Kyoiku-en

5–21–5 Shiroganedai, Minato-ku, Tokyo　東京都港区白金台 5–21–5
☎ (03) 3441–7176
AREA: 20 ha
🚆 Meguro Station, JR Yamanote, Tokyu Mekama lines
🕐 9:00 A.M. to 4:30 P.M. (5:00 P.M. from May 1 to August 31). Closed on Mondays.

Opened to the public in 1949 as a nature education park, this is an ideal place to examine various plants and waterfowl. The Tokyo Metropolitan Garden Museum is next door (admission is ¥210 for adults, ¥60 for children). The park is a 10-minute walk from the station.

---

NAKANO-KU

### Heiwa no Mori Koen

3–37–6 Arai, Nakano-ku, Tokyo　東京都中野区新井 3–37–6
☎ (03) 3385–4150
AREA: 2.5 ha
🚆 Numabukuro Station, Seibu Shinjuku Line; Nakano Station, JR Chuo, Tozai lines

This park has a pond, a playground, and a children's corner. Also here are replicas of Yayoi period (ca. 200 B.C.–A.D. 250) houses and pottery. It is a 6-minute walk from Numabukuro Station and a 17-minute walk from Nakano Station.

### Tetsugaku-do Koen

1–34–28 Matsugaoka, Nakano-ku, Tokyo　東京都中野区松が丘 1–34–28
☎ (03) 3951–2515
AREA: 5.2 ha
�*🚃* Nakano Station, JR Chuo, Tozai lines

This neighborhood park with sandbox, swings, slides, baseball field, and tennis courts has plenty of trees. In summer, kids like to play in the waterfall and climb on the large rocks. From Nakano Station take a bus to Tetsugaku-do.

---

NERIMA-KU

---

### Hikarigaoka Koen

4–1–1 Hikarigaoka, Nerima-ku, Tokyo　東京都練馬区光が丘 4–1–1
☎ (03) 3977–7638
AREA: 60.5 ha
🚃 Narimasu Station, Tobu Tojo Line; Hikarigaoka Station, Toei No. 12 Line

Located in two cities, this is a huge park with vast green open spaces.

### Johoku Chuo Koen

1–3–1 Hikawadai, Nerima-ku, Tokyo　東京都練馬区氷川台 1–3–1
☎ (03) 3931–3650
AREA: 20.2 ha
🚃 Kami Itabashi Station, Tobu Tojo Line; Hikawadai Station, Yurakucho Line

This sports park is good for family picnics.

### Shakujii Koen

1–26–1 Shakujiidai, Nerima-ku, Tokyo　東京都練馬区石神井台 1–26–1
☎ (03) 3996–3950
AREA: 16.8 ha
🚃 Shakujii Koen Station, Seibu Ikebukuro Line

This fairly large park with a picturesque lake in the center of the grounds has an impressive array of cherry trees in spring. A visit to Shakujii Koen can easily become a full-day's outing because of the many attractions available, including swimming and boating.

---

OTA-KU

---

### Garakuta Koen ("Junk Park" inside Haginaka Kotsu Koen)

3–24–26 Haginaka, Ota-ku, Tokyo　東京都大田区萩中 3–24–26
☎ (03) 3743–0991 (park office)
AREA: 2,900 sq. meters

🚃 Otorii Station, Keikyu Kuko Line

This is a playground featuring old pieces of equipment for children to climb on and is popularly called Junk Park. The old bus and trolley car are perhaps the safest and most fun for the under-six set. Kids can sit in the driver's seat and drive or pretend to ride the bus. Adjacent to the park is a grassy area with a large sandbox and climbing equipment. At the nearby Haginaka Traffic Park, children can ride bikes along a small course complete with traffic signs. To get there, go to Keikyu Kamata Station on the Keihin Kyuko Line and transfer to the Keikyu Kuko Line for Otorii Station. If you are like us, you can follow the people with children to the park, or ask at the station for the way to Garakuta Koen, about an 8-minute walk. Another possibility is to get off at Kamata Station on the Keihin Tohoku Line and take a bus bound for Haneda Airport that stops by the park.

### Higashi Chofu Koen

5–13–11 Minami Yukigaya, Ota-ku, Tokyo    東京都大田区南雪谷 5–13–11
☎ (03) 3720–1692
AREA: 25,000 sq. meters
🚃 Ontakesan Station, Tokyu Ikegami Line

A typical playground area where your little ones can enjoy playing. There is also a miniature traffic park where they can learn about safety and traffic rules. In the summer, there are several swimming pools open, and two are just for children. The park is a 10-minute walk from the station.

### Ikegami Hommonji Temple Koen

1–1–1 Ikegami, Ota-ku, Tokyo    東京都大田区池上 1–1–1
☎ (03) 3755–2365
🚃 Ikegami Station, Tokyu Ikegami Line

The grassy areas around this temple are nice for strolling with the children. There is a special festival day at Hommonji temple, ☎ (03) 3752–2331, each year on October 12.

SETAGAYA-KU

### Setagaya Koen

1-chome Ikejiri, Setagaya-ku, Tokyo    東京都世田谷区池尻 1丁目
☎ (03) 3412–7841
🚃 Ikejiri Ohashi Station, Tokyu Shin Tamagawa Line

The highlight of this park is the steam locomotive that actually runs. You can ride it on Saturdays, Sundays, and holidays from 10:00 A.M. to noon and 1:00 P.M. to 3:00 P.M. for a moderate fee. There is also a small playground, outdoor pool, and go-carts.

---

SHIBUYA-KU

### Nabeshima Shoto Koen

2–10–7 Shoto, Shibuya-ku, Tokyo　東京都渋谷区松涛 2–10–7
☎ (03) 3463–1211 (ward office)
AREA: 5,012 sq. meters
🚃 Shinsen Station, Keio Inokashira Line

You'll find a playground with slides and swings, and a nice-size pond surrounded by trees.

---

SHINAGAWA-KU

### Rinshi no Mori Koen

2 Koyamadai, Shinagawa-ku, Tokyo　東京都品川区小山台 2
☎ (03) 3792–3800
AREA: 4.3 ha
🚃 Fudo-mae or Musashi Koyama Station, Tokyu Mekama Line

This park has large and small fields, an adventure forest, and seven play areas with various themes. There is a day camp for children in the forest section from May to September. The park is a 10-minute walk from Musashi Koyama Station.

### Shiokaze Koen

1 Higashi Yashio, Shinagawa-ku, Tokyo　東京都品川区東八潮 1
☎ (03) 5500–2455
AREA: 5.4 ha
🚃 Daiba Station, Yurikamome Monorail Line (from Shimbashi Station)

This is an ocean-side beach park built on reclaimed land. Bring sand toys, and binoculars to view boats and ships.

### Togoshi Koen

2–1–30 Yutakacho, Shinagawa-ku, Tokyo　東京都品川区豊町 2–1–30
☎ (03) 3782–8811
AREA: 1.8 ha
🚃 Togoshi Koen Station, Tokyu Oimachi Line

Mountain scenery and a path around the lake make this small park special. Also here is an outdoor stage and an old locomotive.

### Jingu-gaien Jido Yuen

9 Kasumigaoka-cho, Shinjuku-ku, Tokyo 東京都新宿区霞岳町 9
☎ (03) 3478–0550
🚇 Shinanomachi Station, JR Sobu Line
🕐 9:30 A.M. to 4:30 P.M. daily.
ADMISSION: ¥150 for adults, ¥50 for children

Not a gym, but a terrific little outdoor park with top-quality wooden play equipment. Also has a rock-climbing wall and a waterfall.

### Shinjuku Chuo Koen

2–11 Nishi Shinjuku, Shinjuku-ku, Tokyo 東京都新宿区西新宿 2–11
☎ (03) 3342–4509
AREA: 8.2 ha
🚇 Shinjuku Station (west exit), JR Yamanote and various lines

This park with its lively fountain in a central square is a breath of fresh air in Shinjuku. Also here are a variety of flowering plants and a playground. The park is located behind the Hotel Century Hyatt.

### Wadabori Koen

2-chome, Omiya, Suginami-ku, Tokyo 東京都杉並区大宮 2丁目
☎ (03) 3313–4247 (Zempukuji-gawa Ryokuchi and Wadabori Park office)
AREA: 11.5 ha
🚇 Nishi Eifuku Station, Keio Inokashira Line

A nice, spacious park which not only has many recreational facilities for children but also houses some old relics. It is ideal for family outings, cycling, and picnicking.

### Zempukuji-gawa Ryokuchi

2 Narita Nishi, Suginami-ku, Tokyo 東京都杉並区成田西 2
☎ (03) 3313–4247 (Zempukuji-gawa Ryokuchi and Wadabori Park office)
AREA: 16.4 ha
🚇 Hamadayama Station, Keio Inokashira Line

This is actually two parks along the Zempukuji River.

### Kinshi Koen

4–15–1 Kinshi, Sumida-ku, Tokyo　東京都墨田区錦糸 4–15–1
☎ (03) 3624–4483
AREA: 5.6 ha
🚇 Kinshicho Station, JR Sobu Line

Here there are sports facilities and a square with a fountain and pool.

### Sumida Koen

1–2–5 Mukojima, Sumida-ku, Tokyo　東京都墨田区向島 1–2–5
☎ (03) 3871–1528 (Taito-ku office) or 3625–5495 (Sumida-ku office)
AREA: 16.4 ha (both sides)
🚇 Honjo Azumabashi Station, Toei Asakusa Line; Asakusa Station, Ginza, Toei Asakusa, Tobu Isezaki lines

This is a nice park with an old Japanese garden. There is also a "friendly with water" park to delight any youngster. Sumida Koen is conveniently located two blocks from Honjo Azumabashi Station or just a short walk across the river from Asakusa Station.

TAITO-KU

### Sumida Koen

A large park in both Sumida-ku and Taito-ku. See Sumida-ku for details.

### Ueno Koen

Connected to Ueno Zoo. See chapter 6 zoo listings for information.

TOSHIMA-KU

### Higashi Ikebukuro Chuo Koen

3–1–6 Higashi Ikebukuro, Toshima-ku, Tokyo　東京都豊島区東池袋 3–1–6
☎ (03) 3981–1111 (ward office)
AREA: 6,189 sq. meters
🚇 Ikebukuro Station, JR Yamanote and various lines

This neighborhood park offers a small pond and open space. Leave Ikebukuro Station by the east exit and you'll find the park next to the Sunshine Building, about 8 minutes from the station.

### Minami Ikebukuro Koen

2–21–1 Minami Ikebukuro, Toshima-ku, Tokyo　東京都豊島区南池袋 2–21–1

☎ (03) 3981–1111 (ward office)
AREA: 7,811 sq. meters
🚃 Ikebukuro Station, JR Yamanote and various lines

Here there is a children's swimming pool and lots of open space for playing freely. The park is a 6-minute walk from the east exit of Ikebukuro Station.

### Nishi Ikebukuro Koen

3–20–1 Nishi Ikebukuro, Toshima-ku, Tokyo　東京都豊島区西池袋 3–20–1
☎ (03) 3981–1111 (ward office)
AREA: 8,759 sq. meters
🚃 Ikebukuro Station, JR Yamanote and various lines

There are athletic facilities on the grounds of this park and a "friendly with water" park. The park is a 10-minute walk from the west exit of Ikebukuro Station.

# OUR FAVORITE PARKS, PLAYGROUNDS, AND GARDENS

The following list of parks, playgrounds, and gardens contains descriptions of their facilities and suggestions for enjoying them. All of these places have a diversity that makes you want to visit them again and again. Each time you visit, in different seasons and with different friends, it is a whole new experience!

If you are looking for the children's playground inside one of these vast spaces, just say, *kodomo no yuenchi wa doko desu ka?* which means "Where is the children's playground?" You may have to repeat this phrase along the way, but it should eventually get you there.

To let you know at a glance which of these special spots you might want to visit, we have devised a rating system. We took into account the location, ease of getting there, condition of the park, the cost involved, availability of food, toilets, quiet places, and things kids like. Then we rated the parks in this section using these criteria. Check our ice cream cone (🍦🍦🍦🍦🍦) rating system: one cone for mediocre, three for average, five for great. At the end of the listings by *ku*, or ward, is a section on West Tokyo.

BUNKYO-KU

### Chinzanso Garden and Restaurant　🍦🍦🍦

2–10–8 Sekiguchi, Bunkyo-ku, Tokyo　東京都文京区関口 2–10–8

☎ (03) 3943–1111
AREA: 6 ha
🚇 Mejiro Station, JR Yamanote Line

If you are looking for a special spot to take the kids in Mejiro, you will be pleased to hear about Chinzanso. June is the best time of year to visit Chinzanso because of its famous firefly festival. The many flowers and plants on the premises make it a nice place to observe the change of seasons. We have often made reservations for lunch or dinner and included the children. Not only is the tatami a comfortable choice for infants and toddlers, but you don't have to worry about your noise level interrupting other diners because each party eats in a small house separated from the others. The food is Japanese barbecue, and although the cost is about ¥8,000 for an adult meal, it is well worth it.

Most of the garden winds up and down stone steps, so you will need a firm grip on your toddler if he is not too steady on his feet. As it is not a large area, you do not need a backpack or stroller; just park the car, or take a bus or taxi from Mejiro Station, and enter the rather modern-looking building called Chinzanso Restaurant. The garden area is located out the back door.

CHIYODA-KU

## Hibiya Koen

1 Hibiya Koen, Chiyoda-ku, Tokyo　東京都千代田区日比谷公園 1
☎ (03) 3501–6428
AREA: 16 ha
🚇 Hibiya Station, Hibiya, Toei Mita, Chiyoda lines; Yurakucho Station, Yurakucho, JR Yamanote lines

This sprawling park has a large fountain in the center where our toddlers love to watch the changing water patterns and chase the pigeons. Near the fountain there is a small concession stand selling snacks and drinks. We use the entrance across from the Imperial Hotel that leads directly to the fountain. A minute's walk from there is an excellent playground that never seems to be very crowded, possibly because it is located downtown and away from most residences. After riding the coiled koala bears and playing the giant bead game, the kids can wander over to the pond and throw stones into the water. This park is a refreshing break in the Ginza-Hibiya district. If one parent works in this area or the nearby Otemachi-Marunouchi business district, you could arrange a midday picnic here for the whole family. If you want to drive, parking is available underground.

## Kitanomaru Koen

1–1 Kitanomaru Koen, Chiyoda-ku, Tokyo　東京都千代田区北の丸公園 1–1
☎ (03) 3211–7878　(03) 3234–1948 (boathouse office)
🚊 Takebashi Station, Tozai Line; Kudanshita Station, Tozai, Toei Shinjuku, Hanzomon lines

Near the Imperial Palace grounds you will find a park with grassy lawns and winding paths. Kitanomaru Park is easy to maneuver with strollers, and the outer moat is great for a longer walk. For the young ones, the Chidorigafuchi rowboat area is always lots of fun. Hours are from 9:30 A.M. to 4:00 P.M. from March 1 to December 15; closing time is a little later in July and August. The park is closed on Mondays. The cost is ¥300 per half an hour. This is one of our favorite spots to watch the changing seasons, and it is rarely crowded. The nearby Fairmont Hotel is a good place to park the car, freshen up, and perhaps have an ice cream.

CHUO-KU

## Hama Rikyu Teien (Hama Detached Palace Garden)

1–1 Hama Rikyu Teien, Chuo-ku, Tokyo　東京都中央区浜離宮庭園 1–1
☎ (03) 3541–0200
AREA: 25 ha
🚊 Daimon Station, Toei Asakusa Line; Shimbashi Station, Ginza, Toei Asakusa, JR Yamanote, JR Keihin Tohoku, JR Tokaido, JR Yokosuka lines

Located on the banks of the Sumida River, this spacious Japanese garden is a great place to turn the kids loose. There is a lake on the grounds with a charming Japanese bridge across the middle. At one end of the park is a pier where you can board a double-decker sightseeing boat. The cruise up the river and back is enjoyable for all ages and a great choice for entertaining out-of-town guests. You can purchase snacks on board or take your own picnic lunch.

　　To get there, we suggest taking a cab for the 5-minute ride from either Daimon or Shimbashi stations. If you are driving, you will see the park on the water side as you drive under Shuto Expressway No. 1 between these two stations. Park on the street nearby.

## Gyosen Park  🏞🏞🏞🏞🏞

3–2–1 Kita Kasai, Edogawa-ku, Tokyo　東京都江戸川区北葛西 3–2–1
☎ (03) 3687–3492
🚇 Nishi Kasai Station, Tozai Line

This park boasts a nature zoo, complete with aviaries and a petting zoo, plus an exquisite Japanese garden with tea house, waterfall, and carp-filled pond. Some of the zoo animals are quite exotic (wallabies and iguanas) and, best of all, the whole park is free.

In summer, a large circular fountain provides a place for children to splash in and cool off. Although the zoo has limited operating hours, the rest of the park is open twenty-four hours a day.

MEGURO-KU

## Himonya Koen  🏞🏞🏞🏞

6–9–11 Himonya, Meguro-ku, Tokyo　東京都目黒区碑文谷 6–9–11
☎ (03) 3714–1548
🚇 Gakugei Daigaku Station, Tokyu Toyoko Line

As parents of young children, this park in Meguro was one of our most exciting discoveries. Not only is there a real petting zoo, but there is also a boating pond and pony rides. The petting zoo is open daily from 10:00 A.M. to 11:30 P.M. and 1:30 P.M. to 4:30 P.M., except Mondays and Thursdays. Next to the petting zoo is a ticket machine for the pony rides (¥100). A park worker guides the ponies, so the rides are safe even for the youngest cowboy or cowgirl. There is also an arena for horseback-riding lessons, which can be arranged by calling ☎ (03) 3714–1548. Riding lessons are from 3:00 P.M. to 5:00 P.M., but you must reserve far in advance.

In Himonya Park there is enough space for kicking a ball around and a nice playground with a sandbox. If you are brave enough to row a boat with young children, closed on December to February, the price is ¥50 but each child must be accompanied by an adult. An enjoyable activity for all ages is feeding bread to the ducks.

The park is across the street from Gakugei Daigaku Station and several blocks away from the Daiei department store (see chapter 2) on Meguro Dori. If you drive, you can usually find a parking place on a side street.

## Aoyama Bochi (Aoyama Cemetery) 🌿🌿🌿

2-chome, Minami Aoyama, Minato-ku, Tokyo    東京都港区南青山 2丁目
☎ (03) 3401–3652
AREA: 26.3 ha
🚇 Gaien-mae Station, Ginza Line

Aoyama Cemetery is one of the best spots to view the changing of the seasons in Tokyo. Whether it is autumn leaves or cherry blossoms that you see overhead, you and your family will enjoy a stroll along the paths of this centrally located cemetery (see more on cherry blossom season in chapter 15). Most cemeteries in Japan are not viewed as parks or picnic spots, but Aoyama Cemetery is the exception in Tokyo because of its location and outstanding beauty all year round. There are always joggers and people with children strolling through the grounds. There is a main road cutting through the middle of the area, but the side paths are grassy and safe.

One of the nicest things about Aoyama Cemetery is that it is rarely crowded. Of course, there are more people out in the spring for cherry-blossom viewing, but it is not overrun by hordes of sightseers as some popular spots are.

You can take a taxi to the middle of the cemetery, or walk 10 minutes or so from Gaien-mae Station. If you go by car, be aware that there is no parking in the cemetery, though it is easy enough to find parking nearby. We have had no problem parking on the bridge just before your enter the main intersection.

## Arisugawa no Miya Kinen Koen 🌿🌿🌿

5–7–29 Minami Azabu, Minato-ku, Tokyo    東京都港区南麻布 5–7–29
☎ (03) 3441–9642
AREA: 3.6 ha
🚇 Hiroo Station, Hibiya Line

This is a quiet, rambling park in the heart of Azabu. There is a swing set located near the entrance across from National Azabu Supermarket. The best playground, however, is up the hill near the German Embassy. In addition to jungle gyms, swings, and slides, there is a large sandbox and an open space nearby for playing ball or riding bikes. A 2-minute walk deeper into the park from here will take you to a nice pond. If you bring some bread crumbs, you can feed the ducks or the carp in the pond. This park is conveniently located, and we often use it as an incentive to get our toddlers to sit still in the grocery cart at National Azabu.

From the station, it is a 5-minute walk to the park. If you drive, look for parking on small neighborhood streets.

### Happoen Gardens

1–1–1 Shiroganedai, Minato-ku, Tokyo    東京都港区白金台 1–1–1
☎ (03) 3443–3111
AREA: 5 ha
Meguro Station, JR Yamanote, Tokyu Mekama lines

A visit to this five-hundred-year-old garden in Shiroganedai is best on weekdays since it is a favorite spot for weddings on weekends. Parents will appreciate the quiet serenity of the surroundings, and children will be delighted by the large pond full of colorful mallards and carp. There is a gazebo at the water's edge from where it's fun to watch the fish literally jump into the air to eat the crumbs thrown by children. Since this is a private garden, picnics and excessive noise are discouraged. The restaurant is a good place to stop for an ice cream before heading home.

When you're ready to leave, there are always taxis waiting in front of the restaurant; or you can come by car and park free of charge. From Meguro Station it is a 10-minute bus or taxi ride down Meguro Dori. If you drive, look for the large sign for Happoen restaurant near the Miyako Hotel.

### Kokuritsu Shizen Kyoiku-en (National Park for Nature Study)

5–21–5 Shiroganedai, Minato-ku, Tokyo    東京都港区白金台 5–21–5
☎ (03) 3441–7176
AREA: 20 ha
Meguro Station, JR Yamanote, Tokyu Mekama lines
🕐 9:00 A.M. to 4:30 P.M. (5:00 P.M. from May 1 to August 31). Closed Mondays.

This is a heavily wooded nature reserve full of gigantic old trees. As you walk along the paths, you may see rabbits and squirrels hopping among the trees. In the ponds and marshes are ducks, swans, and geese, and our kids have been enthralled by huge spider webs glistening in the sunlight. When you are looking for some peace and quiet in the hustle and bustle of Tokyo, this is the place to go.

Strollers are a bit difficult to navigate over the pebbled path, so front or back carriers are helpful. For youngsters who are fascinated by insects, be sure to visit the Insect House, open from April to November from 10:00 A.M. to 11:00 A.M., Sundays only. Inside is a marvelous collection of colorful butterflies and other insects.

## Kyu Shiba Rikyu Garden    ୱୱୱ
## (Garden of the Former Imperial Detached Palace)

1–4–1 Kaigan, Minato-ku, Tokyo    東京都港区海岸 1–4–1
☎ (03) 3434–4029
AREA: 4.3 ha
🚇 Hamamatsucho Station, JR Yamanote, JR Keihin Tohoku lines

Located directly down the street from the entrance of Zojoji Temple is this beautifully landscaped garden. On the street side is a playground with swings, slides, and climbing equipment. There are benches here where you can have a picnic, or your can stop at the McDonald's up the street halfway to Zojoji Temple. Just behind this playground is the entrance to the garden. There is no admission charge for children under twelve and adults over sixty-five. Admission for others is ¥150. The garden is open from 9:00 A.M. to 4:30 P.M. daily. This Edo-period (1600–1868) garden, one of Tokyo's oldest, still maintains its miniature landscapes, featuring famous mountains and a pond, connected to the sea, which rises and falls with the tides. It is an excellent choice for photographs, and a good plan is to combine it with one of the attractions in Shiba Koen (see entry later in this section).

For those who drive, we suggest parking along Kaigan Dori, the street that comes out from the front of Zojoji Temple (off Hibiya Dori).

## Nezu Art Museum and Park    ୱୱୱ

6–5–1 Minami Aoyama, Minato-ku, Tokyo    東京都港区南青山 6–5–1
☎ (03) 3400–2536
🚇 Omotesando Station, Ginza, Hanzomon, Chiyoda lines

Your children will enjoy the many features of this Aoyama retreat. We lived nearby when the children were barely walking, and there was always something to interest them. There is a small museum just as you enter the gates, but the exhibits of porcelain are more interesting for adults. The quiet, tree-lined garden is just the place for an adventure walk. Our favorite spot is the bridge over a small pond where giant carp swim. Look for the stone statues of animals as you wander along the paths.

## Odaiba Seaside Park    ୱୱୱୱୱ

1–4–1 Daiba, Minato-ku, Tokyo    東京都港区台場 1–4–1
☎ (03) 5531–0851
AREA: 6.7 ha
🚇 Daiba Station, Yurikamone Monorail Line

This narrow, sandy beach sits on a stretch of newly reclaimed land.

Colorful wind surfers dot the waves while families relax: fishing, swimming, or just playing in the sand. At the far end of the beach you'll find ancient cannons and the remains of the fortress built as a barrier for Commodore Perry's ships in the 1850s. Back at the main beach, you can take a break at Decks Daiba, six floors of restaurants and shops.

### Shiba Koen

4–10–17 Shiba Koen, Minato-ku, Tokyo    東京都港区芝公園 4–10–17
☎ (03) 3431–4359
AREA: 1 ha
Hamamatsu-cho Station, JR Yamanote, JR Keihin Tohoku lines; Daimon station, Toei Asakusa Line; Shiba Koen Station, Toei Mita Line

This park is a collection of buildings and sports centers. Included on its grounds are Tokyo Tower, Zojoji Temple, the Tokyo Prince Hotel, some sports facilities, a bowling alley, a golf range, public tennis courts, and swimming pools. The one real playground with climbing bars and swings is on the other side of Zojoji Temple from Tokyo Tower, down Hibiya Dori to the right as you face away from the temple. There are a couple of other areas with pull-up bars and benches, but they cannot really be called playgrounds.

The sidewalks around the park make for nice strolling with children. The paths inside the park are mostly dirt (mud when it has been raining) or sand, and in some spots they are like hiking trails in the mountains. There is a small waterfall just below Tokyo Tower, and the kids can have some real adventures here if you don't mind the mud.

The best time to visit this area with kids is in conjunction with an outing to one of the attractions on the grounds or a visit to the doctors or pharmacy at the Tokyo Medical and Surgical Clinic. Zojoji Temple is a great background for a photograph, and if you have guests who want to go sightseeing, this is a good spot. You could combine a trip to the temple with a stop at McDonald's (on Kaigan Dori, the street that leads from the front of the temple, about a 5-minute walk toward the bay), then finish up at Kyu Shiba Rikyu Garden (see earlier entry in this section). This park provides plenty of opportunities for a taste of Japanese history without traveling a great distance.

For adults, there are three tennis courts in the park; call ☎ (03) 3431–4359 one month in advance for a reservation. There is also an outdoor public swimming pool complex with three pools of varying depths; ☎ (03) 3435–0470 (pool hours) or ☎ (03) 3578–2111 (ward office). The pools are open from July to mid-September, 9:30 A.M. to

11:30 A.M. and 12:30 P.M. to 5:00 P.M. Night swimming is also available from mid-July to the end of August, 6:00 P.M. to 8:00 P.M. A ¥300 ticket is for two hours' worth of swimming. The pool is open for night swimming in August on Sundays and Mondays. It is closed on Mondays in July and September.

If you drive, it is best to park in a paid lot at one of the attractions or off one of the streets that intersect Hibiya Dori.

OTA-KU

### Nishi Rokugo Koen ("Tire Park")   𝄞𝄞𝄞

1–6–1 Nishi Rokugo, Ota-ku, Tokyo    東京都大田区西六郷 1–6–1
☎ (03) 3731–1811
AREA: 8.5 ha
🚃 Zoshiki Station, Keihin Kyuko Line; Kamata Station, JR Kehin Tohoku, Tokyu Mekama, Tokyu Ikegami lines

A visit to Tire Park is an experience like no other in Tokyo. In the park, there are hundreds of tires in every shape and size imaginable, and they are used in the most creative ways. Some are sculpted into robots or dragons, and there are tunnels and mountains that are perfect for climbing. This park boasts the best swings for parents and babies to swing in together; big, comfortable tire swings that accommodate adults of every shape and size. Because of the tires, it can be a bit dusty on a hot day, so be sure to bring your *oshibori* and use the row of water faucets to clean up afterward. On one side of the park there is a snack bar with Popsicles and ice cream and a few picnic tables.

We are usually fortunate enough to find car parking on the street that runs in front of the park. If you go by train, you can walk the 8 minutes from Zoshiki Station, 15 minutes from Kamata Station, or take a taxi to "Taiya Koen."

### Senzoku Koen   𝄞𝄞𝄞𝄞

2–14–5 Minami Senzoku, Ota-ku, Tokyo    東京都大田区南千束 2–14–5
☎ (03) 3726–2427    (03) 3720–4441 (boat office)
AREA: 2.5 ha
🚃 Senzoku-ike Station, Tokyu Ikegami Line

This very special pond with an adjacent playground is one of the most scenic places you will come across in Tokyo. Children will be delighted by the large swan and duck paddle boats available for rent. The swan boats are roomy and safe, even for two adults and two children. For ¥800 you can paddle across the pond for thirty minutes while your little one mans the steering wheel. Less exotic duck paddle boats are available for ¥600. After a ride on the paddle boats, you can head through the Senzoku Temple grounds to the small playground. A quicker way to get there is to go along a back street to the right of the pond. We have visited this temple on the first weekend in September, during the annual autumn festival. It was especially festive at dusk, with red lanterns reflecting on the surface of the water. In addition to the usual booths of food and games, there was an artist demonstrating the art of candy sculpture. The kids were fascinated as he created various animal shapes from a ball of warm taffy.

If you are driving to Senzoku-ike, go along Nakahara Kaido in Ota-ku and you'll see the pond. There is no parking lot, so you will have to park on the narrow side streets near the playground. The train is quite convenient, as Senzoku-ike Station is located just across the street from the paddle boat entrance. There is a nice terrace cafe for meals or snacks in the building that houses the boats.

SETAGAYA-KU

## Baji Koen ♔♔♔♔

2–1–1 Kami Yoga, Setagaya-ku, Tokyo    東京都世田谷区上用賀 2–1–1
☎ (03) 3429–5101
AREA: 8.5 ha
Shibuya Station, JR Yamanote and various lines
🕐 9:00 A.M. to 5:00 P.M. (4:00 P.M. in winter).

Baji Koen, or Horse Park, is a well-kept, spacious park that was used for equestrian events during the 1964 Olympic Games. Events are held at the park each month, such as free horse rides and carriage races. In addition to the well-designed playground, there is an area of natural woods where the children can go exploring. The park has many lovely details in its layout, such as hedges carved in horse shapes and water fountains with horse-head statues. It is an ideal place for picnics—drinks are available from vending machines—or lunch at the restaurant next to the information office. Baji Koen is open daily all year round. To get there, take a 30-minute bus (bus #24 bound for Seijo Gakuen) or taxi ride from Shibuya Station. Get off at Nodai-mae bus stop and walk 3 minutes to the park. Parking is not available at the park.

## Kinuta Koen 𖢥𖢥𖢥

Kinuta Koen, Setagaya-ku, Tokyo    東京都世田谷区砧公園
☎ (03) 3700–7059
AREA: 38.3 ha
🚇 Yoga Station, Tokyu Shin Tamagawa Line

For residents of Setagaya, this park is a refreshing oasis of green, with excellent facilities for picnics and playing. There is a cycling course and bike rental for children under fifteen years of age. The area is actually divided into two parks, and children will have the most fun in the section where they can climb on an old locomotive and enjoy the playground equipment. The adjacent Setagaya-ku Sports Center has three outdoor swimming pools with shallow pools for the little ones. Even though Kinuta Park is a little difficult to get to (30 to 40 minutes by car or bus from Shibuya), it is a great choice for birthday parties. Not only can you find an abundance of picnic tables just off the playground, but you can also rent a party room in case of rain. There is a water park next door that is fun for older kids as well as adventurous four- or five-year-olds. There is also a miniature water slide for the little ones.

## Komazawa Olympic Koen 𖢥𖢥𖢥𖢥

1–1 Komazawa Koen, Setagaya-ku, Tokyo    東京都世田谷区駒沢 1–1
☎ (03) 3421–6121
AREA: 41 ha
🚇 Komazawa Daigaku Station, Tokyu Shin Tamagawa Line

This large sports complex was built for the 1964 Olympic Games. The park is split in two by Komazawa Dori, and there are three playgrounds spread throughout the park. You will find kilometers of paved paths for bike riding and lots of fresh air and open spaces for exercising and playing all year round.

There is a family area in the park with a small bike course for children (open 9:30 A.M. to 4:00 P.M.; closed Mondays) that is free of charge, and another bike path where you can ride a two-person pedal cart. (If there are two adults on the bike, you cannot put your child in the kid's seat. Only two people total allowed.) Near the bike course is a play area with a few swings and some old climbing structures. There are two other playgrounds, referred to by the regulars as the "squirrel" playground and the "pig" playground, because of the animal-shaped climbing structures. The "pig" playground, preferred by our friends, is on the Tamagawa Dori side of the park, by the track and field stadium.

The "squirrel" playground is across Komazawa Dori, off Jiyu Dori.

The park's public swimming pools are open July 1 to September 15 from 10:00 A.M. to 5:00 P.M. daily except Monday. Tennis courts are available from 8:30 A.M. to 4:30 P.M. daily except Monday and must be reserved two months in advance. Inside the large stadium is a training center where adults can work out from 9:00 A.M. to 5:00 P.M. and from 6:00 P.M. to 8:45 P.M. daily for only ¥350 for two hours. The training center is closed on the third Monday of each month.

If possible, it is best to ride or take your bike to this park so you can make use of the long bicycle course and sidewalks. If you drive, there is parking available in paid lots adjacent to the park, or you can park on one of the side streets. To get to the park from Ebisu Station, take the Sakura Shimmachi bus to the Tokyo Daini Byoin-mae (Tokyo National Hospital No. 2) stop, near the corner of Komazawa Dori and Jiyu Dori. The park is a 10-minute walk from Komazawa Daigaku Station on the Shin Tamagawa Line.

---

| SHIBUYA-KU |
| --- |

### Yoyogi Koen 〰〰〰〰〰

2–1 Yoyogi Kamizono-cho, Shibuya-ku, Tokyo    東京都渋谷区代々木神園町 2–1
☎ (03) 3469–6081
🚇 Harajuku Station, JR Yamanote Line; Meiji Jingu-mae Station, Chiyoda Line

A park for all seasons. Yoyogi Park is located at one end of Meiji Shrine in Harajuku. It is just right for kite flying and picnics, long walks and quiet times, or just about anything you would want to do in an outdoor setting. It is also one of the few parks with convenient parking nearby. If you park at the west end, a stroll up the sidewalks will lead you to the bicycle area where small tricycles and bikes are available for children free of charge from 10:00 A.M. to 4:00 P.M. Tuesday to Sunday (closed Mondays). This is not your typical paved bike lot, but a nice open spot surrounded with trees and lots of grass for parents to sit on and watch the kids.

Heading back across the open spaces will lead you to the perfect picnic spot. You will find a concession stand near the south entrance that sells kites in addition to snacks and drinks. The iris garden of the shrine is famous for its beauty and is an ideal spot to take some pictures. The shrine itself is one of the most popular in Tokyo for residents and tourists alike. The paths of the shrine are gravel, so don't try to take your stroller. This sprawling park becomes fairly crowded on weekends, but Yoyogi has something for everyone.

SHINJUKU-KU

## Shinjuku Gyoen  🌳🌳🌳

11 Naito-cho, Shinjuku-ku, Tokyo    東京都新宿区内藤町 11
☎ (03) 3350–0151
AREA: 9 ha
🚉 Sendagaya Station, JR Sobu Line; Shinjuku Gyoen-mae Station, Marunouchi Line; Shinjuku Station (east exit), JR Yamanote and various lines
🕐 9:00 A.M. to 4:30 P.M. Closed Mondays.

This is a vast, open park with beautiful old trees and a lake. There is no car parking on the grounds, but we sometimes stop by with the kids after a shopping trip in Shinjuku. It is easy enough to park a few blocks away near the Wendy's hamburger restaurant on Yasukuni Dori and walk to the park for a picnic lunch.

There is one playground in a corner of the park, and a large greenhouse on the grounds that houses exotic plants from around the world. The greenhouse is open from 11:00 A.M. to 3:00 P.M., and admission is ¥200 for adults and ¥50 for children.

The park is a 3-minute walk from Sendagaya or Shinjuku Gyoen-mae stations, or a 10-minute walk from Shinjuku Station.

WEST TOKYO

## Inokashira Koen  🌳🌳🌳🌳

1–18–31 Gotenyama, Musashino-shi, Tokyo    東京都武蔵野市御殿山 1–18–31
☎ (0422) 47–6900
AREA: 28 ha
🚉 Kichijoji Station, JR Chuo, Keio Inokashira lines; Inokashira Koen Station, Keio Inokashira Line

Park, small zoo, and pond are all combined here to make for a terrific outing in west Tokyo. The playground facilities located near the pond are excellent, and it is a scenic spot for a picnic. To arrange for boating on the pond, call ☎ (0422) 47–1538. The zoo, called Suiseibutsu-en, has fish and birds and is open from 9:30 A.M. to 4:30 P.M. daily except Monday. Children under twelve are admitted free, and adult tickets are

¥400. Our children delight in petting the guinea pigs and chasing the peacocks. The zoo is actually rather clean if a bit smelly.

Located adjacent to the park is the Inokashira Nature and Culture Park (Inokashira Shizen Bunka-en). Here is an amusement-park atmosphere with ¥100 rides and small carnival rides. There is also a greenhouse and aviary, a small natural history and sculpture museum, and another zoo-type attraction called Hon-en. This zoo has deer and peacocks that are free to roam about. The ticket for Suiseibutsu-en is good for Hon-en, too, so don't throw it away.

The park is a short walk from Kichijoji or Inokashira Koen stations. If you drive, there is parking at the park, although there is often a long line on weekends.

### Koganei Koen 〰〰〰〰〰

1–13–1 Sekino-cho, Koganei-shi, Tokyo    東京都小金井市関野町 1–13–1
☎ (042) 385–5611
🚃 Musashi Koganei Station, JR Chuo Line; Hana Koganei Station, Seibu Shinjuku Line

We are always looking for a new place for a school outing, company picnic, or where we can take visitors from abroad. This park is a great choice, as there is something for everybody here. Unless you live in west Tokyo, it takes a little effort to get there (about one hour on the train from central Tokyo), but it is well worth it.

The grounds of the park are large, with no fences or gates to hem you in, and immediately upon arriving you feel as if you are in the country. The large trees are of many species, and the grounds have a wild look to them that is refreshing in this society where gardeners love to clip and trim. There are many picnic tables, paved and dirt paths, and open areas to choose from. You can stay away from the crowd for a private party, or join the fun with everyone else near the sports center and the playground.

The playground at Koganei Park is one of the nicest we have seen in Tokyo. There is also a small play area for babies (under two years old) with scaled-down slides, swings, and climbing toys, located well away from the older children and their activities.

For older children, there is a pyramid-type structure built into a hill that has stairs, dirt paths, rope ladders, and grassy knolls all around it leading up to the top. There are three levels to the top, all with a variety of slides, hidden sandboxes, and daredevil paths to explore. Just below this pyramid is an open area with an obstacle or workout course. The equipment is made for adult use, but children of all ages play on the balance beam, monkey bars, and pulley swing.

Just next to this course is a hill covered with artificial turf in a fenced-in area that, at first glance, looks like a putting green. There is a gate at the bottom and a pile of red plastic sleds. It is actually a slide and is free of charge. Children do much better on a sled by themselves without an adult to weigh them down or tip them over. (Important to note: The sleds are unstable with two people on them. We watched an adult holding a child in the sled and when the sled tipped over, the child was hurt.) Next door is a paved area for bouncing balls or gently hitting a tennis ball. There is also the usual bike area for children with bikes to use free of charge and a snack stand with drinks, chips, and ice cream for sale.

Also on the grounds is the Edo-Tokyo Tatemono-en, which has a collection of local (Kanto Plain) archaeological objects inside, and some models of old houses and farm structures outside.

Next to the playground is a new members-only sports center. They don't offer anything for children under six years of age, but they have many activities for adults. The phone number for the sports center is ☎ (0423) 81–1336.

To get there, catch bus #3 from Musashi-Koganei Station and get off at Koganei Koen-mae (it's about a 10-minute ride). If you are driving and want to use the parking lot, turn right off Koganei Kaido onto Itsukaichi Kaido. You will see the park to your left; turn at the third street and drive to the lot. The sports center and playground are to your right as you face the park.

### Sagamihara Park

3277 Shimomizo, Sagamihara-shi, Kanagawa　神奈川県相模原市下溝 3277
☎ (042) 778–1653
AREA: 23.8 ha
🚃 Harataima Station, JR Sagami Line; by bus from Sagamiono Station, Odakyu Line

This huge expanse of land was returned to Japan in 1978 from the U.S. military. During the bubble economy, a deluxe park was constructed, featuring top-quality and design playground equipment from the United States. Other features of the park are a zoo with a petting area, a tree house, an observation tower, gardens (including an indoor botanical garden, open from 9:30 A.M. to 4:00 P.M.), and a wading pool in summer.

## Showa Memorial Park  🏵🏵🏵🏵🏵

3173 Midori-cho, Tachikawa-shi, Tokyo　東京都立川市緑町 3173
☎ (0425) 28–1751
AREA: 89 ha
🚃 Nishi Tachikawa Station, JR Ome, Itsukaichi lines
🕘 9:30 A.M. to 5:00 P.M. (4:30 P.M. from November 1 to February 29).

This lovely park has slides, swings, and climbing equipment for all ages. Built on a former U.S. airbase, the Dragon Dunes (six large mosaic dragons) provide hours of fun for little ones who like to climb or play hide-and-seek. A lake with rowboats (¥360 per half hour) and pedal boats for rent (¥710 per half hour) is the centerpiece of the park. Bike courses and jogging courses crisscross the park, and they have over six hundred bicycles of all types for rent. In the winter months, there is ice-skating daily.

To get there, take the JR Chuo Line to Tachikawa Station. Change here for the JR Ome Line to Nishi Tachikawa Station. The park is a 5-minute walk from the station.

## Tomin no Mori  🏵🏵🏵🏵🏵

7146 Kazuma, Hinohara-mura, Nishitama-gun, Tokyo
☎ (0425) 98–6006　東京都西多摩郡檜原村 7146
AREA: 197 ha
🚃 Musashi Itsukaichi Station, JR Itsukaichi Line

This "forest" park is a wonderful chance for Tokyo residents to experience the great outdoors. Built by the Tokyo Metropolitan Government in 1990 in the Chichibu Tama National Park, this park, comprising five "zones," was created to give children a chance to exercise their body and their imagination.

For example, at the entrance is the "Forest of Encounter," where you can get information about the park. Refreshments are available at the forest villa. Here you will also find the wooden craft center, where you can watch craftsmen at work. You can also learn how to make various crafts on the second floor of this building.

Zone 2 is the "Forest of Daily Life." Here you can study how charcoal is made, find out which mountain vegetables are edible, and learn other nature-related skills. Other zones have names such as the "Forest of Adventure," with sports equipment and obstacle courses; the "Forest of Wild Birds," with wildlife exhibits; and the "Forest of Trees," which a breathtaking view of Mt. Fuji.

The park is open from 9:30 A.M. to 5:00 P.M. (depending on the season) and admission is free. To get there, take the JR Chuo Line to Tachikawa Station, change to the JR Ome Line and get off at Haijima Station. From there, take the JR Itsukaichi Line to Musashi Itsukaichi Station, where a shuttle bus leaves for Kazuma. From Shinjuku, the trip will probably take about 2½ hours. If you go by car, take the Shuto Expressway to the Tokaido Interchange and change to the Chuo Expressway. At Kamakawanori, change to the Shinohara Kaido, which will lead you to Kazuma.

# 6
# Amusement Parks, Aquariums, and Zoos

For a special outing with children, you cannot go wrong with an amusement park, aquarium, or zoo. Japan has plenty of all three, with new ones springing up every year. Because of the time involved in getting to many of these places, especially with young children, these outings are often full-day trips.

Most amusement parks, aquariums, and zoos have rest rooms and snack areas. The snacks for sale are the usual chips, ice cream, and pop. Sometimes there are restaurants selling sandwiches and *obento* lunches. You will find souvenir booths full of goodies, and there is almost always a section with ¥100 rides, which are especially delightful for babies and toddlers.

Many of the attractions listed in this chapter could fall under more than one category. The aquariums are generally on the small side and are often combined with another attraction. Some amusement parks have small petting zoos (usually a few rabbits and goats), while most zoos have ¥100 rides. Many of the amusement parks run an ice-skating rink in the winter and swimming pool in the summer. Amusement parks may have a theme, and include playground or athletic equipment as well as the usual rides—roller coasters, tilt-a-whirl, and so on. For the most part, children under age eight or so will be thrilled with the hustle and bustle of these theme parks. Older children may be disappointed at the small scale of things, but if you prepare them, and yourself, in advance, you can all have a great time. If you consider the day trip a cultural experience and an opportunity for the family to spend some time together, these attractions should have something to keep everyone happy.

As with most popular holiday spots in Japan, these attractions will be much less crowded if you visit during the week. However, all the places in this chapter are spacious enough to enjoy on weekends, too, although the gaggles of young couples at the high-tech aquariums on Sundays can be a bit overwhelming. One of the places where lines can be a real problem is Tokyo Disneyland, but *there* the wait is worth it! In all cases, arriving as early as possible any day you go is your best bet.

There is usually a good deal of walking involved if you attempt to see all the exhibits in any of these outings, so be sure to bring a stroller for tired feet. Some places offer strollers for rent, but they go quickly on a busy day.

We suggest that you try at least a few of the outings listed below with your kids. Hours tend to change from season to season so it's a good idea to call for more information before you visit. You may find the zoos and aquariums in Japan a bit more cramped than some of the more spacious and modern habitats in other countries, but if your child is thrilled at the idea of seeing a real giraffe or live dolphin, the trip will be worth the effort.

## AMUSEMENT PARKS

KANTO AREA

### Arakawa Amusement Park (Arakawa Yuen)

6–35–11 Nishiogu, Arakawa-ku, Tokyo　東京都荒川区西尾久 6–35–11
☎ (03) 3893–6003
🚋 Arakawa Yuenchi-mae Station, Toden Arakawa Line
🕘 9:00 A.M. to 5:00 P.M.

This amusement park, which also houses a small zoo, is closed Mondays, except in July and August, and at New Year. There is free admission for children under middle-school age. To get there, take the JR Keihin Tohoku Line to Oji Station and then change to the Toden Arakawa Line.

### Asakusa Hanayashiki

2–28–1 Asakusa, Taito-ku, Tokyo　東京都台東区浅草 2–28–1
☎ (03) 3842–8780
🚋 Asakusa Station, Ginza, Toei Asakusa, and Tobu lines

One of the oldest amusement parks in Tokyo. The park is open from 10:00 A.M. to 6:00 P.M. (9:00 P.M. in the summer), six days a week. It is closed Tuesdays, except during school holidays, when it is open daily. Admission is ¥900 for adults, ¥400 for children up to five years old. The park is just behind Asakusa Kannon Temple.

### Disneyland (Tokyo Disneyland)

1–1 Maihama, Urayasu-shi, Chiba 　千葉県浦安市舞浜 1–1
☎ (0473) 54–0001
🚈 Maihama Station, JR Keiyo Line

This is the real thing. This park is just like the original California Disneyland, with Disney's impeccable landscaping and professional staff. The park has special attractions all year round, including Christmas decorations and shows in December, and late hours and evening fireworks in the summer months. It is open Monday through Thursday from 10:00 A.M. to 7:00 P.M. and Friday, Saturday, and Sunday from 9:00 A.M. to 10:00 P.M. Hours may vary in the winter months so call before you go. The "passport" ticket, valid for all rides, is ¥5,200 for adults and ¥3,570 for four- to eleven-year-olds. There are many ways to get there, but the best option may be to go to Maihama Station, which is right in front of the Disneyland main gate. To get there, take the Yurakucho Line to Shin Kiba Station. Transfer there to the JR Keiyo Line and get off at Maihama Station. You can also take the Tozai Line to Urayasu Station, walk to the shuttle bus terminal, and pay the small fee for the 15-minute ride to Disneyland on its special bus.

Tickets to Disneyland may be purchased in advance at the Disney Resort Ticket Center on the first floor of the Mitsui Building (Hibiya, in Tokyo). The center is open from 10:00 A.M. to 7:00 P.M. daily. For more information call ☎ (03) 3595–1777.

### Fujita Vente

4–6–15 Sendagaya, Shibuya-ku, Tokyo 　東京都渋谷区千駄ヶ谷 4–6–15
☎ (03) 3796–2486
🚈 Yoyogi Station, JR Yamanote, JR Sobu lines; Sendagaya Station, JR Sobu Line
🕐 10:00 A.M. to 6:00 P.M. Closed on Thursdays.

Virtual reality and high-tech entertainment at its best. Fujita Vente is fascinating for kids and their parents. A delightful, well-planned, educational space housed in the headquarters of the Fujita Construction Company. The three floors make for a free fun-filled afternoon. A pamphlet in English helps you discover the "Amusement Space" in the basement, with its amazing virtual stage. Sharks, butterflies, and soccer balls are just a few of the images you will be interacting with. There are also numerous hands-on exhibits. On the first floor, there is a gift shop, toy museum, and cafe. The second floor houses a modern art museum.

## Hikawa Maru

Yamashita Koen, Yamashita-cho, Naka-ku, Yokohama-shi, Kanagawa
☎ (045) 641–4361    神奈川県横浜市中区山下町山下公園
🚇 Kannai Station, JR Negishi Line
🕐 9:30 A.M. to 8:00 P.M. Monday to Friday, 9:30 A.M. to 9:00 P.M. weekends and holidays (varies with each season).

The Hikawa Maru was once a passenger steamer called the "Queen of the Pacific Ocean" that regularly traversed the North American route from 1930 to 1960. Now permanently anchored here, it still preserves the luxury cabins of former times. The ship has a restaurant and an exhibition corner and, in the summer, a beer garden. Admission is ¥800 for adults, ¥400 for children ages six to fifteen, ¥300 for three-to-five-years-olds. Children under three years are free.

## Korakuen Amusement Park

1–3–61 Koraku, Bunkyo-ku, Tokyo    東京都文京区後楽 1–3–61
☎ (03) 3811–2111
🚇 Korakuen Station, Marunouchi Line; Suidobashi Station, JR Sobu Line

This is a typical amusement park, with rides to thrill the teens as well as the usual assortment of smaller rides. It is connected to Tokyo Dome stadium and is next to Koishikawa Botanical Garden. The Park is open from 10:00 A.M. to 6:00 P.M. daily and until 8:00 P.M. in summer (times vary with the seasons). Admission is ¥1,500 for adults, ¥800 for children.

## Lake Sagami Picnic Land

1634 Wakayanagi, Sagamiko-machi, Tsukui-gun, Kanagawa
☎ (0426) 85–1111    神奈川県津久井郡相模湖町若柳 1634
🚇 Sagamiko Station, JR Chuo Honsen Line

Picnic Land is made up of 150 hectares of camping sites with a playland, ranch, and a wading pond. It is open from 9:30 A.M. to 4:00 P.M. (or until 6:00 P.M., depending on the season) every day except Tuesday. The entrance fee is ¥1,400 for adults, ¥800 for children. From Sagamiko Station, take a Kanagawa Chuo Kotsu bus bound for Mikage from bus stop #1 and get off at Picnic Land Mae. The trip takes about 8 minutes.

## Mukogaoka Amusement Park

2–8–1 Nagao, Tama-ku, Kawasaki-shi, Kanagawa
☎ (044) 911–4281    神奈川県川崎市多摩区長尾 2–8–1
🚇 Mukogaoka Yuen Station, Odakyu Line

This park is situated in a twenty-three hectare garden, and much of the beauty of the garden is still here for your enjoyment. There is swimming in the summer, ice-skating in the winter, and the usual small-scale rides and amusements all year round. The park is open from 10:00 A.M. to 5:00 P.M. weekdays, 9:00 A.M. to 5:30 P.M. on weekends and holidays, and closed on Wednesdays. Times vary with the season. Admission is ¥1,500 for adults and ¥800 for children. From Mukogaoka Yuenchi Station, change to the monorail, which takes you directly to the amusement park in just 3 minutes.

### Namco Wonder Egg

Times Park, 1–15 Tamagawa, Setagaya-ku, Tokyo
☎ (03) 3700–3451    東京都世田谷区玉川 1–15　タイムズパーク内
📮 Futako Tamagawa-en Station, Tokyu Shin Tamagawa, Oimachi, Den'en-toshi lines
🕐 10:00 A.M. to 10:00 P.M. daily.

A high-tech adventure park where you can play video games to your heart's content. There are fourteen attractions, plus virtual reality games and the popular Space Age bumper cars. As in addition to the entrance fee, there is a charge for each attraction, you can spend more money here than you intended! Best for older kids.

### Nikko Edomura

470–2 Karakura, Fujiwara-cho, Shioya-gun, Tochigi
☎ (0288) 77–1777    栃木県塩谷郡藤原町柄倉 470–2
📮 Kinugawa Onsen Station, Tobu Kinugawa Line
🕐 9:00 A.M. to 5:00 P.M. daily (9:30 A.M. to 4:00 P.M. in winter).

This unusual park features daily shows by ninja warriors, and all attractions around the sixteen-hectare park are based on the theme of Japan in the Edo period (1600–1868). The admission ticket is from ¥2,300 to ¥4,900 for adults and from ¥1,200 to ¥2,500 for children (depending on the course).

### Nippon Land HOW Amusement Park

2427 Aza Fujiwara, Suyama, Susono-shi, Shizuoka
☎ (03) 3376–1127 (Tokyo office)    静岡県裾野市須山字藤原 2427
📮 Gotemba Station, JR Gotemba Line
🕐 9:00 A.M. to 4:00 P.M. on weekdays, 10:00 A.M. to 5:00 P.M. weekends and holidays. Closed Mondays.

Situated at the foot of Mt. Fuji, this is a combination outdoor sports plaza, amusement park, and resort center. HOW stands for Humanity Opening World, and what it really means is there is something here for everyone, all year round. Golf, ice-skating, skiing, hiking, and a large amusement park are just a few of the attractions. Hotel accommodation is available for those wishing to stay overnight. For reservations, call the Japan Tourist Bureau nearest you. All the attractions are reasonably and individually priced. For information on fees, snow conditions, and hours, call the Tokyo office of Nippon Land. From Gotemba Station, Nippon Land is a 50-minute ride by Fuji Kanko Bus. Admission tickets are ¥800 for adults and ¥500 for children.

## Palette Town

1-chome, Aoumi, Koto-ku, Tokyo    東京都江東区青海 1丁目
☎ (03) 3529–1821 (tape in Japanese)
🚃 Aoumi Station, Yurikamome Monorail Line (from Shimbashi)

The Tokyo area's largest theme park opened here in August 1999, boasting the world's largest Ferris wheel, at one-hundred meters across! The huge complex of Palette Town has much to offer besides the new amusement park. You'll find live music performances and shopping galore in the elegant European-style setting just across the bay from Shimbashi.

## Pony Land

3–12–17 Shinozaki-cho, Edogawa-ku, Tokyo    東京都江戸川区篠崎町 3–12–17
☎ (03) 3678–7520
🚃 Koiwa Station, JR Sobu Line; Shinozakicho Station, Toei Shinjuku Line

At Pony Land, the kids can ride ponies and stagecoaches for free. Park hours are 10:00 A.M. to 11:30 P.M. and 1:30 P.M. to 3:30 P.M. (from July 21 to August 31, open 9:00 A.M. to 11:30 A.M. only). It is closed Mondays and New Year. From the south exit of Koiwa Station, take bus #72 bound for Mizue, Ichinoe, or Edogawa Sports Land. The trip takes about 15 minutes; get off at the Pony Land Mae stop.

## Puroland

1–31 Ochiai, Tama-shi, Tokyo    東京都多摩市落合 1–31
☎ (0423) 72–6500
🚃 Tama Center Station, Keio, Odakyu lines

Sanrio's Puroland is a six-story indoor amusement park. All the attractions are made with the latest technology and with active participation in mind. Sanrio says that each amusement is designed for eighty percent entertainment and twenty percent participation. Once inside the large, domed plaza, you can take your pick from six floors of theme-oriented amusements and restaurants. Much of the park is animated with robots, and all of the restaurants have either entertainment or service by robots. The amusements have themes such as "Fantastic Puro Adventure," where you can ride a boat around Puro Village and learn the story of the birth of Puroland, and "Time Machine of Dreams," where you can experience a trip through time via special effects. Of course, the Sanrio characters are present in abundance, and all the attractions are built with both children and adults in mind. Puroland's controlled admissions policy means that you can enjoy the attractions to the full because the park is never overcrowded. Reserved tickets can also be ordered through the major travel agencies. Passport tickets are ¥4,400 for adults, ¥4,000 for twelve- to seventeen-year-olds, and ¥3,300 for three- to eleven-year-olds. The park is open from 10:00 A.M. to 5:00 P.M. on weekdays and 10:00 A.M. to 8:00 P.M. on weekends. Puroland does close periodically, so it is best to call ahead. The park is a 10-minute walk from Tama Center Station.

## OUR FAVORITE JET-LAG JAUNT

### Tsukiji Fish Market

5–2–1 Tsukiji, Chuo-ku, Tokyo 　東京都中央区築地 5–2–1
☎ (03) 3542–1111
🚇 Tsukiji Station, Hibiya Line
🕐 5:00 A.M. to 1:00 P.M., Monday through Saturday. Closed Sundays, holidays, and second and fourth Wednesdays.

Tsukiji is just about the only place where you can drag the entire family at the ungodly hour of 5:00 A.M. for an interesting outing and a good breakfast too. Not normally early-risers, our family tends to enjoy this adventure most during jet-lagged mornings when we have just arrived back in Japan. It is also a good recommendation to visitors for their first or second day in the city.

Tsukiji's bustling, colorful wholesale market handles tons of fish for all of Japan, and the main auction starts at five in the morning. Even if you arrive a bit later there is still plenty to see, although the market will start closing around noon. After you've checked out the food stalls, you may want to line up for an early breakfast at one of the tiny restaurants at the market. The menu is mostly very fresh sushi so bring snacks for the picky eaters.

## Sanrio Theme Parks

The Sanrio Company, makers of Hello Kitty, The Runabouts, and many more character toys and accessories, opened two new theme parks in the 1990s. These parks were years in the making, and no expense was spared in their design and execution. Although quite different from one another, Puroland in Tokyo (see above) and Harmonyland in Oita Prefecture (see Other Areas) are Japanese theme parks at their best.

## Sega Amusement Theme Park (Yokohama Joypolis)

1–14–18 Shin Yamashita, Naka-ku, Yokohama-shi, Kanagawa
☎ (045) 623–1311    神奈川県横浜市中区新山下 1–14–18
�+Ｔ Sakuragicho Station, JR Keihin Tohoku, Tokyu Toyoko lines; Ishikawacho Station, JR Negishi Line
🕐 11:00 A.M. to 10:45 P.M. Monday through Saturday, 10:00 A.M. to 11:45 P.M. weekends and holidays.

An indoor theme park with virtual-reality attractions, video games, restaurants, and shops. The attractions here (indoor roller coaster, free-fall ride, etc.) are definitely geared toward older kids. Lots of Sega video games will eat up your money fast. To get there, take the bus from Sakuragicho Station and get off at Chobokujo-mae. It is a 15-minute walk from Ishikawacho Station.

## Seibu-en

2964 Yamaguchi, Tokorozawa-shi, Saitama    埼玉県所沢市山口 2964
☎ (0429) 22–1371
🚆 Seibu Yuenchi Station, Seibu Shinjuku Line

At Seibu-en you will find about twenty rides in a big amusement park. During the summer, the hours are Monday through Friday from 10:00 A.M. to 5:00 P.M., Saturday and Sunday from 10:00 A.M. to 8:00 P.M. The park is closed periodically on Tuesday or Wednesday. From November through February it is open on weekends and holidays only, from 10:00 A.M. to 5:00 P.M. Entrance fees range from ¥700 for one- to five-year-olds, to ¥1,500 for adults. The park is connected by train with UNESCO Village (7 minutes from Seibu Kyujo-mae Station on the Yamaguchi Line). UNESCO features scaled-down versions of houses from each country represented in the United Nations. Hours for UNESCO are Saturday through Monday from 10:00 A.M. to 5:00 P.M. The entrance fee is ¥300 for children, ¥600 for students, and ¥1,250 for adults.

## Sesame Place

403 Ajiro, Akiruno-shi, Tokyo 　東京都あきる野市網代 403
☎ (0425) 96–5811
🚃 Akikawa Station, JR Itsukaichi Line

Sesame Place is a theme park based on the popular TV show *Sesame Street*. Built around the theme "play and learn together," the park is set up so that parents and their children can interact and learn with each other. The Tokyo park's special theme is "internationality," and they hire foreign guides—whom they call "play leaders"—to ensure that Japanese children get a taste of international life. At the park you will find Big Bird, Cookie Monster, and many of the other original Sesame Street Characters. There is also a model of 123 Sesame Street, just like the one used on the TV show. Instead of roller-coasters and merry-go-rounds, Sesame Place uses outdoor activities and educational games to give the children their thrills. The park is aimed particularly at children from the age of three to twelve, and so even the youngest child can join in the fun. Besides the restaurants for the general public, there are also nice restroom facilities with baby changing and feeding areas.

The park is located in Akikawa, near Tokyo Summerland (see the entry below). Hours vary with the seasons, but are usually from 10:00 A.M to 5:00 P.M. It is best to call before going. As the park has several attractions for children only, admission is ¥1,000 for children and seniors over sixty-five, and ¥2,000 for adults.

## Tama-tech

5–22–1 Hodokubo, Hino-shi, Tokyo 　東京都日野市程久保 5–22–1
☎ (0425) 91–0820/4
🚃 Tama Dobutsu Koen Station, Keio Line
🕐 10:00 A.M. to 4:30 P.M. daily (winter 9:00 A.M. to 5:30 P.M.).

This is an automobile amusement park run by Honda Motor Co., which is reflected in the various vehicles (battery powered) that feature in some of the rides. The rest are the usual roller coaster, Ferris wheel rides, and so on. There is ice-skating in the winter months. Admission is ¥1,600 for adults, ¥800 for children. Passports for all rides are ¥3,900 for adults, and ¥3,100 for children. To get there from Tama Dobutsu Koen Station, take a bus bound for Tama-Tech or walk for 15 minutes.

## Tobu World Square

209–1 Ohara, Fujiwara-machi, Shioya-gun, Tochigi
☎ (0288) 77–1000 　栃木県塩谷郡藤原町大原 209–1

🚂 Kinugawa Onsen Station, Tobu Kinugawa Line
🕐 9:00 A.M. to 5:00 P.M. daily (in winter to 4:00 P.M.).

Set on eighty hectares in the woods of Nikko, Tobu World Square contains ninety-seven miniature replicas of famous buildings and scenes from around the world. Re-creations of the White House, the Taj Mahal, the Eiffel Tower, the streets of New York, and the old Imperial Hotel can be viewed here. What a great way to take the whole family to see the world without having to travel very far.

### Tokyo Summerland

600 Shiraiwa, Kamiyotsugi, Akiruno-shi, Tokyo
☎ (042) 558–6511　東京都あきる野市上代継白岩 600
🚂 Hachioji Station, JR Chuo Line; Keio Hachioji Station, Keio Line; Akikawa Station, JR Musashi Itsukaichi Line
🕐 10:00 A.M. to 5:00 P.M., closed Thursdays.

This is a medium-size amusement park with a few large rides. The real attraction, and reason for the name, is the unique wave pool. Here, man-made waves wash over swimmers, and intermittent tropical rains fall all year round—all within a domed structure. There are outdoor pools as well, which are open in the summer, and all pools have shallow areas for babies and toddlers. Believe it or not, in the winter months there is ice-skating. Admission for the pool is ¥2,000 for adult and ¥1,000 for children; a "Free Pass" (valid for all attractions) is ¥4,500 for adult, ¥3,000 for children, and ¥2,000 for infants. From the north exit of Hachioji Station take a cab or bus #12 for the 20-minute ride to Tokyo Summerland.

### Toshimaen

3–25–1 Koyama, Nerima-ku, Tokyo　東京都練馬区向山 3–25–1
☎ (03) 3990–3131
🚂 Toshimaen Station, Seibu Ikebukuro Line

This is the oldest amusement park in Tokyo, with fifty attractions. Large adult rides, haunted houses, and a special children's section are all features of the park. Also on the grounds is an outdoor theater with shows nightly during the summer season and every Sunday during the winter. During the summer there is also a fireworks show here that is famous in Japan. Toshimaen is open from 9:00 A.M. to 5:00 P.M. daily, but from mid-November to mid-March the park opens from 10:00 A.M. and is closed on Tuesdays and Wednesdays. A one-day pass including entrance and all rides is ¥2,600 for adults and ¥2,200 for children.

## Wild Blue

2–20–2 Heian-machi, Tsurumi-ku, Yokohama-shi, Kanagawa
☎ (045) 511–2323    神奈川県横浜市鶴見区平安町 2–20–2
🚇 Tsurumi Station, JR Tokaido, JR Tsurumi lines
🕐 10:00 A.M. to 6:00 P.M. Monday through Friday (to 8:00 P.M. weekends and holidays). Closed on Friday from October to March.

Billed as the world's largest indoor water park, Wild Blue seeks to re-create the feel of a tropical island. Attractions including a pool with waves up to 2 meters high for body-boarding, a waterway 350 meters long that goes round the island, and a water slide, all make this spot our kids' favorite adventure year round. They don't even notice that the beach is made of concrete nor that the foliage is artificial. To get there take the bus at Tsurumi Station and get off at Heian Koko.

## Yokohama Cosmo World

2–1 Minato Mirai, Nishi-ku, Yokohama-shi, Kanagawa
☎ (045) 641–6591    神奈川県横浜市西区みなとみらい 2–1
🚇 Sakuragicho Station, JR Negishi, Tokyu Toyoko, Yokohama City lines
🕐 11:00 A.M. to 9:00 P.M. Monday through Friday, 11:00 A.M. to 10:00 P.M. Saturday and Sunday.

A nice little amusement park with a gigantic Ferris wheel left over from the Yokohama Expo of 1989. You'll find many ¥100 rides for the younger crowd and several more adventurous choices for older kids.

## Yokohama Dreamland

700 Matano-cho, Totsuka-ku, Yokohama-shi, Kanagawa
☎ (045) 851–1411    神奈川県横浜市戸塚区俣野町 700
🚇 Totsuka or Ofuna Station, JR Tokaido, JR Yokosuka lines
🕐 10:00 A.M. to 4:30 P.M. (to 5:30 P.M., depending on the season).

An exciting amusement park located southwest of Yokohama City. Among twenty different attractions are the reverse-turning roller coaster, called the Shuttle Loop, a big wheel, a pool (used as an iceskating rink in winter), and bowling alley. Admission is ¥800 for adults and ¥500 for children; a "Free Pass" (valid for all rides) is ¥2,960 for adults and ¥2,600 for children. To get there take the bus from Totsuka or Ofuna stations.

## Yomiuriland

4 Sugasengoku, Tama-ku, Kawasaki-shi, Kanagawa
☎ (044) 966–1111    神奈川県川崎市多摩区菅仙谷 4
🚇 Keio Yomiuriland Station, Keio Sagamihara Line; Yomiuriland Mae Station, Odakyu Line

This is a huge park with thrilling rides, including the "world's fastest roller coaster." There is also an aquarium with dolphin and seal shows and an entire section of children's rides. Roller skating is available year-round, and there are outdoor swimming pools in the summer and ice-skating in the winter. The park is open from 10:00 A.M. to 5:00 P.M. Monday through Friday, 9:00 A.M. to 4:30 P.M. Saturdays (5:00 P.M. on Sundays), and closed on Tuesdays unless it is a school holiday. Times may vary slightly in the winter. Admission is ¥1,600 for adults and ¥800 for children. To get there take the Keio Line from Shinjuku to Chofu Station; change to the Keio Sagamihara Line and get off at Keio Yomiuriland Station, from where you can ride the "skyroad escalator" to the park. An alternative is to take the Odakyu Line from Shinjuku Station to Yomiuriland Station and then catch a special bus to the park.

## OTHER AREAS

### Bampaku Koen Expoland
1–1 Bampaku Koen, Senri, Suita-shi, Osaka　　大阪府吹田市千里万博公園 1–1
☎ (06) 6877–0560
🚇 Ibaraki Station, JR Tokaido Line

This amusement park was built as part of Expo '70, which was held in Osaka. There are a number of large rides and other standard amusements for children. Inside the park there is a playground for younger children, as well as the usual ¥100 rides. A library in the grounds has a large selection of children's books in the international section. The park is open year-round from 9:30 A.M. to 5:30 P.M. (until 9:00 P.M. in summer). It is closed on Wednesdays except in August. Admission is ¥1,000 for adults and ¥550 for children. To get there, take bus #4 from Ibaraki Station. If you are traveling by car, the park is next to Suita Junction just off the Meishin Expressway.

### Festival Gate
3–4–36 Ebisu Higashi, Naniwa-ku, Osaka-shi, Osaka
☎ (06) 6635–1000　　大阪府大阪市浪速区恵美須東 3–4–36
🚇 Dobutsuen-mae Station, Midosuji, Senri lines; Shin Imamiya Station, JR Loop, Nankai lines
🕙 10:00 A.M. to 11:00 P.M. daily (restaurants and shops close earlier).

Since it's debut in 1997, this amusement park has been a big hit in the Osaka area. Several thrilling rides, including a roller coaster, make for a fun outing.

### Harmonyland

5933 Oaza Fujiwara, Hijimachi, Hayami-gun, Oita
☎ (0977) 73–1110　大分県速見郡日出町大字藤原 5933
🚃 Hiji or Kitsuki Station, JR Nippo Main Line

Opened in the spring of 1991, this park exhibits a new concept in children's theme parks. Harmonyland is a vast area filled with miniature villages, parks, and whimsical shops. Focusing on fantasy, a Time Machine and a Dream World are just a couple of Harmonyland's many fairy-tale-like creations. The park is a 35-minute taxi ride from Oita Airport. If you're traveling from the direction of Kitakyushu or Oita airport, the nearest station is Kitsuki on the Nippo Line. From the direction of Beppu and Oita city, the nearest station is Hiji on the same line. From both stations the park is 20 minutes by bus—look for buses with the sign HL (Harmonyland).

### Kobe Portopialand

8–7–1 Minatojima Nakamachi, Chuo-ku, Kobe-shi, Hyogo
☎ (078) 302–2820　兵庫県神戸市中央区港島中町 8–7–1
🚃 Minami Koen Station, Port Island Line

This recently built amusement park on Port Island has plenty of large-scale rides for the older kids but not much here specifically for the under-six set. The park is open 10:00 A.M. to 5:30 P.M. daily (except Wednesday) from March through January, with extended hours in the summer. Admission to the park is ¥1,400 for adults, ¥700 for children, with rides extra. A ¥3,800 pass valid for all rides is available for adults and children.

### Kyoto Monkey Park

Nakao Shitamachi, Arashiyama, Nishikyo-ku, Kyoto-shi, Kyoto
☎ (075) 861–1616　京都府京都市西京区嵐山中尾下町
🚃 Arashiyama Station, Keifuku Line
🕐 9:00 A.M. to 5:00 P.M. daily (4:00 P.M. in winter). Closed on rainy days.

A charming park devoted to  the exotic Japanese snow monkeys of Arashiyama. Admission is ¥500 for adults, ¥400 for junior high school students, ¥300 for elementary school children, and ¥150 for children ages four to six.

### Morino Yuenchi

Yasenose-machi, Sakyo-ku, Kyoto-shi, Kyoto　京都府京都市左京区八瀬野瀬町
☎ (075) 781–9151
🚃 Yase Yuen Station, Eizan Line
🕐 10:00 A.M. to 4:00 P.M. Closed Wednesday.

Previously Sports Valley Kyoto, this space was transformed in 1999 into a new amusement park with rides for all ages. Admission is ¥600 for adults and ¥300 for children.

## Ocean Dome at Miyazaki, SEA GAIA

Hamayama, Yamazaki-cho, Miyazaki-shi, Miyazaki　宮崎県宮崎市山崎町浜山
☎ (0985) 21–1177　🖳 www.seagaia.co.jp
🚃 Miyazaki Station, JR Nippo Main Line

In 1998, *The Guinness Book of Records* listed this resort, with a capacity of ten thousand people, as the world's largest water park. Ocean Dome's idyllic setting next to a real beach enables families to enjoy the best of indoor and outdoor water fun year-round.

## Space World

Edamitsu-cho, Yahata Higashi-ku, Kitakyushu-shi, Fukuoka
☎ (093) 672–3600　福岡県北九州市八幡東区枝光町
🚃 Space World Station, JR Kagoshima Line

Opened in the spring of 1990, this is the world's first space-oriented theme park. Covering more than three hundred thousand square meters, the park includes large-scale rides, pavilions, restaurants, and a "space camp." The space camp gives young people the opportunity to learn about space travel and experience what it is like to travel in space. Besides the youth camp programs, there is a two-day program for adults. Another main attraction at Space World is the Space Dome, which includes several space-simulation attractions. Space World is open from 9:30 A.M. to 6:00 P.M. daily (10:00 A.M. to 5:00 P.M. in winter). Admission to the park is ¥2,400 for adults, ¥1,700 for students, and ¥1,300 for children under twelve. Admission to the attractions is charged separately: either ¥500 or ¥300 each. Passport tickets range from ¥3,500 to ¥4,600. Space World is 30 minutes by bus from Kokura Station on the JR Shinkansen Line, or just a 1-minute walk from Space World Station on the JR Kagoshima Line.

## Universal Studios

2–1 Sakurajima, Konohana-ku, Osaka-shi, Osaka　大阪府大阪市此花区桜島 2–1
☎ (06) 6615–7281
🚃 Osaka Station, JR Tokaido and various lines

Due to open in 2001, this will be a sister park to the original in California. Initial plans call for re-creating some of the most popular stateside attractions and adding a few with local appeal. Information is sketchy as we go to press, but as the opening draws near we are sure a lack of information will be the least of your problems! The park is a 10-minute taxi ride from Osaka station.

## Wan Wan Okoku

2620–5 Imahama-cho, Moriyama-shi, Shiga     滋賀県守山市今浜町 2620–5
☎ (077) 585–7771
🚃 Katata Station, JR Kosai Line
🕐 10:00 A.M. to 4:00 P.M. on weekdays; 9:30 A.M. to 4:30 P.M. on holidays, second and fourth Saturdays, and Sundays. Closed on Thursdays.

About 30 minutes from Kyoto, near Lake Biwa, this unusual theme park features dogs as the main attraction. You can choose a dog to play with or walk, and be entertained by dog performances, as well. A sort of petting zoo for dog lovers. Admission is ¥1,800 for adults and ¥900 for children.

# AQUARIUMS

KANTO AREA

## Enoshima Aquarium, Marineland, and Marine Zoo

2–17–25 Katase Kaigan, Fujisawa-shi, Kanagawa
☎ (0466) 22–8111     神奈川県藤沢市片瀬海岸 2–17–25
🚃 Katase Enoshima Station, Odakyu Line; Enoshima Station, Enoshima Dentetsu Line

The Enoshima Marine Park is actually three outdoor attractions in one. The complex includes a small aquarium, a marineland with dolphin shows daily, and a marine zoo with a sea lion show and other marine life. Located on the beach in Fujisawa, it is open from 9:30 A.M. to 5:00 P.M. daily. Admission is ¥1,890 for adults, ¥840 for students, and ¥525 for children. To get there, take the JR Tokaido Line to Kamakura Station and transfer to the Enoshima Dentetsu Line for Enoshima Station. Alternatively, take the Odakyu Line to Katase Enoshima Station. The aquarium is a 10-minute walk from Katase Enoshima Station or Enoshima Station.

## Hakkeijima Sea Paradise

Hakkeijima, Kanazawa-ku, Yokohama-shi, Kanagawa
☎ (045) 788–8888    📠 (045) 788–9736     神奈川県横浜市金沢区八景島
🚃 Hakkeijima Station, Kanazawa Seaside Line; Minato Mirai Pier, Paradise Line (50-minute boat ride); Kanazawa Hakkei Station, Keihin Kyuko Line; Shin Sugita Station, JR Negishi Line
🕐 8:30 A.M. to 10:30 P.M. (times vary with the season).

An artificial island brimming with leisure facilities, Sea Paradise boasts an aquarium, jet coaster, ninety-meter-high observation tower, underwater tunnel, shopping mall, lodge, and marina. Admission to the island is free. Entrance fees to facilities are priced individually from ¥300 to ¥1,000. The island is a 5-minute walk from Hakkeijima Station or a 50-minute boat ride from Minato Mirai Pier.

### Itabashi Ward Aquarium

3–50–1 Itabashi, Itabashi-ku, Tokyo    東京都板橋区板橋 3–50–1
☎ (03) 3962–8419
🚇 Itabashi Kuyakusho-mae Station, Toei Mita Line

This is a small freshwater aquarium located in Higashi Itabashi Park. It is open from March through November from 10:00 A.M. to 4:30 P.M., and December through February from 10:00 A.M. to 4:00 P.M. It is closed Mondays and holidays. Admission is free.

### Kasai Rinkai Aquarium (Tokyo Sea Life Park)

6–2–3 Rinkai-cho, Edogawa-ku, Tokyo    東京都江戸川区臨海町 6–2–3
☎ (03) 3869–5151, (03) 3869–5152
🚇 Kasai Rinkai Koen Station, JR Keiyo Line; Nishi Kasai Station, Tozai Line

Tokyo Sea Life Park is one of the largest aquariums in Tokyo. Its modern design lets you observe exotic sea life up close—the "room full of tuna" being particularly spectacular. Other attractions include an aviary, a cycling course, a promenade, and "Sea Breeze Square" for ocean viewing. Open from 9:30 A.M. to 5:00 P.M. daily (enter by 4:00 P.M.), except Monday and at New Year's. When Monday is a national holiday, the aquarium is closed the following day. Admission is ¥700 for adults, ¥250 for junior high school students; seniors over sixty-five and children under twelve years old enter free.

### Keikyu Aburatsubo Marine Park

1082 Koajiro, Misaki-cho, Miura-shi, Kanagawa
☎ (0468) 81–6281    神奈川県三浦市三崎町小網代 1082
🚇 Misakiguchi Station, Keihin Kyuko Line
🕐 9:00 A.M. to 5:00 P.M. daily.

This is a three-hectare park with an aquarium where you can see a dolphin and sea lion show. Admission is ¥1,700 for adults, ¥1,300 for high school and junior high school students, ¥850 for elementary students, and ¥450 for children under six. To get there from Misakiguchi Station, take a bus from platform #1 for a 15-minute ride to the terminus at Aburatsubo.

## Shinagawa Aquarium

Shinagawa Kumin Koen, 3–2–1 Katsushima, Shinagawa-ku, Tokyo
☎ (03) 3762–3431　東京都品川区勝島 3–2–1 品川区民公園内
🚈 Omori Kaigan Station, Keihin Kyuko Line

This aquarium is home to a large variety of fish and a school of dolphins that performs daily. The aquarium also features an underwater tunnel allowing visitors a fish's-eye view of life underwater, without getting wet once. Open daily except Tuesdays, hours are from 10:00 A.M. to 5:00 P.M. Admission is ¥900 for adults, ¥500 for elementary and junior high school students, and ¥300 for children age four to seven. The aquarium is a 5-minute walk from Omori Kaigan Station.

## Sunshine Kokusai Aquarium

Sunshine City, 3–1–3 Higashi Ikebukuro, Toshima-ku, Tokyo
☎ (03) 3989–3466　東京都豊島区東池袋 3–1–3
🚈 Higashi Ikebukuro Station, Yurakucho Line; Ikebukuro Station, JR Yamanote and various lines

This is a large aquarium with twenty thousand fish of over four hundred species on display. It is open daily from 10:00 A.M. to 5:30 P.M. (6:00 P.M. on Sundays and national holidays). Admission is ¥1,600 for adults and ¥800 for children. The aquarium is located on the tenth and eleventh floors of the World Import Mart in Sunshine City.

## Tokyo Tower Aquarium

4–2–8 Shiba Koen, Minato-ku, Tokyo　東京都港区芝公園 4–2–8
☎ (03) 3434–8833
🚈 Kamiyacho Station, Hibiya Line; Shiba Koen Station, Toei Mita Line; Hamamatsucho Station, JR Yamanote, JR Keihin Tohoku lines

Centrally located in Shiba Koen, this small aquarium boasts over eight hundred species of fish. The aquarium is open from 10:00 A.M. to 6:00 P.M. daily; admission is ¥800 for adults, ¥500 for children. To get there, take the exit for the Russian Embassy at Kamiyacho Station and walk for 5 minutes. Or, if you take the JR Yamanote Line to Hamamatsucho Station, you'll see Tokyo Tower when you exit the station.

---

KANSAI AREA

---

## Kobe Municipal Suma Aqualife Park

1–3–5 Wakamiya-cho, Suma-ku, Kobe-shi, Hyogo
☎ (078) 731–7301　兵庫県神戸市須磨区若宮町 1–3–5
🚈 Suma Station, JR San'yo Main Line, San'yo Dentetsu Line

This is an excellent aquarium with trained dolphins that perform daily.

Some consider it to be the best of its kind in Japan, and a visit here is a must if you are near Kobe with the kids. Large indoor tanks, outdoor exhibits, and ¥100 rides make up the park. Open daily from 9:00 A.M. to 5:00 P.M. (6:00 P.M. in summer), the park is closed on Wednesdays except in summer. Admission is ¥1,000 for adults, ¥600 for high school students, and ¥400 for children. The park is on Suma Beach—walk from Suma Station or take bus #85 from Kobe Station.

### Osaka Aquarium (Kaiyukan)

1–1–10 Kaigan Dori, Minato-ku, Osaka-shi, Osaka
☎ (06) 6576–5533    大阪府大阪市港区海岸通り 1–1–10
🚂 Osakako Station, Chuo Line and various lines

This spectacular aquarium features water tanks so large that visitors can see fish swimming in a natural-like environment. The Japanese name for this aquarium is Kaiyukan, and its English nickname is "Ring of Fire," referring to the zone of volcanoes that encircles the Pacific Ocean. Plant and animal life from around the Pacific rim are shown both above and below water. Watching penguins swimming underwater is a fascinating sight for all ages. The aquarium is open daily from 10:00 A.M. to 8:00 P.M. The aquarium is a 5- to 8-minute walk from Osakako Station on the Chuo Line.

# Zoos

KANTO AREA

### Edogawa Ward Nature Zoo

3–2–1 Kita Kasai, Edogawa-ku, Tokyo    東京都江戸川区北葛西 3–2–1
☎ (03) 3680–0777
🚂 Nishi Kasai Station, Tozai Line

There are twenty-one kinds of animals at this small zoo. It is open every day from 10:00 A.M. to 4:00 P.M. except Monday and New Year's. Admission is free. To get there, take the Tozai Line to Nishi Kasai Station and walk for about 12 minutes, or take bus #21 bound for Shin Koiwa or Funabori. Located in Gyosen Koen.

### Hamura City Zoological Park

4122 Hane, Hamura-shi, Nishitama-gun, Tokyo    東京都西多摩郡羽村市羽 4122
☎ (0425) 55–2581
🚂 Hamura Station, JR Ome Line

This park is open from 9:00 A.M. to 4:00 P.M. year-round. Admission is ¥300 for adults and ¥50 for children four years old through junior high school. To get there, take the JR Chuo Line to Tachikawa Station and transfer to the JR Ome Line. From Hamura Station, take a bus bound for Hamura Danchi.

### Itabashi Ward Children's Zoo

Higashi Itabashi Koen, 3–50–1 Itabashi, Itabashi-ku, Tokyo
☎ (03) 3963–8003     東京都板橋区板橋 3–50–1 東板橋公園内
🚇 Itabashi Kuyakusho-mae Station, Toei Mita Line

The Itabashi Ward Children's Zoo has farm animals and pony rides. The zoo is open every day except Monday and New Year's from 10:00 A.M. to 4:00 P.M., December through February, and 10:00 A.M. to 4:30 P.M., March through November. Admission is free. The zoo is conveniently located 7 minutes by foot from Itabashi Kuyakusho-mae Station.

### Kanazawa Zoological Gardens of Yokohama

1–15–1 Kamariya Higashi, Kanazawa-ku, Yokohama-shi, Kanagawa
☎ (045) 783–9101     神奈川県横浜市金沢区釜利谷東 1–15–1
🚇 Kanazawa Bunko Station, Keihin Kyuko Line
🕐 9:30 A.M. to 4:30 P.M. Closed on Mondays.
ADMISSION: ¥500 for adults, ¥300 for high school students, ¥200 for junior high and elementary school students

Zoo with koalas, a golden snub-nosed monkey, kangaroos—the whole gang—plus a park. To get there, take the bus from Kanazawa Bunko Station and get off at Natsuyamasakaue.

### Nogeyama Zoological Garden of Yokohama

63–10 Oimatsu-cho, Nishi-ku, Yokohama-shi, Kanagawa
☎ (045) 231–1696, (045) 231–1307     神奈川県横浜市西区老松町 63–10
🚇 Hinodecho Station, Keihin Kyuko Line

This zoological garden comprises a 3.2-hectare garden and a children's petting zoo. It is open from 9:30 A.M. to 4:00 P.M. except Mondays. Admission is free. The park is a 10-minute walk from Hinodecho Station.

### Saitama Children's Zoo

554 Iwadono, Higashimatsuyama-shi, Saitama     埼玉県東松山市岩殿 554
☎ (0493) 35–1234
🚇 Takasaka Station, Tobu Tojo Line

The zoo is in a sixty-six-hectare park, which is situated in a natural mountain setting. Hours are 9:30 A.M. to 4:00 P.M., December to February, and 9:30 A.M. to 5:00 P.M., March to November; it is closed

Mondays. Admission is ¥420 for adults, ¥210 for children. From Takasaka Station, take a bus bound for Hatoyama New Town for a 5-minute trip to the Dobutsu Koen-mae bus stop.

## Tama Zoo

7-chome, Hodokubo, Hino-shi, Tokyo    東京都日野市程久保 7丁目
☎ (0425) 91–1611
🚇 Tama Dobutsu Koen Station, Keio Dobutsuen Line

As many as 210 different kinds of animals roam around in this natural setting. Special attractions include an Insect House with nocturnal animals, a butterfly House, and a bus ride that, for a small fee, takes you through an area with free-roaming lions. The zoo is open from 9:30 A.M. to 5:00 P.M. every day except Monday and New Year's Day. Admission to the zoo is ¥500 for adults, ¥200 for junior high school children, and free for children under twelve and adults over sixty-five.

## Ueno Zoo

9–83 Ueno Koen, Taito-ku, Tokyo    東京都台東区上野公園 9–83
☎ (03) 3828–5171
🚇 Ueno Station, JR Yamanote and various lines

This is where the pandas are! Ueno Zoo is the largest zoo in Tokyo, with over seven thousand mammals, reptiles, amphibians, birds, and other animals. A children's zoo and an aquarium are also here. The zoo is open 9:30 A.M. to 4:00 P.M. every day except Monday. Admission is ¥500 for adults, ¥200 for junior high school students, and free for children under twelve and adults over sixty-five.

## Yokohama Zoological Gardens (Zoorasia)

1175–1 Kamishirane-cho, Asahi-ku, Yokohama-shi, Kanagawa
☎ (045) 959–1000    神奈川県横浜市旭区上白根町 1175–1
🚇 Nakayama Station, JR Yokohama Line; Tsurugamine or Mitsukyo Station, Sotetsu Line
🕐 9:30 A.M. to 4:30 P.M. daily (until 6:00 P.M. in summer). Closed on Tuesdays in fall and winter.

Opened in spring 1999, this well-designed park boasts 315 animals (59 species), including a rare Central African okapi. The animals are kept in their natural habitats, from tropical to sub-Arctic. Zoorasia is a big improvement over most of Japan's zoos, with a huge expanse of land stretching from Asahi to Midori Ward. Admission is ¥600 for adults, ¥300 for high school students, and ¥200 for junior high school and elementary school ages. To get there, take a bus from Nakayama, Tsurugamine, or Mitsukyo stations.

## Kyoto Municipal Zoo

Okazaki, Hoshoji-cho, Sakyo-ku, Kyoto-shi, Kyoto

☎ (075) 771–0210　京都府京都市左京区岡崎法勝寺町岡崎公園内

🚃 Demachiyanagi and Hankyu Shijo Kawaramachi stations, Hankyu Kyoto Line

When your kids have had enough of shrines and temples in Kyoto, take them to this small zoo for a refreshing break. Located in Okazaki Park, just a few blocks from the Kyoto Imperial Palace, this zoo also has a petting area where children can listen to talks about the animals and see them up close. Hours are 9:00 A.M. to 5:00 P.M. (4:30 P.M. in winter); closed on Mondays. Admission is ¥500 for adults, ¥300 for junior high school students, and free for children under twelve. To get there, walk 5 blocks from Demachiyanagi Station or take bus #27 from Hankyu Shijo Kawaramachi Station. An alternative is to take bus #5 from Kyoto Station. The bus trip takes about 30 minutes; get off at the Dobutsuen-mae bus stop.

## Oji Zoo

3–1 Oji-cho, Nada-ku, Kobe-shi, Hyogo　兵庫県神戸市灘区王子町 3–1

☎ (078) 861–5624

🚃 Hankyu Oji Koen Station, Hankyu Kobe Line

Oji Zoo is both a zoo and an amusement park. The zoo is large enough for the kids to get exercise out of doors, while the animals are easy to see and in clean cages. The amusement park is on the small side, but there are sufficient rides and concession stands to thrill anyone under eight or so. The park is open from 9:00 A.M. to 5:00 P.M. (4:30 P.M. in winter) daily except Wednesdays. Admission is only ¥500 for adults, ¥200 for junior high school students, and free for children under twelve. The zoo is in Oji Park, a 3-minute walk from Hankyu Oji Koen Station.

# 7

# Museums, Sports, Activities and classes

NO PROBLEM, DAD!

For kids as well as parents, moving to Japan can seem like accelerating into the fast lane. We have often wondered if we should buy our children their own appointment books to keep track of lessons, play dates, and outings.

There are many opportunities in Japan for parents and children to experience Japanese as well as Western culture in the form of sports, art, and music lessons in a cross-cultural setting. Once children enter the first grade, their free time is at a premium. Therefore, the time to begin taking advantage of these programs is when they are toddlers and preschoolers. Besides teaching your child a new skill, many of these activities will expose him to the Japanese language.

A word about the language difference: when you call to get information about many of the activities listed in this chapter, the voice on the other end of the phone will probably be speaking Japanese. Don't let this deter you. If you do not speak Japanese, one of the obvious phrases to try first is, "*Eigo ga dekimasuka?*" ("Do you speak English?"). Often the person on the phone does have an elementary English vocabulary, and if you are patient you can get the information you need. Don't be afraid to ask for information to be repeated ("*moichido itte kudasai*") or to ask the person to speak more slowly ("*yukkuri hanashite kudasai*"). Other times they will tell you to wait a minute ("*chotto matte kudasai*"), and perhaps someone who speaks English will come to the phone. Whether you end up practicing your latest Japanese lesson or giving someone else a chance to practice his or her English, there are ways to get around the language barrier.

## EXTRACURRICULAR ACTIVITIES

A wide choice of sports, art, and music classes are available to your children. While you live in Japan, your child has a unique opportunity to learn some of Japan's traditional sports in addition to ice-skating, horseback riding, ballet, and other activities. Judo, karate, and many other martial arts teachers hold classes specifically for children. Besides martial arts, the Suzuki music school is here. What better place than Japan for your child to learn by this world-famous music teaching method?

A word of warning about the recitals that go along with some of these classes: Parents are expected to pay a rather exorbitant fee. This large amount of money (often up to ¥100,000 or more) goes toward the cost of renting the performance space and perhaps part of it is the teacher's bonus. Music and dance classes in particular hold such recitals. It would be wise to find out how often recitals would be held and how much money you would be expected to pay before committing yourself to such a class. Private lessons tend to be much more expensive than in your home country. The Yamaha schools are reasonably priced and often they have English-speaking teachers available.

The arrangements for many of these classes must be made in Japanese. Often registration forms can be filled out in English, but you must be able to read the questions. If you do not have anyone who can help you with this, ask one of the parents whose children are in the same class or the instructor. This is a great way to meet some of the other parents. You will find that once you break the ice, the parents will be very willing to include you in other activities that their children may be involved in.

Many Japanese children attend private extracurricular classes after school. Abacus, calligraphy, piano, and art are some of the most popular classes. Try to seek out a Japanese neighbor or friend with a child the same age as yours. Chances are that they will know about private schools in your area.

Kids World, a child care center with over twenty facilities throughout Tokyo, Niigata, and Fukuoka, has one-hour classes in areas such as music, art, and phonics for young children at some of their centers. (For more information see Preschools in chapter 11.) Contact the head office at ☎ 0120–001–537 from 9:30 A.M. to 6:30 P.M. Monday through Friday.

Sakurahorikiri, a complex of stores, located near Asakusabashi, offers classes in doll-making and other Japanese arts and crafts. The address is 1–26–2 Yanagibashi, Taito-ku, Tokyo, ☎ (03) 3864–1773.

Sometimes the American Embassy will have space available for nonembassy children in their classes. In the past, art classes have been held on Saturdays for children ages three and up. Check with the U.S. Embassy preschool for the current schedule (see chapter 11).

Kumon is a private tutorship program that holds lessons year-round throughout the country. Beginning at an early age, children can join these small groups, which often meet in the teacher's home. The fee for these classes is extremely reasonable; in Tokyo, for example, ¥6,000 per month would enable a five-year-old to meet twice a week for a 30- to 60-minute class in Japanese language, English language, or math. Older children can choose from a wider variety of subjects.

Many of our friends use this program in the summer months to keep up their children's Japanese-language skills. The atmosphere is relaxed, and because the lessons are brief the children do not feel as if they are attending school.

For more information, call the Kumon Institute of Education, Tokyo Administrative Office, at ☎ (03) 3234–4401, or write to them at 3–1 Goban-cho, Chiyoda-ku, Tokyo.

## SPORTS

Classes for young children in gymnastics, tumbling, ballet, and the various martial arts are available at either private clubs and gymnasiums or through ward or city programs. Each ward and city offers different kinds of activities, and each season the classes usually change. For very young children, there may be a mother-and-baby class of some sort in swimming or dance, for example. Classes for older children are held on weekends, after school, and during the Japanese school vacation period. For information, contact your local ward or city office.

Private gymnasiums and sports clubs usually hold adult classes, but there are a few that have children's classes as well. Often the international schools offer their space to independent teachers for classes after school hours or on the weekends.

We were disappointed to find no comprehensive listing anywhere of sports organizations or classes for children. Our Japanese friends say that word of mouth is the best resource for finding a class near your home or school. Signboards and advertisements in papers are often written only in Japanese, so don't be afraid to ask if you see something that perhaps would be of interest to your child.

Once in a class, your child may have difficulty understanding the Japanese instructions or feel he is behind at times; if so, just remember that for young children in Japan, the most important thing is not how well the individual performs but how hard he works at it. In the Japanese classes and schools our children have attended, the spirit of *gambare*, or "do your best," is by far the outstanding lesson that comes through, and children of all ages can benefit from that.

## SWIMMING

There are many swimming pools that are open to the public in each ward, often at sports centers or schools. The majority of these pools are indoor and open throughout the year. In Minato Ward, for example, Hommura Elementary School in Azabu, Akasaka Elementary School, and Onarimon Junior High School have indoor pools. The only out-door pool in Minato Ward is the Shiba Pool. Swimmers should bring their Alien Registration Card, as residency is required when using any of the school pools in a ward. At Shiba Pool and at the Minato City Sports Center, you don't have to be a resident. All of the pools listed are well kept and clean. There are a few rules when using indoor pools in Japan: you must wear a swimming cap, no jewelry or makeup is allowed, and no refreshments can be brought in. A shower before entering the pool is mandatory, and you must bring your own towels.

### Central Fitness Club Meguro

2–26–7 Chuo-cho, Meguro-ku, Tokyo　東京都目黒区中央町 2–26–7
☎ (03) 3712–2121
🚆 Gakugeidai Station, Tokyu Toyoko Line
🕐 9:00 A.M. to 11:00 P.M. daily.

The registration fee is ¥3,000. Fees for babies six months and up for the "baby course" are ¥7,800 to ¥10,000 per month, adults and children ¥6,800 to ¥8,500 per month.

### Kugahara Swimming Club

5–12–8 Kugahara, Ota-ku, Tokyo　東京都大田区久が原 5–12–8
☎ (03) 3751–8191
🚆 Ikegami Station, Tokyu Ikegami Line

The registration fee is from ¥5,000 to ¥10,000. For a monthly fee of ¥7,500, the pool can be used once a week; for ¥9,500 per month, access is increased to twice a week; ¥6,000 (free course). From six-month-olds.

## Minato-ku Sports Center Pool

3–1–19 Shibaura, Minato-ku, Tokyo　東京都港区芝浦 3–1–19
☎ (03) 3452–4151
🚃 Tamachi Station, JR Yamanote, JR Keihin Tohoku, Toei Mita, Toei Asakusa lines
🕐 9:30 A.M. to 9:00 P.M. Closed on Mondays.

If you work in Minato Ward, the Sports Center will give you a discount (otherwise the fee is ¥400 for two hours).

## People XAX Futako Tamagawa

2–27 Tamagawa, Setagaya-ku, Tokyo　東京都世田谷区玉川 2–27
☎ (03) 3708–9221
🚃 Futako Tamagawa-en Station, Tokyu Shin Tamagawa, Den'en Toshi lines

Lessons go for ¥7,500 per month (once a week) to ¥8,000 per month (twice a week). There is no registration fee. From four-month-olds.

## Shiba Pool

Shiba Koen, Minato-ku, Tokyo　東京都港区芝公園内
☎ (03) 3435–0470 or (03) 3578–2111 (ward office)
🚃 Hamamatsucho Station, JR Yamanote, JR Keihin Tohoku lines; Daimon Station, Toei Asakusa Line; Shiba Koen Station, Toei Mita Line

This pool is great for families, as it has a kiddie pool with an elephant slide plus an Olympic-size pool where mom and dad can swim laps. Shiba Pool is open from July to mid-September. And the fees are very reasonable. Admission is ¥300 per two hours for adults and ¥100 for elementary and junior high students. The hours are from 9:30 A.M. to 5:00 P.M. daily in August. The pool is closed on Mondays in July and September. Evening swimming (6:00 P.M. to 8:00 P.M.) is available from mid-July to August 31, except Sundays and Mondays.

## Tokyo Itoman Swimming School and Kami Shakujii School

2–13–12 Kami Shakujii, Nerima-ku, Tokyo　東京都練馬区上石神井 2–13–12
☎ (03) 3928–0777
🚃 Kami Shakujii Station, Seibu Shinjuku Line

The registration fee is ¥5,250. Lessons run from ¥6,300 per month (once a week) to ¥9,450 per month (three times a week). From six-month-olds.

## Tokyo Swimming Center

5–4–21 Komagome, Toshima-ku, Tokyo　東京都豊島区駒込 5–4–21
☎ (03) 3915–1012
🚃 Komagome Station, JR Yamanote Line

Two fifty-by-twenty-five-meter pools (one outdoor and one indoor).

The registration fee is ¥8,000. Lessons are ¥7,000 to ¥9,000 per month. From six-month-olds.

### Water Mates Swim Club

1–19–5 Tsunashima Higashi, Kohoku-ku, Yokohama-shi, Kanagawa
☎ (045) 543–0450   神奈川県横浜市港北区綱島東 1–19–5
🚃 Tsunashima Station, Tokyu Toyoko Line

The registration fee is ¥7,000. Lessons are ¥5,300 to ¥6,500 per month. From six-month-olds.

## *BALLET AND GYMNASTICS*

Formal ballet schools abound in Tokyo and most larger cities in Japan. If you want your child to study ballet, there is a listing of most of the schools in the Japanese-language Yellow Pages. If you are more interested in a fun ballet-tumbling-gymnastics class, contact the Nihon Ballet Kyokai at 3–16–5 Shibuya, Shibuya-ku, Tokyo; ☎ (03) 3499–5524. Or, for information on ballet and gymnastics classes for children ages three to fifteen, contact the Nihon Gymnastics Kyokai at Kishi Memorial Hall, 1–1–1 Jinnan, Shibuya-ku, Tokyo; ☎ (03) 3481–2341. Only Japanese is spoken. Here we list some schools in greater Tokyo. For class information in Kansai, call the community center nearest you (see chapter 12).

### Actus Ballet Studio

158 Kashimada, Saiwai-ku, Kawasaki-shi, Kanagawa
神奈川県川崎市幸区鹿島田 158
☎/🖷 (0422) 47–4664 (Helen Price)   💻 hetona3@gol.com
🚃 Shin Kawasaki, JR Yokosuka Line

Director Helen Price is a graduate of the National Ballet School of Canada and has performed, studied, and taught in the United States, Canada, Europe, and Japan. In 1989, she founded the Yokohama Children's Ballet and, in 1991, the Small World Children's Ballet, and eventually consolidated the schools.

Helen's main studio is located in Shin Kawasaki (five minutes from the station), in a large, bright space equipped with a baby grand piano, floor-to-ceiling mirrors, and a sprung dance floor. Helen also teaches classes at Landmark Plaza, in Yokohama. She was certified with the Royal Academy of Dance in 1995. She currently offers ballet classes from age four through adult and a free trial lesson for prospective students.

Pupils with Actus Ballet Studio appear in ballet productions once every two years. Helen has recently formed another company, Actus Ballet Theatre, whose aim is to bring dance to the community while providing additional performing experience for her students. Using dancers, live music, and narrative, Actus Ballet Theatre has performed for schools, hospitals, and on television.

## Ana's School of Dance
International Dance School

Green House, 5–2–9 Denenchofu, Ota-ku, Tokyo
☎ (03) 3721–5495   📠 (03) 3721–7429   東京都大田区田園調布 5–2–9 グリーンハウス
🚃 Denenchofu Station, Tokyu Toyoko, Tokyu Mekama lines

This is one of the best-known ballet schools for foreigners in the Tokyo area, founded by Ana Keates in 1982. "Miss Ana," a graduate of the Royal Ballet in London, is a registered teacher of the Royal Academy of Dance and has danced professionally throughout Europe and Japan.

Miss Ana's teachers form an international, highly qualified team, specializing in a variety of dance forms. The school offers a wide range of dance classes for children and adults, with classes held at most of the international schools in Tokyo. Classes include classical ballet, character, tap, modern, jazz, national, song and dance, *pas de deux*, folk dancing, and fitness. Major productions featuring all the students are staged at the end of each year, complete with elaborate costumes and guest artists.

Over the years, Miss Ana's pupils have regularly achieved high marks in ballet examinations. Several students have been accepted to some of the best ballet schools in the world, including the Royal Ballet School at Whitelodge, England, and the National Ballet School of Canada.

## Chacott

1–20–8 Jinnan, Shibuya-ku, Tokyo   東京都渋谷区神南 1–20–8
☎ (03) 3476–1311
🚃 Shibuya Station, JR Yamanote and various lines

Located directly across from the Seibu Seed store in Shibuya, Chacott is not a ballet school but rather a store for all types of dance supplies. Leotards, tap shoes, ballet shoes—everything for dancers, both adult and children—can be found at this store. The store is also a good resource for brochures from the many ballet schools around town, and they may be able to give you a lead on the right school for your child.

### Diana Ishiyama Song and Dance School of Musical Theater

3046–25 Nogawa, Miyamae-ku, Kawasaki-shi, Kanagawa
☎/🖷 (044) 798–5320　神奈川県川崎市宮前区野川 3046–25
🚆 Nakagawa Center Kita and Center Minami stations, Yokohama Subway Line

At this school, students can take song and dance musical theater, or more advanced classes in jazz, tap, hip-hop, and ballet. In the song and dance classes, pupils learn basic vocal skills for stage along with various dance styles, including ballet, modern, jazz, and tap. All music and spoken lines are in English, and the classes are open to anyone from age four through adult. Contact director Diana Ishiyama for a complete course description.

### International Dance School (IDS)

Matsuishi Bldg., 2F, 1–8–9 Hiroo, Shibuya-ku, Tokyo
☎/🖷 (03) 3444–2180　東京都渋谷区広尾 1–8–9　松石ビル 2F
🚆 Ebisu Station, JR Yamanote, Hibiya lines

Conveniently located in Hiroo, IDS offers classes taught in a professional studio by highly trained, bilingual instructors. Classical ballet, jazz, tap, and creative dance are on the curriculum, including Royal Academy of Dance testing. Teacher assistants help with the younger classes (children are accepted from age three), while adult classes are also available. Annual performances and recitals are held at the studio.

### International Gymnastics Club (IGC)

3–39–5–301 Ebisu, Shibuya-ku, Tokyo　東京都渋谷区恵比寿 3–39–5–301
☎ (03) 3440–0384　🖷 (03) 3440–0628　📧 igcjapan@gol.com

IGC is run by Lance Lee, an American fitness coach and gymnast. The club holds after-school and Saturday classes at a number of the international schools. The club's motto, "Reaching for the stars," is embodied in the "I Can!" attitude encouraged in classes to build confidence and a positive approach. Gymnastics, along with some fitness classes for adults, are the means through which the teachers communicate this message to everyone they come in contact with.

### Jenny Hosmer Ballet School

Sun Square Bldg., M–3, 1–4–1 Oji, Kita-ku, Tokyo
☎/🖷 (03) 3927–2772　東京都北区王子 1–4–1　サンスクエアビル M–3
🚆 Oji Station, JR Keihin Tohoku, Toden Arakawa, Namboku lines

In operation for the past fifteen years, the school is run by longtime resident of Japan Jenny Hosmer, a graduate of the Johannesburg School of Ballet, Music and Drama, in South Africa. Jenny offers ballet classes for children ages three and up. She also holds adult classes for beginners as well as for the serious student of dance. Her ballet school follows the Royal Academy of Dance course of study, and enters pupils in the RAD exams. Jenny is a certified teacher with the Royal Academy.

### Saiga Ballet

2–20 Kagurazaka, Shinjuku-ku, Tokyo　東京都新宿区神楽坂 2–20
☎ (03) 3268–3183
🚇 Iidabashi Station, JR Sobu, Tozai, Namboku, Yurakucho lines

For nearly forty years Saiga Ballet has offered classes in classical ballet for children aged three and up. The founder of the school, Toshiko Saiga, is a former principal ballerina with the Komaki Ballet. Ms. Saiga speaks excellent English and encourages foreign children to study with her. Saiga Ballet students are invited to participate in the annual Music for Youth (see music section in this chapter) performances of such classics as *The Nutcracker*.

#### Dance Supplies Online

Check out the discount prices and large selection available through the following two dance supply catalogs:

*Dance Supplies, Etc.*
🖥 <www.dancesupply.com>, 🖨 (410) 647–2905

*Ultimate Dance Catalogue*
🖥 www.ridgewood_nj.com/dance/index.html

### *TENNIS*

In Tokyo, the Krissman Tennis School (KTS), founded in 1984, offers professional tennis instruction in Roppongi, Setagaya, and some of the international schools. Classes are available for children, age five and up, and for adults. Both group (six to eight students) and private lessons are available. KTS has access to night courts in Tokyo, plus a resort in Chiba. Students are eligible to participate in various tournaments and events throughout the year. You may also want to check out its summer camp program (see Summer Programs in this chapter). For more information, call or fax ☎/🖨 (03) 3325–0924.

If you aren't interested in tennis lessons but just want to play a little tennis with the family, there are many public courts available in Tokyo. Contact your ward office to find out the locations nearest your home. The procedure for reserving a public court varies, but a lottery is usually held, as there aren't enough courts to go around. The ward office will tell you where to submit a postcard with your name, address, phone number, and date and time you want to play. You'll probably have better luck if you request a morning time slot during the week.

Several of the public parks in Tokyo have tennis courts. You can reserve these courts through any of the thirty-two public park administration offices, or by visiting the public park office where the tennis court is located. When you first apply for a court, bring your Alien Registration Card or passport, so you can be issued a membership card. To reserve a particular date, submit your application during the first ten days of the previous month. A lottery will then be held. You can get the results by calling or visiting the park office between the fifteenth and twentieth of the month. Court fees are approximately ¥1,500 an hour, ¥1,800 on weekends and holidays.

## TENNIS COURTS

### Komazawa Olympic Park Tennis Court

1–1 Komazawa Koen, Setagaya-ku, Tokyo　東京都世田谷区駒沢公園 1–1
☎ (03) 3421–6121
🚈 Komazawa Daigaku Station, Tokyu Shin Tamagawa Line
🕐 8:30 A.M. to 6:30 P.M. (10:30 A.M. to 4:30 P.M. in winter).

For those with an open schedule! A raffle for court times is held the third Monday of each month at 9:00 A.M. Applicants should petition court times two months in advance. The fee is ¥2,000 for two hours.

### Meiji Jingu Gaien Tennis Court

2-chome, Kita Aoyama, Minato-ku, Tokyo　東京都港区北青山2丁目
☎ (03) 3403–0923　📠 (03) 3403–5666
🚈 Gaien-mae Station, Ginza Line; Aoyama 1-chome Station, Ginza, Hanzomon lines
🕐 7:00 A.M. to 11:00 P.M.

Reservations in person are required a month in advance. Nevertheless, you can make multiple reservations in one visit. A two-hour slot costs ¥3,000 to ¥4,000 on weekdays and ¥6,000 to ¥14,000 on weekends. Weekend playing times are often booked.

### Wadabori Koen Tennis Court

Wadabori Koen, Omiya 2-chome, Suginami-ku, Tokyo
☎ (03) 3311–7410　東京都杉並区大宮2丁目 和田堀公園
🚈 Nishi Eifuku Station, Keio Inokashia Line
🕐 9:00 A.M. to 5:00 P.M. daily.

Reservations are made by mail. Send a self-addressed postcard two months in advance. Envelopes must be postmarked by the twenty-fourth of the month. Rate: ¥800 for two hours.

## Zempukuji Riverside Tennis Court

1–30–27 Narita Nishi, Suginami-ku, Tokyo　東京都杉並区成田西 1–30–27
☎ (03) 3313–4247
🚉 Hamadayama Station, Keio Inokashira Line
🕐 9:00 A.M. to 4:00 P.M. September through March.

These three courts are part of the green Zempukuji riverside sports area. Reservations are made through the Tokyo Metropolitan Sports Utility Center at 1–2–5 Nakano, Nakano-ku, Tokyo, ☎ (03) 5330–1321, or through the park office before the twentieth of the previous month. Rate: ¥1,500 an hour.

## *MARTIAL ARTS*

The various forms of martial arts all have their origins in the Orient. The most popular and easiest forms are taught throughout Japan in private training halls, or *dojo*, or under the auspices of the wards and cities. Students can begin in some of the classes at the tender age of four, though there are classes for all levels, from housewives to senior citizens. The brief descriptions that follow may help you in choosing a class for your child. The information phone numbers given are the central headquarters—not only the most likely place to find an English speaker, but also the best place to get information for all of Japan.

### AIKIDO

Call the Tokyo office of the International Aikido Federation at ☎ (03) 3203–9236 for information in Japanese or English on aikido classes, or write to them at 17–18 Wakamatsu-cho, Shinjuku-ku, Tokyo. Children may study this martial art form from as early as age five. Aikido was developed in the beginning of the twentieth century and is based on an old art form called *aikijutsu*. Its philosophy is based on the idea of overcoming an opponent by using only the minimum amount of force necessary. Known as the Way of the Spirit and Harmony, aikido is a system of joint locking, throwing, and striking, quite different from judo or karate. Practitioners attempt to follow the attacker's line of motion, overbalancing him at first and then locking either a wrist or joint to subdue him.

## JUDO

Call or write the All-Japan Judo Federation, c/o Kodokan, 1–16–30 Kasuga, Bunkyo-ku, Tokyo, ☎ (03) 3818–4171 or (03) 3818–4199, for information in Japanese.

Judo is world famous as a system of throwing and grappling with an unarmed opponent. Beginners first learn falling methods, followed by throws, strangles, and hold-downs. Boys and girls from fourth grade and up are eligible for classes in most wards and private facilities. For adults, universities provide excellent training facilities that often nonuniversity members can use. Contact the university nearest you for more information.

## KARATE

Call or write the Federation of All Japan Karate-Do at No. 2 Sempaku-shinko Bldg., 1–11–2 Toranomon, Minato-ku, Tokyo, ☎ (03) 3503–6640, for information in Japanese or English. Classes are available for children from the age of six on. Karate, which originated in Okinawa, is a system of empty-hand fighting with the emphasis on punching, kicking, and blocking. Beginners first exercise to improve their fitness and then practice basics in groups, gradually progressing to working with a partner for speed and timing. Karate is split into some twenty different styles, or *ryu*, and you will need to decide which style you prefer to learn.

## KENDO

Call or write the Tokyo Kendo Federation at Shinkokusai Bldg. 934, 3–4–1 Marunouchi, Chiyoda-ku, Tokyo, ☎ (03) 3211–5967, for information in Japanese. For information in English, call or write the All Japan Kendo Federation, International Section, c/o Nippon Budokan, 2–3 Kitanomaru Koen, Chiyoda-ku, Tokyo, ☎ (03) 3211–5804. Kendo classes are available for children from around the age of eight. Kendo, or the Way of the Sword, is practiced with both *katana*, the long Japanese sword, and *shinai*, its bamboo counterpart. Combatants wear protective armor and attempt to strike each other with the *shinai* on the head, torso, or forearms in imitation of the medieval Japanese art of actual sword fighting. In kendo, the sword is gripped with both hands, as opposed to the one-hand grip used in Western fencing.

## T'AI CHI CHUAN

For more information on classes for all ages (children can start studying from the age of four), call the Japan T'ai Chi Association at ☎ (03)

3367–8044, 📠 (03) 3367–8587, or write them at Poreporeza Building, 5F, 4–4–1 Higashi Nakano, Nakano-ku, Tokyo. Alternatively, contact the All-Japan Soft Style Martial Arts Federation, ☎ (03) 3400–9371. They will answer questions in Japanese.

T'ai Chi Chuan, known as *taikyokuken* in Japanese, is a martial art form that has been imported unchanged from China. It is probably the softest and least aggressive of the combative sports, consisting of a slow, rhythmic flow of motion aimed at promoting balance, timing, and general good health. It is also designed to promote a balance between the body and the spirit as well as between the yin and yang elements— motion and stillness, emptiness and fullness, hardness and softness. It is distinguished by its unusually slow, circular movements.

### HORSEBACK RIDING

Horseback riding is one of the more difficult sports to pursue as a regular hobby in Japan, especially in Tokyo. Besides the hefty cost, there is also distance to consider. Most of the horseback riding clubs are an hour or more out of the city by public transportation.

For those who simply want an opportunity for their children to ride on a horse, pony rides are given at several of the large parks (see chapter 5). At Baji Koen, 2–1–1 Kamiyoga, Setagaya-ku, Tokyo, ☎ (03) 3429–5101, twenty minutes by taxi from Shibuya Station, one Sunday a month is set aside for a horse show at which free horse rides are offered for children age four to ten. The children are allowed to ride the large thoroughbreds with volunteers from the police equestrian unit. This is a very special event; you must pick up your free tickets for the horse rides two hours before the show. As the date and time of the event varies from month to month, so call the park at the beginning of the month to find out when the horse festival will take place.

In the Kobe area, riding is available at the Kobe Joba Club and the Rokko-san Model Pasture Stables. See "Kids in Kobe" in *Living in Kobe* (chapter 12) for more information.

GREATER TOKYO AREA

For the serious equestrian, there are horseback-riding clubs that you can join. Like other sports clubs, the riding clubs ask for an initial membership fee and then an annual fee. Many of the clubs will provide transportation from the nearest train station to the club if you let them know when you are coming. Boots and riding gear can be rented or purchased at most of the clubs. Visitor passes are available at an hourly rate, and both visitors and members must make a reservation in advance. Below is a short list of some of the larger and more accessible riding clubs available to Tokyo residents.

## Avalon Riding Club

3–19–2 Noge, Setagaya-ku, Tokyo　東京都世田谷区野毛 3–19–2
☎ (03) 3701–0573
🚇 Futako Tamagawa-en Station, Tokyu Shin Tamagawa, Oimachi, Denentoshi lines

## Crane Horse Riding Club

286 Kitayatsu-cho, Wakaba-ku, Chiba-shi, Chiba
☎ (043) 228–5531　千葉県千葉市若葉区北谷津町 286
🚇 Chiba Station, JR Sobu and various lines

## La Hacienda Riding School

1–6–5 Akuwa Nishi, Seya-ku, Yokohama-shi, Kanagawa
☎ (045) 363–2501　神奈川県横浜市瀬谷区阿久和西1–6–5
🚇 Mitsukyo Station, Sotetsu Line

## Machida Riding Center

37 Hayamajima, Shiroyama-machi, Tsukui-gun, Kanagawa
☎ (042) 782–0262　神奈川県津久井郡城山町葉山島 37
🚇 Hashimoto Station, JR Yokohama Line

## Nagisa Ponyland

7–3 Minami Kasai, Edogawa-ku, Tokyo　東京都江戸川区南葛西 7–3
☎ (03) 5658–5720
🚇 Kasai Station, Tozai Line

Free pony rides for elementary school children. Nagisa Ponyland offers rides from 10:00 A.M. to 11:30 A.M. and 1:30 P.M. to 3:00 P.M. every day except Mondays and rainy days. Ponyland is a 10-minute bus ride from the station.

## Pony Rides—Higashi Itabashi Park

3–50–1 Itabashi, Itabashi-ku, Tokyo　東京都板橋区板橋 3–50–1
☎ (03) 3962–8419
🚇 Itabashi Kuyakusho-mae Station, Toei Mita Line
🕐 10:00 A.M. to 4:30 P.M. Closed on Mondays.

Children ages three to twelve can ride ponies at this park free of charge. Tickets can be picked up starting at 10:10 A.M. for the rides, which begin at 10:30 A.M., 1:10 P.M., and 1:30 P.M. only.

## Shinozaki Riding Academy

3–12–17 Shinozaki-cho, Edogawa-ku, Tokyo　東京都江戸川区篠崎町 3–12–17
☎ (03) 3678–7520
🚃 Shinozaki Station, Toei Shinjuku Line

Free horseback-riding classes are offered at this academy for girls age thirteen and up. The classes are held in January, March, May, September, and November. Participants are chosen by lottery.

For children age twelve and under free pony and stagecoach rides are available at Shinozaki Ponyland from 10:00 A.M. to 11:30 A.M. and 1:30 P.M. to 3:00 P.M. every day except Monday or in the case of rain.

## Tokyo Horseback Riding Club

4–8 Yoyogi Kamizono-cho, Shibuya-ku, Tokyo　東京都渋谷区代々木神園町 4–8
☎ (03) 3370–0984
🚃 Sangubashi Station, Odakyu Line

## FAMILY OUTINGS

I always found skiing and bicycling to be two of the most enjoyable —not to mention invigorating—sports for families. Back in the U.S., our family frequently took to the slopes or spent weekends exploring new bike paths, yet initially we were hesitant to pursue these activities upon moving to Japan. Ski trips seemed too complicated to plan in a foreign country, and perhaps too expensive. And although our whole family loved bicycling, we limited outings to local parks for fear of being run over in Tokyo traffic!

Fortunately, we met up with two families who helped us see the error of our ways. Through the Greens and the Warfields, we learned just how enjoyable and affordable biking and skiing in Japan can be. For guided bicycling tours with the Greens, see the Hakkakuso Bicycling Lodge entry in this chapter.

For several years now, Marsh and Tomoko Warfield have operated a series of ski and snowboard trips that have proved quite popular with the foreign community. The price of the trip includes a round trip on the Shinkansen, bus transfers, lodging with two meals daily and Japanese baths, and ski lessons (optional). Contact Marsh or Tomoko Warfield by phone or fax at ☎/🖷 (03) 3707–3908.

There is a comprehensive new guide to skiing and snowboarding in Japan on the Internet. SkiJapan includes information on more than one hundred resorts, a daily weather report, and even a newsletter and bulletin board, all in English! Go to 🖳 <www.skijapanguide.com>.

## BICYCLING

Bicycling is a great way for the whole family to get exercise on the weekend. Bring your own bicycles or let the kids (under twelve) borrow one free from any of the parks listed in this section.

### Haginaka Kotsu Koen (Traffic Park)

3–24–26 Haginaka, Ota-ku, Tokyo　東京都大田区萩中 3–24–26
☎ (03) 3743–0991
🚃 Otorii Station, Keikyu Kuko Line
🕐 9:00 A.M. to 11:25 A.M. and 1:00 P.M. to 3:55 P.M. daily.

Petal down make-believe streets with traffic signals and road signs. Bicycles, tricycles, and pedal carts are free for kids under twelve.

### Hakkakuso Bicycling Lodge

422–1 Sunomiya, Tateyama-shi, Chiba　千葉県館山市洲宮 422–1
☎/🖨 (0470) 28–2824　✉ dgreen@gol.com

Long-time residents of Tokyo, David and Yoshiko Green are both teachers in the local international schools and are renowned for their annual community ski trips and bicycling lodge.

The couple first began cycling back in 1976. Since then, David has become an avid cyclist, touring extensively throughout Japan. For the past seventeen years, David and Yoshiko have been leading bicycle tours for students, families, and other groups. Seven years ago, with the completion of their lodge for Japan Bicycle Tours, in Hakkakuso, they realized their dream.

Located near the ocean in Tateyama, this area is a bit of paradise only two hours from Tokyo. The beach, just five minutes away, is a series of traditional fishing villages that dot the coastline of Minami Boso Peninsula. Also nearby are tennis courts, botanical gardens, and Kamogawa Seaworld.

Hakkakuso Lodge itself is surrounded by brilliant fields of poppies and *nanohana*, for which the area is famous. The yellow and red flowers are in bloom from January through April, when the fields are then planted with rice. Sunsets any time of year are magnificent.

Comfortable and well designed, the lodge sleeps twenty people and is operated on a reservation-basis only. It is open on weekends and holidays. English and Japanese are spoken. Food and accommodations are a combination of Western and Japanese style.

For a daily charge of ¥7,200 (¥6,700 per child), breakfast and dinner are included with lodging. Bicycles are available at no extra charge.

The Greens have ten mountain bikes for use or, if you want to transport your own by car, David will loan you one of his racks. Visitors to Hakkakuso can request any number of routes that are mapped out especially for the area: from a two-hour trip to all-day adventures, all the while taking in the beautiful scenery and fresh air.

Hakkakuso Lodge is the perfect place for groups of families traveling with kids or for school groups. David can organize barbecues on the beach or other special touches, depending on the needs of the group. He has put together *shakuhachi* concerts by famed musician (and Kamogawa neighbor) John Kaizan Neptune, in addition to paper-making workshops, and so on.

Each spring and autumn, Japan Bicycle Tours organizes weekend bicycle trips for parents and children. These trips are designed mostly for the beginner or intermediate cyclist, generally grades three through six. Each student must be accompanied by a responsible adult. Other tours for grades seven and over offer a slightly faster pace, greater distance, and perhaps a few more hills. If your children are younger or you prefer a less strenuous challenge, David can set you up with a map and his phone number, and you can take off on your own. Further information can also be obtained by writing to Japan Bicycle Touring, 1–3–3–202 Okamoto, Setagaya-ku, Tokyo, or by contacting David Green in Tokyo by phone and fax ☎/🖷 (03) 3708–4012.

### Jido Kotsu Koen (Children's Traffic Park)

2–22 Narita Nishi, Suginami-ku, Tokyo　東京都杉並区成田西 2–22
☎ (03) 3315–4564
🚃 Hamadayama Station, Keio Inokashira Line; Kichijoji Station, JR Chuo, Keio Inokashira lines; Nakano Station, JR Chuo, Tozai lines
🕘 9:00 A.M. to 12:00 P.M. and 1:00 P.M. to 4:15 P.M. Closed on Mondays.

This small "traffic park" combines fun and traffic safety for kids. There are bikes, go-carts, and tricycles. Admission is free. From Kichijoji or Nakano stations, take the bus to Suginami Dai-ni Shogakko-mae bus stop.

### Kinuta Park

Kinuta Koen, Setagaya-ku, Tokyo　東京都世田谷区砧公園
☎ (03) 3700–0414
🚃 Yoga or Futako Tamagawa-en Station, Tokyu Shin Tamagawa Line
🕘 9:00 A.M. to 4:00 P.M. Closed on Mondays.

A winding two-and-a-half-kilometer course. On the premises are a bird sanctuary, museum (Setagaya Bijutsukan), a play area, and a restaurant.

Bikes are for children only and free for those under twelve. Take the bus from Futako Tamagawa-en Station to Bijutsukan Iriguchi. Parking is available.

## Koganei Koen Cycling Course

Sekino-cho, Koganei-shi, Tokyo　東京都小金井市関野町
☎ (042) 388–1165
🚃 Musashi Koganei Station, JR Chuo Line
🕐 9:00 A.M. to 4:30 P.M. Closed on Mondays.

Bikes are free for children under sixteen. Take bus #3 to Koganei Koen.

## Kokyo (Imperial Palace)

1–1 Kokyo Gaien, Chiyoda-ku, Tokyo　東京都千代田区皇居外苑 1–1
☎ (03) 5572–6412 (weekdays), (03) 3211–5020 (Sundays only)
🚃 Nijubashi-mae Station, Chiyoda Line
🕐 10:00 A.M. to 3:00 P.M. (last bike out) on Sundays only.

This course runs from Hibiya Koen to Takebashi, about five and a half kilometers. There are free bikes behind Babasakimon Police Station. For adults and children.

## Komazawa Olympic Park

1–1 Komazawa Koen, Setagaya-ku, Tokyo　東京都世田谷区駒沢 1–1
☎ (03) 3421–6121
🚃 Komazawa Daigaku Station, Tokyu Shin Tamagawa Line; Ebisu Station, JR Yamanote, Hibiya lines
🕐 10:00 A.M. to 4:00 P.M. Closed on Mondays.

The park's course is just over two kilometers. Bikes are free for children under fifteen. From Ebisu Station take bus #2 to Tokyo Dai-ni Byoin-mae.

## Showa Memorial Park

3173 Midori-cho, Tachikawa-shi, Tokyo　東京都立川市緑町 3173
☎ (042) 528–1751
🚃 Nishi Tachikawa Station, JR Ome, Itsukaichi lines
🕐 9:30 A.M. to 5:00 P.M. daily (4:30 P.M. in winter).

Over six hundred bicycles of all types for rent. Many bike courses throughout the one-hundred-and-eighty-hectare park.

## Tamagawa Cycling Course

4–18–14 Nishi Rokugo, Ota-ku, Tokyo　東京都大田区西六郷 4–18–14
☎ (03) 3731–9388
🚃 Rokugodote Station, Keihin Kyuko Line
🕐 9:00 A.M. to 12:00 P.M. and 1:00 P.M. to 3:00 P.M. (last bike out) daily.

A two-and-a-half-kilometer course. Free bikes for children over ten.

## Ueno Park

Ueno Koen, Taito-ku, Tokyo　東京都台東区上野公園
☎ (03) 3828–5644
🚇 Ueno Station, JR Yamanote and various lines
🕐 9:00 A.M. to 4:00 P.M. Closed on Mondays.

The course continues for four hundred meters behind the National Science Museum (Kokuritsu Kagaku Hakubutsukan). Bikes are free for children under twelve. Take the Ueno Park exit from Ueno Station.

## Yoyogi Park Cycling Center

2–1 Yoyogi Kamizono-cho, Shibuya-ku, Tokyo　東京都渋谷区代々木神園町 2–1
☎ (03) 3469–6081
🚇 Harajuku Station, JR Yamanote Line; Meiji Jingu-mae Station, Chiyoda Line
🕐 10:00 A.M. to 4:00 P.M. Closed on Mondays.

A two-kilometer course. Bikes are free for children age fifteen and under. Children over fifteen not allowed.

## *SKIING* (INDOOR SKI RESORT)

### SSAWS

2–3–1 Hamamachi, Funabashi-shi, Chiba　千葉県船橋市浜町 2–3–1
☎ (047) 432–7000 (tape recording)
🚇 Minami Funabashi Station, JR Keiyo Line
🕐 8:00 A.M. to 10:00 P.M. (varies with season and day).

Billed as the world's largest indoor ski slope, this four-hundred-and-ninety-meter course is quite an experience. The one-day fee is ¥5,400 for adults, ¥4,800 for middle school students, and ¥4,100 for children. A pool and restaurants are also on the premises. Ski rental equipment is available.

## *ICE-SKATING*

Ice-skating can provide exercise and fun for the entire family. There are many rinks open all year round for those who wish to take lessons or maintain their form. For all the rinks, opening and closing dates and times can vary from year to year, so it is a good idea to call first to be on the safe side. Some rinks are open only in the winter months, others are located within or adjacent to an amusement park (see chapter 6). All of the large rinks have rental skates for adults and children; the rental fee is usually an extra charge above admission. For lessons, call the rink—preferably in Japanese—to inquire. We have many friends who take their children to lessons with a Japanese teacher. Ice skaters face a universal set of challenges and, therefore, the children are able to learn the basics despite the language difference.

If you are outside the Tokyo area, call Nihon Ice-Skating Remmei at ☎ (03) 3481–2351 for information about local rinks.

### ICE HOCKEY

There are several leagues in the Tokyo area. Ask around at the international schools, where chances are a few of the students participate.

---

OUTDOOR SKATING RINKS

---

### Children's Land (Kodomo no Kuni)

700 Naramachi, Aoba-ku, Yokohama-shi, Kanagawa
☎ (045) 961–2111　神奈川県横浜市青葉区奈良町 700
🚇 Tsurukawa Station, Odakyu Line
🕐 9:30 A.M. to 4:30 P.M. Closed on Mondays.

Admission to the park, open until February 27, includes use of the skating rink and two-hour skate rental. Skates from sixteen centimeters are available. Rates: ¥1,300 for adults, ¥700 for students, and ¥600 for preschoolers. From Tsurukawa Station, take the bus to Kodomo no Kuni.

### Dreamland Skating Rink

700 Matano-cho, Totsuka-ku, Yokohama-shi, Kanagawa
☎ (045) 851–1411　神奈川県横浜市戸塚区俣野町 700
🚇 Ofuna Station, JR Negishi, JR Yokosuka, JR Tokaido lines
🕐 10:00 A.M. to 5:30 P.M. weekdays, 10:00 A.M. to 7:00 P.M. on weekends and holidays.

Open from mid-November to early March. Rates: adults ¥1,500, children ¥800. No lessons available.

### Fujikyu Highlands

5–6–1 Shin Nishihara, Fujiyoshida-shi, Yamanashi
☎ (0555) 23–2111　山梨県富士吉田市新西原 5–6–1
🚇 Fujikyu Highland Station, Fujikyu Line (via Otsuki Station, JR Chuo Main Line)

The two rinks at the Highlands are open November 1 to March 21, from 9:00 A.M. to 5:00 P.M. Monday through Saturday, 9:00 A.M. to 8:00 P.M. on Sundays and holidays. Additionally, on Saturday and before holidays, there is all-night skating. Closed on the third Tuesday of each month. Rates: ¥1,000 for the day and ¥1,000 for skate rental.

## Hibiya City Ice-Skating Rink

Hibiya Kokusai Bldg., 2–2–3 Uchisaiwaicho, Chiyoda-ku, Tokyo
☎ (03) 3595–0295    東京都千代田区内幸町 2–2–3 日比谷国際ビル
🚇 Uchisaiwaicho Station, Toei Mita Line

This rink, modeled on New York's Rockefeller Center, is open from mid-November to the end of February. The hours are 3:00 P.M. to 8:00 P.M. Monday through Saturday, 11:00 A.M. to 7:00 P.M. Sundays and holidays. Rates: ¥800 for adults, ¥600 for children. Lessons available for children only.

## Karuizawa Skate Center

Sengataki Onsen, Karuizawa-machi, Kita Saku-gun, Nagano
☎ (0267) 46–1111    長野県北佐久郡軽井沢町千ヶ滝温泉
🚇 Karuizawa Station, JR Shin'etsu Main Line
🕐 9:00 A.M. to 5:00 P.M. Sunday through Friday, 9:00 A.M. to 6:00 P.M. Saturday.

The center's indoor rink is open October to March, Golden Week, and summer holidays, while the four-hundred-meter outdoor rink is open until February 28. Rates: adults ¥700, children ¥500 for a half-day ticket.

## Nikko Kirifuri Skate Center

2854 Tokorono, Nikko-shi, Tochigi    栃木県日光市所野 2854
☎ (0288) 54–2401
🚇 Nikko Station, Tobu Nikko Line
🕐 10:00 A.M. to 4:00 P.M. Sunday through Friday and holidays, 10:00 A.M. to 5:30 P.M. Saturday, and the day before holidays.

The indoor rink is open from July to early May and the outdoor rink, from the middle of November to early March. Rates: adults ¥1,500, children ¥800 for the outdoor rink; adults ¥1,280, children ¥640 for the indoor rink. Skate rentals are ¥1,000. From Nikko Station, take a shuttle bus or 5-minute taxi ride.

## Nippon Land HOW Yuenchi

2427 Aza Fujiwara, Suyama, Susono-shi, Shizuoka    静岡県裾野市須山字藤原 2427
☎ (0559) 98–1111 (Yuenchi), (03) 3376–1113 (Tokyo Information Center)
🚇 Gotemba Station, JR Gotemba Line, Fuji Kyuko bus

This snow-time amusement park claims it's natural lake is the world's largest rink. There is also a triple-course ski slope with nighttime skiing and a play slope for sleighing. Hours are 9:00 A.M. to 10:00 P.M. Monday through Friday, 8:00 A.M. to 10:00 P.M. Sundays and holidays, and all night on Saturdays. Open daily from the end of October to the end of March. Rates: adults ¥3,000, children ¥2,200 for weekdays; adults ¥4,000, children ¥3,000 for weekends and holidays.

## INDOOR SKATING RINKS

### Citizen Skate Rink

4–29–27 Takadanobaba, Shinjuku-ku, Tokyo　東京都新宿区高田馬場 4–29–27
☎ (03) 3371–0910
🚇 Takadanobaba Station, JR Yamanote, Seibu Shinjuku, Tozai lines

Open year-round from 12:00 P.M. to 7:45 P.M. Monday through Saturday, 10:00 A.M. to 7:45 P.M. Sunday and holidays. Rates: adults ¥1,300, children ¥800. Lessons are available for both children and adults.

### Edogawa Sports Land

1–8–1 Higashi Shinozaki, Edogawa-ku, Tokyo　東京都江戸川区東篠崎 1–8–1
☎ (03) 3677–1711
🚇 Shinozaki Station, Toei Shinjuku Line

Open 9:00 A.M. to 8:00 P.M. daily, October to May. Closed on Tuesdays and Thursdays. Rates: adults ¥500, children ¥200. Skate rental is adults ¥300, children ¥200.

### Hama Ice Palace

Hama Bowl, 2F, 2–2–14 Kitasaiwai, Nishi-ku, Yokohama-shi, Kanagawa
☎ (045) 311–4321　　神奈川県横浜市西区北幸 2–2–14 浜ボウル 2F
🚇 Yokohama Station, JR Tokaido and various lines

Open year-round, from 12:00 A.M. to 6:30 P.M. on weekdays, 10:00 A.M. to 6:30 P.M. on weekends and holidays. Rates: ¥1,300 adults, ¥900 a day for children. Skate rental is ¥700. Admission plus rental is ¥1,800 for adults and ¥1,400 for children.

### Higashi Fushimi Ice Arena

3–1–25 Higashi Fushimi, Hoya-shi, Tokyo　東京都保谷市東伏見 3–1–25
☎ (0424) 67–7171
🚇 Higashi Fushimi, Seibu Shinjuku Line

Open year-round from 2:00 P.M. to 6:00 P.M. on weekdays, 10:00 A.M. to 4:00 P.M. on weekends and holidays. Rates (includes skate rental): ¥1,700 for adults, ¥1,000 for children.

**SURVIVAL TIP**

If you find sporting equipment expensive in Japan (or if you hate to invest until you know whether junior is serious about the sport), try United Rent All, 2–17–1 Meguro Honcho, Meguro-ku, Tokyo; ☎ (03) 3794–3431. Also, check out newspaper classified ads (see chapter 12) or the mail-order section in chapter 3.

## Kanagawa Skating Rink

1–1 Hirodai Otamachi, Kanagawa-ku, Yokohama-shi, Kanagawa
☎ (045) 321–3561　神奈川県横浜市神奈川区広台太田町 1–1
🚈 Higashi Kanagawa Station, JR Tokaido, JR Keihin Tohoku lines

Open year-round. Hours are 10:00 A.M. to 6:30 P.M. daily. Closed on Thursdays. Rates: adults ¥1,600, children ¥1,200 (including skate rental). Lessons are available for both children and adults.

## Meiji Jingu Skating Rink

5 Kasumigaoka-cho, Shinjuku-ku, Tokyo　東京都新宿区霞岳町 5
☎ (03) 3403–3456 (tape recording)
🚈 Sendagaya Station, JR Sobu Line

Open Monday through Saturday 10:00 A.M. to 6:30 P.M., Sundays and holidays 10:00 A.M. to 3:00 P.M. Rates: children fifteen and over ¥1,300, under fifteen ¥900. Skate rental is ¥500. The rink is open year-round. Lessons are available for both children and adults.

## Shin Yokohama Prince Hotel Skate Center

2–11 Shin Yokohama, Kohoku-ku, Yokohama-shi, Kanagawa
☎ (045) 474–1112　神奈川県横浜市港北区新横浜 2–11
🚈 Shin Yokohama Station, JR Yokohama, JR Tokaido Shinkansen lines

The center is open year-round from 3:30 P.M. to 6:30 P.M. daily (times vary slightly according to the season and day). The fee is ¥1,200 for adults, ¥700 for children. Skate rental is ¥600 for adults, ¥400 for children.

## ROLLER-SKATING

For information in Japanese on classes and rinks nearest you, call Zen-Nihon Roller-Skating Remmei, #3 Lions Mansion 506, 1–31–13 Higashi Ikebukuro, Toshima-ku, Tokyo, ☎ (03) 3983–6335. Classes are available for children from the age of two or three.

### Tokyo Dome Inline Skate Rink

Korakuen Yellow Bldg., 4F, 1–3–61 Koraku, Bunkyo-ku, Tokyo
☎ (03) 3817–6113　東京都文京区後楽 1–3–61 後楽園黄色いビル 4F
🚈 Suidobashi Station, JR Sobu, Mita lines; Korakuen Station, Marunouchi Line

Open from 9:30 A.M. to 9:00 P.M. on weekends and from 10:00 A.M. on weekdays. Rates for two-hour time blocks are ¥1,400 adults, ¥1,000 middle school, ¥700 children. Skate rental is ¥500.

## FISHING

Just because you're living in a city of twelve million people, it doesn't mean you can't go fishing! Various points along Tokyo Bay have the following to offer kids (accompanied by serious anglers!).

### Atsugi Fishing Center

1928 Mita, Atsugi-shi, Kanagawa　神奈川県厚木市三田 1928
☎ (0462) 41–2535
🚃 Hon Atsugi Station, Odakyu Line
🕐 8:00 A.M. to 5:00 P.M. daily.

Twelve ponds on the Nakatsugawa River. The focus is chiefly on carp and, from June on, *ayu*, the popular and pricey Japanese river fish. Fee: ¥500 including fishing rod and bait. For an extra charge you can take the day's catch home. Take a bus from the station.

### Benten-ya

2–22 Seto, Kanazawa-ku, Yokohama-shi, Kanagawa
☎ (045) 701–9061　神奈川県横浜市金沢区瀬戸 2–22
🚃 Kanazawa Hakkei Station, Keihin Kyuko Line

Mackerel (from 7:30 A.M.), smelt (from 8:00 A.M.). Fee: ¥5,500 to ¥9,500 (including bait).

### Ichihara-shi Umizuri Shisetsu

1–12 Minami Kaigan, Goi, Ichihara-shi, Chiba　千葉県市原市五井南海岸 1–12
☎ (0436) 21–0419
🚃 Goi Station, JR Uchibo Line
🕐 6:00 A.M. to 7:00 P.M. (April to June), 6:00 A.M. to 9:00 P.M. (July to October), 7:00 A.M. to 5:00 P.M. (November to March). Closed Mondays.

A spot by the sea. From the observatory there is a view of Tokyo Bay and Mt. Fuji. Chiefly *mebaru*, croaker (*ishimochi*), *anago*, *iwashi*, and *bora*. Fee: adults ¥920 for the day, junior high school students ¥460; free for children under twelve and adults over sixty-five.

### Isehara Masu Tsuriba

1582 Hinata, Isehara-shi, Kanagawa　神奈川県伊勢原市日向 1582
☎ (0463) 95–4150
🚃 Isehara Station, Odakyu Line
🕐 6:00 A.M. to 5:00 P.M. daily.

A fishing spot that appeals to children. Shared barbecuing facilities. Fee: ¥3,000 to ¥5,000. A 20-minute bus ride from the station.

## Ishikawa Tsuribune-ten

4–12–44 Shibaura, Minato-ku, Tokyo   東京都港区芝浦 4–12–44
☎ (03) 451–1228
🚇 Tamachi Station, JR Yamanote Line

Smelt (from 7:45 A.M.). Fee: ¥8,500 (including bait, minimum ten people).

## Isogo Umizuriba

388 Shin Isogo-cho, Isogo-ku, Yokohama-shi, Kanagawa
☎ (045) 761–1931   神奈川県横浜市磯子区新磯子町 388
🚇 Isogo Station, JR Negishi Line
🕐 8:00 A.M. to 6:00 P.M. (April to June, September, and October), to 5:00 P.M. (November to March), to 8:00 P.M. (July and August). Closed Tuesdays.

This fishing hole stocks *kisu*, *anago*, *karei*, and croaker. Fee: adults ¥500 for the day, children ¥300.

## Isotsuri Center

Futomi Flower Center, 67 Futomihama, Kamogawa-shi, Chiba
☎ (0470) 92–1311   千葉県鴨川市太海浜 67  太海フラワーセンター
🚇 Futomi Station, JR Sotobo Line
🕐 8:00 A.M. to 5:00 P.M. daily.

Fees: entrance to the center, ¥450 to ¥600. For fishing, ¥500 (catch and release) or ¥300 plus ¥2,500 to ¥3,500 a kilogram. Rates include rod and bait.

## Shizen Kyuyomura Keiryu Tsuriba

3882 Oguno, Hinode-machi, Nishitama-gun, Tokyo
☎ (0425) 97–4911   東京都西多摩郡日の出町大久野 3882
🚇 Musashi-Itsukaichi Station, JR Itsukaichi Line

Trout fishing on the Hiraigawa River. Fees: trout ¥2,500, fishing rod and bait ¥250. Open daily, except Tuesday, from 9:00 A.M. to 4:30 P.M.

## Suzukien

3–38–33 Asagaya Minami, Suginami-ku, Tokyo   東京都杉並区阿佐谷南 3–38–33
☎ (03) 3398–0607
🚇 Asagaya Station, JR Chuo Line

Carp and goldfish. Open from 8:00 A.M. to sunset. Closed on Fridays. Fee: ¥600 per hour.

## Teganuma Fishing Center

1 Akebonobashi, Shonammachi, Higashi Katsushika-gun, Chiba
☎ (0471) 85–2424   千葉県東葛飾郡昭南町曙橋 1
🚇 Tennodai Station, JR Joban Line; Kohoku Station, JR Narita Line
🕐 8:00 A.M. to dusk. Closed Mondays and Thursdays.

Carp and *herabuna*. Fees: men ¥1,500 a day and ¥1,000 a half day; women ¥1,200 a day and ¥800 a half day.

### Todoroki Fishing Center

1–1 Todoroki, Nakahara-ku, Kawasaki-shi, Kanagawa
☎ (044) 711–3257　神奈川県川崎市中原区等々力 1–1
🚃 Musashi Kosugi Station, JR Nambu Line
🕐 8:30 A.M. (from 6:30 A.M. in July and August) to 5:00 P.M. daily. Open Saturdays and Sundays at 6:30 A.M., from April to October. Closed on Mondays.

Several kinds of fish are stocked, including carp. Fee for four hours: adults ¥500, children ¥200. The center is a 5-minute bus ride from the station.

### Yoshino-ya

5–7–10 Nekozane, Urayasu-shi, Chiba　千葉県浦安市猫実 5–7–10
☎ (047) 351–2544
🚃 Urayasu Station, Tozai Line

Smelt (from 8:00 A.M.), mackerel (7:00 A.M.). Fee: ¥9,000 (including bait).

### *BASEBALL*

Baseball is very popular in Japan. If your child's school doesn't have a team, be on the look-out for a neighborhood league (you'll notice the kids in their spiffy uniforms playing on local fields most weekends). Ask if you can join the team. A couple of foreign kids have done just that and were welcomed by their neighborhood league.

## BOY SCOUTS AND GIRL SCOUTS

Boy Scouts and Girl Scouts are both international organizations concerned with the development and education of young people. Boy Scouts of Nippon is a large organization whose meetings and business are conducted in Japanese. Boy Scouts of America (Japan) is the name under which the international and foreign communities operate their troops. There are more than one hundred packs of Boy Scouts in Japan, and they include Scouts from all over the world.

The Boy Scouts of America (Japan) troops are tightly controlled and organized, and there are strict requirements that must be met before a troop may be formed. Children may enter the Scouting program in first grade (age six) and continue to be active in Scouting the rest of their lives. Those who do not live near an organized Scout troop can participate in the Lone Scout program. In this program, the parent and child work together toward the goals and achievements that normally the child would be working on independently. This program also allows children who have been Scouts, or who want to become Scouts when they return to their home country, to keep up with other Scouts their age.

For information on the Boy Scouts of America (Japan) program, contact the Boy Scouts of America, Far East Council, Yokota Air Base, Bldg. 2000, Fussa-shi, Tokyo; ☎ (0425) 52–2511 ext. (22) 57388.

For those interested in the Boy Scouts of Nippon, contact the National Headquarters, Boy Scouts of Nippon, 4–11–10 Osawa, Mitaka-shi, Tokyo; ☎ (0422) 31–5161 or ☎ (0422) 32–0010.

Besides the Girl Scouts of Nippon, the Girl Scouts of America are also in Japan. Their organization is not as tightly controlled as the Boy Scouts of America (Japan), making it fairly simple to start up your own troop. Girls from first grade on can become involved. The Girl Scout troops do not need a sponsor in the way that the Boy Scouts do, and so troops often start up and then disband when a particular leader moves away.

The best way to find out about Girl Scouts of America (Japan) programs in your area is to ask at the international schools near you or to contact the West Pacific Girl Scout Council, Yokota Air Base, Bldg. 2000, Fussa-shi, Tokyo; ☎ (0425) 52–2511 ext. (22) 57349.

For information on the Girl Scouts of Nippon, contact their office at 1–40–3 Nishihara, Shibuya-ku, Tokyo; ☎ (03) 3460–0701 or ☎ (03) 3460–8383.

## MUSIC

### KAWAI MUSIC SCHOOLS

Kawai music schools are located throughout Japan. They offer classes for children from the age of three in both piano and electric piano. For information about classes in your area, contact the Kawai Music School at Kawai Music Shop Aoyama, 5–1 Jingu-mae, Shibuya-ku, Tokyo. The phone number is ☎ (03) 3409–2511, and hours are from 11:00 A.M. to 9:00 P.M.

### SUZUKI METHOD

The world-famous Suzuki method of teaching music to children began right here in Japan some sixty years ago. The founder, Shin'ichi Suzuki, believed that children can learn to play instrumental in much the same way that they learn to speak. This means that beginning at a very young age, perhaps even before the child is born, he or she can be influenced toward becoming a musician.

Lessons for children usually begin around age three. Before age three, the Suzuki method maintains that the child can be prepared for music lessons by listening and observing those around him. Usually the parents of a child under age three are encouraged to learn an instrument themselves by the Suzuki method, to pave the way for the child's lessons. Whenever the child start lessons, the parent must understand that he or she, too, is going to learn along with the child. A parent must attend all music classes with the child, and in essence learn how to play the instrument with the child. The parent can then direct and observe the child's progress when practicing at home.

Children may start piano, violin, or cello lessons at the age of three and flute lessons at the age of four or five. The Suzuki office in Tokyo, ☎ (03) 3295–0270, can provide you with information in Japanese on classes and teachers anywhere in Japan. The Suzuki head office, ☎ (0263) 32–7171, will supply you with a contact number, perhaps someone who speaks English. Teachers are available throughout Japan, and many are able to speak a little English.

## Music for Youth

Daido Bldg., 5F, 2–39–9 Nishi Shimbashi, Minato-ku, Tokyo
☎/🖷 (03) 3437–3422 (office)　東京都港区西新橋 2–39–9 大同ビル 5F
🚇 Shimbashi Station, JR Yamanote, JR Keihin Tohoku, Ginza lines

Music for Youth has been in existence since 1939 and was the first group to introduce educational symphony concerts to Japan. This non-profit, educational association serves the international community by presenting concerts at low cost for students and family groups. They also provide musical opportunities for handicapped young people and run a summer music camp at Karuizawa in Nagano-ken.

The force and founder behind this organization is Eloise Cunning-ham, a remarkable lady who works tirelessly to bring music and education together for children of all ages and races. Music for Youth sponsors a number of concerts by professional and amateur artists and groups (ballet, opera, symphony) each year. The group is financed by membership dues, special grants, and sales of tickets.

Call or write if you would like to become a member or want more information. Music for Youth re-opens at the new Shimbashi location listed here in the summer of 2000.

## Theater for Children

2–8–13–402 Azabu Juban, Minato-ku, Tokyo　東京都港区麻布十番 2–8–13–402
☎ (03) 3451–8102, (03) 3420–1947
🚇 Roppongi Station, Hibiya Line

Theater for Children began more than twenty-five years ago when a group of foreign women saw a need for children's theater for the English-speaking community. The group produces two shows annually, one in the fall in Tokyo and a road show in spring that it takes to the major international schools around Tokyo. A volunteer, nonprofit organization, it is always in need of adults to help with sets, costumes, music, and, of course, acting.

## Yamaha Music Center

7F, 3–34–32 Nakano, Nakano-ku, Tokyo　東京都中野区中野 3–34–32  7F
☎ (03) 3383–7381
🚇 Nakano Station, JR Chuo Line

Yamaha music classes are available at numerous locations in Tokyo and other major cities around Japan. For information about class curriculum and school locations in your area, call toll-free: ☎ 0120–329–808. English-speaking teachers are available at some locations.

### *FOREIGN STUDENTS MUSIC CONTEST*

## Japan International Cultural Exchange Foundation

2–15–5–507 Shoto, Shibuya-ku, Tokyo　東京都渋谷区松濤 2–15–5–507
☎ (03) 3467–7422　🖨 (03) 3467–7317

Held every two years, this contest is open to all foreign students under age eighteen. Singers or musicians are invited to perform a piece in their native language, and the talent is often quite impressive. Contestants appear for one night. Prizes, ranging from bicycles to pearls, are awarded to the lucky winners.

# So You Want to Be a Star . . .

Upon hearing the words "talent agency," many parents assume their child must have some sort of showbiz-type talent or experience in order to register with an agency. For foreign kids in Japan, this is definitely not the case. There are lots of opportunities out there for your aspiring model-narrator-movie star child.

To promote a product, a talent agency is usually hired by an advertising agency to round up kids for an audition. If the ad is a photo that will appear in a magazine, catalog, or as a subway poster, it is known as a print job. These jobs usually pay pretty well, and there is the added bonus of having a photo souvenir of your kid, the star.

An audition for a print job usually requires a brief interview where a Polaroid snapshot will be taken of your child. You may have to fill out a form with basic information, although the agency often handles that. Sometimes a print job will be cast by picture selection only. In this case, the agency submits the pictures it has on file, then informs you whether or not you got the job. Note, however, that while the client's decision is pending, you will be asked to hold the job date open.

Some agencies cast for fashion shows, which means they need your kid to model clothes on a fashion runway. Unlike the grown-up world of fashion modeling, this kind of job is not limited to beautiful children only. All types of kids are used, although it does help if your kid likes being on stage and takes direction well.

Working as a runway model can be tiring for some children, as it involves a good bit of waiting time while rehearsing. There will also be at least one fitting session.

Both fashion and print jobs fall into the modeling category. Agencies that specialize in modeling for children are always on the lookout for new faces. Babies grow and change so quickly and, in the foreign community, children and their families relocate frequently.

Television commercials are usually the highest paying jobs, depending on the part. They are also the most time-consuming. Most agencies cast for TV commercials.

There are two kinds of roles your child may be asked to play. A modeling part requires no acting ability, just the child's presence on the screen. Even without a speaking part, be prepared for a long day, especially if there are several children in the cast. For a speaking part in a TV commercial, your child will have to memorize lines, do some acting, and be able to follow the director's instructions. Usually the client has a certain look in mind for promoting the product and, who knows, maybe your kid has just what they're looking for.

From time to time, a casting call goes out for a specific talent, such as a red-haired girl who plays the violin, or a chubby boy who can do somersaults. So if any of the kids in your family can sing, dance, play an instrument or just like to ham it up, sign them with an agency and see what happens.

If you attend an audition for a TV commercial or any other on-camera work, the casting people will videotape your interview-audition. First, your child will be given a sheet of paper with his or her name on it to hold up in front of the camera. The child will be asked to slowly turn around for the camera, then to introduce himself or herself. Sometimes the director will ask your child to improvise a scene ("Pretend you're begging your mom for another helping of ice cream!") or act out one from a script. If it is a script reading, it will probably have been distributed in the waiting room.

Have your child take time to read the script over and over, becoming familiar with the words and trying to imagine how he or she would feel. At the audition, the director may ask for the scene to be read several ways.

Another field open to foreign children is singing for English-language video and cassette tapes, most of which are marketed to Japanese children who want to learn English. The work consists of simple childhood songs and nursery rhymes. Besides these recordings, there is also work for children to sing jingles in TV commercials, as well as to sing back-up for Japanese CD recordings. If your child enjoys singing (and can carry a tune), these jobs can be fun.

Narration and voice-over work is another choice for children who read copy easily and expressively, with no strong regional accent. Sometimes the voice work is just a couple of lines, as in a commercial for radio or TV. Other jobs require more skill, for example, when dubbing a Japanese cartoon character's voice into English.

To be considered for most narration work, the agency will submit a demo tape of your child's voice to the client. For work in Japan, a demo tape can be a simple recording done on a boom box, consisting of a couple of reading samples and perhaps a few bars of a song. Some agencies may ask to put your child's voice on their master demo tape.

If you decide to pursue any of these possibilities for your child or yourself, remember that the motto of this industry is "Hurry up and wait." Being prepared with healthy snacks and drinks, books, and quiet games will make the job much less tedious for everyone.

Unfortunately, there are no regulations governing how many hours a child may work here in Japan, so be clear with the agency about your child's tolerance level. Because there are no unions either, there is no pay scale for this kind of work. Children, as a rule, get paid less than adults, even when they work the same hours. Nevertheless, the yen is still strong enough to make even the cheapest jobs enticing for most kids.

Many children get a real boost to their self-esteem from appearing in a video, seeing their picture in a magazine, or hearing their voice on the radio. If your kid has dreams of stardom, Tokyo is a good place to start. As they say in showbiz, "Here's looking at you, kid!"

The agencies listed below represent children for modeling, print jobs, television, film, and some narration work.

## AGENCIES IN TOKYO

### *MODELING*

#### Carrotte

Sengokuyama Annex, #205, 5–30–20 Toranomon, Minato-ku, Tokyo
東京都港区虎の門 5–30–20　仙石山アネックス 205
☎ (03) 3432–0170　📠 (03) 3432–1088
🚇 Kamiya-cho Station, Hibiya Line

Carrotte represents foreign and Japanese children, from newborns to eighteen-year-olds.

#### Echo

Takano Bldg., 5F, 3–12–2 Tsukiji, Chuo-ku, Tokyo
東京都中央区築地 3–12–2　高野ビル 5F
☎ (03) 3542–4731　📠 (03) 3542–4733　🖥 echo_model@msn.com
🚇 Tsukiji Station, Hibiya Line

Echo handles foreigners of any age, from babies to grandparents. They have been in business for over thirty years.

#### E Promotions

2–11–9 Nishi Nakanobu, Shinagawa-ku, Tokyo　東京都品川区西中延 2–11–9
☎ (03) 3784–9851　📠 (03) 3784–9855
🚇 Ebara Nakanobu Station, Tokyu Ikegami Line

One of the oldest agencies in Tokyo, E Promotions has been in business for over three decades. They will represent foreigners or Japanese of all ages.

#### I.M.O.

1–6–6 Nishi Azabu, Minato-ku, Tokyo　東京都港区西麻布 1–6–6
☎ (03) 3405–0425　📠 (03) 3405–0509
🚇 Roppongi Station, Hibiya Line

Established in 1988, this company represents foreigners of all ages.

# THE RUNDOWN ON MODELING AND TALENT AGENCIES

It was some years ago that my then seven-year-old son begged me to let him register with a talent agency in Tokyo. His interest had been piqued when a good friend purchased a Game Boy with earnings from modeling and acting jobs. Concerned that these jobs might interfere with school work, I hesitated to pursue this extracurricular activity. I also imagined that an acting career for my son would involve lots of extra work for me: accompanying him to auditions, fittings, and so forth.

However, when summer vacation arrived and we had some free time, I agreed to take him around to a few agencies. First, we made some phone calls to set up appointments. Then, at each talent agency we visited, I filled out a standard form, listing my child's measurements, clothing, and shoe sizes. It wasn't necessary for me to bring any photographs of my son. Most agencies took their own pictures, either for free or a ¥1,000 service charge. No agency charged a registration fee.

We ended up registering initially with five agencies. Unlike in the United States, it is acceptable to freelance with as many agencies as you want in Japan. Once in a while your child may be offered an exclusive contract, but that's pretty rare. You may, however, be called by more than one agency for a job. It is then best to go with whomever calls you first.

My son's first audition was for a fashion show. Together with about twenty other kids and parents, we met our agent at the designated subway station. After a fifteen-minute walk in the scorching heat, we arrived at the audition place, only to find hordes of kids from other agencies already there. We spent an hour waiting for our turn. It was an exhausting day, and we didn't get the job.

Just as I was giving up the idea of taking my son to any more auditions, a friend told me about the way she handles them. Instead of meeting at the station, she requests that the agency fax her the map of where the audition is to take place. She then takes her child directly there. By going a little early, her kid is one of the first to be seen, and the whole process often takes about fifteen minutes.

The next week we got a call from an agency that specializes in extras for TV work. Both my sons and I (yes, there are parts for moms too!) had been cast in a TBS drama. Each child was paid ¥15,000 (adults got ¥20,000) for the day's work, which started at 1:00 P.M. and was to end at 8:00 P.M. Unfortunately, the taping dragged on until 11:00 P.M., at which point my children were a bedraggled, whining mess. We have since sworn off offers to work as extras, unless the studio or location is nearby and the job is absolutely guaranteed to be brief.

At my son's next fashion show audition, we went directly to the site. Sure enough, it was quicker and easier. The next week my son received a call from the agency saying that he had gotten the job. For modeling in the fashion show he would receive ¥20,000. He would be required to attend one fitting and a rehearsal for about two hours on the day of the show.

I was surprised at how much fun my child had modeling in the fashion show. He got to wear some really "cool" clothes, and the whole production with lights, music, and props was quite a spectacle. I did notice that the waiting time was a bit much for some of the younger children.

After the success of the fashion show, I agreed to let my son audition for a narration job that would require him to sing and speak in English for an educational children's video. This same company has hired him for several more jobs, usually paying ¥15,000 for three hours' work. For two sessions in one day, he is paid ¥30,000.

Most agencies will deposit the payment into your child's (or your) bank account. The timing for the payment varies from two to three weeks after the job to two months. A few agencies will pay cash at the job. Another option is to stop by the agent's office and pick up the money.

Now that my son is older, he loves doing narration work. He is no longer interested in the modeling or print jobs, although he will jump at the chance to do an acting part. These days, narrating (especially cartoon voices!) and singing are his hobbies. I don't even mind taking him to the jobs, since he enjoys the work so much.

Earning a substantial amount of money has been an education in itself for my son. He is allowed to spend ten percent of his earnings on whatever he wants. Another ten percent goes to our household charity fund, and the rest goes into his savings account for college. He keeps up with the yen-dollar exchange rate and has learned that money doesn't grow on trees.

My son has learned some other valuable lessons from his work experience, such as the importance of punctuality, cooperation, and a commitment to doing a good job (otherwise you don't get hired again). Perhaps the best thing to come out of this whole experience is his enhanced self-esteem. Every child needs to find something at which he or she excels, no matter what the age.

## Isop

Imperial Akasaka Ichibankan, #317, 8–13–19 Akasaka, Minato-ku, Tokyo
☎ (03) 3405–7151   📠 (03) 3405–6704   東京都港区赤坂 8–13–19 赤坂一番館 317
🚈 Nogizaka Station, Chiyoda Line

This agency will take foreigners of any age. They have been in business since the late 1980s.

## K and M Promotions

3–40–2 Jingu-mae, Shibuya-ku, Tokyo   東京都渋谷区神宮前 3–40–2
☎ (03) 3404–9429   📠 (03) 3403–6675   📧 kandm@netlaputa.or.jp

This agency has been representing foreigners of all ages since 1980.

## R & A Promotions

TSI-Funamachi Bldg., 5F, 5–25 Funamachi, Shinjuku-ku, Tokyo
☎ (03) 3225–3561   東京都新宿区舟町 5–25   TSI 舟町ビル 5F
🚈 Yotsuya 3-chome Station, Marunouchi Line

A new agency that handles children and adults for all kinds of jobs.

## Sugar and Spice

Room B–2, 5–4–11 Hiroo, Shibuya-ku, Tokyo   東京都渋谷区広尾 5–4–11, B–2
☎ (03) 3280–5481   📠 (03) 3280–5480
🚈 Hiroo Station, Hibiya Line

Known for its work with children, this company accepts foreign children from newborn to eighteen years.

## *VOICE-OVERS*

### Jarico International

1–51–3 Sakura, Setagaya-ku, Tokyo   東京都世田谷区桜 1–51–3
☎ (03) 3420–1947   📠 (03) 3420–2012
🚈 Kyodo Station, Odakyu Line

Gerri Sorrells, who has had many years of experience as a voice-over artist, also works as a casting director and producer for television, educational tapes, and other jobs involving children. Look for her series of bilingual books and tapes for kids.

### Tip Top Co.

601 Grand Maison, Shinjuku Gyoen, 1–7–10 Shinjuku, Shinjuku-ku, Tokyo
東京都新宿区新宿 1–7–10   グランドメゾン新宿御苑 601号
☎ (03) 3359–8331   📠 (03) 3359–8332
🚈 Shinjuku Gyoen-mae Station, Marunouchi Line

This agency specializes in voice-overs, including kids' voices for cartoons. If possible, send a demo tape, otherwise they will tape you.

## Voiceland

Palais Crystal, 601, 1–1 Katamachi, Shinjuku-ku, Tokyo
東京都新宿区片町 1–1 パレスクリスタル 601
☎ (03) 3358–8261　🖷 (03) 3353–8710　🖳 minowa@gol.com
🚈 Akebonobashi Station, Shinjuku Line

Owned by the talented Rumiko Varnes Minowa, this company hire children as well as adult for all types of recordings, both voice-overs and singing.

### *SINGING*

## Eric Jacobsen

2–8–36 Zoshigaya, Toshima-ku, Tokyo　東京都豊島区雑司ヶ谷 2–8–36
☎/🖷 at the studio (03) 3987–2455, home (03) 3987–2426　🖳 ericj@gol.com
🚈 Kishibojin-mae Station, Toden Arakawa Line

Eric does not run an agency, but is a musical director-musician who works on kid-oriented projects: pop music CDs, educational videos, and multimedia "edutainment." He is always looking for enthusiastic kids who can sing. If possible, send a short demo tape and photo to the above address.

---

KANSAI AREA

### *MODELING*

## Creamy and D Guys

Ekimae Dai 2 Bldg., 2F, 1–2–2 Umeda, Kita-ku, Osaka-shi, Osaka
☎ (06) 6347–7705　🖷 (06) 6347–7784　大阪府大阪市北区梅田 1–2–2 駅前第2ビル 2F
🚈 Osaka Station, JR Tokaido and various lines; Umeda Station, Hankyu, Hanshin, Midosuji, Yotsubashi lines

Creamy and D Guys has been in business in Osaka since the 1980s, representing both foreigners and Japanese, from newborns up to twenty. The agency also represents adults who have modeling experience.

# SUMMER PROGRAMS

Summer programs for children range from intensive language courses to outdoor recreation. Some of the offerings will be in a bilingual setting, others all in English or all in Japanese. Below, we have listed some summer offerings, but there are many more throughout Japan. Often an individual city or prefecture will run what they call a youth symposium, where Japanese and foreign children come together for a weekend of cultural exchange. Many of the international schools, and especially the preschools, offer day camp or summer school programs (see chapter 11). Large corporations also sponsor camps for children with special interests or needs. The best way to find out about these kinds of activities is to call the international school nearest you, starting in April. Usually the organizers of these events will send information to the schools for publicity.

During the Japanese school summer holiday, the wards and cities offer special classes in sports, language, and art. The *jido-kan*, or children's centers, and the national Children's Castle in Tokyo (see the Rainy-Day Activities and Ideas section in this chapter) also offer special one- or two-week classes during this time.

If you plan to send your children to summer camp in the United States, you'd be wise to start planning as early as February. For children living overseas, summer camp can offer a chance to experience life back in their home country, as well as an opportunity to learn new skills and polish existing talents. With international moves, some children may find that a favorite sport or activity is no longer accessible in their new posting. Parents can ease this loss by seeking out specialized camps. If you have an academically gifted child who needs more of a challenge than his regular school offers, there are exciting summer programs available through some of the American universities. For the largest resource on summer camps, check out Petersons at 💻 <www.petersons.com> or fax 📠 (609) 243–9150 in the United States. This annual guide has over one thousand six hundred listings. Another good source for camp ideas is the National Camp Association at 💻 <www.summercamp.org>, ☎ 800–966–2267. The association also offers a free camp advisory listing.

### Kids World

☎ 0120–00–1537 (toll-free)

A summer day camp for children up to age eight, complete with excursions, arts and crafts, music, and games. The camp also offers fun-and-fitness classes, in the indoor gym, for children age one and two (with mothers) and, in the Young Explorer and Discovery programs, for children ages two through six. Kids World has nineteen locations in the greater Tokyo-Yokohama area and one in Fukuoka.

## Nihon UNESCO Kyokai Remmei

Asahi Seimei Ebisu Bldg., 12F, 1–3–1 Ebisu, Shibuya-ku, Tokyo
☎ (03) 5424–1121　東京都渋谷区恵比寿 1–3–1　朝日生命恵比寿ビル 12F

The UNESCO association seeks to promote international relations and the use of English. It offers a variety of programs, camps, and homestays.

## Okutama Bible Camp

3–839 Yugi-machi, Ome-shi, Tokyo　東京都青梅市柚木町 3–839
☎ (0428) 76–0931

This Bible camp facility was founded in 1942. During the summer, the Christian Academy (see chapter 11) runs two one-week Bible camps for international kids. The camp runs from Monday to Saturday, and there are two sessions, one for grades three to five, and one for grades six to eight. The camp also runs summer programs for Japanese-speaking children. Activities include hiking, Bible study, and all sorts of outdoor pursuits. The cost is extremely reasonable—below ¥20,000 for the week.

## YMCA Japan

7 Honshio-cho, Shinjuku-ku, Tokyo　東京都新宿区本塩町 7
☎ (03) 5367–6640 (head office)

YMCA Japan runs day camps and overnight camps year-round. There are branches of the YMCA throughout Japan, and each runs its own programs. Most of the summer camps are overnight outdoor camps. Children come for two to five days to a YMCA facility and enjoy outdoor recreation at that location. The YMCA has camp facilities all over Japan. For example, in Okinawa, the emphasis is on water sports. In Hokkaido, hiking and skiing are the main activities. Overnight camps are generally for children age eight to eighteen and are staffed by college-age leaders.

YMCA facilities offer three kinds of camp programs. English-speaking participants and leaders are most likely to be present at the YMCA international programs. YMCA language camps are camps that are run in English to give Japanese children an opportunity to experience an all-English-speaking environment. Native English speakers are welcome at these camps as well. Finally, at the YMCA handicapped camps, programs are run for children with special needs.

Day camps may be held in some areas; these are generally for children age eight to twelve, but some programs may be offered for younger children. To find out about camps and activities in your area, call the head office number listed above or the regional office nearest you.

In Tokyo call ☎ (03) 3293–1921, Yokohama ☎ (045) 662–3721, Osaka ☎ (06) 6441–0894, Kobe ☎ (078) 241–7201, and Kyoto ☎ (075) 231–4380.

### GYMNASTICS SUMMER PROGRAMS

The International Gymnastics Club (see the Sports section in this chapter) runs a spring program in early April and a summer program from June through August. At each location, the program lasts from two to four hours and entails an intensive gymnastic workout. Also on the itinerary is a weekly "meet" where the children are judged and scored by the head instructor.

### TENNIS SUMMER PROGRAMS

The Krissman Tennis School (see the Sports section in this chapter) runs four-day summer courses for one hour per day. Geared toward children age five to fifteen.

## RAINY-DAY ACTIVITIES AND IDEAS

There are many wonderful things about living in Japan, but the rainy season is not one of them. As the parents of young children, we dread the dreary days of rain, rain, and more rain. This season of precipitation is supposed to fall in June, but the actual time period varies. Some years, we thought we could escape the rain by going on vacation in June, only to find the rainy season beginning in July. Other years, it seems that the rain starts in the spring and continues through August. At any rate, you can count on an extended period of wetness at some point during the summer in Japan.

When the kids cannot go outdoors and play, you will need to find other alternatives to keep them happy. Rainy days can mean visits to museums, movies, or other special indoor outings. If you do not have that kind of energy—and you won't after the eighth straight day of rain—then you will need some resources for keeping the kids busy at home.

No matter what you do with the kids, you will want them to have the proper rainwear. Fortunately, Japan has the world's greatest selection of rain gear for kids. Who can resist the adorable boots, hats, coats, and umbrellas in bright colors and cute designs. When the kids want to get out of the house in the summer rain, send them outside with this gear on and let them puddle-jump and play to their hearts content—after all, it is only water! One friend pays her kids a few yen to "wash" the windows outside with a spray bottle and towel when it rains. Because of the humidity, it is rare for the children to catch a cold, and if they get really dirty, you can always have a hot bath waiting when they come inside.

If everybody has cabin fever and you need a break, try taking the kids to a car wash. This probably sounds ridiculous, but ¥1,000 will buy you an exciting trip through the car wash and a clean car as well. There is something soothing to mom, yet thrilling to the kids, about sitting in the car as it gets soaped, sprayed, and shined.

When you decide to brave the weather, plan a special outing to a place where the kids can enjoy indoor activities and burn off some energy. Department stores (see chapter 2), aquariums (see chapter 6), and book and toy stores (see chapter 4) all make great rainy-day outings with the children. Also check out the amusement parks (see chapter 6), as some of them are indoors. The places listed below are of special interest to children and are all worth a visit in any kind of weather.

### A TRIP TO THE MOVIES

All of the blockbuster hit films come to Japan, even though the ticket price might be a bit steeper than what you would pay back home. Most of the U.S. movies are subtitled in Japanese, so you can enjoy the original English dialogue. An IMAX theater has opened on the second floor of the Takashimaya Department Store in Shinjuku (Times Square, 12F), ☎ (03) 5361–3030. Their two- and three-dimensional movies about sea life, wildlife, and space are a treat for the whole family on a rainy day.

### OBSERVATORIES, PLANETARIUMS, AND MUSEUMS

There are a few planetariums and many excellent museums throughout Japan—certainly too many to list here. There are, however, some museums that are more interesting to children than others, and we have listed a few of these. If you have a special interest in a particular type of museum, or want to find one for your children outside of Tokyo, check the English-language newspapers or the listings in *Tokyo Journal* and *Kansai Times Out.*

## Antique Toy Museum

239 Yamate-cho, Naka-ku, Yokohama-shi, Kanagawa
☎ (045) 621–8710　神奈川県横浜市中区山手町 239
🚆 Ishikawacho Station, JR Negishi Line
🕘 9:30 A.M. to 7:00 P.M. daily.

More than three thousand toys on display, the oldest dating back to the nineteenth century. Much comes from the owner's private collection. Located behind the Toys Club. Admission is ¥200.

## Drum Museum (Taikokan)

Miyamoto Unosuke Store, 4F, 2–1–1 Nishi Asakusa, Taito-ku, Tokyo
☎ (03) 3842–5622　東京都台東区西浅草 2–1–1　宮本卯之助商店 4F
🚆 Tawaramachi Station (Kokusai Dori exit), Ginza Line

Children can enjoy trying out drums from around the world. Admission: adults ¥300, children ¥150.

## Fire Museum (Shobo Hakubutsukan)

3–10 Yotsuya, Shinjuku-ku, Tokyo　東京都新宿区四ッ谷 3–10
☎ (03) 3353–9119
🚆 Yotsuya 3-chome Station, Marunouchi Line
🕘 9:30 A.M. to 5:30 P.M. (entry until 4:30 P.M.). Closed on Mondays. Open holidays.

Big fire trucks and all the firefighting gadgets you could ever imagine. The first museum of its kind. Ten floors of display material. Some explanations in English. Admission is free.

## Fujisawa Shonandai Bunka Center

1–8 Shonandai, Fujisawa-shi, Kanagawa　神奈川県藤沢市湘南台 1–8
☎ (0466) 45–1500
🚆 Shonandai Station (east exit), Odakyu Line

This center houses a small children's museum, a planetarium, and an omnimax theater. Open from 9:00 A.M. to 5:00 P.M. Closed on Mondays.

## Goto Planetarium and Astronomy Museum (Goto Planetarium to Temmon Hakubutsukan)

Tokyu Bunka Kaikan, 5F, 2–21–12 Shibuya, Shibuya-ku, Tokyo
☎ (03) 3407–7409　東京都渋谷区渋谷 2–21–12　東急文化会館 5F
🚆 Shibuya Station, JR Yamanote and various lines

This planetarium, located across from Shibuya Station, offers a program of shows that is changed regularly. It is often open in the evening for special programs. For up-to-date program information, call the museum or check the museum listings in the monthly city magazines. Note that the programs are in Japanese and a bit on the dull side for young children, with the emphasis more on star charts than entertainment. Closed Mondays.

### Hachioji Children's Science Museum (Hachioji-shi Kodomo Kagakukan)

9–13 Oyoko-machi, Hachioji-shi, Tokyo　東京都八王子市大横町 9–13
☎ (0426) 24–3311
🚾 Hachioji Station, JR Chuo Line

This museum has a planetarium and computers that children can play with. Open from 9:30 A.M. to 4:30 P.M. Closed on Mondays. From the north exit of Hachioji Station take a bus to the Fukushi Kaikan stop.

### Katsushika Museum and Planetarium (Katsushika-ku Kyodo to Temmon no Hakubutsukan)

3–25–1 Shiratori, Katsushika-ku, Tokyo　東京都葛飾区白鳥 3–25–1
☎ (03) 3838–1101
🚾 Ohanachaya Station, Keisei Line

Museum and planetarium are open 9:00 A.M. to 7:00 P.M. Tuesday through Thursday, 9:00 A.M. to 9:00 P.M. Friday and Saturday, 9:00 A.M. to 5:00 P.M. Sunday and holidays. Closed on Mondays and the second and fourth Tuesday each month.

### Kite Museum (Tako no Hakubutsukan)

1–12–10 Nihombashi, Chuo-ku, Tokyo　東京都中央区日本橋 1–12–10
☎ (03) 3275–2704
🚾 Nihombashi Station, Ginza, Tozai Lines
🕐 11:00 A.M. to 5:00 P.M. Closed Sundays and holidays.

Kites from around the world, including Brazil, Indonesia, Malaysia, and Japan. Admission: adults ¥200, children ¥100. The museum is located behind Nihombashi Tokyu Department Store.

### Mechanical Toy Museum (Kikaijikake no Omochakan)

Marine Tower, 3F, 15 Yamashita-cho, Naka-ku, Yokohama-shi, Kanagawa
☎ (045) 641–1595　神奈川県横浜市中区山下町15　マリンタワー 3F
🚾 Ishikawacho Station, JR Negishi Line

Sixty-odd movable displays that start up at preset intervals. Open Monday through Friday 10:00 A.M. to 7:00 P.M., 10:00 A.M. to 9:00 P.M. on Saturday, Sunday, and holidays. Admission: adults ¥200, children ¥100.

## Min-On Music Museum (Min-On Ongaku Shiryokan)

Min-on Bunka Center, 8 Shinanomachi, Shinjuku-ku, Tokyo
☎ (03) 5362–3555  東京都新宿区信濃町8 民音文化センター内
🚇 Shinanomachi Station, JR Sobu Line

Some one hundred thousand CDs and LDs on hand, all of which may be rented. Nine antique pianos. Open 11:00 A.M. to 4:00 P.M. Closed on Mondays. Admission is free.

## Musashino University of Music and Musical Instrument Museum (Musashino Ongaku Daigaku Gakki Hakubutsukan)

1–13–1 Hazawa, Nerima-ku, Tokyo  東京都練馬区羽沢 1–13–1
☎ (03) 3992–1121 (school), (03) 3992–1410 (museum)
🚇 Ekota Station, Seibu Ikebukuro line
🕐 10:30 A.M. to 3:00 P.M. Wednesdays only.

Three floors filled with musical instruments from around the world. Admission is free.

## Museum of Maritime Science (Fune-no-Kagakukan)

Higashi Yashio, Shinagawa-ku, Tokyo  東京都品川区東八潮
☎ (03) 5500–1111  📠 (03) 5500–1336
🚇 Fune-no-Kagakukan Station, Yurikamome Monorail Line; ferry from Takeshiba South Pier or Hinode Pier.
🕐 10:00 A.M. to 5:00 P.M. Monday through Friday, 10:00 A.M. to 6:00 P.M. Saturday and Sunday.

An incredible boat-shaped structure houses this collection of ships and their parts. You will find interesting displays and exhibitions inside.

## National Science Museum (Kokuritsu Kagaku Hakubutsukan)

7–20 Ueno Koen, Taito-ku, Tokyo  東京都台東区上野公園 7–20
☎ (03) 3822–0111
🚇 Ueno Station, JR Yamanote and various lines

The natural history museum is adjacent to Ueno Park (see chapter 6 under Zoos) and has exhibits on astronomy, botany, geology, and much more. If your child wants to see dinosaur bones, this is the place. Open from 9:00 A.M. to 4:30 P.M. daily. Closed on Mondays.

## Ome Railroad Park (Ome Tetsudo No Koen)

2–155 Katsunuma, Ome-shi, Tokyo  東京都青梅市勝沼 2–155
☎ (0428) 22–4678
🚇 Ome Station, JR Ome Line

The highlight of the Railroad Park is to see the "trains" run at 10:00 A.M., 11:00 A.M., 1:00 P.M., 2:00 P.M., and 3:00 P.M. You can also play on the locomotives in the park and view the miniature railways panorama.

Park hours are 9:15 A.M. to 5:00 P.M. It is closed on Mondays. To get there, take the JR Chuo Line to Tachikawa Station and change to the JR Ome Line. The park is a 15-minute walk from Ome Station.

### Orgel Music Box Museum (Orgel no Chiisana Hakubutsukan)

3–25–14 Mejirodai, Bunkyo-ku, Tokyo　東京都文京区目白台 3–25–14
☎ (03) 3941–0008
📍 Gokokuji Station, Yurakucho Line
🕐 1:30 P.M. and 3:00 P.M. Closed on weekends and holidays. Admission is ¥1,000. Call for reservations.

A display of cylinder and disk orgels, automats, and automatic pianos. A 1905 Orgel Diorama, made in Paris, sets windmills and boats in motion to the tune of *Beautiful Blue Danube.*

### Printing Bureau Museum

9–5 Ichigaya Hommura-cho, Shinjuku-ku, Tokyo　東京都新宿区市ヶ谷本村町 9–5
☎ (03) 3268–3271
📍 Ichigaya Station, JR Sobu, Yurakucho lines
🕐 9:30 A.M. to 4:30 P.M. Tuesday through Sunday. Closed on Mondays.

Really fascinating museum for kids old enough to be interested in money. You'll see a stack of one million dollars on display (which you can try to lift!), as well as examples of money from 122 countries around the world. There is a special section on counterfeiting and another on postage stamps.

### Science Museum (Kagaku Gijutsukan)

2–1 Kitanomaru Koen, Chiyoda-ku, Tokyo　東京都千代田区北の丸公園 2–1
☎ (03) 3212–8544
📍 Takebashi Station, Tozai Line

A museum with something for everyone, this large building houses exhibits on electronics, transportation, architecture, space exploration, and much, much more. Many of the displays are set up so that children can learn "hands on" about the subject. The museum is open from 9:30 A.M. to 4:50 P.M. daily.

### Shinkansen Museum (Shinkansen Shiryokan)

Kokubunji-shi Hikari Plaza, 1–46–8 Hikari-cho, Kokubunji-shi, Tokyo
☎ (0425) 73–4370　東京都国分寺市光町 1–46–8　国分寺市ひかりプラザ
📍 Kunitachi Station, JR Chuo Line

This fascinating bullet train museum showcases all the models, from the early Hikari of 1969 and 1972 to the latest Nozomi models. Open 10:00 A.M. to 4:30 P.M. (the railway exhibit room is open 9:00 A.M. to 5:00 P.M.). Closed the second and fourth Monday each month.

## Subway Museum

6–3–1 Higashi Kasai, Edogawa-ku, Tokyo　東京都江戸川区東葛西 6–3–1
☎ (03) 3878–5011
🚇 Kasai Station, Tozai Line
🕙 10:00 A.M. to 5:00 P.M. Closed Mondays.

The Subway Museum offers multisensory experiences—all featuring subways and how they work—for children and adults. There are many things here for children to do first-hand, such as blow train whistles and drive in a subway simulator. The museum is across the street from Kasai Station east exit.

## Sumo Museum (Sumo Hakubutsukan)

Kokugikan (Sumo Association Headquarters and Hall), 1F, 1–3–28 Yokoami, Sumida-ku, Tokyo　東京都墨田区横網 1–3–28　国技館 1F
☎ (03) 3622–0366
🚇 Ryogoku Station, JR Sobu Line

The history and highlights of sumo. Admission is free, except during tournaments, when access is limited to ticket holders.

## Sunshine City Planetarium

Sunshine City, 3–1–3 Higashi Ikebukuro, Toshima-ku, Tokyo
☎ (03) 3989–3466　東京都豊島区東池袋 3–1–3　サンシャインシティ
🚇 Higashi Ikebukuro Station, Yurakucho Line; Ikebukuro Station (Sunshine City exit), JR Yamanote and various lines

This planetarium (there is also an aquarium, see chapter 6) is the largest in Tokyo. As well as viewing the stars at night, you can have a grand view of the entire Kanto plain from the observatory on the top floor of the building. Call ahead or check the local city magazines for current program information. The planetarium is open daily from 10:00 A.M. to 8:00 P.M. (from 11:00 A.M. on Sunday and holidays).

## TEPCO Electric Energy Museum (TEPCO Denryokukan)

1–12–10 Jinnan, Shibuya-ku, Tokyo　東京都渋谷区神南 1–12–10
☎ (03) 3477–1191
🚇 Shibuya Station, JR Yamanote and various lines

Everything you ever wanted to know about electricity. The museum includes a variety of displays, question-and-answer computers, and video showings.

## Tokyo Tower

4–2–8 Shiba Koen, Minato-ku, Tokyo　東京都港区芝公園 4–2–8
☎ (03) 3433–5111
🚇 Kamiyacho Station, Hibiya Line; Daimon Station, Toei Asakusa Line

Tokyo Tower, the world's tallest self-supporting iron tower, holds a variety of amusements for you and your children. Besides the breathtaking view from the observatory, there is an aquarium (see chapter 6), a wax museum, and something called the Holographic Mystery Zone. There is also a floor full of ¥100 rides and games. The tower is open daily from 10:00 A.M., with extended evening hours in the summer months.

### Transportation Museum (Kotsu Hakubutsukan)

1–25 Kanda-Sudacho, Chiyoda-ku, Tokyo　東京都千代田区神田須田町 1–25
☎ (03) 3251–8481
🚃 Kanda Station, JR Yamanote, JR Keihin Tohoku, JR Chuo, Ginza lines; Akihabara Station, JR Yamanote, JR Sobu, JR Keihin Tohoku, Hibiya lines

This is mainly a rail museum, but you will also find exhibits of cars, bikes, airplanes, and ships. Much of the equipment can be climbed on or operated by children. Open from 9:30 A.M. to 5:00 P.M. The museum is closed on Mondays.

### Yokohama Children's Museum

5–2–1 Yokadai, Isogo-ku, Yokohama-shi, Kanagawa
☎ (045) 832–1166　神奈川県横浜市磯子区洋光台 5–2–1
🚃 Yokodai Station, JR Negishi Line

This is a museum with a planetarium, an omnimax theater, and a variety of displays and exhibits that can be used by children. For current program information, call the museum or check the listings in one of the city magazines. Hours are 9:30 A.M. to 5:00 P.M. Tuesday through Saturday, and 9:00 A.M. to 5:00 P.M. Sundays and holidays. Closed on Mondays. The museum is located behind the Yokohama Bank. The Children's Museum is located in the Yokohama Science Center.

### Yokohama Doll Museum (Yokohama Ningyo no Ie)

18 Yamashita-cho, Naka-ku, Yokohama-shi, Kanagawa
☎ (045) 671–9361　神奈川県横浜市中区山下町 18
🚃 Ishikawacho Station, JR Negishi Line; Yokohama Station, JR Tokaido and various lines

The Yokohama Doll Museum boasts over four thousand dolls from around the world, and it also hosts special arts events and performances. For more information, call the museum or check the local arts listings. Hours are 10:00 A.M. to 5:00 P.M. (until 7:00 P.M. in the summer). It is closed on Mondays. From Ishikawacho Station take the south exit and walk toward the Marine Tower. To get there from

Yokohama Station, leave by the east exit and take a bus (stop #2) from the bus terminal on the first floor of Sogo Department Store. Get off at the Yamashita Futo Iriguchi bus stop. The doll museum is easily recognizable by its pink, triangular-shaped roof.

## Yokohama Science Center

5–2–1 Yokodai, Isogo-ku, Yokohama-shi, Kanagawa
☎ (045) 832–1166　神奈川県横浜市磯子区洋光台 5–2–1
🚃 Yokodai Station, JR Negishi, JR Keihin Tohoku lines

"Space and Yokohama" is the museum's theme. Favorite pitstops include the planetarium, with its thirty-degree inclination dome, and the astronaut cockpit simulator. Admission to the center is ¥400 for adults, ¥200 for children (additional fee for Space Theater). Open 9:30 A.M. to 5:00 P.M. daily, 9:00 A.M. to 5:00 P.M. on Sunday and holidays. Closed on Monday and the day after a holiday.

THROUGHOUT JAPAN

Here are a handful of museums that are outstanding for one reason or another and should be visited if you live near them or are traveling in the area with your children.

## Himeji Museum of History (Hyogo Kenritsu Rekishi Hakubutsukan)

Hommachi 68, Himeji-shi, Hyogo　兵庫県姫路市本町 68
☎ (0792) 88–9011
🚃 Himeji Station, JR San'yo Main Line, JR Bantan, JR Kishin lines

This is an impressive history museum with many exhibits where children can enjoy hands-on experience. Hours are 10:00 A.M. to 5:00 P.M. It is closed on Mondays. To get there from Himeji Station, take a Shinki bus bound for Hirano-minamiguchi to Hakubutsukan-mae. You will be on the bus for about 15 minutes.

## The Hiroshima City Culture and Science Museum

5–83 Motomachi, Naka-ku, Hiroshima-shi, Hiroshima
☎ (082) 222–5346　広島県広島市中区基町 5–83
🚃 Gembaku Dome Mae Station, tramway line

This is a science museum that includes a planetarium with seasonal programs. It is open from 9:00 A.M. to 5:00 P.M. and closed on Mondays. From Gembaku Dome Mae Station, turn left. The museum is 5 minutes down the road past the city's baseball ground.

## Japan Toy Museum

671–3 Nakanino, Kodera-cho, Kanzaki-gun, Hyogo
☎ (0792) 32–4388　　兵庫県神崎郡香寺町中仁野 671–3
🚉 Koro Station, JR Bantan Line

The Japan Toy Museum houses changing exhibits of toys from around the world. Hours are from 10:00 A.M. to 5:00 P.M. It is closed on Wednesdays. Change to the Bantan Line at Himeji Station for the 20-minute ride to Koro Station. On foot, it takes about 20 minutes from the station to the museum.

## Kobe Maritime Museum (Kaiyo Hakubutsukan)

2–2 Hatoba-cho, Chuo-ku, Kobe-shi, Hyogo　兵庫県神戸市中央区波止場町 2–2
☎ (078) 391–6751
🚉 Motomachi Station, JR Tokaido Main Line, Hanshin Line

This is a maritime museum with exhibits of model ships and educational displays about the geography of the local area and how it was formed. Hours are 10:00 A.M. to 4:30 P.M., closed on Mondays. Call for information on summer opening times. The museum is located south of the station, about 12 minutes on foot.

## Modern Transport Museum (Kotsu Kagakukan)

3–11–10 Namiyoke, Minato-ku, Osaki-shi, Osaka
☎ (06) 6581–5771　　大阪府大阪市港区波除 3–11–10
🚉 Bentencho Station, Osaka Loop Line

Conveniently located next to the station, the Modern Transport Museum has real trains and other exhibits that children can climb on and pretend to drive. Hours are from 10:00 A.M. to 5:30 P.M. Closed on Mondays.

## Port Island Science Center and Planetarium (Kobe Shiritsu Seishonen Kagakukan)

7–7–6 Minatojima Nakamachi, Chuo-ku, Kobe-shi, Hyogo
☎ (078) 302–5177　　兵庫県神戸市中央区港島中町 7–7–6
🚉 Minami Koen Station, Port Liner

This museum and planetarium occupies a three-story building on Port Island. Call for special program information. The center is located near Kobe Portopia Land (see chapter 5). It is open from 9:30 A.M. to 4:30 P.M. Monday through Saturday and 10:00 A.M. to 5:00 P.M. on Sundays and holidays. It is closed on Wednesdays.

## World Children's Art Museum

1–1 Toriido, Oka-machi, Okazaki-shi, Aichi　愛知県岡崎市岡町鳥井戸 1–1
☎ (0564) 53–3511
🚆 Miai Station, Meitetsu Line

A unique complex adjacent to the Parent-Child Formative Center, in Okazaki City, this museum displays drawings by children from all over the world. In addition to the children's art, there are works by world-famous painters that were done in the artists' teenage years. Five permanent exhibits and five special exhibits are presented each year. The museum is open from 9:00 A.M. to 4:30 P.M. every day except Mondays. In summer, hours are extended to 5:30 P.M. To get there, take the Shinkansen (Tokaido Line) to Toyohashi. Change to the Meitetsu Line and get off at Miai Station. The museum is a 5-minute taxi ride from the station.

## *ALTERNATIVE LEARNING EXPERIENCES*

### Kobekko Land

1–3–1 Higashi Kawasaki-cho, Chuo-ku, Kobe-shi, Hyogo
☎ (078) 382–1300　兵庫県神戸市中央区東川崎町 1–3–1
🚆 Kobe Station, JR Tokaido and various lines

In 1987, the municipal government built Kobekko Land as a children's indoor center for play and learning. The facilities include not only play and exercise areas, but a performance hall and computer rooms as well. Kobekko Land is free for children up to age eighteen and accompanying parents or guardians. The center, located in Harbor Land, a 7-minute walk from Kobe Station, is open daily, except Monday, from 9:30 A.M. to 5:00 P.M.

Some of the attractions include video booths, where children can select and watch videos; an arts and crafts room with daily supervised projects; a music studio equipped with recording facilities; concerts, films, and plays in the three-hundred-seat Kobekko Hall; and a ham-radio corner. For the little ones, there is a play hall with a ball pool that toddlers adore.

### National Children's Castle

5–53–1 Jingu-mae, Shibuya-ku, Tokyo　東京都渋谷区神宮前 5–53–1
☎ (03) 3797–5665
🚆 Omotesando Station, Ginza, Hanzomon, Chiyoda lines

This unique establishment in Tokyo was built by the Ministry of Health and Welfare at a cost of ¥32.2 billion in 1985. It was entrusted into the hands of the Child Welfare Foundation of Japan as a place for children to dream, learn, play, and grow together. From its inception, the National Children's Castle has offered an outstanding selection of programs and activities for children and their parents.

To meet the increasing needs of international visitors and members, the castle has an International Division. Several Japanese staff members can speak English, and English-language information and catalogs are also available. Bilingual family theater programs are also held. For English information about the castle, you are welcome to call or inquire at the International Division, ☎ (03) 3797–5665, or write to the above address.

The complex consists of two main buildings that house numerous recreational and educational facilities. On the rooftops of both buildings are outdoor play areas. Our younger children prefer the vast Play Hall, on the third floor, where they can run and play on the indoor climbing equipment or engage in quiet play in the child-size kitchen and playhouse. Mothers of crawling babies will appreciate the tatami area and the soft toys provided for little ones.

Across from the Play Hall, the Fine Arts Studio always has art projects going on that the children can participate in. A favorite activity of ours is the long, white drawing board and jars of paint that even the youngest child can use. To the rear of the Play Hall is the Computer Play Room that houses the Computer Challenge Game, the first of its kind in the world. On the same floor there are also bathrooms, a rest area, and vending machines for drinks.

On the fourth floor, the Audio Visual Library has viewing booths for watching a favorite video or cartoon, available from the castle video library, which has over six thousand titles. Also on the fourth floor are the Music Lobby and Music Studios. Miniconcerts featuring international and ethnic music are put on here, and instruments are available for hands-on experiences.

There are two theaters in the castle. The Aoyama Theater puts on musicals, ballets, concerts, and plays, such as *Annie, Big River,* and *Hans.* The Aoyama Round Theater is smaller and more informal.

On the rooftop is an enclosed net area for frisbees and balls, and a Playport system jungle gym from the United States.

There is a restaurant on the first floor that offers everything from coffee to breakfast, lunch, and dinner; there is also a sushi bar on the first floor. On the second floor is a coffee shop, and on the eighth floor there is a French restaurant.

Other facilities at the castle include a health club with a swimming pool (for adults only). Also located in this building are the Child Care Center and Well Child Clinic, a hotel, a personal computer room, a gallery for exhibits, and rooms that may be rented for lectures, seminars, dinners, and luncheons. The hotel at the National Children's Castle is one of the best deals in town, offering very reasonable rates for families visiting Tokyo.

Classes are offered at the castle in everything from mother-and-baby swimming to percussion ensembles to recycled art. Unusual offerings also include classes for children with Down's syndrome and counseling for overweight or asthmatic children. You will find many events and classes to occupy the entire family all year round. The class schedule begins in April in accordance with the Japanese school system. When you register for classes, you will be charged a class fee and a ¥1,000 registration fee that is good for three years. While enrolled in a class, you will receive a membership card which entitles you to free admission to the castle. Registration for classes must be done in person, but you may call for class information. All classes are taught in Japanese except for a few that are taught bilingually (in English and Japanese).

Even if you do not take a class, you might consider becoming a member of the Children's Castle by joining the Tomo no Kai membership circle. Initial membership costs ¥1,500 (the application fee), and yearly dues are ¥2,000 per family. Members receive the colorful Castle Newsletter in Japanese six times per year; free general admission tickets; prior notice, early reservation, and discount privileges for castle events and theater programs; and discounts on purchases made in the castle shops.

The castle hours are weekdays (Tuesday through Friday) from 12:30 P.M. to 5:30 P.M.; Saturdays, Sundays, and holidays from 10:00 A.M. to 5:30 P.M.; winter, spring, and summer vacations (Japanese school system) from 10:00 A.M. to 5:30 P.M. The castle is closed on Mondays or Tuesdays when Monday is a national holiday. It is open for all national holidays except at New Year's.

Admission is ¥500 for adults and ¥400 for children. When accompanied by an adult, children under three enter free. Group rates are available. Special activity programs for school groups are held in the morning.

### Tokyo Metropolitan Children's Museum (Tokyo-to Jido Kaikan)

1–18–24 Shibuya-ku, Shibuya, Tokyo　東京都渋谷区渋谷 1–18–24
☎ (03) 3409–6361
🚃 Shibuya Station, JR Yamanote and various lines

This is a wonderful place for children and parents to come and play, learn, and explore. The Jido Kaikan is a children's center located near Shibuya Station. Renovated in 1990, this six-story building is overflowing with interesting things to entertain the kids.

There is a small outdoor playground next to the building, but the real fun is inside. Starting in the basement level, there are small rides and electronic games for the children to play. For young children, the wooden toy corner is full of cars, blocks, pretend food, and riding toys, all made of top-quality wood. The first floor is the lobby and information center, and on the second floor is an indoor playground and infant-nursing room. The third floor has science and computer games, and the fourth floor has conference rooms that are used as music space and for lectures. The fifth floor is a small library (most books are Japanese), and the roof boasts yet another playground.

The layout of the building is easy to figure out, and bathrooms with baby changing facilities are clearly marked on each floor. There are a couple of restaurants in the building where you can get a light meal or snack, and there are plenty of chairs for weary parents to rest in while the kids burn off some energy.

The Jido Kaikan is the only one of its kind in Tokyo. However, many of the wards and cities in Tokyo run local *jido-kan*, or children's halls. Some wards have only one or two, while others, such as Minato-ku, have as many as twelve. These children's centers are smaller in scale than the one in Shibuya and do not offer as many services, but they can be convenient resources if there is one in your neighborhood. Some of them offer after-school programs, called "schoolchildren's clubs," for children who come home to an empty house after school.

For information on what programs are run in your area, contact your ward or city office and inquire about the local *jido-kan*.

## CHILDREN'S TELEVISION PROGRAMS

Japanese television programs for toddlers and teens include numerous cartoons of one type or another. Some of these are long-running character cartoons that have spawned all types of accessories featuring the same characters. Others are stories in the Disney style, or old

Disney cartoons dubbed in Japanese, and still others are Japanese action-adventure with too much violence for our taste. Just be aware that the cartoon scene is a mixed bag, and the smartest thing to do before allowing your children to watch any cartoon is to preview it yourself. One Japanese friend says that maybe half of the cartoons on TV are suitable for young children.

As for TV in general, there are many more choices in programming with the advent of cable. A recent development is the availability of the Discovery Channel, which offers educational programs in English with Japanese subtitles. For more information, contact your local cable operator, or PerfecTV Customer Center at ☎ (0570) 03–9888.

# Celebrating in Japan

31 DECEMBER

THESE LONG "SOBA" NOODLES
REPRESENT HOPES FOR A LONG LIFE.

For young children, life in a foreign country is a fun-filled adventure. One of the most fascinating aspects of living in a foreign country is the chance to experience the native culture and its traditions. We are continually surprised at how many opportunities there are for our children to participate in Japan's festive offerings. Often, the very fact that we have young children makes it more likely that we will come across these celebrations. There is no better way to get into the spirit of things than to participate in the festivities of your host country with your children.

## CELEBRATING JAPANESE HOLIDAYS

Japan has many national holidays. Some, such as the ones listed here, are more meaningful and fun for children than others. For the Japanese, national holidays are often just a day to stay at home and either relax or get some projects done around the house. Other holidays are times for traveling with the family, while still others are for dressing up and visiting the local shrine for a ceremony or formal portrait to mark the day. When asked about the visits to the shrine, most Japanese will reply that for them it is more of a cultural tradition than a religious rite. You will soon learn which shrines are popular in your area, and which holidays are for traveling or for staying at home.

There are also other holidays that are important in different regions of the country. For example, Tanabata (July 7) is a relatively quiet holiday in most of the country, perhaps marked by a small celebration at home. Sendai (in Miyagi Prefecture), however, is famous for its Tanabata Festival. It is one of the largest festivals of the year, and people from all over the country know that if you want to celebrate Tanabata in a big way, you have to go to Sendai. (However, be aware that in many places, including Sendai, the festival is celebrated on August 7.)

Celebrations may differ from neighborhood to neighborhood as well. During our first year here, on *keiro no hi* (Respect for the Aged Day), all the children in the neighborhood lined up to carry the *omikoshi,* or portable shrine, to the park where the old people in the neighborhood gather. Japanese mothers urged us to join the procession with our children, and upon arrival at the park we were greeted by elderly people from the neighborhood who had prepared bags of goodies for all the children. To this day, *keiro no hi* (September 15) remains our children's favorite national holiday. Nevertheless, when I told my friends—both Japanese and foreign—about this event near our house, they replied that they had never heard of, or experienced, anything like it in their neighborhood. The best advice we have for you on this matter is just to keep your eyes open!

Many festivities are cause for children—and adults—to dress in traditional costume. Even the international schools have celebrations where Japanese dress is appropriate. Besides being a useful item while you are here, investment in a kimono for your daughter or *hakama* for your son can serve as a memento of your stay long after you have moved on to another country.

There are many opportunities to obtain these traditional costumes at reduced prices. Rental companies often sell off their stock at big discounts in department store sales. Such sales are usually advertised in English newspapers and magazines. Once you attend a sale and register your name, you will receive announcements of upcoming sales. You can also rent traditional clothes for a special occasion from the catalog companies listed in chapter 2.

Another option for purchasing these costumes is the small stores on neighborhood shopping streets, where prices are often lower than at the department stores. If you do purchase an outfit at a neighborhood store, they will show you how to dress your child. For the girls, it's a bit complicated, unless you have a Japanese grandmother to teach you! Or you can make an appointment at your local hairdresser or a nearby hotel. They will usually have an employee experienced in the intricacies of putting on a kimono. They will also put up your daughter's hair using exquisite hair ornaments which you can buy to match her costume.

Tokyo's major festivals and events are listed in the monthly

"Calendar Events," available at the Tourist Information Center, in Yurakucho (see Visiting Japan in chapter 1). You can pick up a copy toward the end of each month, or call the Teletourist Information Line, at ☎ (03) 3201– 2911 for twenty-four-hour recorded information.

Food plays an integral part in any holiday, and in Japan there are a few basic foods that are prepared for holidays or special events. For example, *osekihan*, a mixture of sticky rice and red beans, is a traditional festive food. The red beans make the rice pinkish red; red is considered an auspicious color, and so *osekihan* is served on any festival day or birthday in the family. Many traditional foods can be found ready-made in your local grocery store. Others are easy to make at home, and a basic Japanese cookbook can tell you how.

Every month in Japan brings a new and different holiday or event. To experience Japan through a child's eyes, try to incorporate some of these holidays into your own family traditions.

### *THE NEW YEAR HOLIDAY* (OSHOGATSU)

The first three days of January are all national holidays to celebrate the New Year. On December 31, or *omisoka*, the Japanese hurry about preparing for the new year and participate in events geared to getting rid of all the bad fortune accumulated during the past year. On New Year's Eve, the traditional food is *soba* noodles, eaten around midnight. These long noodles represent hopes for a long life. Homes are  decorated with *kadomatsu*, or arrangements of pine branches and bamboo, and ropes hung with white paper strips decorate gateways and doorways to ensure luck in the new year. At midnight, the bells in the shrines and temples toll 108 times to symbolize the banishing of man's 108 sinful desires. The shrines and temples are filled with throngs of people not only at midnight, but for the duration of the holiday. People greet one another with congratulations for the new year, "*akemashite omedeto gozaimasu*" is the greeting you will hear everywhere.

New Year's Day is the most important day for children, although this national holiday is rather solemn compared with some of the other holidays. At New Year's, children receive money from relatives in specially decorated envelopes called *otoshidama*. Although some parents insist that their children save a portion of the gift, many allow them to spend the full amount on whatever their hearts desire. Now you know why kids look forward to the New Year's celebration so much! Other than receiving money and playing a number of traditional Japanese games, there is not much else going on for children at New Year's.

On January 1, the new year is welcomed by eating *mochi*, a paste made by pounding cooked rice in a mortar with a pestle. Most of the Japanese schools and some of the international schools will have a *mochi*-pounding ceremony at school. If you travel to any of the winter resorts in Japan over the New Year holiday, you will possibly get a chance to experience these foods at the lodge where you stay. *Osechi ryori* is another traditional New Year's food. This *obento* smorgasbord of Japanese delights can be ordered and delivered to your home from department stores and restaurants, but be sure to place your order early. One of our Japanese friends told us that many people now order from a store and that few people actually make these traditional foods at home anymore.

Most stores and businesses are closed for the first few days of January, and the cities tend to be rather deserted because many families travel to their hometown or ancestral home over the holidays. Once January 3 comes, the stores reopen and all the children rush to department stores and toy stores to spend their *otoshidama*.

### FEBRUARY 3 OR 4: BEAN-THROWING FESTIVAL (SETSUBUN)

Although early February still seems like winter in much of Japan, *setsubun* celebrates the first day of the new year, according to the ancient solar calendar, and the traditional beginning of spring. This is celebrated by throwing beans and shouting, "*oni wa soto*" ("Out with evil") and "*fuku wa uchi*" ("In with good luck"). This act of purification, said to date from the Muromachi period (1333–1568), was believed to be essential to prepare oneself for the coming year and the spring planting season. You can join the crowds who go to the temple to throw beans, but it's much more fun for the kids to do it at home.

Look in your supermarket for dried soybeans, which are prominently displayed at this time of year. (One mother told us she switched to roasted peanuts in the shell because they were easier to clean up.) Usually children are allowed to throw the number of beans that correlate to their age, which makes the mess minimal for preschoolers.

In most Japanese homes with small children, a devil-like monster mask is made, and the father wears it while the children chase him around the house. Eventually, they chase him outside while they shout "*oni wa soto*" as they throw the beans out of the door or window, and "*fuku wa uchi*" when they toss beans around the house.

## MARCH 3: DOLL FESTIVAL OR GIRLS' DAY (HINA MATSURI)

This festival for girls features a set of *hina* dolls arranged on a tier of shelves covered with bright red cloth. We were shocked to find out how expensive these miniature dolls are. Sets in department stores range from ¥50,000 to ¥200,000 and up. Traditionally, when the first daughter is born, she inherits her mother's set of dolls or the grandparents buy a new set. In other cases, girls may receive one doll each year until they have a full set. The basic set consists of an emperor and empress and attendants and musicians in ancient court dress. Some families opt for just the emperor and empress. Most foreigners decide not to indulge in this expensive souvenir and settle for viewing the lavish displays of dolls at the department stores. Some parents have procured "antique" dolls at flea markets at very little cost. This is perfectly acceptable for foreigners, but you would not find the Japanese using a discarded doll set. The set of dolls can be put out any time beginning in February, but they are always put away on March 3, because of the superstitious belief that, otherwise, a girl won't get married until late.

It is a real treat to be invited by a Japanese family to view their daughter's doll collection. If you feel that you must have at least one doll to commemorate this special day, look for the dolls at one of the discount stores, or rent the whole set from one of the rental companies (see chapter 3).

On Girls' Day, you will see young girls celebrating with their families, wearing their best kimono or Western dress and eating traditional foods, such as *osekihan*. A special dish for this day is *chirashi-zushi*, or sushi rice with cooked vegetables mixed in. You will also see in the grocery stores the *hishimochi* (diamond-shaped rice cake) colored pink, green, and white, and colorful puffed rice "*hina* snacks." These pastel colors for Girls' Day are a pleasant reminder that spring is just around the corner.

## EARLY APRIL: CHERRY-BLOSSOM VIEWING (OHANAMI)

Perfect pink blossoms suddenly arrive to fill the sky and just as quickly are blown away. This short period of beauty is celebrated by all Japanese in early April or sometimes late March, depending on when the blooms are at their best. Watch the newspapers for reports on the approaching cherry blossom "front."

Children love the cherry blossom season. Favorite places for picnics under the trees in Tokyo are Aoyama Cemetery, Yasukuni Shrine, and Ueno Park. A group of mothers with their children meet for a big picnic in Aoyama Cemetery every year. All you need are blankets and food to make a special outing. The sky is hidden by a cover of blossoms, and toward the end of the peak week they flutter down on your face like snowflakes.

If you are more adventurous, you might want to attempt an *ohanami* party at night. To do this, go to a park early in the morning of the picnic and stake out a spot for your group. Cherry blossoms by moonlight give the picnic another flavor entirely. Be sure to bring enough flashlights or lanterns so you can see what you are eating! There will be a party going on every few feet, but the park is surprisingly dark at night and you won't feel as if you're in a crowd. *Ohanami* is fun to do with several other families. Just park the car, pile all your gear on the stroller, and head for the site. It is safe, night or day, and you and your children will probably be asked to join in some of the other parties nearby. Everyone is friendly and often a little drunk during the annual week of cherry blossoms.

### APRIL 29 TO MAY 5: GOLDEN WEEK

Golden Week is the name given to the series of holidays that come in quick succession at the end of April and the beginning of May. It is the "spring break" of Japan, and everyone who is able to takes off work and travels. The first day of Golden Week, April 29—formerly Emperor Showa's birthday—is called Greenery Day. At the end of Golden Week is *kodomo no hi*, or Children's Day. In between, there is Constitution Day (May 3) and Citizens' Holiday (May 4). Depending on the days on which the holidays fall, it's possible to take just one day off, combine it with the national holidays, and end up with a week-long break. Bear in mind that most Japanese will also be taking advantage of the holidays to travel; if you plan to take a trip, you will need to make reservations as far in advance as possible. Many people even make reservations a year ahead to be sure of taking a holiday. Recently, companies are tending to shut down for the whole of Golden Week, but the practice has not spread to all Japanese schools yet. Even so, you can be sure that all amusement parks and tourist spots will be very crowded on these holidays.

### MAY 5: CHILDREN'S DAY (KODOMO NO HI)

Formerly known as Boys' Day, this national holiday involves some special rites for the sons in the family. Streamers with a carp (*koi*) design are flown from the rooftop, balcony, or flagpole in the garden. The carp is recognized for its strength in swimming against the current and parents hope that their sons will have this same strength and determination.

For May 5, boys sometimes set up a display of dolls on a tiered platform. These dolls are feudal warriors clad in miniature armor. If you decide to invest in a set of these *gogatsu ningyo*, be aware that the red cloth and tiers come together with the dolls. Some people have just one samurai figure as their display. The figures are set up in April and can be taken down anytime after May 5.

Festive food is a big part of the Children's Day celebration. Families serve *osekihan* and *chimaki*, a mixture of *mochi* and rice. Another special dish is *tai* (sea bream), which can be elaborately prepared for you by most department stores. At this time you can easily spot accessories and foods in all the local shops, which makes joining in these celebrations fun and easy.

### JULY 7: STAR FESTIVAL (TANABATA)

The celebration of the Tanabata Festival originates in a Chinese legend about two stars who are lovers but are separated by the Milky Way. The two stars can meet only once a year on the seventh day of the seventh month. On this day, everyone writes down his wish—it's always fun to see what the little ones have to say—and hangs it on a cut bamboo branch that is placed in front of the house. The wish, or sometimes poem, is written on a strip of paper and hung on the branch together with origami ornaments. At the end of the festivities, the branch is usually thrown into a river to symbolize the ridding of misfortune or sometimes put in a field and used as a scarecrow.

### OCTOBER, SECOND MONDAY: SPORTS DAY (TAIIKU NO HI)

Sports Day in Japan is a national holiday focusing on fitness. Around the time of this holiday, many schools and communities hold their annual field day, or *undokai*. If you live in an area where a community sports day is held, be sure to take part in the fun. The whole family can get involved in races, games, and all manner of good-natured competition.

Most schools hold some form of sports day during the autumn. These competitions often resemble a mini-Olympics, with banners, prizes, and the students decked out in team colors. Parents are encouraged to attend these events, so be prepared to do your part in the name of team spirit!

### NOVEMBER 15: SEVEN-FIVE-THREE DAY (SHICHI-GO-SAN)

On this day, children all over Japan are celebrated. How wonderful to live in a society where children are so precious! *Shichi-go-san* literally means "seven-five-three" and describes the day when three- and seven-year-old girls and five-year-old boys are taken to a Shinto shrine by their parents to give thanks to the deities for their children and to pray for their good health.

This is a day that parents mark with a formal photograph. You will see children of all ages dressed in their best on this day. Children of the designated ages, in particular, are decked out in their first kimono or in Western-style clothes. Most shrines conduct a brief ceremony in which you are welcome to participate. At the larger shrines, pay the fees (¥5,000 or so) at the counter and wait in an adjoining room for your group to be called. After the priest has chanted and waved his wand of streamers across the row of children standing with their parents, it is time to file out. In addition to the ceremony, children receive a good-luck souvenir and *chitose ame*, or one-thousand-year-candy, to ensure a long life. You can purchase these at one of the counters even if you don't want to take part in the ceremony. At the smaller shrines, the priest is more likely to greet you personally and give your children a private ceremony.

Foreigners in Japan can make this day a memorable one for their children by cooking a favorite food for dinner, baking a cake, or planning a special family activity.

### DECEMBER 25: CHRISTMAS IN JAPAN

This holiday is listed under both the Japanese and the Western traditions. Most Japanese families with children celebrate Christmas. The religious aspects of Christmas are nonexistent, however, except for those Japanese who are Christians.

Santa Claus comes to Japan, just as he does to other countries, with a gift for good little boys and girls. Since Saint Nick is a tradition borrowed from Western culture, customs vary from house to house. Instead of coming down the chimney and leaving gifts under the Christmas tree, Santa may leave them outside on the balcony on Christmas morning. One Japanese mother told us that the presents at their house appear on Christmas Eve while the children are having their bath!

As with many other Western customs, the Japanese have tailored Christmas to suit their own lifestyle. The bakeries have come up with "Christmas cakes" that have become an indispensable part of Christmas celebrations. However, you'll be surprised to find that a Japanese Christmas cake is a plain sponge cake covered in cream and decorated with strawberries, which is much more to the Japanese taste than a rich fruit cake. You can order these elaborately decorated cakes (sleighs and Santas are the usual motifs) at all bakeries and some grocery stores. Just look for the poster of the cream-covered cake—but be warned that they usually look better than they taste! Also, the Japanese eat roast chicken on Christmas rather than the turkey that is popular in the United States.

In the past few years it has become trendy for young couples to make Christmas Eve a romantic night out. Your Christmas Eve date is all-important, and hotels and fine restaurants offer special Christmas Eve packages. Young people make plans early for what is becoming for many Japanese the most romantic night for the year.

Christmas is for children all over the world, and Japan is no exception. However, adults do not often exchange presents, nor is it traditionally a time for a family gathering (this takes place over the New Year). Santa is the primary gift-giver in Japan, and he usually brings one present for each child.

## CELEBRATING WESTERN HOLIDAYS IN JAPAN

Before we had children, we never gave much thought as to how traditional Western holidays could be celebrated in Japan. Once we became parents, it suddenly was important to know where we could get Halloween costumes, stocking stuffers for Christmas, valentines, and Easter-egg dye. Like most parents, we wanted our children to experience the same holiday traditions we had enjoyed, despite the fact that we were far from our native country. Keeping family traditions alive is important wherever you live. When you live overseas, it takes forethought, time, and money, but the result is worth it.

During the past few years, trendy Tokyo and much of the rest of Japan have embraced many popular Western customs. For the majority of holidays, especially the more commercial ones, the Japanese have begun to celebrate in their own way to some degree. Often the celebration is a variation of the holiday we know as Westerners, but at least there is a festive air on that day, and some essential holiday items are available in the stores. The list in the holiday supplies section of this chapter will lead you to the basic items and the mail-order companies will fill the gap.

### FEBRUARY 14: VALENTINE'S DAY

Valentine's Day in Japan is one of those holidays with which the Japanese have taken more than a few liberties. In essence, it is the day when women give the men in their lives (boyfriends, co-workers, bosses) a token of their affection, usually candy, called *giri choko*, or "obligation chocolate." Then on White Day, March 14, the men must reciprocate with gifts for the women who gave them candy. A well-known underwear manufacturer has even tried to turn this holiday to its advantage by urging men to buy white lingerie for their loved ones.

From the end of January, you will see Valentine candy in many stores in creative styles for everyone in the family. Because in the West, Valentine's Day is for giving candy, flowers, and cards to your sweetheart, this selection comes in handy for foreigners. Its quality varies widely, and as with anything in Japan, you get what you pay for.  Chocolate animal, toy, and doll shapes are all available, and they make perfect valentines for children and the young at heart. There are also valentine card displays in some shops, but the cards are usually expensive. We like to let the children make their own to give to friends or to send to relatives overseas. Paper, doilies, heart stickers, and a little glue are all you need.

### EASTER

Yes, the Easter bunny does come to Japan. You can buy egg dye here and even cellophane grass for your basket. Most good florists have a selection of straw baskets; this can be the year that you hand-paint your child's basket with his name and some Easter decorations.

For young children, Easter usually means fancy clothes, the Easter bunny, and Easter egg hunts. This is one of those holidays that is extra fun in Japan because of the relative safety of the parks and playgrounds. The weather is usually beautiful at this time of year, and you can gather a group of friends with children and have a real old-fashioned Easter egg hunt in a park. One family we know invites twenty to thirty friends to meet in Yoyogi Park each Easter for a picnic and egg hunt. Any nearby park is suitable for such a gathering, and perhaps this will become an annual tradition for your family, too.

### JULY 4: INDEPENDENCE DAY IN THE UNITED STATES

Because we are Americans, we decided to list this holiday for all those who wonder how to celebrate Independence Day while in Japan. In fact, our suggestions can be used to help families from any foreign country understand and participate in their home country's special patriotic day.

In the United States, the Fourth of July involves barbecues, swimming, watermelon, and fireworks. Even though you will miss the picnics back home, if you are like us, you may want your children to experience some of the pride and excitement that go along with any patriotic celebration. Some of the ways to do this require a little forethought, but they are well worth it. Here are some ideas we have tried: hang your country's flag around the house or even outside; cook the  traditional foods for the celebration during the week and let the children participate, perhaps relating to them stories of your childhood or what their relatives will be doing back home on the day of celebration; read stories about your home country and this particular event in its history; play traditional patriotic music, your national anthem, or other favorite songs, and dance around the house; on the holiday itself, have the entire family dress in the colors associated with your country (in the U.S., of course, red, white, and blue). Even a two-year-old can learn the name of the country he comes from and enjoy the festivities that you have planned to make this day special.

### OCTOBER 31: HALLOWEEN/ALL SAINTS' EVE

Halloween is another Western holiday that is gaining popularity with the Japanese, especially among teenagers and young adults. In the West, the door-to-door quest for treats is the highlight of Halloween for the under-twelve set (and their parents). In Japan, however, that part of the tradition has not caught on, and the holiday is usually celebrated the weekend before with costume parades, parties, and contests. These are activities the whole family can enjoy. Look for signs on the street and in the paper each year for the annual Halloween festival in Tokyo at Kiddyland on Omotesando, in Daikanyama-Ebisu area, and in Aoyama. Unfortunately, jack-o'-lanterns have not become a common sight during Halloween, although pumpkins are available at some supermarkets such as National Azabu, in Hiroo.

In Japan, door-to-door trick-or-treating is a safe activity for young children. The foreign community often practices this tradition within their own neighborhoods. If you don't live where there are other foreigners nearby, you can always call a few friends and ask them if you can come by with your ghosts and goblins to give them a chance to pick up a few treats and show off their costumes.

## NOVEMBER 23: LABOR THANKSGIVING DAY
## (KINRO KANSHA NO HI)

No matter what country you are from, the harvest season is a good opportunity for children to learn about the traditions and history of their own country, and to learn to give thanks for all they have. Every culture has a harvest celebration in the fall, and Japan is no exception. Japan's harvest celebration, commonly known as Labor Thanksgiving Day, is a Japanese national holiday. Because it falls in late November, when Americans traditionally celebrate Thanksgiving, some expatriate families find it convenient to have their Thanksgiving Day dinner on this Japanese holiday. American Thanksgiving foods are freely available in Tokyo and other large cities. Turkeys, canned or fresh pumpkin, and fall foods such as apples and chestnuts are in abundant supply.

## DECEMBER 25: CHRISTMAS

You may be surprised to hear Christmas carols in your supermarket as early as October, but the Japanese merchants go all out for Christmas. When you are downtown shopping, keep your eyes open for some spectacular decorations.

The commercialization of this Christian holiday means that you will have no trouble getting a tree and all the trimmings in Japan. The trees are rather expensive—¥10,000 and up in Tokyo—and they often come as live trees in a pot. Recently, artificial trees have become popular with the Japanese; they are sold in large department stores.

In Tokyo, we take the children to see the lighted tree at Aoyama Gakuin University, where they also have handbell and choral concerts in early December. Refugees International Japan sponsors a large tree at Tokyo Station, and they have special concerts and events there during the weeks before Christmas. Hibiya City Ice-Skating Rink is Tokyo's version of Rockefeller Center and is a great outing for the entire family.

Throughout Japan, the Japanese have what they call the season of *daiku*, when groups get together to perform Beethoven's Ninth Symphony. It runs through December, and you can choose from a vast number of performances by first-rate orchestras. Other Christmas favorites are the *Messiah* and the *Nutcracker Suite*. Look for listings of these events in English-language newspapers and magazines. When our children were too young to attend these performances, we played recordings of the music around the house at Christmastime to get in the spirit of the season.

Some families take advantage of the long holiday that includes Christmas and New Year's to take a vacation trip to an exotic place in the South Pacific or Asia. The Philippines, being primarily a Catholic country, is a special place to visit at Christmastime. Many resorts offer Christmas packages for families with children; if you plan on doing this, be sure to make reservations well in advance.

If you decide to stay in Japan over the holidays, you can still make Christmas without your extended family a memorable occasion. Organize a festive meal with friends and neighbors. Get in the Christmas spirit by spending time together decorating the house and preparing traditional holiday foods.

### Christmas Cards

Each year, Refugees International Japan sells greeting cards designed especially for them by major artists living in Japan. The cards make attractive and original Christmas or New Year's greetings, and the proceeds go to Refugees International Japan, a nonprofit organization run by volunteers. For information, contact Refugees International Japan; ☎ (03) 5500–3093, from 10:00 A.M. to 3:00 P.M. UNICEF Japan also has a beautiful catalog of Christmas cards from Japan. For a catalog, call ☎ (03) 3355–3255 or write to UNICEF House, 2F, 31–10 Daikyo-cho, Shinjuku-ku, Tokyo.

Christmas cards that feature photographs can be ordered at a very reasonable rate from Associated Photo Co. in the United States. The cards come with matching envelopes, and there are a variety of Christmas patterns to choose from. This company also prints photo birth announcements, invitations, and We've Moved cards. For information, contact ☎ (513) 421–6620, 🖷 (513) 421–6622, or write to the company at Box 14270, Dept. R, Cincinnati, Ohio 45250, USA. Visa and Master-Card are accepted.

### New Year's Cards (*Nengajo*)

Your local photo shop can make up fairly inexpensive New Year's postcards in a week or so with your family photo on the front. These cards usually say "Happy New Year" in Japanese. There is, however, room on the border for you to write your own greeting and sign your name. At larger photo shops, you will find a variety of Christmas and New Year's photo postcards that can be printed for you in English. For a little bit more money, you may have a fully personalized greeting on the card, such as "Merry Christmas and Happy New Year from the Smith Family."

## BIRTHDAY PARTIES

When it comes to celebrating birthdays overseas, many parents go to extra lengths to make birthdays special for their children. You may miss having relatives around, but even without them there are usually more than enough people to invite to your child's party. School friends, neighbors, and just about anyone who knows and cares about your child will want to be invited. This can be a problem if you do not live in a house or apartment large enough for a crowd. We have some alternative locations for you. Of course, for very young children you may want to follow the rule of thumb that says invite one guest for each year of your child's life (i.e., one child guest for a one-year-old's party, two for a two-year-old's, and so on).

Many of the stores listed in this chapter will become your sources for all types of birthday-party supplies. From paper goods to game prizes, balloons to party hats, these stores have them.

Chances are that one of the local McDonald's restaurants has a special room available for birthday parties. Since each restaurant is independently owned, you will have to check on your own. As an example, the McDonald's in Musashi Koyama Mall, ☎ (03) 3781–3417 (see chapter 2 under Shopping Districts), offers to provide, for a minimum of six children, a birthday cake (about ¥1,000) and a McDonald's lunch for the birthday boy or girl and guests. There are no other charges—except the hamburgers, of course. The big advantage to this plan is that you do not risk demolition of your house, and when the party is over you can get up and go and simply leave the mess behind.

Rooms are available at other restaurants, and the wards usually have some sort of public space available for rent for a small fee. Call your ward office to see what they have and plan on reserving these rooms weeks or even months in advance. The Sizzler Restaurant chain has a birthday club for ages two to six. Just fill out a form at the restaurant and give it to your server. They will mail you a coupon good for a free salad bar (all you can eat!), a cake, and a present for the boy or girl. The Sizzler on Meguro Dori, 6–13–11 Todoroki, Setagaya-ku, Tokyo, ☎ (03) 3705–3339, is a favorite with many families due to the playground just across the street. There is also free parking. The Rock 'n' Roll Diner in Shimokitazawa, ☎ (03) 3111–6565, has a Birthday Club for kids.

For those of you who are lucky enough to live near a large park, outdoor parties can be easy. That is, of course, unless it rains. Check beforehand to see if the park has covered facilities for reservation or rent. Kinuta Park in Setagaya (see chapter 5) has a large carpeted room available for a small rental fee. You can have the cake and presents inside and, if the weather is nice, have the children play games outside.

Other alternative locations are the amusement parks or zoos in your area. This is a big adventure and, if you are paying, it can be a big expense. If you decide to do this, enlist the other mothers' help, and put the kids on a budget. For party favors, you could give the kids matching T-shirts or badges to wear on the outing. If you wish to have fast food delivered to your home for a party, Domino's and Pizza Hut both deliver (they accept faxes) and are English-friendly. Check the TownPage telephone directory for the ones nearest you.

## PHOTOGRAPHY STUDIOS

During your stay in Japan, you may want to visit a professional studio to have some commemorative photos taken. The following studios are known for their excellent work.

### Ark Photo Salon / Formal Wear Rental

1–21–7 Ebisu Nishi, Shibuya-ku, Tokyo　東京都渋谷区恵比寿西 1–21–7
☎ (03) 3476–4141
🚋 Ebisu Station, JR Yamanote, Hibiya lines

At Ark, your whole family can dress up in fancy clothes (Japanese or Western style) and pose for a portrait in the shop's digital camera photo salon.

### Clique Productions

☎ (03) 3584–0548   📠 (03) 3584–0549
💻 <neil-clique@shrine.cyber.ad.jp>, <simon-clique@shrine.cyber.ad.jp>

Neil Krivonak, the professional photographer behind Clique Productions, has gained quite a reputation for his photos of children. His specialty is family portraits, which he will take at any location.

### Igarashi Studio

Hotel Okura Annex, 2F, 2–10–4 Toranomon, Minato-ku, Tokyo
☎ (03) 3586–1690   東京都港区虎の門 2–10–4　ホテルオークラ別館　2F
🚈 Toranomon Station, Ginza Line; Kamiyacho Station, Hibiya Line

This studio has been a favorite with foreigners in Tokyo for many years. Prices are around ¥15,000 a sitting, with special prices for children offered several times a year. Look for their ad in the *Japan Times*.

## HOLIDAY SUPPLIES AND GIFT SHOPS

There are a few stores that you can always count on to have a supply of seasonal decorations, cards, costume supplies, and gifts. The following list should help you find most of what you will need to celebrate the holidays.

### Itoya

2–7–15 Ginza, Chuo-ku, Tokyo   東京都中央区銀座 2–7–15
☎ (03) 3561–8311
🚈 Ginza 1-chome Station, Yurakucho Line; Ginza Station, Marunouchi, Ginza, Hibiya lines
🕐 10:00 A.M. to 7:00 P.M. Monday through Saturday, 10:30 A.M. to 7:00 P.M. Sunday and holidays.

There are six branches of this stationery shop in Tokyo: the main shop in Ginza and the other branches in Tamagawa Takashimaya Mall (see chapter 2), Shibuya Design House, Marunouchi File Shop, Garden Plaza Hiroo, and the Kasumigaseki Building. Itoya has every stationery item you could ever wish for, as well as many clever ones you did not know you needed. It also has a good selection of seasonal cards, pins, stickers, small decorations, and art supplies.

## Bungu Star

5–2–2 Roppongi, Minato-ku, Tokyo　　東京都港区六本木 5–2–2

☎ (03) 5474–2128　　🖷 (03) 5474–5845

🚈 Roppongi Station, Hibiya Line

🕐 11:00 A.M. to 8:00 P.M. Closed on Sundays and holidays.

Although at first glance this appears to be a stationery store, it also carries wrapping paper, seasonal decorations, and all kinds of unique gifts. Conveniently located on Gaien-Higashi Dori near Starbucks.

## Office Depot

•TOC, 1F, 7–22–17 Nishi Gotanda, Shinagawa-ku, Tokyo
東京都品川区西五反田 7–22–17　TOC 1F

☎ (03) 3494–5555　　toll-free 0120–77–8700 (catalog shopping: 8:00 A.M. to 6:00 P.M.)

•Ginza branch: 1–2–3 Ginza, Chuo-ku, Tokyo　　東京都中央区銀座 1–2–3

☎ (03) 5524–1211

🕐 8:00 A.M. to 8:00 P.M. Monday through Friday, 9:00 A.M. to 8:00 P.M. Saturday, 10:00 A.M. to 6:00 P.M. Sunday and holidays.

Maybe you wouldn't consider Office Depot for holiday stuff, but it's worth a visit. They have a large selection of greeting cards and paper supplies at discount prices. Other branches are located in Nishi Shinjuku, Shibuya, Ichigaya, Shimbashi, and Ginza.

## Sakurahorikiri

1–26–2 Yanagibashi, Taito-ku, Tokyo　　東京都台東区柳橋 1–26–2

☎ (03) 3864–1773

🚈 Asakusabashi Station, JR Sobu, Toei Asakusa lines

🕐 9:30 A.M. to 5:30 P.M. Closed Sundays and holidays.

A complex of stores with all kinds of arts-and-crafts goodies. Check out their doll-making classes for kids and grown-ups, too.

## Kiddyland

6–1–9 Jingu-mae, Shibuya-ku, Tokyo　　東京都渋谷区神宮前 6–1–9

☎ (03) 3409–3431

🚈 Omotesando Station, Hanzomon, Chiyoda, Ginza lines

🕐 10:00 A.M. to 8:00 P.M. Closed third Tuesdays.

Located on Omotesando, 5 minutes from Harajuku Station (see chapter 2 under Harajuku in the Shopping Districts section), Kiddyland has costumes, gag gifts, kids' toys, and paper products (napkins, plates, streamers, etc.).

## Seibu Loft

21–1 Udagawa-cho, Shibuya-ku, Tokyo　　東京都渋谷区宇田川町 21–1

☎ (03) 3462–3807

🚃 Shibuya Station, JR Yamanote and various lines
🕐 10:00 A.M. to 8:00 P.M. Saturday through Thursday (Friday to 9:00 P.M.).

Located in Shibuya and part of Seibu Department Store (see chapter 2 under Department Stores), this is a fun store to visit. Year-round you will find goods running the gamut from neon to nice, trendy to traditional. For each holiday, the store carries the cheaper disposable-type decorations, as well as some exquisite handcrafted items. There are also many things that you can put to use for original decorating or gift giving. Seibu Department Store in Ikebukuro also has an impressive three floors of Loft items, from stationery to party favors.

### National Azabu Bookstore

Located over National Azabu Supermarket, in Hiroo, this bookstore-cum-gift shop always has a reasonable supply of holiday goods. For a more detailed description, see chapter 4 under Bookstores.

### Christmas Depot

For Christmas decorations, recipes, cards, and gifts, check out "The Largest Christmas Superstore on the Net" at 🖥 <www.christmasdepot. com>.

### Tokyu Hands

Tokyu Hands is the place to shop for parties in general. It has lots of supplies for do-it-yourself decorations and gifts (see chapter 2 under Specialty Shops).

### Tuxedo Bear Balloon Shop

1–4–1 Minami Azabu, Minato-ku, Tokyo　東京都港区南麻布 1–4–1
☎ (03) 3457–5241
🚃 Hiroo Station, Hibiya Line
🕐 11:00 A.M. to 8:00 P.M. on weekdays (to 6:00 P.M. on Sundays and holidays). Closed Tuesdays.

This shop can provide helium balloons of all shapes and sizes.

## DISTRICT SHOPPING FOR PARTY FAVORS

Other sources for decorations and gifts at great prices are Sanrio stores and the three large shopping districts (see chapter 2): Akihabara, Asakusabashi, and Kappabashi. For costumes, see the section on resale shops in chapter 2.

## Asakusabashi Shopping District

🚈 Asakusabashi Station (exit A3), JR Sobu, Toei Asakusa lines

From October, you'll find four to five blocks of Christmas decoration and craft stores here. Don't forget to check out the side streets. One year, we found miniature Japanese instruments (shamisen, koto, etc.), which made special ornaments for the tree at ¥150 each!

## Christmas Store

239 Yamate-cho, Naka-ku, Yokohama-shi, Kanagawa
☎ (045) 621–8710 (Toys Club Museum)　神奈川県横浜市中区山手町 239
🚈 Ishikawa-cho Station, JR Negishi Line
🕐 9:30 A.M. to 7:00 P.M. daily (6:30 in winter).

Located in the Toys Club Museum, open 365 days a year.

## Sweden Center

6–11–9 Roppongi, Minato-ku, Tokyo　東京都港区六本木 6–11–9
☎ (03) 3403–1351
🚈 Roppongi Station, Hibiya Line
🕐 11:00 A.M. to around 7:00 P.M. daily.

Traditional Swedish Christmas decorations and seasonal delicacies, such as Christmas cookies and cakes in December. The deli carries other yummy goodies year-round, such as salmon and cheese. Decorations range from wreaths to exquisite glass figurines.

## Kate Wohlfart's

4–24–40 Takanawa, Minato-ku, Tokyo　東京都港区高輪 4–24–40
☎ (03) 3443–1560
🚈 Shinagawa Station, JR Yamanote and various lines
🕐 11:00 A.M. to 7:00 P.M. Closed Mondays.

A German Christmas store with beautiful ornaments and decorations that can be had for a few hundred yen.

# COSTUMES FOR RENT

## Big Kids

Hashimoto Bldg., 4F, 1–4–3 Sanno, Ota-ku, Tokyo
☎ (03) 3777–0707　📠 (03) 3777–1978　東京都大田区山王 1–4–3　橋本ビル 4F
🚈 Omori Station, JR Keihin Tokaido Line

Costumes for Halloween, from ¥5,000 to ¥18,000, include native Japanese dress, traditional outfits from other cultures, and animal suits. Open 10:00 A.M. to 7:00 P.M. Monday through Saturday. Closed on Sunday and holidays.

## Tokyo Isho (Tokyo Costume)

3–21–8 Nishihara, Shibuya-ku, Tokyo　東京都渋谷区西原 3–21–8
☎ (03) 3485–2101, (03) 3467–1451 (Yoyogi branch)

Costumes ranging from sumo garb to period outfits. Rental fees start at ¥15,000 (for two nights). Open 10:00 A.M. to 6:00 P.M. Closed on Sunday, holidays, and the first and second Saturday each month.

# HOLIDAY MAIL ORDER FROM ABROAD

Unless otherwise specified, VISA and MasterCard are accepted.

## Maid of Scandinavia

7009 Washington Avenue South, Edina, Minnesota 55439, USA
☎ (612) 943–1661　🖨 (612) 943–1688

This two-hundred-page catalog is filled with party supplies, such as crepe-paper streamers, paper plates and cups, party signs, even piñatas. It also has cake decorating supplies.

## Oriental Trading Company, Inc.

P.O. Box 3407, Omaha, Nebraska 68103–0407, USA
☎ 800–875–8480　🖥 www.oriental.com/home.htm

Here it is, the company with treat-bag fillers, costumes, decorations, and even holiday candy. The price is right, although for international shipping you initially pay half the order price and any overpayment will be refunded. Considering the volume that you get for your dollar, this is more than reasonable!

## The Party Basket, Ltd.

734 Nashville Avenue, New Orleans, Louisiana 70115, USA
☎ (504) 899–8126　🖨 (504) 897–2239

This catalog offers the largest selection we have ever seen of children's party goods. From piñatas and party favors to personalized napkins, this company sells everything you need for a perfect party. Besides carrying over fifty choices of table settings and decorations for birthday parties, the Party Basket is full of ideas for major holidays and religious occasions.

## Stik-ees

1165 Joshua Way, P.O. Box 9630, Vista, California 92083, USA
☎ (760) 727–7011　🖨 (760) 727–9099

This company has been in business since we were kids, selling color decals for all occasions. The designs stick on windows, bathtubs, and most smooth surfaces, and they can be used over and over again. They have packets for sale for all major holidays (cutouts of witches and pumpkins for Halloween, Santa for Christmas, etc.), enabling children to decorate the windows in the house or their rooms for each season.

## PARTY ENTERTAINMENT

### David Letendre

203 Revelto Court, 1–4–9 Motoizumi, Komae-shi, Tokyo
☎ (03) 3489–5330　東京都狛江市元和泉 1–4–9　リベルトコート 203

David has been entertaining kids and families in Tokyo for twenty years. His show includes comedy, magic, and balloon sculpturing. The entertainment is especially designed for kids and families. We have seen him perform many times and know him to be fun and reliable. Book early for weekend engagements and Christmas parties.

### Terry O'Brien

1–8–2 Hyakunin-cho, Shinjuku-ku, Tokyo　東京都新宿区百人町 1–8–2
☎ (03) 3209–4319 or (03) 3379–3511

Terry's magic act is very professional, and he performs in major clubs and hotels throughout Japan. If his hectic schedule allows, he also performs for private parties, and he is especially good with children.

### Kyle's Good Finds

Sun Heights Nakano, 2–7–10 Arai, Nakano-ku, Tokyo
東京都中野区新井 2–7–10　サンハイツ中野
☎ (03) 3385–8993　📧 kyle@crissicross.com

Kyle Sexton's mouth-watering concoctions have won the hearts of kids (and parents, too) since he first opened his bakery in 1990. His homemade pies, cakes, brownies, and cookies are available for take-out or delivery by Takyubin, anywhere in Japan. Kyle's custom-made birthday cakes (Winnie the Pooh, Mickey Mouse, and others) are much in demand. In addition to the character molds, Kyle can even create a cake design from a photograph. Two days' notice is necessary for Takyubin delivery and one day for pick-up orders.

### Baskin Robbins

☎ (03) 3442–3181 (National Azabu)　📧 www.31ice.co.jp

From Hokkaido to Tohoku, Baskin Robbins has invaded Japan. In Tokyo alone, there are over fifty shops. Our kids love their ice cream birthday cakes (order two to three days ahead) and theme cakes (Aladdin and Hello Kitty). The latter are available at prices from ¥2,000. Another option is individual cupcake-size cakes in the shape of an animal or clown. For the store nearest you, check the TownPage telephone directory.

## SPECIAL EVENTS

In addition to national holidays, there are many special events throughout Japan that your children may enjoy. You may find that some of these regional events are worth planning a vacation around.

### JANUARY 6: NEW YEAR PARADE OF FIREMEN (DEZOME SHIKI)

There is nothing children like better than firemen, right? Well, this parade is full of them, all dressed in traditional attire and performing acrobatic stunts on bamboo ladders. What a treat! The firemen's parade takes place in Harumi Dori in Chuo-ku. It's a bit crowded but the view from Dad's shoulders is usually pretty good.

### EARLY FEBRUARY: SNOW FESTIVAL IN SAPPORO (YUKI MATSURI)

This unique event is well worth the trip to the northernmost island of Hokkaido. Young children delight in seeing elaborate life-size (and larger) snow sculptures. It is a crowded event, and a sturdy backpack helps toddlers get a better view. Strollers are difficult to navigate, and walking the entire route is exhausting even for parents. A better idea is to choose one section of the park and let the kids investigate. The ice slides, sculptures kids can climb on, and their favorite cartoon characters larger than life in ice will captivate the kids for hours.

### LAST SATURDAY IN JULY: FIREWORKS DISPLAY ON THE SUMIDA RIVER (HANABI TAIKAI)

From late summer to early fall, fireworks displays are held all around the country. They are traditionally held over water, where their reflection can be enjoyed. For a memorable evening on the Sumida River, rent a cruise boat with other families and watch the magnificent display from the water. You can also watch from the central point, but it is very crowded. The view is exciting even from a distance, however, which is sometimes better for young children who may be frightened by the noise. Also in mid-August there is a fireworks display located in Jingu Stadium. This is visible from many rooftops in the Shibuya area. For more information, watch the papers for details and look out for colorful posters at subway stations.

### LATE AUGUST: GOODBYE TO SUMMER RALLY (NORYO TAIKAI)

From late August into early October, neighborhood festivals (*matsuri*) take place throughout Japan. The following description of the Azabu Juban festival in Tokyo is typical of other celebrations at this time of year. At the Juban festival, the crowds have become so huge in recent years that it is best to go in late afternoon just after the stalls have been set up. Dress your children in their cool summer *yukata*, a casual cotton kimono. It is possible to purchase adult and children's *yukata* at a Juban shop in the middle of the festival, which we did one year. The owners were quite gracious about dressing us all up in our finery! Cotton *yukata* are more comfortable than you can imagine in the August heat and humidity.

Even if you don't feel like dressing up, you can still stroll down the long shopping street, which is gaily decorated for the event. There are stalls offering cool treats, such as "ice candy" (Popsicles) and *kakigori* (snowcones). Most of the vendors have something especially for children. There are goldfish-catching games and numerous small toys for sale. One of our favorite booths is full of miniature plastic food at bargain prices. A collection of realistic sushi rolls, soy sauce bottles, and chopsticks is available in addition to fruit, hamburgers, and tiny cartons of milk. We always buy several bagfuls to send back home for children's birthdays, and we keep some for our own grocery shopping games at home.

At the festival, when you hear the drum beat, make your way to the end of the street where a tall platform is erected. On the top you will see a drummer sounding out a traditional beat for the townspeople to dance to. The drummers—young men and women from the neighbor-hood—are quite impressive to watch. They are accompanied by Japan-ese folk songs played over the loudspeakers. A procession of locals winds its way around the platform performing simple dances. From grandmothers to toddlers, everyone is welcome to join in the fun. Usually some of the older residents know the dances well, so watch their movements a few times before joining in. Our preschoolers often pick up the dances before we do!

Some of your fondest memories of Japan will be of the nights full of music, food, and fun at your neighborhood festival. There will be some sort of festival in almost every neighborhood either in summer or autumn. The ward office can give you information on your area, but also be on the look-out for signs of preparation. A few days before the festival, the portable shrine (*omikoshi*) will be set up under a tent where people will be making offerings of fruit, sake, and other gifts to the gods. The shopkeepers may also be lining the streets with paper lanterns and streamers. On the day of the *matsuri*, the shrine is paraded around several blocks on the shoulders of the residents. Many neighborhoods also have a shrine for children to carry, and they get a big thrill from being part of the procession. Inquire at the tent about taking part. Usually foreigners are more than welcome. After all, it's your neighborhood too!

### EARLY OCTOBER: GINZA FESTIVAL (GINZA MATSURI)

There are several large festivals in the first week of October in Tokyo, including Ginza *matsuri*. These are more commercial and elaborate than the neighborhood festivals, with parades, floats, and streets full of open-air bazaars. Since the main streets are blocked to traffic, it is safe to walk with children, but the crowds can be overwhelming on a nice day. For more information about the Ginza *matsuri*, call the festival office at ☎ (03) 3561–0919.

### EARLY NOVEMBER: AUTUMN FESTIVAL AT MEIJI SHRINE (AKI MATSURI)

This is an excellent opportunity to absorb some of the culture of Japan without buying tickets and sitting in a theater. In the crisp autumn air you can watch Noh plays, see ancient dances, and hear music played on traditional instruments. There is also Japanese archery and a variety of martial arts performances. We have found that these events usually have a special section for children. Some years there is a petting zoo or appearances by favorite cartoon characters. The Meiji Shrine grounds are quite large, so you might want to bring a picnic meal and take your time to wander around and enjoy the events. For more information about the festival, call the shrine office at ☎ (03) 3379–5511.

# 9

# Having a Baby in Japan

AH.... BACH... I HOPE YOU
LIKE HIM TOO.

The idea of giving birth in a foreign country can be unsettling. Fortunately, Japan has one of the lowest infant mortality rates in the world, and those foreigners who have had children here have found that many facilities in Japan do not differ greatly from those in their home country. The Westernization of facilities and practices in the field of obstetrics makes it easy to seek out hospitals with high standards of hygiene and state-of-the-art equipment.

It is interesting to note that the Japanese count the period of pregnancy as ten lunar months of twenty-eight days each whereas Westerners count nine months of thirty-one days. Home pregnancy tests are available at most drugstores in Japan, although for instructions in English you may have to purchase one from an international pharmacy (see the Family Planning section in this chapter).

After you have visited a doctor to confirm your pregnancy, you will need to go to your local ward or city office to register the pregnancy. You must take your Alien Registration Card and fill out a form with your doctor's name and the address of the clinic or hospital with which he or she is associated. You will then receive the booklet, the *boshi kenko techo*, commonly referred to as the *boshi techo*, which will be a record of your health during pregnancy, labor, delivery, and that of your child's subsequent development. You will also receive information concerning pregnancy and birth, and a health card entitling you to free checkups at Japanese hospitals during your pregnancy.

The *boshi techo* is an important little book, and you should carry it with you, particularly during your last weeks of pregnancy. The hospital or clinic staff will write in this booklet at each prenatal checkup and many times during your hospital stay. If you take your child to a Japanese hospital or public health center for checkups and shots, or use Japanese National Health Insurance, the *boshi techo* will also serve as your child's record for the first six years. The handbook is also necessary if your child will be registered as a Japanese citizen. A copy of the *boshi techo* in English can be obtained from many of the obstetricians and gynecologists in private practice in Tokyo, and also by writing to the Japanese Organization for International Cooperation in Family Planning Incorporated (see listing under Family Planning in this chapter). This English-language book is only for your convenience; officially you must register your pregnancy at the ward or city office and receive the Japanese-language *boshi techo*.

## MATERNITY CLOTHES

Can't quite zip those jeans? Are you feet starting to swell? You may feel panicked at the thought of finding comfortable and stylish maternity wear in Japan, but we have some suggestions for you. If you need some immediate relief, use the old trick with the rubber band. All you have to do is get a medium-size rubber band, loop it through the button hole of your pants until it is secure, and then pull the other end over the button on the other side. You can also borrow your husband's old shirts and sweaters for baggy tops. Do not forget the option of asking friends and relatives back home to send you a care package of Western-size maternity wear for the last mile.

All department stores have a selection of maternity clothes (see chapter 2 under department stores). You can also buy Japanese maternity clothes and undergarments from the Japanese baby equipment catalogs listed in chapter 3. Japanese maternity clothes are, of course, made for Japanese women, and they are often not large enough for Western women, especially after six months of pregnancy.

You can also make use of bulletin-board ads, newspaper and magazine ads, and friends' maternity clothes if you do not want to spend much money. Another possibility is to look in local resale shops (see chapter 2 under Resale Outlets) or to order from abroad.

### MAIL-ORDER MATERNITY AND NURSING CLOTHES FROM ABROAD

The catalogs listed here offer clothes that range from inexpensive, homey fashions to stylish, formal maternity wear. Whatever your style or budget, there is probably something here to get you through those nine long months.

## Garnett Hill

P.O. Box 5005, Littleton, New Hampshire 03561–5005, USA
☎ (603) 823–5545    🖶 (603) 823–9578

This company's catalog offers wonderful cotton maternity clothes and bras. The styles are comfortable and stylish and never fussy. The primary focus of the catalog is on fine bed linens and comforters. Besides the maternity clothes, we like its European-style children's clothes as well.

## J. C. Penney Company

Circulation Dept., Box 2056, Dept. PR22, Milwaukee, Wisconsin 53201–2056, USA
🖳 www.jcpenney.com

This company has a large selection of maternity clothes and nursing bras in addition to baby furniture and accessories. Prices are extremely reasonable.

## La Leche League International

P.O. Box 4079, Schaumburg, Illinois 60168–4079, USA
☎ (847) 519–9585    🖶 (847) 519–0035    🖳 www.lalecheleague.org

This group issues a catalog full of material on breastfeeding, nutrition, and childbirth. They also carry a range of accessories for nursing mothers, such as breast pumps, milk storage systems, and breast shields and shells.

## Motherwear

320 Riverside Drive, Northampton, Massachusetts 01060, USA
☎ (213) 455–1426    🖳 www.motherwear.com

This company has a good selection of nursing bras, breast pumps, nursing garments, pillows, and just about anything else to do with nursing your baby.

# Choosing a Place of Birth

Whether you decide to give birth in Japan or in your hometown hospital, the most important thing for expectant couples is to be informed. All options should be considered, and when searching for the ideal doctor or place of birth do not be afraid to get a second opinion. Attending a class on choosing a place of birth is an important first step. There are many options for pregnant women in Japan. A childbirth education class in your area can inform you of possible places of birth and answer many of your questions.

## CHILDBIRTH EDUCATION CLASSES

For many years, the Tokyo Childbirth Education Association (TCEA) did an outstanding job of guiding thousands of women through pregnancy, preparing them for childbirth, and offering support in the early stages of parenting. Julie Pearse, the Australian midwife who founded TCEA back in 1984, taught pregnancy, childbirth, and breastfeeding classes at Aiiku Hospital and assisted women in labor until her return to Australia, in 1990. Her successor, Canadian nurse Diana Bond, took over briefly before she, too, was transferred from Tokyo. Both women are remembered fondly for their many contributions to TCEA.

In 1991, the dynamic childbirth educator, Elena de Karplus, arrived on the scene and became TCEA's new director. She was the driving force behind the organization until the Tokyo office closed in the fall of 1998. In addition to teaching childbirth preparation classes, Elena added many new programs for expectant and new parents. Her team of qualified instructors taught classes at many locations throughout Tokyo but Elena herself was available practically twenty-four hours a day for labor support or counseling.

Elena's selfless dedication, professional integrity, and passion for her work endeared her to hundreds of families faced with having a baby in a foreign country. Over the years she worked closely with the Japanese medical community and hosted such visiting dignitaries as Sheila Kitzinger and Michel Odent. Elena continued helping new mothers after the birth of their children with Tokyo Moms Club and also through TCEA's monthly newsletter, *Tokyo Stork.*

Even after Elena was transferred back to New York, in 1996, she continued to run TCEA with the invaluable assistance of Elizabeth Walther. Finally, in the fall of 1998, with Elizabeth's departure from Tokyo imminent, Elena felt that it would be impossible to continue to run TCEA long distance. Despite her absence from Japan, Elena maintains an informative website, 💻 <www.birthintokyo.com>, and continues birth counseling through e-mail, 💻 <kartcea@cyburban.com>, and by fax 📠 (914) 725–0150.

Fortunately for foreign women in the Tokyo area, two different groups have stepped in to offer comprehensive childbirth education in English. Sherry Thornburg, a former instructor with TCEA, organized Birth Education Services in Tokyo (BEST), in 1998. Sherry has had many years of experience in public health in the United States and Australia and is a member of International Childbirth Education Association.

BEST offers a variety of childbirth programs taught by a team of experienced health educators, most with medical backgrounds. Individual counseling is also available. For additional information or for a free brochure, contact Ann Tanaka at Birth Education Services in Tokyo, 3–16–5 Nishi Azabu, Minato-ku, Tokyo; ☎/🖷 (03) 3482–0728, 💻 <q.sherry@worldnet.att.net>.

Childbirth Education Center (CEC) was started by Brett Iimura and Kalli Matsuhashi in 1997. Both are American mothers who had their own children in Japan and have lived in this country for many years. Their Japanese language ability, together with knowledge of the Japanese medical system, are helpful in accessing the latest information about pregnancy and childbirth here.

Brett and Kalli teach a core class, Birthing Your Baby: Preparation for Labor. This class focuses on the process of labor and how women and their partners can make the choices that will ensure the best outcome for them. Topics covered include stages of labor, self-help measures in labor, drugs and medical intervention, breastfeeding and postpartum care. Additional classes in Early Pregnancy and Becoming a Parent are also available; group or individual sessions are offered.

CEC holds monthly Moms-'n'-Babies meetings where new mothers can gather to share information and make friends. All classes and meetings are held at the Tokyo Women's Plaza in Omotesando. For more information contact Brett Iimura at ☎/🖷 (03) 5721–0399, or Kalli Matsuhashi at ☎/🖷 (048) 267–4634.

Ward and city offices usually have a series of birth preparation classes taught by a team of nurses, midwives, and at least one doctor, all in Japanese. The content and tone of the classes varies tremendously, some being very good and others mediocre. The good thing about these classes is the opportunity they provide for expectant mothers to meet other women and to hear opinions other than those of her doctor. Through the classes, the mother can also become familiar with her *hokenjo* (health department), since it will also be where she will take her child for free immunizations and health checks, if she chooses to take advantage of these services. The health department may also have classes on breastfeeding, baby care, weaning, and so on. Many hospitals also offer these types of classes to their patients. Besides these classes, there are often doctors and health-care professionals who give lectures and advice to parents at other centers. Check the department store listings (in chapter 2) for stores that provide this service.

In the greater Tokyo and the Kansai areas, there are several classes taught in English, and some instructors may be willing to correspond with expectant mothers living in other parts of the country. A short list of independent childbirth education services and programs follows.

### Aqua Birth House Underwater Birth Group (Suichu Shussan Renraku Kai)

4–16–21 Sakuragaoka, Setagaya-ku, Tokyo　東京都世田谷区桜ヶ丘 4–16–21
☎ (03) 3427–1314　📠 (03) 3427–1223

Lessons in preparing for an underwater birth are given. English-speaking staff available.

### Baby Healthy

500–1 Minami Ota, Inamachi, Tsukuba-gun, Ibaraki
☎ (0297) 58–3708　　茨城県筑波郡伊奈町南太田 500–1

Midwife Fusaka Sei is experienced in underwater birth.

### The Childbirth School

1–24–8 Takadanobaba, Shinjuku-ku, Tokyo　東京都新宿区高田馬場 1–24–8
☎ (03) 3232–0006

This school was started in 1979. Classes are taught by independent midwives and doctors who not only train couples in the Lamaze method of childbirth but also teach them the latest theories of child-rearing and infant care.

## MIDWIVES

For generations, midwives have played a valuable role in pregnancy and childbirth in Japan. Today there are more than twenty-three thousand registered midwives, and even in large hospitals midwives may be involved in the majority of deliveries. A home birth is an option considered by some women in Japan because of the access to experienced independent midwives. However, only a small percentage of babies are born at home, with the majority of Japanese women delivering in hospitals and clinics. If you are considering a home birth, be aware that it may be difficult to arrange for emergency backup at a nearby hospital. There are no official support services for midwives although you could arrange for your own transportation.

The following associations can give you information about midwives throughout Japan: Japan Academy of Midwifery, 1–12 Katamachi, Shinjuku-ku, Tokyo, ☎ (03) 3357–2506; Japanese Midwives' Association, 1–8–21 Fujimi, Chiyoda-ku, Tokyo, ☎ (03) 3262–9910; Japanese Nursing Association—Midwife Division, 5–8–2 Jingu-mae, Shibuya-ku, Tokyo, ☎ (03) 3400–8331; and JIMON, the Japan Midwives' Organization Network, ☎ (03) 3414–3207.

The childbirth educators in your area may also be able to provide you with some names and phone numbers of midwives. The midwives listed below offer a variety of services in the greater Tokyo area. Some of them work through a clinic while others will deliver your baby at home.

| Head Midwife | Place | Telephone | Type of Service |
|---|---|---|---|
| Mizuochi | Adachi-ku | (03) 3899–5205 | Clinic |
| Kamiya | Bunkyo-ku | (03) 3812–0707 | Home |
| Sakuma | Chiba-ken | (0479) 76–2357 | Clinic |
| Yachiyo | Chiyoda-ku | (03) 3261–0626 | Clinic |
| Nomoto | Chofu-shi & Mitaka-shi | (0424) 82–2973 | Clinic |
| Fukasa | Ibaraki-ken | (0297) 58–3708 | Clinic |
| Aoyagi | Ota-ku | (03) 3761–4138 | Clinic |
| Kurihara | Saitama-ken | (0492) 31–1046 | Clinic |
| Aqua Birth House/Yamada | Setagaya-ku | (03) 3427–1314 | Home, Clinic |
| Terajima | Shibuya-ku | (03) 3376–5972 | Home, Clinic |
| Sugiyama | Suginami-ku | (03) 3313–5658 | Clinic |
| Fukuoka | Sumida-ku | (03) 3611–7563 (03) 3611–0301 (evening) | Clinic |
| Motoyama | Yokohama-shi | (045) 391–1169 | Clinic |
| Tabata | Yokohama-shi | (045) 751–7685 | Home |

## CLINICS AND HOSPITALS

If you plan to deliver in a clinic or a hospital, take the time to find one whose facilities and philosophies suit you. You will find that most major hospitals have strict birth policies. Some hospitals do not allow husbands to be present at the birth. Others may require a new mother to stay in the hospital for a set period—usually about a week—and also restrict the length of time she can spend with her baby. In general, smaller clinics offer a more personal and flexible service. Of course, your special needs must be taken into consideration. The place of birth that you choose will greatly depend on whether you have a high-risk pregnancy or whether you are expecting your third child.

No matter what the policies are at your place of birth, do not hesitate to question the practices and to request certain changes if necessary. Although doctors are not used to discussing options with Japanese patients, they expect to hear plenty of questions from foreigners. It helps if your doctor speaks English, or if you can communicate in Japanese. If there seems to be a communication problem, try to arrange for an interpreter to come along for at least one visit so that the important issues can be discussed. If you are submitting a birth plan, it is a good idea to have it written in Japanese as well as your native language so that there is no confusion.

Some hospitals are more rigid than others, but we have found that insistence in a firm but polite manner can achieve results. This is especially effective if you are dealing with a situation such as separation from baby at birth. Many mothers enjoy rooming-in with their baby, or at least want unlimited access to their newborn. This is especially important for a breastfeeding mother. Some hospitals have a policy that the baby must be separated from the mother for up to twenty-four hours after birth for observation. Often, with persistence, this rule can be eliminated or at least relaxed.

In Japan today, the trend is toward delivering in large hospitals. Doctors usually have delivery "rights" at certain hospitals, so you should find out which doctors deliver where. Of course, there is often no guarantee at a large hospital that a specific doctor will deliver your baby.

Small ob-gyn clinics are also fairly popular in this country, both with Japanese and with foreigners. Many of these clinics are not luxuriously decorated, but they do offer a cozy environment in which to give birth. A similar atmosphere can be found in maternity homes, which are small clinics run by midwives. Most small clinics have some form of emergency backup, but you should check to see exactly what the situation would be in case of an emergency.

Prenatal and postnatal vitamins are not routinely prescribed in Japan. If you would like to take them, or if you are anemic, your doctor will provide them. Be aware that the iron content—the main reason pregnant and nursing women take these vitamins—may not be as high as even regular multivitamins from the United States. You can also ask your doctor in your home country to give you a supply of prenatal vitamins, or you can order vitamin supplements from the Foreign Buyer's Club (see chapter 10).

Some medical interventions are common in this country both before and during childbirth. For example, ultrasound is frequently used for prenatal exams, and many hospitals require fetal monitors during labor. Induction of labor is not uncommon, especially in small clinics with limited staff. Episiotomies are also quite routine. You will want to discuss these and other issues with your doctor ahead of time. In their birth plan, foreign women sometimes state which interventions they would prefer to eliminate in a normal childbirth.

Many smaller clinics do not offer any pain-relief drugs during childbirth. In some clinics and in the hospitals, epidural is available, but the majority of Japanese midwives and doctors advocate a "natural" birth without drugs. For true emergencies, a general anesthetic is usually given, but for other situations it is possible to request an epidural. In case of a cesarean, check to see what anesthesia will be administered and be sure to ask your doctor what sort of incision he will make. A transverse uterine scar is supposedly stronger and will increase your chances of avoiding a cesarean with your next baby. The ten percent cesarean rate in Japan is much lower than in Western countries. Vaginal birth after cesarean (VBAC) is a new concept here, but some doctors are receptive to the idea.

Amniocentesis, the procedure of drawing fluid from the womb to test for abnormalities in the fetus, is offered by a few specialists, but it is not the common procedure for women over thirty-five years of age that it is in the United States and some other Western countries. If a mother does face some problem in her pregnancy, it is a good idea to contact some of the experts in the field. Several hospitals in Japan are world-famous for their work on special problems in conception and childbirth. See the listings of hospitals and ob-gyn clinics later in this section.

Circumcision, the operation in which the foreskin is cut from a male infant's penis, is another procedure that is rarely done in Japan. Because Japanese newborns are not traditionally circumcised, most doctors have rarely performed this surgery. Parents planning to have their infant circumcised should take care to find an experienced doctor. In Japan, this surgery is usually performed by surgeons who specialize in male urinary tract surgery. A good book to read if you want further information on circumcision is *Circumcision* (Edward Wallerstein, Springer Publishing Co., New York, 1980), or check out websites such as The National Organization of Circumcision Information Resource Center at ⌨ <www.nocirc.org>.

Some of the routine procedures administered to newborn babies in Japan are antibiotic eye drops to prevent eye infection, vitamin K shots, screening tests for rare metabolic problems such as phenylketonuria (PKU), and checks for jaundice. The baby's blood type may not be tested unless specifically requested. Also, an imprint of the baby's footprint is not usually taken as it is in many Western countries. Instead, the baby's dried umbilical cord stub is preserved and sometimes given to the parents in a little box.

We suggest that before leaving the hospital, you ask the doctor or nurse to write down all of the baby's tests and results, in English if possible. This information is not recorded in detail in the *boshi techo*, and you will want to have it for your baby's records.

## RECOMMENDED HOSPITALS

Both large and small hospitals with ob-gyn, maternity, and pediatrics departments are listed below. Some of them may be affiliated with a university or teaching facility, while others may have their origins as Christian hospitals. If you visit these hospitals, you will be seen by one of the doctors on the staff there. Usually, it is not possible to make an appointment; you must go and wait your turn. Other doctors may have delivery "rights" at the hospital but see patients by appointment in their own office or clinic.

GREATER TOKYO AREA

### Aiiku Hospital

5–6–8 Minami Azabu, Minato-ku, Tokyo
☎ (03) 3473–8321    東京都港区南麻布 5–6–8

### Hiroo Hospital

2–34–10 Ebisu, Shibuya-ku, Tokyo
☎ (03) 3444–1181　東京都渋谷区恵比寿 2–34–10

### International Catholic Hospital (Seibo Byoin)

2–5–1 Naka Ochiai, Shinjuku-ku, Tokyo
☎ (03) 3951–1111　東京都新宿区中落合 2–5–1

### International Goodwill Hospital

1–28–1 Nishigaoka, Izumi-ku, Yokohama-shi, Kanagwa
☎ (045) 813–0221　神奈川県横浜市泉区西ヶ丘 1–28–1

### Jikei University Hospital

3–19–18 Nishi Shimbashi, Minato-ku, Tokyo
☎ (03) 3433–1111　東京都港区西新橋 3–19–18

### Kanagawa Children's Medical Center

2–138–4 Mutsukawa, Minami-ku, Yokohama-shi, Kanagawa
☎ (045) 711–2351　神奈川県横浜市南区六ッ川 2–138–4

### Keio University Hospital

35 Shinanomachi, Shinjuku-ku, Tokyo
☎ (03) 3353–1211　東京都新宿区信濃町 35

### Red Cross Hospital (Nisseki Byoin)

4–1–22 Hiroo, Shibuya-ku, Tokyo
☎ (03) 3400–1311　東京都渋谷区広尾 4–1–22

### St. Luke's International Hospital (Episcopal)

9–1 Akashi-cho, Chuo-ku, Tokyo
☎ (03) 3541–5151　東京都中央区明石町 9–1

### Seventh Day Adventist Hospital (Eisei Byoin)

3–17–3 Amanuma, Suginami-ku, Tokyo
☎ (03) 3392–6151　東京都杉並区天沼 3–17–3

### Showa University Hospital

1–5–8 Hatanodai, Shinagawa-ku, Tokyo
☎ (03) 3784–8615　東京都品川区旗の台 1–5–8

KANSAI AREA

### Hamada Hospital

1–6–9 Uriwari, Hirano-ku, Osaka-shi, Osaka
☎ (06) 6708–7200　大阪府大阪市平野区瓜破 1–6–9

## Itoh Byoin

3–2 Inokoda-cho, Shimogamo, Sakyo-ku, Kyoto
☎ (075) 781–5188　京都府京都市左京区下鴨狗子田町 3–2

## Iwasa Ladies' Clinic

9–22 Korien-cho, Hirakata-shi, Osaka
☎ (072) 831–1666　大阪府枚方市香里園町 9–22

## Kaisei Hospital

3–11–15 Shinohara-kitamachi, Nada-ku, Kobe-shi, Hyogo
☎ (078) 871–5201　兵庫県神戸市灘区篠原北町 3–11–15

## Kobe Adventist Hospital

8–4–1 Arinodai, Kita-ku, Kobe-shi, Hyogo
☎ (078) 981–0161　兵庫県神戸市北区有野台 8–4–1

## Konan Hospital

1–5–16 Kamokogahara, Higashi Nada-ku, Kobe-shi, Hyogo
☎ (078) 851–2161　兵庫県神戸市東灘区鴨子が原 1–5–16

## Morimoto Women's Hospital

4–26–4 Hoshin, Higashi Yodogawa-ku, Osaka-shi, Osaka
☎ (06) 6328–6410　大阪府大阪市東淀川区豊新 4–26–4

## Nihon Baptist Hospital

47 Yamanomoto-cho, Kita Shirakawa, Sakyo-ku, Kyoto-shi, Kyoto
☎ (075) 781–5191　京都府京都市左京区北白川山ノ元町 47

## St. Barnabus Hospital (no English spoken)

1–3–32 Saikudani, Tennoji-ku, Osaka-shi, Osaka
☎ (06) 6779–1600　大阪府大阪市天王寺区細工谷 1–3–32

## Santa Maria Hospital

13–15 Shinjo, Ibaraki-shi, Osaka
☎ (0726) 27–3459　大阪府茨木市新庄 13–15

## Ueda Hospital

1–1–4 Kunika-dori, Chuo-ku, Kobe-shi, Hyogo
☎ (078) 241–3305　兵庫県神戸市中央区国香通 1–1–4

## Yodogawa Christian Hospital

2–9–26 Awagi, Higashi Yodogawa-ku, Osaka-shi, Osaka
☎ (06) 6322–2250　大阪府大阪市東淀川区淡路 2–9–26

## Yoshida Hospital

1–7–1 Akatamachi, Saidaiji, Nara-shi, Nara
☎ (0742) 45–4601　奈良県奈良市西大寺赤田町 1–7–1

## PRIVATE OB-GYN CLINICS

The ob-gyn doctors listed below are in private practice, as opposed to being on the staff at a large hospital. What this means to you as a patient is that you will most likely be able to make an appointment instead of waiting your turn at a hospital. These doctors may have delivery "rights" at one or more hospitals, or they may deliver in their own clinic. Private clinics may or may not take Japanese National Health Insurance. This list is by no means complete, but these are doctors and clinics that have been recommended by the foreign community and where, for the most part, you will have no problem being understood English.

---

GREATER TOKYO AREA

### Dr. Tsuneo Akaeda, Akaeda Roppongi Shinryojo

6–11–35 Roppongi, Minato-ku, Tokyo
☎ (03) 3405–1388　東京都港区六本木 6–11–35

### Dr. Ryoko Dozono (female), International Medical Crossing

4–2–49, #401, Minami Azabu, Minato-ku, Tokyo
☎ (03) 3443–4823　東京都港区南麻布 4–2–49–401

### Dr. Shin Juzoji, Higashi Fuchu Hospital

2–7–20 Wakamatsu-cho, Fuchu-shi, Tokyo
☎ (0423) 64–0151　東京都府中市若松町 2–7–20

### Dr. Sayoko Makabe (female), Kanda Clinic

3–20–14 Nishi Azabu, Minato-ku, Tokyo
☎ (03) 3402–0654　東京都港区西麻布 3–20–14

### Dr. Hisami Matsumine (female), Toho Fujin Women's Clinic

5–3–10 Kiba, Koto-ku, Tokyo
☎ (03) 3630–0322　東京都江東区木場 5–3–10

### Miyamoto Clinic for Women

15–10 Wakamatsu-cho, Shinjuku-ku, Tokyo
☎ (03) 3209–8315　東京都新宿区若松町 15–10

### Naganuma Clinic

1–20–2 Takadanobaba, Shinjuku-ku, Tokyo
☎ (03) 3232–1501　東京都新宿区高田馬場 1–20–2

## Rose Lady's Clinic

2–3–18 Todoroki, Setagaya-ku, Tokyo
☎ (03) 3703–0114   東京都世田谷区等々力 2–3–18

## Sanno Clinic, Dr. Gen'ichi Nozue, Dr. Hiroko Shinno (female)

8–5–35 Akasaka, Minato-ku, Tokyo
☎ (03) 3402–3151   東京都港区赤坂 8–5–35

## Dr. Hiroko Shinno (female), Tokyo Women's Clinic

Roppongi Denki Bldg., 2F, 6–1–20 Roppongi, Minato-ku, Tokyo
東京都港区六本木 6–1–20   六本木電気ビル 2F
☎ (03) 3408–6950   🖷 (03) 3408–8453

## Dr. Ryutaro Tojo, Tojo Women's Clinic

2–34–7 Maruyamadai, Konan-ku, Yokohama-shi, Kanagawa
☎ (045) 843–1121   神奈川県横浜市港南区丸山台 2–34–7

## Kazuo Yamanaka Obstetrics and Gynecology Clinic

28–11 Wakamatsu-cho, Shinjuku-ku, Tokyo
☎ (03) 3200–6913   東京都新宿区若松町 28–11

## Dr. Yoichiro Yanagida, Tokyo Maternity Clinic

1–20–8 Sendagaya, Shibuya-ku, Tokyo
☎ (03) 3403–1861   東京都渋谷区千駄ヶ谷 1–20–8

## Dr. Takumi Yanaihara, Tokyo Medical and Surgical Clinic

No. 32, Mori Bldg., 2F, 3–4–30 Shiba Koen, Minato-ku, Tokyo
☎ (03) 3436–3028   東京都港区芝公園 3–4–30 32森ビル 2F

## Yotsuya Obstetrics and Gynecology Clinic

1–1 Sanei-cho, Shinjuku-ku, Tokyo
☎ (03) 3351–3224   東京都新宿区三栄町 1–1

---

KANSAI AREA

## Dr. Yuriko Hashimoto (female), Ito Sanfujinka Clinic

5–6–6 Izumi-cho, Suita-shi, Osaka
☎ (06) 6388–0141   大阪府吹田市和泉町 5–6–6

## Dr. Hiroko Kimura (female), Kimura Clinic

4–12–17 Nishitemma, Kita-ku, Osaka-shi, Osaka
☎ (06) 6365–9646   大阪府大阪市北区西天満 4–12–17

**Dr. Masahiro Nishikawa, Nishikawa Clinic**

2–16–10 Tennoji-kita, Abeno-ku, Osaka-shi, Osaka

☎ (06) 6714–5218　大阪府大阪市阿倍野区天王寺北 2–16–10

**Dr. Seishiro Oida, Oida Clinic**

Nishihairu Manjuji, Karasuma-Dori, Shimogyo-ku, Kyoto-shi, Kyoto

☎ (075) 351–5786　京都府京都市下京区烏丸通万寿寺西入ル

**Tanaka Maternity Clinic**

1–8–15 Yahata, Nada-ku, Kobe-shi, Hyogo

☎ (078) 851–2284　兵庫県神戸市灘区八幡 1–8–15

**Dr. Rokuro Ueda, Ueda Maternity Clinic**

1–1–4 Kunika-dori, Chuo-ku, Kobe-shi, Hyogo

☎ (078) 241–3305　兵庫県神戸市中央区国香通 1–1–4

## RECOMMENDED READING

We would like to recommend some books that we think cover nearly everything you need to know about the childbirth experience. *A Good Birth, A Safe Birth* (Harvard Common Press) by Diana Korte provides an excellent overview of pregnancy and childbirth, including normal delivery, special situations, and a sample birth plan. We also recommend any of the numerous books by Penelope Leach or Sheila Kitzinger. Most of these are available through La Leche League, or the Foreign Buyers Club in Japan.

The *Japan Health Handbook* (Kodansha International), heavily revised in 1998, contains valuable information about childbirth in Japan as well as modern-day procedures. We highly recommend it. Of particular importance are chapter 6, on sexual and reproductive health, and chapter 7, on having a baby.

## BREASTFEEDING

The vast majority of Japanese women choose to breastfeed their babies. At one stage, bottle feeding was strongly recommended in Japan, but after peaking in the 1970s, it is now on the decline. There are various views about breastfeeding management in this country, so you may hear conflicting advice from doctors, midwives, and well-meaning friends. Breast massage—the Oketani method in particular—is quite popular with the Japanese. This method was started by a midwife who believed that massage could help relieve breastfeeding problems and also increase a mother's ability to produce milk. While in the hospital, new mothers are often offered breast massage by the nurses.

If you are interested in breastfeeding, we suggest that you contact La Leche League International (LLL). This is a nonprofit organization interested in helping mothers to breastfeed their babies. LLL has an international network of trained volunteer leaders who conduct monthly meetings and counsel mothers over the phone. They are backed up by a medical advisory board of doctors and other health-care professionals whose advice is available in case of an unusual problem. There are English- and Japanese-speaking LLL groups throughout Japan, with at least two groups in the Tokyo area. LLL groups in Japan offer a wide selection of books in English on pregnancy, childbirth, and breastfeeding that are available for loan. To find a leader in the greater Tokyo area, call TELL (Tokyo English Life Line) at ☎ (03) 3498–0261 or 🖷 (03) 3498–0272. In the Kansai area, contact one of the community centers listed in chapter 12. For a list of leaders in Japan, both English- and Japanese-speaking, write to La Leche League International Headquarters at P.O. Box 4079, Schaumburg, Illinois 60168–4709, USA, or call ☎ (847) 519–9585. Their website is at 🖳 <lalecheleague.org>.

## AFTER THE BABY IS BORN

Because you live in a foreign country, there are a number of important documents that you will need to obtain after the baby is born. The first item you will want to consider is the child's passport. Most likely you will need to visit your embassy or consulate to find out about the rules and regulations concerning the nationality of your baby.  The baby need not be present, but if you want to get a passport for him you will need two identical pictures, just as you would for an adult passport. Some hospitals have access to a photographer who will take your baby's picture while still in the hospital. Children's passports are generally valid for only five years, but it still seems pretty silly to have a picture of a two-week-old baby in a passport! The other papers you may need include both parents' passports, parents' marriage certificate (original), parents' Alien Registration Card, and copies of visa applications. Again, the requirements depend on your nationality, so call before you go to make sure that you take all of the necessary documents.

You must also register your child at the local ward or city office within fourteen days of the birth. For this you will need to take both parents' passports and Alien Registration Cards, the original birth certificate (this is a paper in Japanese from the hospital), and the *boshi techo.*

For registration at immigration, you will need to take both parents' passports, the child's passport if he is not registered on a parent's, the alien registration cards of both parents and child, the original birth certificate, and the *boshi techo.*

## PARENT SUPPORT GROUPS

There are a number of groups that have met regularly in the past to help parents with special needs. Some of these groups are Adoptive Parents Support Group, Children of Single and Divorced Parents Group, Family Problem Discussion Group, Parents of Children with Special Needs, and Infant Death Support Group. To find a current contact person for these groups, or to find out if a group for your special need exists, call TELL at ☎ (03) 3498–0261, in Tokyo, and, in the Kansai area, call the Community House and Information Center at ☎ (078) 857–6540 or the Kobe International Community Center at ☎ (078) 322–0030.

The Association of Foreign Wives of Japanese (AFWJ), the group of foreign wives of Japanese men, ☎ (045) 742–6979 (Beverly Nakamura), may also have up-to-date information about parent support groups.

### Ma-Ma Service Office Pocket

No. 5 Lions Mansion, #314, 1–5–2 Aobadai, Aoba-ku, Yokohama-shi, Kanagawa
神奈川県横浜市青葉区青葉台 1–5–2　第5ライオンズマンション 314
☎ (045) 982–7715, (03) 3496–6515 (Tokyo)

This company, which offers a new and unique service in Japan, was founded to help new mothers cope with those first few days or weeks at home with a new baby. The employees all have experience with babies, and they also undergo special training before being sent out to work. The helpers will clean, shop, cook, bathe the baby, baby-sit, and do any other baby care that you request. There is a twenty-eight-hour minimum and a four-hour daily minimum. Requests for help should be made as far in advance as possible. Payments are to be made in advance, and transportation costs are paid directly to the helper.

# BIRTH STORIES

Foreign women may well feel apprehensive about giving birth in Japan. To offer encouragement and to help allay fears, three foreign women, Diane, Becky, and Mary, relate their very different experiences of birth in Japan.

## *CESAREAN SECTION AND VAGINAL BIRTH AFTER A CESAREAN — DIANE*

I experienced the births of two children in Tokyo. My first baby was born without complication by cesarean section, and three years later I had an easy vaginal birth with my second baby.

My first pregnancy was uneventful until the last two weeks, when the baby turned into the breech position. My doctor tried to turn the baby, without success, and then suggested a planned cesarean section because of the baby's position and size.

I entered Sanno Clinic on my due date feeling comfortable with the situation. I was introduced to the anesthesiologist, who explained the procedure of the epidural and surgery to me. My husband was allowed into the delivery room and held my hand throughout the operation.

The surgery was performed quickly and expertly. I felt no pain, just a slight grogginess due to the antinausea tranquilizer. A sheet shielded my view of the birth, but as soon as my baby was born he was lifted up for me to see.

My husband carried the baby as I was wheeled back to my room, and there I breastfed my baby for the first time when he was only forty minutes old. The anesthesia had not worn off, so I was in no pain.

In spite of the initial disappointment over having to undergo a cesarean birth, I was delighted with my healthy son and the warm, friendly surroundings of the clinic. During my recuperative stay of nine days at Sanno, I enjoyed delicious Western meals and was treated very well. Their policy of a twenty-four-hour private nurse [no longer available] and rooming-in for the baby was ideal, particularly after a cesarean birth. (Incidentally, the scar from the surgery is almost invisible, due to a low, horizontal incision.) The staff honored my requests for breast milk only, although some of the nurses suggested sugar water or formula so that I could get some rest.

Two and a half years later I became pregnant with my second child and, after much research, I decided to attempt a vaginal birth.

My doctor was not enthusiastic about the idea, but he gradually agreed that I was not a high-risk candidate and that a vaginal birth should certainly be possible. I informed the hospital at this point that I would be bringing a female labor assistant (LA), as well as my husband, to offer support during the birth.

Again, I had a joyous and completely uneventful pregnancy and I gained fifty pounds, exactly the same as with my first baby. It is interesting to note that Japanese doctors seem to be stricter concerning weight gain than their Western counterparts.

Four days after my due date, I went into labor. My LA (who is a trained midwife) and I decided that I should continue to labor at home as long as I felt comfortable, because Sanno is only a five-minute drive from my house. This was technically my first birth, so there was the possibility of a long labor.

The LA checked my pulse and the baby's heartbeat. I felt excited yet calm, and the contractions continued to be bearable. After three hours, the labor pains accelerated, and I felt that it was time to go to Sanno.

In my birth plan I had specified that I wanted no intervention as long as the birth was progressing normally. With the exception of an external fetal monitor, which was attached to me for only a few minutes upon arrival, there were no interventions or restrictions during the labor.

Specifically, this meant that I continued to wear my favorite cotton nightgown, I was not subjected to a shave or an enema, and I had complete freedom in choosing my labor position. I used various positions that I found comfortable and was not made to lie on my back. Finally, I requested that the midwife break my waters, which she did three hours after I arrived.

Two hours later, I knelt onto the trolley and, leaning on a stack of pillows, was wheeled down to the delivery room. I moved from the trolley onto the delivery table, still in a kneeling position. I'm sure that this was a little unorthodox for the staff, but they continued to allow me to make my own decisions because the birth was progressing quickly and normally.

Still in a kneeling position, I immediately began pushing, and the baby's head popped out before the doctor arrived. Although the head midwife was still washing up, another midwife jumped into position and caught him just in time. There was a little confusion at this point as a kneeling position for birth is not usually encouraged. However, it all happened so quickly and easily that no one was upset. Once the midwife figured out how to flip me over without my sitting on the baby, we cut the umbilical cord and I put the baby to my breast.

The doctor came in to inspect me—I had not had an episiotomy and there was no tear, so I was soon wheeled back to my room. The baby had been washed and weighed and was carried by my husband. Once again we enjoyed the convenience of rooming-in. After such an easy birth, I was discharged after two days, at my own request.

### PREMATURE BIRTH—BECKY

My son was born by cesarean section; he was two months premature (gestational age: twenty-nine weeks, five days) and weighed 1,746 grams [3.85 pounds]. At birth he had edema [fluid retention], severe anemia, extremely low immunity (even for a premature infant), and weak respiration.

I first saw my baby two days after his birth in the neonatal intensive care unit (NICU). I knew nothing about premature babies and was very upset and shocked to see all the medical equipment and my son's scrawny, sickly appearance. He had been given a blood transfusion because of his anemia and was breathing with the aid of a respirator. Two IVs were attached to him—one containing glucose, the other a general antibiotic.

During my first visit to the NICU I met the doctor only briefly because I was too stunned by my baby's condition to ask many questions, and the doctor did not volunteer any information. As the weeks passed, I naturally began to have more and more questions about my son's treatment and condition. I had heard that Japanese doctors are far less likely than Western doctors to give detailed information unless specifically asked to do so and I found that I had to work hard at digging the answers to my questions out of my doctor. Particularly frustrating was the fact that the doctor seemed more prepared to give information to my husband than to myself.

I found that especially during the crisis points of my son's hospitalization, communication broke down between the staff and myself. Looking back, I realize that part of this was perhaps due to the fact that Japanese and Americans take different approaches to emotional or life-threatening situations.

On the positive side, the doctors allowed me to visit my son at any time, day or night. The studies I have read on premature baby care stress the importance of maternal bonding and touching, even with a very sick premie like my son. In this respect, the NICU was wonderful. I was allowed to hold my son's hand and touch him at any time, although I was not permitted to hold him until he was out of the incubator.

In retrospect, I feel that my son is alive today because of the care he received in the NICU and, now that we are back in Tokyo for a second posting, I take my son back to the same doctor for checkups.

### HOME BIRTH—MARY

When I became pregnant with my first child, I decided, after much research and reflection, that giving birth at home would offer our baby and myself the best chance of a happy, healthy birth. I wanted a good, safe birth, but I was not able to find a hospital or clinic that I felt good and safe going to. I wanted to have freedom of movement in labor and birth. In particular, I wanted to avoid being forced onto my back and having to push the baby up and out against the force of gravity. Another major factor in the decision process was that I wanted to avoid the unnatural and often unnecessary separation from my baby after birth.

You might think that an awful lot of paraphernalia is necessary to prepare for a birth at home, but in fact relatively little is required. Your midwife or doctor will bring any essential equipment along, such as a stethoscope, sterile sheets, etc. I decided to try to be as prepared as  possible in the highly unlikely event that we would be on our own without anyone to attend to us. I ordered a stethoscope (about ¥1,000), an oxygen kit (about ¥30,000), and postpartum large-size sanitary napkins from our neighborhood drugstore. Our midwife suggested sterilizing a few squares of white cotton to use to clear away excess fluids and vernix from the baby's face to make breathing easier. As we didn't have a waterproof mattress cover, I used a plastic shower curtain instead.

Through the midwife's contacts, we were able to arrange an ambulance if emergency help was needed. A month before my due date, I visited the hospital to see the facilities and meet the staff. In the end, everything went as planned and I gave birth to a healthy girl in the comfort of my own bedroom.

With this happy experience in mind, I decided on a home birth again when I became pregnant with my second child a few years later. Even though I had learned of a couple of maternity clinics that were indeed very good—minimal intervention, no unnecessary separation of mother and baby, visits by children allowed, the possibility of returning home soon after the birth, and so on—this time, I had our three-year-old daughter to think about. I didn't want to have to disappear suddenly and then show up a few days later with a stranger in my arms, and so I opted for another home birth.

My most recent home birth experience was again positive and without complications. With our wonderful midwife, my sister, and my husband in attendance, I went into labor in our own bedroom. I was able to take a hot bath, which made the rushes of labor easier to bear. In bed I felt I had to breathe consciously to "blow away" the pain, but in the warm water I felt far more relaxed. As our three-year-old daughter slept downstairs, I gave birth to her baby brother, and I was able to greet her the next morning in my own bed with her new brother. I was very happy to be able to give our lives a semblance of continuity so that my daughter would feel secure and that her brother's birth would be a joyous rather than traumatic experience for her. I can't help feeling that the kind of birth experience that we have had with our children helps to develop family closeness and stability.

I would urge anyone who is planning on having a baby at home to read any books that they can find on the subject. It is also helpful to interview doctors and midwives before hiring someone to care for you at this most important time. If you are interested in having a home birth in Japan, you can consult the list of midwives in this book. Most of the midwives speak only Japanese, so if you do not, you may want to have a translator accompany you to at least some of your prenatal visits and possibly for the actual birth as well.

## FAMILY PLANNING

In Japan, the most popular kinds of contraceptives are condoms (eighty percent), followed by natural family planning, also known as the rhythm method. Also available but less frequently used are the IUD and the birth control pill. Other forms of contraception, such as diaphragms, cervical caps, vaginal jellies, and creams can be obtained in Japan. In case of unwanted pregnancy, some doctors are now prescribing the "morning-after" pill. Abortions are performed frequently and safely in this country (as many as 350,000 a year) and are considered a back-up form of birth control.

Condoms in Japan are unusually thin, yet strong. Since this is the contraceptive of choice for many Japanese couples, you can easily find a selection (in rainbow-colored hues if you wish) in any pharmacy, as well as in supermarkets and vending machines. Size and proper fit may be a problem for some foreigners, in which case you may want to bring a supply with you from home. A source for larger-size condoms in Japan is the American Pharmacy in Tokyo, Hibiya Park Bldg., 1F, 1–8–1 Yurakucho, Chiyoda-ku, ☎ (03) 3271–4034. Condoms can also be ordered from the Foreign Buyers Club.

The Ministry of Health and Welfare in Japan now allows doctors to prescribe the birth control pill. Previously there were restrictions about the use of the pill, and the government did not consider it to be safe. Now, however, the pill is becoming more acceptable among Japanese women. There is some confusion about the strength of the dosage in the Japanese pill—although some doctors will offer you a "low dosage" pill, it may well be a bit stronger than a similar pill in the United States. However, new varieties of contraceptive pills with lighter dosages have recently been introduced to Japan, and the smaller clinics seem to have the latest information on this. The simplest way to get a birth control pill prescription in Japan is to visit a gynecologist at a small clinic. Of course, if you want to continue on exactly the same pill that you used back home, we suggest that you bring it with you. If you plan to receive birth-control pills through the mail, be aware that the Japanese post office only allows a three-month supply of prescription drugs to enter the country in any one package.

For more information about family planning and contraception, contact the Japanese Organization for International Cooperation in Family Planning Incorporated (JOICFP), Hoken Kaikan Shinkan, 1–10 Ichigaya Tamachi, Ichigaya, Shinjuku-ku, Tokyo; ☎ (03) 3268–3450, 🖷 (03) 3235–9776. The English version of the Japanese government mother and child health handbook (*boshi techo*) is available from this organization for ¥920 (plus postage fee).

## Infertility

For help and information about infertility, contact Resolve Inc. This support group publishes information on medical issues as well as a directory of infertility specialists. You can contact them at 1310 Broadway, Somerville, Massachusetts 02144–1731, USA; ☎ (617) 623–0744, 🖵 <www.resolve.org>.

In Japan, the following clinics are among those that specialize in infertility.

### Hara Infertility Clinic

1–7–8 Sendagaya, Shibuya-ku, Tokyo
☎ (03) 3470–4211　東京都渋谷区千駄ヶ谷 1–7–8

### International Medical Crossing (Dr. Ryoko Dozono)

4–2–49 Minami Azabu, Suite 401, Minato-ku, Tokyo
☎ (03) 3443–4823　東京都港区南麻布 4–2–49　#401

### Kanda Clinic (Dr. Sayoko Makabe)

Umeda Bldg., 2F, 3–20–14 Nishi Azabu, Minato-ku, Tokyo
☎ (03) 3402–0654　東京都港区西麻布 3–20–14　梅田ビル 2F

### Odawara Women's Clinic

Ito Bldg., 3F, 4–4–7 Ebisu, Shibuya-ku, Tokyo
☎ (03) 3473–1031　東京都渋谷区恵比寿 4–4–7　伊藤ビル3F

### Toho Women's Clinic (Dr. Hisami Matsumine)

5–3–10 Kiba, Koto-ku, Tokyo
☎ (03) 3630–0322　東京都江東区木場 5–3–10

## ADOPTION

Adopting a baby in Japan—indeed in any country—is not without obstacles, but we have heard numerous success stories in the years we have lived here. Although one must be prepared for a long wait, many of our friends have received babies within months of making the commitment to adopt. The key to getting a child seems to be perseverance and a positive attitude. Many of the parents we spoke with mentioned the importance of keeping in regular contact with the adoption agencies. One mother noted that she thought she and her husband were given a baby just so that she would stop calling every week!

The following organizations, both in Japan and overseas, may be able to give you more information about adoption.

### Adoptive Families of America

2309 Cono Avenue, St. Paul, Minnesota 55108, USA
☎ (612) 645–9955　📠 (612) 645–0055

This national support organization for adoptive families produces a bimonthly magazine containing descriptions and pictures of children waiting to be adopted, in addition to parenting articles. This group also publishes an annual list of adoption agencies.

## Ai no Kesshin

10–15 Hinode-cho, Shizuoka-shi, Shizuoka　静岡県静岡市日出町 10–15
☎ (054) 250–0217　toll-free 0120–428–277 (hotline in English)

This Christian organization offers adoption information, counseling, and foster care. Babies are sometimes available for adoption.

## Americans for International Aid and Adoption

877 S. Adams, Birmingham, Michigan 48009, USA
☎ (313) 642–2211

This organization places children from Asia and South America in adoptive homes. A free information packet is available.

## Families for Private Adoption

P.O. Box 6375, Washington, D.C. 20014, USA
☎ (202) 722–0338

This support group for parents who wish to adopt or have babies adopted privately issues a quarterly newsletter which is available free to members or for a small charge to nonmembers.

## International Concerns Committee for Children

911 Cypress Drive, Boulder, Colorado 80303, USA
☎/🖷 (303) 494–8333　🖳 www.fortnet.org/icc

This organization helps families interested in adopting children from other countries. Although this group does not actually place children, it provides information and counseling free of charge.

## International Family Services (IFS)

Koenji Sun Heights, 408, 1–5–4 Koenji Minami, Suginami-ku, Tokyo
☎ (03) 3312–9515　🖷 (03) 5377–1348　東京都杉並区高円寺南 1–5–4–408

Adoptions are possible through IFS, which also does home studies and adjustment surveys for babies and children who were adopted overseas and now reside in Japan.

## National Council for Adoption

1930 17th Street N.W., Washington, D.C. 20009–6207, USA
☎ (202) 328–1200　🖷 (202) 332–0935

Many books and pamphlets about adoption are available from this organization for adoptive parents and children, including their own *Adoption Factbook*. A list of publications as well as adoption agencies is also available.

## Wa no Kai

4–14–13 Shimo Ochiai, Shinjuku-ku, Tokyo
☎ (03) 3951–7270　東京都新宿区下落合 4–14–13

This organization offers help with such problems as unwanted pregnancy and infertility. Sometimes has babies for adoption.

### ONLINE SOURCES

**Adoption.com**, 🖳 <www.adoption.com>, offers everything you might want to know about adoption, including registries of adoptable children and families hoping to adopt.

**The Adoption Guide**, 🖳 <www.theadoptionguide.com>, dispenses advice and resources on adoption, as well as a guide to adoption agencies.

**National Adoption Information Clearinghouse**, 🖳 <www.calib.com/naic>, is a comprehensive site on all aspects of adoption, with helpful links to other related sites and databases.

**Rainbow Kids**, 🖳 <www.rainbowkids.com>, is an online magazine about international adoption.

### HELPFUL PUBLICATIONS

*The Report on Foreign Adoption.* Available from the International Concerns Committee for Children, listed above under Adoption.

*The Private Adoption Handbook*, by Stanley B. Michelman and Meg Schneider with Antonia Van Der Meer (Villard Books).

*A Handful of Hope*, by Suzanne Arms (Celestial Arts).

*Guide to Adoption Agencies*, by Julia Posner. Available from the Child Welfare League of America, 440 First Street N.W., Suite 310, Washington, D.C. 20001, USA.

## BIRTH ANNOUNCEMENTS

Heralding the arrival of your precious bundle is one of the best parts about having a baby. In Japan, you can either have the announcement made up here, or you can order from an overseas mail-order source. If you choose to have your announcements printed here, check with a well-known stationery company such as Itoya (see chapter 8 under Holiday Supplies and Gift Shops). A small neighborhood printer can probably do the same job for less money, but communication may be difficult.

At Itoya, you will find a nice selection of fine stationery, such as Crane's, although most are rather expensive. Itoya does not have the variety of personalized birth announcements that are available in similar stores in the United States, but they will try to accommodate your design ideas.

If you want a Japanese touch, consider printing the information on *washi* paper, with a matching envelope. Another choice is the blank greeting cards with various Japanese scenes on the fronts available in stationery stores. We once used a greeting card with a picture of a little girl in a kimono for an announcement. You can either have the message inside printed, or you can write it in yourself. Postcards with pictures of children on the front, often available around the Japanese holidays, can be used in a similar way.

Probably the easiest and cheapest method is the one that most of our Japanese friends use. At your local photo shop you can order a postcard with your baby's picture plus a few words about the birth. Most large photo stores will print your announcement in English if you so request. These postcards can be addressed and mailed without an envelope, which saves time and money. You can pick out the style beforehand, and then add the baby picture and the facts later. This kind of birth announcement can usually be ready in a few days.

If you want to order birth announcements from an overseas catalog, plan ahead. You can often order the birth announcement of your choice, and then call or fax the final information after the birth. Ask about this when you write for a brochure. Usually, the company will send you the envelopes ahead of your due date so that you can address them and have them ready to mail when the baby arrives. This method is the least time-consuming—and, of course, it helps to get as many of the little tasks like birth announcements out of the way before the baby does arrive.

### MAIL-ORDER BIRTH ANNOUNCEMENTS

#### Babies 'n' Bells

☎ (972) 416–2229    🖨 (972) 418–5723    🖥 babiesnbells.com

This Internet site offers you a wide variety of custom paper products, announcements, and photo cards to announce the addition to your family. These beautiful personalized cards come on fine-quality paper, and orders are processed quickly. They also feature thank-you cards to match your announcement.

**Webbaby**

🖳 webbaby.com

This Internet site offers you the opportunity to show all the folks back home the new baby on the web. They offer you a private site to post your pictures with your choice of background and music. What better way to welcome a new millennium baby than using an Internet announcement.

## SPECIAL GIFTS AND MEMENTOS

The birth of a new baby is a blessed event anywhere in the world. To commemorate your own baby's birth or that of a friend's baby, here are some of our favorite gift ideas.

Japanese baby blankets are made of the softest toweling imaginable. We have not seen these lovely blankets, which are practical as well as pretty, in any other country. For little girls, you may want to start a collection of dolls, and here the selection is vast, from porcelain to plastic to wood. The Japanese teething rings and other toys for young babies are unique and delightful. If you want to buy baby clothes, some of the soft, one-hundred-percent-cotton sleepwear is ideal. Another big hit with many of our friends has been the Hard Rock Cafe Tokyo T-shirts or Tokyo Disneyland T-shirts, in baby sizes, of course. Ornate photo albums, embroidered with the baby's name and date of birth, are available in any department store. The style of these albums is uniquely Japanese, and they make a gift that every proud parent can use.

A gift indicating the baby's year of birth in the Japanese zodiac is a good way to commemorate a birth in Japan. These mementos, from statues to soap in the shape of the zodiac animals, are prominently displayed around the New Year, so pick something up then if you will have use for it later in the year.

Even the ward and city offices get into the act when it comes to welcoming a new addition to the household. For example, the Minato-ku office presents potted plants to any household with a new baby.

These families are usually notified by postcard as to when they can pick up their plant. Check with your local office to see if any special gift is offered to newborns in your area.

## VOCABULARY LIST

Knowing a few key words in Japanese can make all the difference when you are staying in the hospital in Japan, or if you are caught in an emergency situation. The following words and phrases will be helpful during your pregnancy and stay in hospital.

### CALLING AN AMBULANCE

The national number for ambulance service is ☎ 119. You must give the request and directions in Japanese:

Please send an ambulance: *kyukyusha o onegaishimasu*
I have a sudden illness, please come quickly: *Kyubyo desuga, hayaku kite kudasai*
Please take us to _____ hospital: (hospital name) *byoin ni tsurete itte kudasai*
My address is _____: *jusho wa _____ku, _____shi, _____chome*
My name is _____: *namae wa* (your name) *desu*

### GENERAL VOCABULARY

anemia: *hinketsu*　貧血
backache: *senaka ga itai*　背中が痛い
bleeding: *shukketsu*　出血
contraception: *hinin*　避妊
delivery: *osan, bumben*　お産, 分娩
doctor: *oisha-san, dokuta*　お医者さん, ドクター
ectopic pregnancy: *shikyugai ninshin*　子宮外妊娠
endometrium (uterine wall): *shikyu naimaku*　子宮内膜
fallopian tubes: *rankan*　卵管
fetus: *taiji*　胎児
indigestion: *shoka furyo*　消化不良
infection: *kansen*　感染
infertility: *funin*　不妊
menstruation: *gekkei, seiri*　月経, 生理
midwife: *osamba-san, josampu*　お産婆さん, 助産婦
miscarriage: *ryuzan*　流産

morning sickness: *tsuwari*　つわり
nurse: *kangofu-san, naasu*　看護婦さん，ナース
obstetrics and gynecology: *sanfujinka*　産婦人科
oral contraceptive pills: *keiko hininyaku, piru*　経口避妊薬，ピル
ovarian cyst: *ransoo-noshu*　卵巣のう腫
ovary: *ransoo*　卵巣
ovulation: *hairan*　排卵
pelvic examination: *naishin*　内診
pelvis: *kotsuban*　骨盤
placenta: *taiban*　胎盤
pregnancy: *ninshin*　妊娠
swelling: *hare*　はれ
toxemia: *ninshin chudokusho*　妊娠中毒症
uterus: *shikyu*　子宮
vagina: *chitsu*　膣
vaginal discharge: *taige, orimono*　帯下，おりもの

### GENERAL HOSPITAL VOCABULARY

What are you doing?: *nani o shitemasu ka?*　何をしてますか
Who are you?: *donata desu ka?*　どなたですか
Please call the doctor: *oisha-san o yonde kudasai*　お医者さんを呼んで下さい
Please call the nurse: *kangofu-san o yonde kudasai*　看護婦さんを呼んで下さい

### LABOR

breaking of waters: *hasui*　破水
breech birth: *sakago*　逆子
cesarean section: *teio sekkai*　帝王切開
contraction: *itami, shushuku*　痛み，収縮
fetal monitor: *taiji kanshi sochi*　胎児監視装置
induced labor: *yuhatsu bumben*　誘発分娩
labor has begun: *jintsu ga hajimarimashita*　陣痛が始まりました
labor pain: *jintsu*　陣痛
labor room: *jintsu shitsu*　陣痛室
pain or discomfort: *itami, itai desu*　痛み，痛いです
shaving: *teimo*　剃毛

How many minutes apart are your contractions?: *nampun oki ni itami ga arimasu ka?*　何分おきに痛みがありますか
　one minute apart: *ippun oki desu*　1分おきです
　two minutes apart: *nifun oki desu*　2分おきです

three minutes apart: *sampun oki desu*　3分おきです
four minutes apart: *yompun oki desu*　4分おきです
five minutes apart: *gofun oki desu*　5分おきです
six minutes apart: *roppun oki desu*　6分おきです
seven minutes apart: *nanafun oki desu*　7分おきです
eight minutes apart: *happun oki desu*　8分おきです
nine minutes apart: *kyufun oki desu*　9分おきです
ten minutes apart: *juppun oki desu*　10分おきです

enema: *kanchoo*　浣腸
episiotomy: *ein sekkai*　会陰切開
general anesthetic: *zenshin masui*　全身麻酔
　　local anesthetic: *kyokubu masui*　局部麻酔
　　　epidural anesthetic: *komakugai masui*　硬膜外麻酔
　　　spinal anesthetic: *sekizui masui*　脊髄麻酔
injection: *chusha*　注射
medicine: *kusuri*　薬

## DELIVERY

delivery room: *bumben shitsu*　分娩室
delivery table: *bumben dai*　分娩台
pillow: *makura*　枕
dilation: *kakucho*　拡張
full dilation: *zenkaidai*　全開大
transition: *ikoki, henka*　移行期，変化

I feel like pushing/I want to push: *ikimitai desu*　いきみたいです
bag of waters: *yomaku*　羊膜
afterbirth: *atozan*　後産
placenta: *taiban*　胎盤
umbilical cord: *heso no o*　へその緒

## POSTPARTUM

bowel movement: *otsuuji, haiben*　お通じ，排便
catheter: *kuda, kateteru*　管，カテーテル
constipation: *bempi*　便秘
diarrhea: *geri*　下痢
heavy bleeding/hemorrhage: *shukketsu*　出血
laxative: *shikanzai, kangezai, bempi yaku*　弛緩剤，緩下剤，便秘薬
lochia (normal bleeding after delivery): *orimono*　おりもの

perineum: *eimbu*　会陰部
sanitary pads: *napukin*　ナプキン
stool: *ben*　便
urine: *o-shosui*　お小水

I want to go to the toilet: *toire ni ikitai*　トイレに行きたい
Please may I get up?: *okitai no desu ga ii desu ka?*　起きたいのですがいいですか

## THE BABY

baby: *akachan*　赤ちゃん
birth certificate: *shussei shomeisho*　出生証明書
circumcision: *katsurei*　割礼
jaundice: *odan*　黄疸
meconium: *taiben*　胎盤

May I see my baby?: *akachan ni attemo ii desu ka?*　赤ちゃんに会ってもいいですか
May I hold my baby?: *akachan o daitemo ii desu ka?*　赤ちゃんを抱いてもいいですか
Please bring my baby: *akachan o tsurete kite kudasai*　赤ちゃんを連れて来てください
nursery: *shinseiji shitsu*　新生児室

## BREASTFEEDING

breast: *oppai, o-chichi*　おっぱい，お乳
breastfeeding room: *junyu shitsu*　授乳室
breast massage: *o-chi-chi no massaji*　お乳のマッサージ
breast milk: *bonyu*　母乳
breast pump: *sakunyuki*　搾乳器
colostrum: *shonyu*　初乳
glucose water: *budoto eki*　ブドウ糖液
nipples: *chikubi*　乳首

I am going to breastfeed: *o-chichi o agetai desu*　お乳をあげたいです
May I feed my baby?: *akachan ni o-chichi o agetemo ii desu ka?*　赤ちゃんにお乳をあげてもいいですか
My breasts are full: *o-chichi ga hatte imasu*　お乳が張っています

# 10

# Kids' Health

# In

# Japan

THE DRINKING WATER IN JAPAN
DOES NOT CONTAIN FLUORIDE.

Nothing is more important to parents than their children's general health and well-being. Living in Japan is becoming a healthier prospect all the time as hospitals and emergency services continually update equipment and modernize procedures. Once you become accustomed to Japanese medical procedures and medications, and find out what is and what is not available here, you will be able to feel confident that you are doing all you can to keep your kids healthy.

## TAKING CARE OF THE KIDS' HEALTH

Many Western pharmaceutical goods are available in this country, but there are a few products that the parents of young children should bring from home. The first is Children's and Infant Tylenol or a similar acetaminophen product to reduce fever and discomfort in a sick child. We suggest that you bring a year's supply of the drops or chewable tablets. Remember that Japanese post office regulations prohibit sending more than a three-month supply of a prescription drug through the mail. Tylenol is not considered a prescription drug in other countries, but as it is not available over-the-counter here, it may be considered one by the post office. Have your contact person send it in small amounts to be on the safe side.

The second medicine-cabinet essential that we miss is teething gel, a great help when babies are teething. Some infants do not care for the stuff, while others just about live on it for their first two years of life. Borrow some from a friend or fly it in just in case your child is of the latter persuasion. Also worth bringing is a children's decongestant for colds, expectorant for coughs, and a sudafed (pseudoephedrine) product for adults.

Bring an extra pair of eyeglasses or contact lenses if possible. Both are available in Japan, but can be quite expensive. For English-speaking opticians, visit one of the Wasin Optical Stores in Ginza or Shibuya. Other stores are located in Shinjuku, Ikebukuro, Urawa, and Yokosuka. The head office is located at 6–4–4 Ginza, Chuo-ku, Tokyo; ☎ (03) 3572–3693.

If your child suffers from allergies or asthma, you should bring enough medication to get through the first few months. Inhalers and bronchiodilators are available in Japan, as are allergy shots and other medications. For help with allergic reactions or asthmatic attacks, contact a doctor (see the listing at the end of this chapter), or see a specialist at one of the following clinics.

### Japan Allergy Clinic

New Shimbashi Bldg., 3F, 2–16–1 Shimbashi, Minato-ku, Tokyo
☎ (03) 3591–5464　東京都港区新橋 2-16-1　ニュー新橋ビル 3F
🚇 Shinjuku Station, JR Yamanote and various lines

### Takagi Skin Clinic, Dr. Chieko McKinstrey

Kuken Bldg., 3F, 36–1 Udagawa-cho, Shibuya-ku, Tokyo
☎ (03) 3462–2807　🖶 (03) 3461–8178　東京都渋谷区宇田川町 36-1　空研ビル 3F
🚇 Shibuya Station, JR Yamanote and various lines

### Yokohama Children's Allergy Center

469 Futatsubashi-cho, Seya-ku, Yokohama-shi, Kanagawa-ken
☎ (045) 365–3601　神奈川県横浜市瀬谷区二橋町 469
🚇 Mitsukyo Station, Sotetsu Line

For noncontrolled prescription drugs, you may also order from International Pharmaceutical Services (IPS), a company experienced with overseas shipping regulations. You may contact them for more information at 320 Judah St., Suite 1, San Francisco, California 94122, USA; 🖥 <www.internationalpharmacy.com>, ☎ (415) 664–6100, 🖶 (415) 664–6125.

## FEEDING THE KIDS

Recently, many mothers are wisely choosing to breastfeed their babies. For information and support about breastfeeding, call La Leche League International (see chapter 9). There are English- and Japanese-speaking groups throughout Japan. Mothers who plan to feed their babies formula can choose from several Japanese brands—Meiji, Morinaga, and

Snow—as well as SMA, a U.S. product, and Nestle, from Switzerland. The instructions for mixing the formula are often in Japanese, but you can ask your doctor which formula he would recommend and how to mix it. Unfortunately, as well as being expensive, formula in Japan (as in other countries) is often made with palm and coconut oils high in saturated fat. For those children who are allergic to milk products, a few stores carry soy formula. If you decide to use formula, you will need to use bottled or purified water to mix it with, as the canned liquid formula is not available in Japan.

For bottles and nipples, check any department store or baby supply store. You will find Nuk brand nipples sold here. Playtex disposable bottles are available at some of the international supermarkets and the American Pharmacy in Tokyo located in the Hibiya Park Bldg., 1F, 1–8 Yurakucho, Chiyoda-ku; ☎ (03) 3271–4034.

When it comes to baby food, you won't run into many problems finding good-quality, healthy food to feed your baby in Japan. Jars of Gerber prepared baby food are sold in large supermarkets. Even if the label is in Japanese, you can tell what is in the jar by the picture on the front. There is a good alternative to Gerber, however, from a Japanese company. Wakodo makes freeze-dried baby food, to which you add hot water to reach the desired consistency. The food comes in packets just large enough for one serving, with fish and vegetables being predominant. Look for the white box with "Wakodo" written on it in English. Kewpie Co., too, makes its own freeze-dried baby food, which is packaged in a box similar to Wakodo. Look for the Kewpie baby food in jars as well. Snow, Meiji, and Morinaga also carry a wide variety of baby food.

The drinking water in Japan does not contain fluoride, so some parents opt for supplementing it with fluoride drops or tablets. If you want your children to have fluoride supplements, you will have to buy them overseas because they are not available in Japan. Check with your doctor back home for his advice on fluoride supplements.

There is a company called COMFO Inc. (Shimbashi 5-chome, Minato-ku, Tokyo) that will set up a water server and deliver natural drinking water to your home or office on a regular basis in ten- and fifteen-liter bottles. For inquires in English, call ☎ toll-free 0120–30–4132 or fax ☎ (03) 3435–0124. There is also a pamphlet in English and Japanese that describes its services.

A word about cow's milk in Japan: because of the high temperature of pasteurization, most milk here has a different taste and smell. However, there are a few brands which are pasteurized at the lower 63°C and these have a less distinctive taste. Look for the Takanashi brand that has "63C.30" on the label.

Children's multivitamins are available in stores, but all the information is in Japanese and the dosage may not be what you are accustomed to in your home country. The Foreign Buyers' Club has a catalog for vitamins and health-food products from the United States (see the listings in the next section of this chapter).

Another favorite source for vitamins outside of Japan, and at discount prices, is Puritan's Pride. They can be reached at 1233 Montauk Hwy, P.O. Box 9001, Oakdale, New York 11769–9001, USA; ☎ 800–645–1030, 🖷 (516) 471–5693, 🖳 <www.puritan.com>.

Amway in Japan carries an extensive line of vitamins, hypoallergenic products, plus water and air treatment systems. For a catalog contact Nihon Seimei, Minami Azabu Bldg., 2–8–12 Minami Azabu, Minato-ku, Tokyo; ☎ toll-free 0120–12–3777 or in English at ☎ (03) 3928–9357, 🖷 (03) 3928–4226.

Herbal and homeopathic remedies specifically for children are available from Red Mountain Remedies. The herbalist-mom at Red Mountain also sells a must-have Remedies for the Road travel kit. Ask for a free brochure at ☎ 888–791–8333 or 🖳 <www.redmtremedies.com>.

Another source for herbal remedies is Herbs for Kids, ☎ (406) 587–0180 or 🖳 <www.herbsforkids.com>.

Nutritional favorites of little ones in Japan are *yakiimo*, or sweet potatoes, which we buy from vendors on the street. Kids also enjoy strips of *nori* (edible seaweed) and *shirasuboshi* (the tiny fresh fish you see in the refrigerated section of grocery stores). Get a rice cooker and cook rice; you can mix it with any number of dishes that your children will enjoy.

## A TASTE OF HOME

Whether you are looking for food products from abroad, pesticide-free produce, a special treat from home, gourmet delicacies, or just a supermarket that takes phone orders and will deliver, you can find it here. Many of these companies are run by foreigners, therefore language is not a problem. Call or write the companies below for their catalogs, and you should never have to go too long without that important something from home.

## Benten Supermarket

16–2 Wakamatsu-cho, Shinjuku-ku, Tokyo　　東京都新宿区若松町 16–2
☎ (03) 3202–2421　📠 (03) 3202–2423
🚇 Akebonobashi Station, Toei Shinjuku Line

No home should be without a Benten catalog. This supermarket, in business over forty years, has Western food products similar to those available at supermarkets catering to foreigners, such as National Azabu or Kinokuniya, but at somewhat lower prices. Price is not the only reason for shopping at Benten's, however. Just the fact that you can look in the catalog and place an order for your week's groceries and have them delivered the next day—free of charge if you spend over ¥5,000—makes the catalog a necessity for every household. There is no membership fee, and deliveries in metropolitan Tokyo are daily, except for the Fuchu, Mitaka, and Kurume areas, where delivery is only on Wednesday and Friday afternoons. For long-distance deliveries, you can place your order by mail, and it will take one to two weeks to arrive. There is a packing charge of ¥1,500, and you pay the shipping charges on delivery.

## Chikyujin Club System

Shin Yokohama, Kohoku-ku, Yokohama-shi, Kanagawa-ken
☎ (045) 474–5458, 0120–733–550 (toll-free)　　神奈川県横浜市港北区新横浜

Chikyujin Club is more of a food co-op than just a mail-order company. Once a week, you will receive an order list in the mail. There are over five hundred items available, from nonhomogenized milk and low-pesticide produce to whole grains and bakery goods. The fruits and vegetables are harvested the day before delivery, so freshness is assured. The order form itself is in Japanese, but there is a computer printout of all the products in English, so all you have to do is match the number on the order form to the item on the printout. The two-thousand-member club is based in Yokohama, and they deliver once a week to the Tokyo-Yokohama area free of charge with a minimum order of ¥3,500. There is a membership fee of ¥5,000.

## Farmland Freezer Club

1–27–11 Higashi Tamagawa, Setagaya-ku, Tokyo
☎ (03) 3720–4651　📠 (03) 3720–5959　　東京都世田谷区東玉川 1–27–11
🚇 Okusawa Station, Tokyu Mekama Line

Farmland Freezer Club is a great resource for those who like to shop ahead or have a large freezer! Most of their offerings are frozen, and imported meats and seafood make up the majority of the list. Also available are some frozen fruits and vegetables. The meats are offered at lower prices than you would pay elsewhere, and there are many types of meat not available in your local stores. Ground lamb, whole bone-in hams, and a wide variety of fresh sausages are just some of the "not available in Japan" items you can order.

## Foreign Buyer's Club

5–15 Koyocho-naka, 3F, Higashinada-ku, Kobe-shi, Hyogo
兵庫県神戸市東灘区向洋町中 5–15 3F
☎ (078) 857–9001　🖷 (078) 857–9005/1089　🖳 www.fbcusa.com

The FBC is a wonderful co-op run by a foreign couple in Kobe. It is a nonprofit organization, and they import goods from the United States through a large wholesale house. What that means to you and me is that we can get almost any item we want from the United States delivered to our door, and at a reasonable price. Orders must be made by the case, so unless you have adequate storage space, get together with a friend to order. For ¥200 each, FBC also offers specialty catalogs for baby goods, health food, coffee and teas, and vitamins. There is a ¥1,000 membership fee, and you pay delivery charges. Usually delivery takes four to five weeks.

## Japan-Europe Trading Company

PMC Bldg., 3F, 1–23–5 Higashi Azabu, Minato-ku, Tokyo
☎ (03) 3582–1490　🖷 (03) 3583–9060　東京都港区東麻布 1–23–5 PMCビル 3F
🚇 Shiba Koen Station, Toei Mita Line; Kamiyacho Station, Hibiya Line

This company offers an exclusive catalog of imported goodies for the gourmet. Many of the items are of the hard-to-find variety, and often they are discounted below retail price. If you have a craving for fine cheeses, wines, or specialty meats, this is the catalog to have. There is no membership fee, and you pay the delivery costs.

## Natural House

3–6–18 Kita Aoyama, Minato-ku, Tokyo　東京都港区北青山 3–6–18
☎ (03) 5469–1411
🚇 Omotesando Station, Ginza, Hanzomon lines

Natural House is a large chain of stores that offers an assortment of "healthy" products. There are eleven Natural House stores in the Tokyo area and eight in the Kobe-Osaka region. Since it is such a large operation, the controls on all of their products may not be as strict as some of the smaller companies. Natural House does not deliver, but stores in Tokyo are centrally located.

### Nissin World Delicatessen

2–34–2 Higashi Azabu, Minato-ku, Tokyo 東京都港区東麻布 2–34–2
☎ (03) 3583–4586
〰 Shiba Koen Station, Toei Mita Line; Kamiyacho Station, Hibiya Line

Opened in 1998, this spacious and modern store is an expansion of Meat Rush, the discount deli next door. The new store is stocked with an array of international foods in addition to seafood, fresh produce, and dairy products, all at competitive prices.

### Radish Bohya

For catalog and to place orders, call ☎ (03) 5228–3333 (Tokyo, Chiba), ☎ (048) 422–4080 (Saitama, Northern Kanto area), ☎ (046) 228–9994 (Kanagawa, Shizuoka).

### Seikatsu Club Seikyo

4–2–1 Chitosedai, Setagaya-ku, Tokyo 東京都世田谷区千歳台 4–2–1
☎ (03) 5490–8311 🖷 (03) 5490–8312 🖵 www.jca.ax.apc.org/seikatsu/
〰 Chitose Funabashi Station, Odakyu Line

For those days when it's difficult to get out of the house or when you're tired of carrying home heavy bags along with those screaming children, why not become a member of your local cooperative and have goods delivered to your door? For more information on the cooperative nearest you and how to join, call the Seikatsu Club.

### Tengu Natural Foods

50–2 Umehara, Hidaka-shi, Saitama 埼玉県日高市梅原 50–2
☎ (0429) 85–8751 🖷 (0429) 85–8752

Tengu Natural Foods is a company that offers healthy foods imported from the United States and Canada at reasonable prices. Granola, wholewheat flour, and an assortment of whole grain breads are just some of the goodies offered that are also good for you. Tengu is constantly expanding its line of health-food products and will send a catalog upon request. Delivery is made to your home, usually within a few days of placing your order, and payment can be made through your local post office.

## *OBENTO* TIPS

Now that you've got those cute little *obento* containers, you are probably wondering what to squeeze into them. I found that the key is to use lots of tiny things. At first I used to cram oversized peanut-butter-and-jelly sandwiches into them, but eventually my children were embarrassed. I progressed to cutting different kinds of sandwiches into shapes and then I started to get adventurous. Now, I buy bags of miniature frozen food: meatballs, chicken wings, tiny hotdogs, or vegetables such as acorn squash, corn, and English peas. All that is needed is a quick microwave in the morning with a little seasoning and then they can be arranged artfully in the box along with a helping of rice. For dessert, I skewer various fruit, or include a mini-container of pudding or jello.

Purchasing a rice cooker made life even simpler. I lay down a bed of rice and top it with tasty treats or simply use it as a staple food. One day I found those little plastic triangular molds in the supermarket and discovered I could make my own professional-looking riceballs (*onigiri*)! Most children enjoy rice balls, but my first attempts didn't look so appealing. I would tuck a bit of tuna into a wad of rice, which I would then squeeze in my fist. Even with *nori* delicately wrapped around it, my rice balls looked like lumpy stones. But once I found the little molds it was incredibly easy to make neat, triangular *onigiri* that looked as good as they tasted.

Another lunch favorite is chicken on a stick, which I often buy at the corner *yakitori* stand. Even my pickiest eater, who basically eats no vegetables, enjoys a slice of a Japanese sweet potato, purchased the night before from the vendor on the street. This child's only acceptable green vegetable is another *obento* staple: Japanese soybeans, or *edamame*. The beans are popped out of their pods and eaten cold and lightly salted, sort of like boiled peanuts.

At first I worried about the temperature of food in the *obento* box, but it doesn't seem to be a big concern except in the summer when I am extra cautious about not using mayonnaise or anything that might cause salmonella. If you are running out of *obento* ideas, I suggest you buy one of those magazines or "mooks," a "book-magazine," usually available at local Japanese bookstores. With dozens of glossy photos of the most elaborate *obento* creations imaginable, these publications will supply even more ideas!

## VACCINATIONS AND JAPAN

"Vaccines and vaccinations have some side-effects and unknown factors related to them and are therefore controversial."

This quotation was taken from a paper, "Immunizations in Japan." This section is not intended as a recommendation, but rather as a resource to help you understand what vaccinations are available in Japan, compared with those available in some other countries. The final decision on when and which vaccinations should be given to your child can be taken after you consult with your doctor.

Because of the Vaccinations Law and the Tuberculosis Prevention Law, the Japanese government implements vaccinations "in order to protect society from communicable diseases" (quoted from the *boshi techo*, the mother-and-child health record). All babies resident in Japan are entitled to free polio, TB, DPT (diptheria, pertussis, and tetanus), and measles immunizations. To receive your free immunization coupons, contact the Health Department (*hokenjo*) of your ward or city office, and you will receive a *boshi techo* if you do not already have one (see chapter 9 for information on obtaining the *boshi techo* during pregnancy if your baby is to be born in Japan).

The DPT and measles injections must be done by a doctor in your ward; polio and BCG (for increased resistance to tuberculosis) must be administered at the Health Department. The vaccinations are administered on designated dates, and because some vaccinations are given in a series, none of the vaccinations should be missed. If your child cannot make one of the designated dates, it may be necessary to make special arrangements to receive them. Call your Health Department to check the dates (it may be that only Japanese is spoken).

Of course, you do not have to use the coupons for free vaccinations. You may go to a private doctor and pay for the vaccinations with cash or by using whatever foreign insurance coverage you would normally use.

The BCG, the vaccination for tuberculosis, is one of the most controversial vaccinations because it provides only limited protection. It is generally recommended for areas with low overall hygiene. Presently, in Europe a BCG vaccination is administered after birth; in Japan, it is given in infancy. The United States does not ordinarily give the vaccination. However, at public schools in the United States, skin tests are done annually for TB. If a child has had a BCG,

## SCHEDULE OF VACCINATIONS

|  | JAPAN | USA | UK |
|---|---|---|---|
| DPT | 3 times between 3 months and 7 years, booster 12 to 18 months after initial series | 2, 4, and 6 months 18 months, 5 years | 3 months, 4 1/2 to 5 months, and 6 to 8 weeks later |
| DT | 12 years | 15 years and every 10 years throughout life | with polio at 4 1/2 to 5 years |
| POLIO | twice between 3 months and 4 years (4 to 18 months) at 6-week intervals | 2, 4, and 18 months, 5 years | with tetanus at 15 years |
| MEASLES | once from 1 year to 6 years (recommended at 18 months) | part of MMR | part of MMR |
| MUMPS | once at 12 months | part of MMR | part of MMR |
| RUBELLA | 5 years, 15 years | part of MMR | part of MMR |
| MMR | not available as one injection | 15 months, 5 years | ―― |
| BCG | birth to 4 years (3 to 12 months if prior TB skin test is negative) | not recommended | 10 to 13 years if prior TB skin test is negative |
| CHICKEN POX | once after 1 year | 15 months | not available |
| HEPATITIS B | given to newborn of carrier mothers | 3 times in first 2 months | 3 times for child of carrier mother |
| INFLUENZA | 3 to 15 years | ―― | ―― |
| HEMOPHILUS INFLUENZA (Hb) part of DPT | ―― | 3 times in the first 15 months | ―― |

he may then test positive for TB and will then have to have a chest X-ray and possibly have further tests for TB.

The common vaccinations are DPT, DT (diptheria and adult tetanus), MMR (measles, mumps, and rubella; multishot), and BCG.

The schedule for administering the various kinds of vaccinations and serial vaccinations differs from country to country. The general trend, however, is to cut down the number of vaccinations given. It is less important which schedule you follow; *completing the vaccinations on schedule is what is important.* If you plan to leave Japan while in the process of getting your child vaccinated, it is advisable to follow a schedule most adaptable to your move. Be sure to bring all vaccination records for your family upon moving to Japan. Most schools will require proof of immunization.

The schedule of vaccinations (from *Accessible Medical Services for Foreign Residents of Tokyo*, Dai-Ichi-Hoki Shuppan Co., Ltd., 1988) is reproduced here with permission from the Kansai Childbirth Education Organization, with the guidance of Dr. G. Barraclough.

## BE PREPARED

During your stay here, you will want to have your own library of medical and developmental books in your native language, and many of the best books in English are available from the mail-order sources discussed in chapter 4. Especially useful is a help-at-a-glance reference book on medical emergencies. The National Safety Council, in the United States, publishes two such books on emergency medical treatment, *Emergency Medical Treatment: Infants* and *Emergency Medical Treatment: Children.* The books are made of thick paper with tabs for quick reference in case of emergencies. Large-print, step-by-step instructions are given with pictures of what to do in case of injuries, such as choking, poisoning, burns, broken bones, and more.

The single most important book we recommend is *Japan Health Handbook* (Kodansha International) by Meredith Enman Maruyama, Louise Picon Shimizu, and Nancy Smith Tsurumaki: two nurses and one childbirth educator. The authors have compiled vast amounts of information in this book covering everything from birth to death. The chapters on children's health, having a baby, and nutrition are specially helpful.

There are many websites which can help you find answers to

your medical questions. Kids Doctor, 🖳 <www.kidsdoctor.com>, is a twenty-four-hour resource on everything a parent needs to know to keep the children healthy. Check out the many articles and health tips. MedicineNet, 🖳 <www.medicinenet.com>, provides information on diseases, treatments, and medications. Get advice from physicians on the "Ask the Experts" bulletin board. Many of the parenting websites listed in chapter 12 have medical resources.

Most doctors recommend that parents take an infant CPR course when they have a baby. Infant and adult CPR courses and basic first-aid courses are offered in English through the community centers (see chapter 12), churches, private clubs, and some of the childbirth educators (see chapter 9).

It is wise to plan what you would do in case of an emergency—when you move to Japan, locate the hospital nearest you that has a twenty-four-hour emergency room. There are three levels of emergency room care, and you should find out what is available in your area. Tertiary emergency facilities can handle life-threatening emergencies, secondary emergency care hospitals can care for serious but not life-threatening emergencies, and primary emergency care is available at a large number of hospitals and clinics.

## CALLING AN AMBULANCE

The ambulance and emergency procedures and services in Japan are most likely not what you are used to in your home country. Ambulance drivers in Japan are not trained paramedics as in the United States and other countries, and often foreigners are advised to get to the nearest emergency hospital on their own if the situation is not a true emergency. Your doctor can also arrange for an ambulance to pick you up and take you to the hospital of his or her choice.

Throughout Japan, ☎ 119 is the emergency number for fire and ambulance services. Call ☎ 110 for police. You must be able to give the information in Japanese.

For ease in calling during an actual emergency, it is a good idea to place a memo near your telephone with the emergency phone numbers and Japanese-language phrases written down for stating your address, phone number, and name.

To call an ambulance, dial ☎ 119. Useful phrases include:

Please send an ambulance: *kyukyusha o onegai shimasu*

My address is _____: *jusho wa _____ku, _____machi _____chome, _____banchi,* (house name), and _____*go* (apartment or house number)

My name is _____: *namae wa _____desu*

My telephone number is _____: *denwa bango wa* (your phone number)

I live near (some landmark): (_____) *no chikaku desu*

Once you have telephoned, the ambulance will be dispatched even if you stay on the line. If you are not able to make yourself understood, do not hang up. In many areas, they will be able to direct an ambulance to you by tracing your call.

## Poison Control Centers

In case of accidental poisoning, call the following numbers for help in English.

U.S. Air Force Hospital at Yokota ☎ (0425) 52–2511 ext. 2257740
U.S. Navy Hospital at Yokosuka ☎ (0468) 21–1911 ext. 5247
New York Poison Control Center ☎ (212) 340–4494
Los Angeles Poison Control Center ☎ (213) 664–2121

In Japanese, there are two phone numbers for poison information: the Tsukuba Chudoku Center, ☎ (0990) 52–9899 (open 9:00 A.M. to 5:00 P.M. daily), and the Nihon Chudoku Joho Center at ☎ (0990) 50–2499 (open twenty-four hours every day).

## Earthquakes—Preparing For the Big One

To help sensitize your child to earthquakes and related safety issues, you can take him on a field trip to the Earthquake Science Hall, in the Kita Ward Disaster Prevention Center at 2–1–16 Nishigahara, Kita-ku, Tokyo; ☎ (03) 3940–1811. Though there are no interpreters, a pamphlet is available in English, Chinese, and Korean. Added to this, the hands-on nature of the exhibits explain the major earthquakes that have occurred in Japanese history. The whole course, including simulation of how to handle emergencies, such as smoke, fire, the collapse of a building, and first-aid injuries, takes about an hour. Hours are 9:00 A.M. to 5:00 P.M. Closed on Monday, holidays, and from December 28 through January 4. Admission is free.

The Yokohama Disaster Prevention Center (4–7 Sawatari, Kanagawa-ku, Yokohama-shi, Kanagawa-ken) offers a similar program, with an English-language video that can be viewed on the premises or borrowed to watch at home. For more information, call ☎ (045) 312–0119.

Your ward office can provide you with a handbook in English and a map showing Tokyo's 137 evacuation sites. Find out which site is closest to you. Visit the site (often a park) with your children and pick a meeting spot.

In your home, it is a good idea to prepare an emergency kit. You could start by checking out the pre-assembled kits available in the disaster prevention section (*bousai yohin uriba*) of the Loft in Shibuya (21–1 Udagawa-cho, Shibuya-ku, Tokyo). In addition, you will find a whole range of products and devices here for earthquake-proofing your home, above all gadgets to secure the furniture. We bought protective earthquake helmets for the whole family secondhand. These items are often for sale through expats who are leaving Japan. Check the bulletin boards or want ads (see chapter 12).

### EMERGENCY KITS

An emergency kit should include the following items:

Backpack
Water and food (three days' worth)
Can opener
Rope
Radio
Medicine
Flashlight, candles, and matches
Extra batteries (for radio and flashlight)
Tissue paper (they won't be handing it out at Shibuya station)
Soap and small towels
Knife
Gloves
Underwear and socks
Blanket

### *EMERGENCY PRECAUTIONS AND PROCEDURES*

A certain amount of secondary damage can be avoided by securing all furniture and thereby keeping things from toppling. One method is to wedge something underneath the front edge of the furniture so that it tips backward toward the wall. You can also secure furniture to the wall or ceiling by wires. Keep a fire extinguisher in your home (check to see whether it is for general, oil, or electrical fires). Powder extinguishers are long-lasting. To determine what is left in the can, shake it; if you can hear the powder, it is still effective.

Practice tuning in to NHK radio (693 kHz on the AM band), Inter FM (76.1) or NHK-TV (general) to hear English-language broadcasts. Label these stations on your radio.

Participate in the Citizens' Anti-Disaster Group of your community (information available at your ward office). You can join an existing volunteer brigade or form your own. In either case you will be trained and become part of your Japanese community in an immediately intimate way.

## PEDIATRIC CARE

Finding a reliable doctor who makes you and your child feel comfortable is important to all parents. In Japan, there are many pediatricians and general practitioners with training and experience overseas, and many who speak English. You can visit a nearby hospital and see any one of the doctors in the pediatrics department, or you can go to a private clinic by appointment. Be aware, however, that, as with the ob-gyn doctors in chapter 9, you will not usually be able to make an appointment, and you may have to wait until a doctor is available to see you. At the private clinics, Japanese National Health Insurance may or may not be accepted.

There are a number of doctors in the Tokyo-Yokohama area and in the Kobe-Osaka area that we know of—both pediatricians and general practitioners—who have been in private practice for years. Many of them are foreigners, and they all have experience in helping foreigners in Japan with their medical problems. If you live in an outlying area and need advice or referral, most of these doctors will be happy to assist you. For a list of maternity or children's hospitals frequented by foreigners and where you are likely to find English-speaking pediatricians, see chapter 9.

### Dr. A. Altinbay

254 Yamashita-cho, Naka-ku, Yokohama-shi, Kanagawa
☎ (045) 681–2113　神奈川県横浜市中区山下町 254

### Dr. Claudine Bliah

☎ (03) 3436–3028

Dr. Bliah works at several clinics and speaks both English and French.

### Bluff Clinic

82 Yamate-cho, Naka-ku, Yokohama-shi, Kanagawa
☎ (045) 641–6961　神奈川県横浜市中区山手町 82

### Endo Clinic, Dr. Norio Endo

Meguro Nishiguchi Mansion #305, 2–24–13 Kami Osaki, Shinagawa-ku, Tokyo
☎ (03) 3492–6422　東京都品川区上大崎 2–24–13　目黒西口マンション 305

### International Clinic, Dr. Aksenoss

1–5–9 Azabudai, Minato-ku, Tokyo
☎ (03) 3583–7831　東京都港区麻布台 1–5–9

### King Clinic, Dr. Theodore King

Olympia Annex Bldg., 6–31–21 Jingu-mae, Shibuya-ku, Tokyo
東京都渋谷区神宮前 6–31–21　オリンピア アネックス
☎ (03) 3409–0764　🖥 member.nifty.ne.jp/the-king-clinic

### Konno Clinic (English-speaking doctor, mornings only)

7–21–7 Nishi Shinjuku, Shinjuku-ku, Tokyo
☎ (03) 3371–5813　東京都新宿区西新宿 7–21–7

### Dr. George Mikasa

101 Yamashita-cho, Naka-ku, Yokohama-shi, Kanagawa
☎ (045) 641–6991　神奈川県横浜市中区山下町 101

### Dr. Hideki Mukaiyama

22–1 Hommoku Sannotani, Naka-ku, Yokohama-shi, Kanagawa
☎ (045) 623–7311　神奈川県横浜市中区本牧三ノ谷 22–1

### National Medical Clinic, Dr. Endo, Dr. Okubo, Dr. Sakakihara

Room 202, 5–16–11 Minami Azabu, Minato-ku, Tokyo
☎ (03) 3473–2057　東京都港区南麻布 5–16–11　ラガールビル 202

### Sanno Byoin

8–5–35 Akasaka, Minato-ku, Tokyo
☎ (03) 3402–3151　東京都港区赤坂 8–5–35

### Dr. Joseph Sato

1–18 Hommoku, Naka-ku, Yokohama-shi, Kanagawa
☎ (045) 621–4403   神奈川県横浜市中区本牧 1–18

### Dr. Yoshiro Shioda and Dr. Chieko Shioda

6224–6 Izumi-cho, Izumi-ku, Yokohama-shi, Kanagawa
☎ (045) 804–6655   神奈川県横浜市泉区和泉町 6224–6

### Shiraki Clinic (English-speaking doctor, mornings only)

4–1–3 Nishi Ochiai, Shinjuku-ku, Tokyo
☎ (03) 3951–3070   東京都新宿区西落合 4–1–3

### Tokyo British Clinic, Dr. Gabriel Symonds, Dr. Evelyn Lewis

Daikanyama Y Bldg., 2F, 2–13–7 Ebisu, Shibuya-ku, Tokyo
☎ (03) 5458–6099   東京都渋谷区恵比寿 2–13–7   代官山Yビル 2F

### Tokyo Medical and Surgical Clinic (across from Tokyo Tower), Dr. Fair, Dr. Marshall, Dr. Fuji

No. 32 Mori Bldg., 2F, 3–4–30 Shiba Koen, Minato-ku, Tokyo
☎ (03) 3436–3028   東京都港区芝公園 3–4–30   32森ビル 2F

---

KANSAI AREA

---

### Dr. Geoffrey Barraclough

4–23–11 Ninomiya-cho, Chuo-ku, Kobe-shi, Hyogo
☎ (078) 241–2896   兵庫県神戸市中央区二ノ宮町 4–23–11

### Dr. Masanori Kyogoku's Clinic

8–13 Kusunoki-cho, Ashiya-shi, Hyogo
☎ (0797) 31–2735   兵庫県芦屋市楠町 8–13

### Dr. Yukio Sono

3–13–16 Nishimidorigaoka, Toyonaka-shi, Osaka
☎ (06) 6848–0057   大阪府豊中市西緑ヶ丘 3–13–16

### Dr. Toshio Watanabe

5–2–16 Sakaguchi-dori, Chuo-ku, Kobe-shi, Hyogo
☎ (078) 221–5111   兵庫県神戸市中央区坂口通 5–2–16

## DENTAL HEALTH

Families relocating to Tokyo have many more choices in dental care than they did a decade ago. Many of the dentists we mention have studied in the U.S. or at least have a good command of the English language. Orthodontic treatment and pediatric dentistry are two of the fields that are expanding in Japan.

Resin sealants to protect against cavities are now available here, but not all dentists use them so its best to ask if the treatment is available. As there is no fluoride in the water here, you may want to purchase fluoridated toothpaste for your family.

My first experience with a dentist in Japan was when my son, six years old at the time, needed a retainer to correct his cross-bite. I had always waited until annual summer vacations to take the children to our hometown dentist for checkups.

When we realized that my son's cross-bite problem needed attention sooner, I made an appointment with Dr. Takehiko Ono, of the Royal Dental Clinic, in Roppongi. Our first visit to Dr. Ono was pleasant and painless. It was also relatively inexpensive, as Dr. Ono accepts Japanese National Health Insurance.

Dr. Ono fitted my child with a retainer made of clear plastic, which was hardly noticeable. It was to be worn on his lower teeth for a few months to see if his teeth would shift. If not, then we would abandon the retainer until his permanent teeth came in, at which point he might need braces.

I found it reassuring that Dr. Ono took the time to explain the procedure he was using, and he answered all of my questions in excellent English. My son was fascinated by a large display case, which featured toothbrushes from all over the world, and was quite relaxed by Dr. Ono's gentle manner.

The only difficulty we encountered had to do with keeping track of the retainer which my six-year-old was supposed to take out whenever he ate. I vividly remember sorting through the garbage at Shakey's pizza after he had left it on a tray there. And then there was the time he lost it during lunch at school. After combing every inch of the classroom, the retainer was nowhere to be found (although it did show up several months later in the bottom of his backpack!). Imagine my relief and gratitude when Dr. Ono offered to replace the retainer for free.

Since our initial visit, Dr. Ono has become our family dentist, and we have always been pleased with his work. One of his specialties is working with the orthodontia (braces) that have already been applied by a previous dentist. This is quite helpful for families whose children can't get back to their home country often enough for adjustment of their braces. The address of Royal Dental Clinic is 4–10–11 Roppongi, Minato-ku, Tokyo; ☎ (03) 3404–0819.

The husband-and-wife team of Drs. John and Maori Kaku offer the Tokyo community a clinic specializing in both orthodontics and pediatric dentistry. Both of them graduated from Tokyo Dental College, then went on to complete their residencies at the University of California. After that, at Boston University, Maori specialized in pediatric dentistry while John became a certified orthodontist. Upon returning to Japan, they opened their clinic, Shinjuku Orthodontics and Pediatric Dentistry.

Quite a few friends have taken their children to the Kakus' clinic, and have been very pleased with the results. One child, who was self-conscious about his braces, was made to feel not quite so strange when he attended a picnic with other adolescent patients, all of whom sported mouths full of braces. John and Maori are sensitive to the embarrassment some children feel about their braces on their teeth and organize support gatherings from time to time.

John and Maori Kaku operate two dentist offices in Tokyo. Shinjuku Orthodontics and Pediatric Dentistry is located at 1–28–3 Kabuki-cho, Shinjuku-ku, Tokyo, ☎/📠 (03) 3200–8661. Their clinic is open from 10:00 A.M. to 7:00 P.M. Tuesday, Wednesday, Friday, and Saturday, and every other Sunday.

The Tokyo Clinic Dental Office, conveniently located across the street from Tokyo Tower, is another reputable clinic staffed by three well-educated dentists. Dr. Thomas Ward, an American who received his education in the U.S., joined the practice in 1990, after working in Kobe for several years at the Oriental Dental Office there. Before that he was required to pass the national dental exam in Japanese, no small feat for a non-native speaker.

Also on staff is Dr. Hirokazu Enatsu, who grew up attending international schools in Okinawa and then went on to receive his doctorate in dentistry at UCLA. Upon his return to Japan in 1980, he spent two years at Tokyo Medical and Dental University to learn more about dentistry in Japan. Now Dr. Enatsu works three days a week at his own clinic in Hachioji and three days at the Tokyo Clinic.

Dr. Yoshimi Okuda received his Ph.D. from Josei Dental University in 1986, and spends Wednesdays at the Tokyo Clinic. The rest of the week he operates his own clinic in Azabu Juban, which accepts national health insurance. Altogether, the team at Tokyo Dental Clinic is well liked and respected by the foreign community in Tokyo. Their general dentistry services range from pediatric dentistry to after-hour emergencies.

Tokyo Dental Clinic is located in No. 32 Mori Building, 2F, at 3–4–30 Shiba Koen, Minato-ku, ☎/🖨 (03) 3431–4225. Hours of operation are from 9:00 A.M. to 6:00 P.M. Monday through Saturday. The clinic is closed on Tuesdays and Sundays.

For patients requiring more extensive dentistry. Dr. Kazuya Nakashima's clinic specializes in periodontics (oral surgery) and cosmetic dentistry. Educated in the U.S., Dr. Nakashima works with the latest in porcelain laminate veneers and other advanced techniques for cosmetic surgery. He also does implants, adult orthodontics, root canals, as well as gum and bone grafts. Dr. Nakashima's clinic is located in Roppongi. Office hours are from 10:00 A.M. to 6:00 P.M. Monday through Friday. For directions call his office at ☎ (03) 3479–2726.

In addition to the above dentists, there are several others who were also recommended by satisfied patients. Feel free to call them for more information. For information about dentists in other parts of Japan, see *Japan Health Handbook*.

In Akasaka:  Dr. Kenji Tsubota, ☎ (03) 3585–8519 (Cosmetic dentistry)
Dr. Harry Okamoto, ☎ (03) 3505–5910 (General dentistry)

In Aoyama:  Tanaka Dental Clinic, ☎ (03) 3475–1188 (General dentistry)

In Ebisu:  Dr. Naoomi Narisawa, ☎ (03) 3476–5585 (General dentistry)
Kyoritsu Dental Associates, ☎ (03) 3770–5515 (Orthodontics, pediatrics, oral surgery)

In Gotanda:  Dr. Yoshinobu Shoji, ☎ (03) 3495–0811 (General dentistry)

In Meguro:  Dr. Jason Wong, ☎ (03) 3473–2901 (Orthodontics)

In Setagaya:  Yamazaki Family Dentistry, ☎ (03) 3418–6611 (General dentistry)

In Shinjuku:  Dr. Yoshihiro Kubo, ☎ (03) 3356–2910 (General dentistry)
Usui Dental Clinic, ☎ (03) 3260–7448 (General dentistry)

## SPECIAL NEEDS

For those children with learning or physical disabilities, contact the Tokyo International Learning Community (see chapter 11) for referral or advice.

## VOCABULARY LIST

First of all, the phrase _____ *ga itai* (my _____ hurts) will work wonders in communicating the nature of your problem to the doctor.

arm: *ude* 腕
broken leg: *ashi no kossetsu* 足の骨折
bronchitis: *kikanshien* 気管支炎
chicken pox: *mizuboso* 水疱瘡
a cold; catch a cold: *kaze; kaze o hiku* かぜ、かぜをひく
constipation: *bempi* 便秘
convulsions: *hikitsuke* ひきつけ
cough: *seki* せき
diaper rash: *omutsu kabure* おむつかぶれ
diarrhea: *geri* 下痢
earache: *mimi ga itai* 耳が痛い
eczema: *shisshin* 湿疹
fever: *netsu* 熱
food poisoning: *shokuchudoku* 食中毒
German measles: *fushin, mikkabashika* 風疹、三日ばしか
headache: *atama ga itai* 頭が痛い
jaundice: *odan* 黄疸
leg: *ashi* 足
measles: *hashika* はしか
mumps: *otafukukaze* おたふくかぜ
pediatrician: *shonika i* 小児科医
pediatrics: *shonika* 小児科
pneumonia: *haien* 肺炎
polio: *porio, shonimahi* ポリオ、小児麻痺
rash: *hosshin* 発疹
roseola: *toppatsusei hosshin* 突発性発疹
scarlet fever: *shoko netsu* 猩紅熱
sneeze: *kushami* くしゃみ
sore throat: *nodo ga itai* のどが痛い
sprained finger: *tsukiyubi* 突き指
stomachache: *onaka ga itai, fukutsu* おなかが痛い、腹痛
tetanus: *hasshofu* 破傷風
tonsils; tonsilitis: *hentosen; hentosenen* 扁桃腺、扁桃腺炎
tuberculosis (TB): *kekkaku* 結核
whooping cough: *hyakunichizeki* 百日ぜき

# 11
# Educating the Kids

## PRESCHOOLS

Preschools are big business, especially in Tokyo, and the number of these schools serving the international community continues to grow each year. Often it is hard to determine what is meant by the name "preschool." Preschool as most Westerners know it means a preparatory program for the first grade. This traditional preschool education is available at a number of schools listed here. Many of the international schools have preschool/kindergartens affiliated with them.

All the international schools run from September to June, and often preschool or kindergartens run a summer school program in June and July. The admission process for the fall semester usually begins in February of the previous school year, and screening of the child is often involved. In Tokyo, most of the schools save a few openings for those people moving to Japan during the summer, and there are usually openings during the school year because many families are transferred in the middle of the year.

For information about day-care centers and nurseries see chapter 12.

TOKYO AREA

### ABC International School

AGES: 10 months to 3 years
2–1–21 Moto Azabu, Minato-ku, Tokyo    東京都港区元麻布 2–1–21
☎ (03) 5791–4358    🖳 www2.gol.com/users/abcintl
🚇 Hiroo or Roppongi Station, Hibiya Line

A small preschool where the ratio of teachers to students is low.  ABC focuses not only on play activities but works to increase children's social skills and ability to learn.

## Ai International School

AGES: 2 to 6 years
2–21–8 Mita, Minato-ku, Tokyo (office at 5–4–4 Mita)　東京都港区三田 2–21–8
☎ (03) 3769–3372　🖳 aioffice@gol.com
🚅 Tamachi Station, JR Yamanote, Keihin Tohoku lines; Mita Station, Toei Mita, Toei Asakusa lines

A preschool with a maximum capacity of sixty students and one teacher for every eight to ten students. All instruction is conducted in English. Ai International also offers after-school tutoring and a special summer program for elementary school students.

## American World International

AGES: 9 months to 3 years; ESL, 3 to 12 years
☎ (03) 5464–6966　🖷 (03) 5464–6955　🖳 usaworld@ea.mbn.or.jp

American World has an enthusiastic staff and five locations in and around Tokyo: Shibuya, Kamata, Saginuma (Kawasaki), and two in Okurayama (Yokohama). Call the above number for details.

## Child's Play

AGES: 1 1/2 to 4 years
18–8 Motoyoyogi-cho, Shibuya-ku, Tokyo　東京都渋谷区本代々木町 18–8
☎ (03) 3460–8841　🖷 (03) 5709–0552
🚅 Yoyogi Uehara Station, Chiyoda, Odakyu lines

Child's Play is a preschool education center. Children may attend two, three, or five days a week. Three-year-olds are eligible for a full-day program three days a week. The staff for each session consists of one fully qualified kindergarten/nursery school teacher and two qualified teaching assistants, with one teacher for every four to seven children. The day is scheduled into segments for free play, crafts, music, and tumbling. Daily outings to the park are scheduled. Reading and writing skills for preschoolers are also taught.

## Children's House

AGES: 3 to 4 years
3–18–16 Meguro Honcho, Meguro-ku, Tokyo　東京都目黒区目黒本町 3–18–16
☎ (03) 3710–1160　🖷 (03) 3710–1193　🖳 www.tokyois.com
🚅 Musashi Koyama Station, Tokyu Mekama Line

A coed, nondenominational school, Children's House was founded in

1994 by international parents who wanted to provide a child-centered education for their children.

It uses a hands-on approach in small multicultural group settings to develop each child's social, emotional, physical, cognitive, and creative development. Craft activities, field trips, music, art, drama, and study skills are incorporated into the weekly schedule.

This preschool is currently searching for a larger facility due to their increasing enrollment. Children's House accepts students who will turn 3 before October 1, and is part of Tokyo International School (see International Schools).

### Cooperative Playgroup, Franciscan Chapel Center

AGES: 1 1/2 to 5 years
4–2–37 Roppongi, Minato-ku, Tokyo　東京都港区六本木 4–2–37
☎ (03) 3401–2141
🚇 Roppongi Station, Hibiya Line

The Cooperative Playgroup is a private nonprofit organization that meets in the Franciscan Chapel Center hall in Roppongi. The group's organization is left entirely to the committee of mothers whose children are enrolled in the group each year. To be eligible, a child must be an English speaker with an English-speaking mother, and the child must be two years old by the New Year. The contact person for this group changes from year to year; call the Franciscan Chapel Center to get the current phone number.

### EWA Children's Garden (American Embassy Preschool)

AGES: 2 to 5 1/2 years
American Embassy Compound, 2–1–1 Roppongi, Minato-ku, Tokyo
☎ (03) 3224–6796　🖷 (03) 3224–6788　東京都港区六本木 2–1–1
🚇 Roppongi Station, Hibiya Line

The goal of this school is to meet the physical, emotional, and social needs of preschoolers. The outdoor play area has climbing equipment, slides, and swings as well as a field for athletic activities. Reading readiness and small-muscle activities are also part of the curriculum. Three classes meet from 9:00 A.M. to 12:00 P.M., September to June.

### Gregg International School

AGES: 2 to 8 years
1–14–16 Jiyugaoka, Meguro-ku, Tokyo　東京都目黒区自由が丘 1–14–16
☎ (03) 3725–6495　🖷 (03) 3724–2554
🚇 Jiyugaoka Station, Tokyu Toyoko, Tokyu Oimachi lines

Gregg International School is a part of the Gregg International College of Languages, headquartered in Tokyo. They offer full- or half-day programs for two- to four-year-olds. The kindergarten program is full-day. Classes are conducted in English, and the teacher-student ratio is 1:6. Art, music, and gym are included in the weekly schedule of games, crafts, stories, and free time. Eight weeks of summer school is also offered for ages five to seven.

### Junior Athletic Club (JAC) Prekindergarten

AGES: 1¹/₂ to 5 years
2–1–17 Moto Azabu, Minato-ku, Tokyo　東京都港区元麻布 2–1–17, 2F
☎ (03) 3445–6326　🖷 (03) 3445–5676
🚊 Hiroo Station, Hibiya Line

JAC Prekindergarten is a community of children from all over the world. The school attempts to give an international and bilingual education that emphasizes social skills. The school is run in a Montessori-like fashion in that children are encouraged to pursue activities which best suit their own personality. All the teachers and assistants are trained and have teaching experience. The school is divided into two classes: a junior class with children age one and a half to three years and a senior class with children age three to five. The school runs from 10:00 A.M. to 2:00 P.M. daily, with options for two-, three-, four- and five-day programs. It is located near Arisugawa Park in Hiroo.

### Kids World Preschool

AGES: 2 to 4 years
☎ 0120–00–1537 (toll-free)

With numerous locations throughout Tokyo, Kids World offers a preschool program with at least one English-speaking teacher on the premises, in addition to other bilingual staff. An offshoot of the day-care facilities for ages one to eight years.

### Komazawa Park International Preschool

AGES: 2¹/₂ to 6 years
4–26–17 Fukasawa, Setagaya-ku, Tokyo　東京都世田谷区深沢 4–26–17
☎ (03) 5707–0979　🖳 www.nnliij4u.or
🚊 Komazawa Daigaku Station, Tokyu Shin Tamagawa Line

A preschool with a teacher for every seven students and classes designed around the teachings of leading early childhood educators. Komazawa combines indoor activities with special, structured outings to the nearby park of the same name.

## QUESTIONS TO ASK WHEN VISITING A PRESCHOOL

1. Does the school provide a healthy and safe environment for children? Are children under adult supervision at all times? Does the building have good lighting, ventilation, smoke detectors, fire extinguishers, window/balcony guards, and easy access to exits in case of fire?

2. Is there a wide variety of materials and equipment? Are they age-appropriate? Do they promote gross motor and fine motor skills, language development, social development, and creative and expressive arts?

3. Does the school provide nutritious meals and/or snacks? How does the school handle special nutritional needs such as food allergies?

4. Are there enough adults to respond to each child individually? What is the teacher-child ratio? Given the classroom ratio, can teachers respond to each child's varying degrees of development?

5. Are interactions between adults and children frequent, respectful, warm, and caring? Do teachers foster a love of learning, promote self-esteem, and develop self-confidence?

6. What is the school's philosophy about learning? Are teachers provided training on the school's philosophy? Are the teachers specially trained in keeping with the school's particular philosophy? Can the staff adequately answer your questions about the program's specifics? What are the staff qualifications? Are there trained specialists on staff for art, music, drama, computer, language, and physical education?

7. Are planned activities appropriate to a child's age and development? Does the program stimulate a child creatively, intellectually, physically, and socially with a balance of free play, outdoor play, and group activities?

8. Does the school have a discipline policy? Does the policy have clear and consistent behavioral expectations and consequences? Does the school have a consistent discipline policy? Does the policy encourage positive behavior or is it punitive? What methods are used during the discipline process?

9. Is regular communication with parents encouraged? Are parents welcome visitors to the school? What mediums are used to communicate with the parents? Is parent involvement welcomed and encouraged in the classrooms? If so, what type of activities are parents involved with?

10. Are parent-teacher conferences scheduled at least once a year, and at other times when requested, to discuss a child's progress, accomplishments, or any difficulties at home or school? How does the school assess the children? (What tools are used to observe and record the child's progress throughout the year?)

11. Has the school developed a standard plan with regard to emergency procedures? If a child needs emergency medical treatment, where will he or she be taken? In the event of disaster (earthquake, fire, etc.), what is the proposed course of action? Does the school keep adequate equipment and supplies (food, water, first aid, and tools) on hand?

12. Does the school have a toileting policy? Is there a specific age by which a child must be toilet trained?

13. Are children taken off the school grounds on a regular basis? If so, what precautions are taken?

14. What is the make-up of the class: size, gender, age, nationalities, and ESL (English as a Second Language) students?

15. Does the school have any after-school programs?

16. Are there parents of enrolled children that could be contacted to get a personal account of the school?

17. What is the admissions process? Is there a waiting list? How is the waiting list managed? Are applications carried over to the next year automatically or must an applicant reapply? What is the timeframe for the admissions process?

Contributed by Kirsten Sansom

## Little People Montessori School

AGES: 2 to 4 years

1–36–11 Sakura Shimmachi, Setagaya-ku, Tokyo　東京都世田谷区桜新町 1–36–11
☎ (090) 1204–2565　📠 (03) 5706–4572　🖥 www.montessorijapan.com/littlep.html
🚃 Sakura Shimmachi Station, Tokyu Shin Tamagawa Line

The school is run in a home (capacity twelve students) and provides children with positive educational experiences in a warm and secure environment. Sessions are held from 9:00 A.M. to 12:15 P.M., either three days or five days a week. Teacher-student ratio is 1:6. Students come from many countries, and all instruction is given in English. There is a cooking or baking activity once a week. Through a variety of creative activities, the school tries to foster independence and build self esteem. Open from September to June, followed by a three-week summer school.

## Maria's Babies Society

AGES: 7 months to 5 years

3–36–20 Jingu-mae, Shibuya-ku, Tokyo　東京都渋谷区神宮前 3–36–20
☎ (03) 3404–3468　📠 (03) 3404–3625
🚃 Gaien-mae Station, Ginza Line; Omotesando Station, Ginza, Hanzomon, Chiyoda lines

Billed as Japan's first bilingual and bicultural institution for children, Maria's Babies employs mostly British women to teach proper English, games, and etiquette to babies and children up to age six.

There are mother-and-child programs in addition to classes geared toward groups of children only. Lessons in teaching English to your child are available for mothers whose children are students. This school emphasizes exposure to Western culture through music, language, art, and culture classes. Open Monday through Friday, with both morning and afternoon sessions.

## Pacific International School

AGES: 2¹/₂ to 6 years

5–11–5 Shimouma Setagaya-ku, Tokyo　東京都世田谷区下馬 5–11–5
☎/📠 (03) 5481–9425
🚃 Gakugei Daigaku Station, Tokyu Toyoko Line

A preschool kindergarten program for ages two and a half to six. Three separate classes (ages two and a half to three, four to five, and five to six) are held daily from 8:15 A.M. to 2:30 P.M. Japanese is spoken at the school, although English classes are taught for forty minutes each day. Children study math, science, music, and art. Special activities include field trips. Educators are trained in child development. Some English is spoken.

### PAL International School
AGES: 18 months to 5 years
3–5–38 Nishi Azabu, Minato-ku, Tokyo　東京都港区西麻布 3–5–38
☎ (03) 5770–8166　📠 (03) 5770–8167
🚇 Roppongi Station, Hibiya Line

Classes, held from 9:00 A.M. to 1:30 P.M., are divided into three age groups: one and a half to two and a half, two and a half to three and a half, and three and a half to five. The teacher-student ratio is 1:4. Classes are taught in English by an experienced and bilingual staff. The curriculum is adjusted for each child's educational, physical, and social development.

### Rainbow International Preschool
AGES: 18 months to 6 years
•Denenchofu School: 3–12–15 Denenchofu, Ota-ku, Tokyo
　東京都大田区田園調布 3–12–15
　☎/📠 (03) 3722–0312　💻 www.rainbowschool.co.jp/typi/html
　🚇 Denenchofu Station, Tokyu Toyoko, Tokyu Mekama lines
•Hiroo School: 3–17–4 Hiroo, Shibuya-ku, Tokyo　東京都渋谷区広尾 3–17–4
　☎/📠 (03) 3406–4320　💻 www.rainbowschool.co.jp
　🚇 Hiroo Station, Hibiya Line

Open year round, this school was founded by Eriko Salamack to provide a Montessori-type environment for young children. Japanese and English are both used at the school. Activities include arts and crafts, math games, etiquette, and exercise. Sessions are from 8:45 A.M. to 2:25 P.M. and from 3:00 P.M. to 6:00 P.M.

### Saint Alban's Nursery Program
AGES: 2 to 4 1/2 years
3–6–25 Shiba Koen, Minato-ku, Tokyo　東京都港区芝公園 3–6–25
☎ (03) 3431–8534
🚇 Kamiyacho Station (exit 1), Hibiya Line

The nursery program at Saint Alban's Anglican Church is part of the church's group of community programs. Designed to provide educational activities for children in the two to four age group, it is not technically a preschool, but rather a pre-preschool, helping to prepare children for a more formal preschool/kindergarten education elsewhere. There are two teachers in charge of the morning program. Two-year-olds may come two mornings a week, three-year-olds may come three or five mornings, and four-year-olds attend five mornings a week.

### Saint Cecilia Preschool

AGES: 3 to 5 years
4–7–23 Shiroganedai, Minato-ku, Tokyo　東京都港区白金台 4–7–23
☎ (03) 3446–9884
Shibuya Station, JR Yamanote and various lines

Saint Cecilia is a Catholic, Japanese-speaking preschool that operates six days a week. In past years, it has had a number of international students. Fees are very reasonable compared with international schools. Children are at school from 9:00 A.M. to 1:30 P.M., and they must bring their own lunch. Saturday is a half day, and the school follows the Japanese school year schedule. There is an outdoor play area. The school is affiliated with another preschool called Seishin Gakuen, ☎ (03) 3312–5701, in Suginami Ward. From Shibuya Station take bus #87 bound for Tamachi.

### Shirogane International School

AGES: 3 to 5 years
5–5–2 Shiroganedai, Minato-ku, Tokyo　東京都港区白金台 5–5–2
☎ (03) 3442–1941　🖷 (03) 3442–1942
Meguro Station, JR Yamanote, Tokyu Mekama lines / Bus 77 or 86

Shirogane International School offers a program from 8:50 A.M. to 2:00 P.M., five days a week for three- to four-year-olds and four- to five-year-olds. Teaching is all in English, and the teacher-student ratio is 1:7. Besides regular classroom activities, outside teachers are brought in for music and gymnastics classes each week.

### Sunshine Montessori School

AGES: 2¹/₂ to 6 years
3–8–8 Hiroo, Shibuya-ku, Tokyo　東京都渋谷区広尾 3–8–8
☎/🖷 (03) 5706–4572　🖳 www.montessorijapan.com/sunshine.html
Hiroo Station, Hibiya Line

Originally opened in 1984, Sunshine has been run on Montessori lines since 1993. It is a nonsectarian school, open to children of any nationality or language. Sessions are mornings only or full day. Instruction is given in English. Full-day children are exposed to the Japanese language and culture twice a week. Children are instructed in the use of a computer, and there are also woodwork classes twice a week. There is a large outdoor play area where both structured activities and free play are available to children at all times. The teacher-student ratio is 1:7. A three-week summer school is also offered.

### Tokyo Union Church Preschool/Kindergarten

AGES: 3 to 5 years
5–7–7 Jingu-mae, Shibuya-ku, Tokyo　東京都渋谷区神宮前 5–7–7
☎/🖷 (03) 3400–1579　💻 tvcplc@twics.com
🚈 Omotesando Station, Ginza, Hanzomon, Chiyoda lines; Harajuku Station, JR Yamanote Line

Tokyo Union Church Preschool operates both morning and afternoon half-day programs for three- to four-year-olds and a full-day kindergarten program for five-year-olds. Children may attend two, three, or five days a week. The underlying aim of the school is to foster growth according to Christian principles, and the program is designed for international families. The curriculum includes library time, kinder music, Japanese culture class, and a weekly Bible story. The teacher-student ratio is 1:6 for the three-year-olds and 1:10 for the older class.

### Unida International School

AGES: 2 to 6 years
3–25–2 Ebisu, Shibuya-ku, Tokyo　東京都渋谷区恵比寿 3–25–2
☎ (03) 3443–6850　🖷 (03) 3443–7867
🚈 Ebisu Station, JR Yamanote, Hibiya lines

Unida offers full- and half-day classes for children from two to six years old. Preschool activities are conducted in English, with fifteen minutes of Japanese or English lessons daily. Both native and nonnative English speakers are on the staff, and the teacher-student ratio is 1:5. The curriculum includes art, music, dance, exercise, reading, writing, and speaking.

### Willowbrook International School

AGES: 22 months to 5 years
KS Flat, 2F, 3–8–26, Nishi Azabu, Minato-ku, Tokyo
東京都港区西麻布 3–8–26 KSフラット 2F
☎ (03) 5474–8334　🖷 (03) 3405–6484　💻 IBS-Tokyo@msn.com
🚈 Roppongi Station, Hibiya Line

Founded in 1998 by early childhood educators, the school offers an integrated educational curriculum for all nationalities, with an emphasis on human values and interpersonal skills. The classes are held in the morning for ages, two, three, and four- to five-year olds, with the option of extended day care in the afternoon. At Willowbrook, kids explore nature, music, art, even cooking and drama. English is used in the classrooms, along with daily Japanese lessons.

KANSAI AREA

### Aotani International Preschool

AGES: 3 to 4 years
1–3–10 Kagoike-dori, Chuo-ku, Kobe-shi, Hyogo
☎ (078) 221–3805　兵庫県神戸市中央区篭池通 1–3–10
🚇 Oji Station, Hankyu Kobe Line

The Aotani International Preschool was founded in 1984 by Sole Bruggemann. She is an accredited teacher with many years of teaching experience in the international schools in the Kobe area. Three-year-olds may attend either three or five days a week, and four-year-olds attend five days. The curriculum is designed to help prepare students for kindergarten at any of the international schools, and there are many extracurricular activities and outings during the school year.

### Peter Pan International Pre-School

AGES: 2 to 6 years
• Kobe Rooms: East Court 2, #304, #302, 1–14 Koyo-cho Naka, Higashi Nada-ku, Kobe　兵庫県神戸市東灘区向洋町中 1–14 イーストコート2 #304, #302
☎ (078) 857–9626　🖷 (078) 857–5144　📧 LkMaynard@aol.com
🚇 Island Center Station, Rokko Liner Line
• Kawanishi Rooms: Mosaic Box 3F, 11–1 Sakaemachi, Kawanishi-shi, Hyogo
☎/🖷 (0727) 40–2505　兵庫県川西市栄町 11–1　モザイクボックス 3F
🚇 Kawanishi Noseguchi Station, Hankyu Takarazuka Line

This preschool uses the Montessori method in their bilingual classrooms. Morning classes are for ages two to three and three to four, and afternoon classes are for ages five to six. The majority of the program is in English, but Japanese is taught for twenty minutes daily and is also incorporated in games and songs.

# INTERNATIONAL SCHOOLS

English-speaking international schools have been serving the foreign community in Japan since 1872. In 1965, these schools met formally to discuss matters of administration and curriculum and formed the Japan Council of International Schools (JCIS). This body facilitates open communication between the schools and provides the teaching and administrative staff with in-service and professional growth opportunities.

There are also a number of smaller international schools that are not affiliated with JCIS. These schools usually represent a particular nationality (e.g., the German schools in Tokyo and Kobe) and were founded for the purpose of educating those foreign nationals who intend to continue their education in their home country after a stay in Japan. Classes at these schools are conducted in the native language, and the lessons usually follow the national curriculum of the related country. Some of the schools accept students who are not of that nationality, but the student must be able to speak the language of the school fluently. To find out more about these schools, contact the embassy of the country you are interested in.

Schools located outside the greater Tokyo area are listed at the end of this section.

Each school has a distinct personality, the result of the school's founding principles, the current administration, and the philosophy of education. The best method to use when deciding which school best suits your child is to go and visit the school personally. You will find that the school administrators welcome the parents of prospective students and encourage interested parents to learn more about all the schools before choosing one for their child. Some schools have large, modern facilities; others have small classrooms and a more informal feel. For some parents, accessibility (location near a subway or the use of a school bus service) is an important criterion. Still other parents are swayed by the quality of the playground equipment. It all depends on your priorities and what you and your child feel is important at this time in your child's life.

A word about admissions. Rumors fly fast and furious about the difficulty of being admitted to this or that school. It is true that these schools have a limited number of places for new students each term. They may also have quotas for the number of nonnative English speakers allowed in each class, as well as a fixed boy-girl ratio. As a parent, such variables may be beyond your control, and all you can do is follow the admission process carefully and keep your fingers crossed.

For more information on a particular school, call the school directly or consult the American Chamber of Commerce publication *Living in Japan*, available at English-language bookstores.

## The American School in Japan (ASIJ)

GRADES: Preschool to 12th      Founded in 1902

• 1–1–1 Nomizu, Chofu-shi, Tokyo　東京都調布市野水 1–1–1
☎ (0422) 34–5300　🖶 (0422) 34–5304　🖳 www.asij.ac.jp

• Nursery School/Kindergarten Campus: 2–15–5 Aobadai, Meguro-ku, Tokyo
☎ (03) 3461–4523　🖶 (03) 3461–2505　東京都目黒区青葉台 2–15–5

The American School in Japan (ASIJ) offers students a long and rich heritage of educational excellence. ASIJ is home to students from over thirty countries; one of the school's goals is to prepare these students to be citizens of the world.

The school is under the administration of a headmaster and is overseen by a board of directors. The large campus in west Tokyo offers an abundance of fresh air and open spaces. The campus houses modern school buildings as well as a sports complex and playing fields. There is a private bus service to the Chofu campus, and the average bus ride is forty-five minutes from central Tokyo. There is no uniform requirement.

Students from kindergarten to grade twelve may attend the Chofu campus. The school also has a small campus in Meguro that is home to the early childhood and kindergarten program. Children from age three to five are eligible to attend the Meguro campus (children must be three by September 1). All nursery/kindergarten programs are full-day. There are six classes at the Meguro campus, each staffed by one teacher and one assistant teacher. The number of pupils per class ranges from eighteen to twenty-two, depending on the age. All classes are conducted in English, and if the child is not a native English speaker, the parents must be able to speak English. Parent involvement is encouraged at all levels of the nursery/kindergarten program.

The kindergarten program at the Chofu campus is similar in content to the one in Meguro. Children must be five years old by September 1 to qualify. As at the Meguro campus, each kindergarten class has up to twenty-two pupils and is taught by one teacher and one assistant. Some parents say that the Chofu campus has a more mature feel to it, perhaps because of the proximity of the older children in the elementary school. The children at the Chofu campus also have access to the music, library, sports, and computer facilities at the elementary school. If your child is of kindergarten age and you are not sure which campus you would prefer, the best thing to do is to visit both schools and talk with the teachers.

The elementary, middle, and high schools at the Chofu campus all offer a wide range of academic and extracurricular activities. Japanese language classes are required for all students from grades one through five, and in the middle and high school, Japanese is offered as part of the foreign language program. Students at both campuses are given numerous opportunities to experience Japanese culture and to interact with Japanese schoolchildren. Instruction in English as a second language is available for children in all grades of the elementary school.

Many elective and summer educational opportunities are offered through the school and summer school. ASIJ also offers a postgraduate year for serious students who desire an extra year of personal enrichment or intensive preparation for college.

### The British School in Japan

AGES: 3 to 13 years      Founded in 1989
1–21–18 Shibuya, Shibuya-ku, Tokyo    東京都渋谷区渋谷 1–21–18
☎ (03) 5467–4321    🖷 (03) 5467–4322    💻 www.bst.ac.jp
🚃 Shibuya Station, JR Yamanote and various lines; Harajuku Station, JR Yamanote Line; Jingu-mae Station, Chiyoda Line

The British School in Tokyo is an independent co-educational day school offering a British-style education to children from three to thirteen years. As a nonprofit organization, it is administered by a Board of Trustees representing the British community in Tokyo.

The school has an enrollment of 380 nursery to year 8, offering a complete preparatory-style program. Class sizes average 22 pupils. The majority of pupils are British, but students of all nationalities are welcomed provided that each child, relative to age, is fluent in English. Twenty-nine nationalities are presently represented.

The headmaster and all full-time teachers are U.K. qualified and experienced in the delivery in the national curriculum of England. Specialist staff provide additional instruction in music, drama, P.E., computer skills, and languages. Campus facilities include a fully-equipped gymnasium, dance-drama Studio, library, science and music rooms, and up-to-date computer equipment. Students may choose from an extensive range of after-school clubs and activities.

The British School in Tokyo is located in Shibuya, in the heart of the city. It is a short walk from Yoyogi Park and is easily accessible by public or private transport. Admission is by assessment and interview with the Headmaster.

### The Christian Academy in Japan (CAJ)

GRADES: Kindergarten to 12th    Founded in 1950
1–2–14 Shinkawa-cho, Higashi Kurume-shi, Tokyo
東京都東久留米市新川町 1–2–14
☎ (0424) 71–0022    🖷 (0424) 76–2202    🖳 don.rudd@jemanet.or.jp
🚃 Higashi Kurume Station, Seibu Ikebukuro Line

The Christian Academy in Japan is located on a four-acre campus in Kurume and provides a Christian-based education in English for the missionary community and other international families. The school is owned and operated by a twelve-member board of directors selected from six sponsoring evangelical mission organizations.

Two-thirds of the student body are the children of missionaries, and the school has an average enrollment of three hundred students. Kindergarten applicants must be five years old by September 1.

The school accepts students from non-English-speaking homes, but the children must be able to pass an English-language screening test. Enrollment of students from non-English-speaking homes is limited to a maximum of twenty percent in each year. Non-Christian enrollment is also limited to twenty percent per grade.

The majority of the faculty members are hired from the United States, and the curriculum is also from the United States. Participation in Bible studies is required of all students, and non-Christian students make a commitment to comply with this rule at the time of registration. Other religious activities include devotions during the day and weekly chapel meetings. The school offers a wide variety of other extracurricular activities, and the sports teams compete with other international schools in the Tokyo area.

### International School of the Sacred Heart

GRADES: Kindergarten (coed); 1st to 12th (girls)    Founded in 1908
4–3–1 Hiroo, Shibuya-ku, Tokyo    東京都渋谷区広尾 4–3–1
☎ (03) 3400–3951    🖷 (03) 3400–3496    🖳 www.iac.co.jp/~issh3/
🚃 Hiroo Station, Hibiya Line

The International School of the Sacred Heart is a girls' school that is directed by the Catholic Sisters of the Worldwide Society of the Sacred Heart and provides an education in English for children of the international community. Located near the Azabu district in central Tokyo, Sacred Heart's student body is made up of approximately 650 students of diverse faiths from over fifty countries. From the first grade, the school uniform is compulsory.

The kindergarten program is open to both boys and girls from ages three to five, although the program for three-year-olds is only available for children who have siblings attending the school. All kindergarten programs are full-day, and emphasis in the kindergarten is on developing the whole personality and helping children to become self-learners.

All classes at Sacred Heart are taught in English, and in general parents of students are expected to be fluent English speakers. The school accepts some nonnative English speakers who are not Japanese. This number changes from year to year. Enrollment of Japanese nationals is usually limited to returnees from an English-speaking country who do not wish to reenter the Japanese school system.

Sacred Heart hires native English-speaking teachers who are qualified in their home countries. The curriculum and materials used are primarily from the United States and Great Britain. Sports teams from Sacred Heart compete in the leagues with the other international schools and occasionally with Japanese schools as well. Extracurricular activities are offered for students in grade two and above. Also from grade two, Catholic students begin preparation for confirmation. At grade five, students are offered a program of religious studies and can choose to study Christianity (Catholicism or Protestantism) or other world religions.

### International School Support Services (ISSS)

3–18–16 Meguro Honcho, Meguro-ku, Tokyo　東京都目黒区目黒本町 3–18–16
☎ (03) 3710–1331
🚃 Musashi Koyama Station, Tokyu Mekama Line

Established in 1992, ISSS offers educational support to students through tutoring, home schooling programs, or attention to special needs. With an enrollment of over two hundred, ISSS fills a crucial gap in educational services. Programs include an intensive ESL course, junior high and high school correspondence courses to make up missed classes or complete graduation requirements, and a summer school session. If your child is having difficulty adjusting to school academically or emotionally, contact ISSS for its individualized services.

### Japan International School (JIS)

•Grades: 1st to 9th　　Founded in 1980
2–10–7 Miyamae, Suginami-ku, Tokyo　東京都杉並区宮前 2–10–7

☎ (03) 3335–6620   📠 (03) 3332–6928   💻 www.ajis.co.jp
🚆 Fujimigaoka Station, Keio Inokashira Line

• Affiliated kindergarten: Aoba International School
AGES: 1 1/2 to 6 years      Founded in 1976
2–10–34 Aobadai, Meguro-ku, Tokyo   東京都目黒区青葉台 2–10–34
☎ (03) 3461–1442   📠 (03) 3463–9873
🚆 Shibuya Station, JR Yamanote and various lines; Daikanyama Station,
Tokyu Toyoko Line

Japan International School is a nonparochial, bilingual, and multi-cultural elementary and middle school. Affiliated with the school is Aoba International School, a four-year kindergarten. Both schools were founded by Regina Doi, who now acts as headmistress, to offer an international education to all children, especially nonnative English speakers.

There are no quotas at the schools for the number of Japanese students accepted, and although all classes are taught in English, Japanese is often the language used among students. Both schools welcome students who want to experience Japanese culture on a daily basis.

At the four-year kindergarten in Meguro, children are prepared to enter a first-grade class in either a Japanese or an international school. The children come from a wide variety of backgrounds, and all of the classes are taught in English. At both schools, those students whose English is not up to standard are given special help and are offered a Saturday program of English instruction.

The Japan International School is located in a five-story building in the heart of Shibuya. There is bus transportation to and from school, and students are required to wear uniforms. The curriculum is basically from the United States, but it is oriented toward Japan and the world at large in social studies, history, and geography. The school prides itself on its advanced math program, and children are instructed in the abacus up to grade three. Qualified teachers and staff are hired from around the world, and most of them have a strong background in teaching students whose native tongue is not English.

There are approximately 280 students in the elementary and middle school, and all children go to various locations each week for sports and outdoor recreation. The school does not compete in sports with other schools. Aikido is taught to students from third grade.

The school places many students in boarding schools abroad for high school studies upon completion of middle school. Help with placement in other international schools in Japan is also available.

## K. International School

AGES: 3 to 14 years
3–31–5 Higashisuna, Koto-ku, Tokyo　東京都江東区東砂 3–31–5
☎ (03) 5632–8715　🖷 (03) 5632–8715
🚃 Higashi Oshima Station, Toei Shinjuku Line

With classes through the ninth grade, K. International's curriculum emphasizes independent thinking. On-campus facilities include a state-of-the-art library, computer laboratory, swimming pool, and two playgrounds.

## Nishimachi International School

GRADES: Kindergarten to 9th　　Founded in 1949
2–14–7 Moto Azabu, Minato-ku, Tokyo　東京都港区元麻布 2–14–7
☎ (03) 3451–5520　🖷 (03) 3456–0197　🖥 www.nishimachi.ac.jp
🚃 Hiroo Station, Hibiya Line

Nishimachi International School, located in the Azabu district of central Tokyo, is a private, nonsectarian, coeducational day school founded with a commitment to provide children with an international perspective. The program is for students from five to fifteen years of age, extending from kindergarten through grade nine.

Both foreign and Japanese parents who wish their children to learn English and Japanese find an educational haven in the school's unique dual-language, multicultural program. Approximately four hundred children from twenty-five countries attend Nishimachi.

The school requires its students to study the Japanese language daily, while the rest of the curriculum is taught in English. Its curriculum is basically American, with supplementary materials used from other countries. Nishimachi believes that a second language provides the opportunity for children to grow beyond a single culture and that education should promote the well-rounded development of individuals through the cultivation of their intellectual, creative personal, social, and physical abilities.

Nishimachi International School prides itself on its familylike atmosphere and small classes. The faculty consists of teachers from around the world, the majority of whom are from the United States, Japan, and Great Britain.

In addition to Nishimachi's outdoor education center, located one hundred and fifty kilometers northwest of Tokyo, local facilities include the Ushiba Gymnasium, the Reischauer Memorial

Library (with both English and Japanese volumes), modern classroom facilities, state-of-the-art elementary and junior high computer labs, sophisticated science rooms, an expanded art facility, a music performance studio, and a rooftop observatory dome. All buildings are networked and all classrooms have access to the Internet and the online catalog.

Nishimachi is accredited by the Western Association of Schools and Colleges.

### Saint Mary's International School
GRADES: Pre-first grade to 12th (boys)　　Founded in 1954
1–6–9 Seta Setagaya-ku, Tokyo　東京都世田谷区瀬田 1–6–9
☎ (03) 3709–3411　🖷 (03) 3707–1950　🖳 www.smistokyo.com
🚃 Futako Tamagawa-en Station, Tokyu Shin Tamagawa, Tokyu Oimachi lines

Saint Mary's International School is located near Seisen International School (see separate listing) in the residential area of Setagaya. Saint Mary's is run by a Roman Catholic order, the Brothers of Christian Instruction. The school includes boys of all faiths and nationalities and strives to blend these diverse backgrounds to give students a worldwide perspective and teach respect for one another. All students at Saint Mary's wear school uniforms.

As Seisen is nearby, many boys attend the kindergarten program there before moving to Saint Mary's in the first grade. Saint Mary's elementary school has its own Reading Readiness program for five-year-olds, but boys must be five years old on or before September 1 to be eligible. Extracurricular activities are offered at all grade levels.

All classes are taught in English, but special efforts are made to meet the needs of all students. Non-English-speaking students receive special instruction in English as a second language. As a school serving the international community, Saint Mary's limits acceptance of Japanese students to those returning from living abroad. The school curriculum is basically American, and the majority of the teachers come from North America. For high school students, Saint Mary's offers classes leading to an international baccalaureate diploma. This course consists of a two-year (grades eleven and twelve) program leading to a diploma that qualifies students for admission to universities throughout the world. Advanced college standing is offered in many U.S. colleges for those holding this diploma.

Saint Mary's shares a private bus service with neighboring Seisen.

## Santa Maria School

GRADES: Preschool to 6th      Founded in 1959
2–2–4 Minami Tanaka, Nerima-ku, Tokyo    東京都練馬区南田中 2–2–4
☎ (03) 3904–0509
🚇 Nerima Takanodai Station, Seibu Ikebukuro Line; Iogi Station, Seibu
Shinjuku Line

Santa Maria School was established by a Roman Catholic order—
The Sisters Adorers—at the request of parents from the nearby U.S.
military facility. Since then, the school has grown and it now serves
both the military and civilian communities near Yokota Air Base and
in the Tokyo area. In total, the school enrolls approximately two hundred students from kindergarten to grade six.

The curriculum at Santa Maria is typical of a parochial school in
the United States. There are American and Japanese faculty members,
and instruction in English as a second language is available for those
students who need it.

All students attend classes full-time and are required to wear the
school uniform from first grade. Light religious training is part of the
curriculum, and Catholic students are prepared for first communion
in the second grade.

The school observes some American and some Japanese holidays and encourages all parents to participate in the PTA.

## Seisen International School

GRADES: Kindergarten to 12th (girls)      Founded in 1962
1–12–15 Yoga, Setagaya-ku, Tokyo    東京都世田谷区用賀 1–12–15
☎ (03) 3704–2661    🖨 (03) 3701–1033    🖥 www.twics.com/-dcj/sishome.htm
🚇 Yoga Station, Tokyu Shin Tamagawa Line

Seisen International School is a Roman Catholic girls' school run by
the Handmaids of the Sacred Heart of Jesus. The school serves a truly
international student body with over five hundred students representing
some sixty countries. The school's educational program is based on
reverence for God as the basic attitude of humanity. The faculty strives
to realize the full potential of its students and to help them understand
the essence of humanity uniting world cultures.

The coed kindergarten follows the Montessori system of education.
Children age three to six are grouped together, and three-year-olds
are only eligible for half-day programs. Two-and-a-half-year-olds may
be eligible depending on their level of maturity, and those older than
three may choose half- or full-day programs. There is also a pre-first
grade class to prepare five-year-olds for first grade.

Religious instruction is compulsory for all students at Seisen. Classes in Catholic instruction are available as well as other world religions. All classes are taught in English, and ESL courses are available for international students who are nonnative English speakers. Although children with two Japanese parents are generally not eligible for acceptance at Seisen, as with many other international schools, those Japanese children who are returning from a long stay abroad may be accepted.

From grade one of elementary school, Japanese language classes are given twice a week. Extracurricular activities are available for students in all grades. Seisen's sports program offers a wide range of sports for girls, and the school competes with the other international schools as well as with U.S. military and Japanese schools.

Seisen International School shares a private bus service with nearby Saint Mary's International School.

### Tokyo International School (TIS)

3–18–16 Meguro Honcho, Meguro-ku, Tokyo　東京都目黒区目黒本町 3–18–16
☎ (03) 3710–1160　🖷 (03) 3710–1193　🖳 www.tokyois.com
🚝 Musashi Koyama Station, Tokyu Mekama Line

Tokyo International School (TIS) is a coed, nondenominational school started by international parents who wanted to provide a child-centered education for their children. First, they opened their preschool (see Children's House) and then TIS, the elementary school, in 1997.

TIS has become very popular due to its dedication to cultural diversity and a curriculum which was developed using models from the United States of America, England, Canada, and Australia. Their low teacher-to-student ratio, teaching approach that integrates subjects into common themes to stimulate interest, and ability to bring out a student's potential have also contributed to their success.

Students receive Japanese lessons, use computers in their classroom, and go on a variety of field trips. Gymnastics, swimming lessons, and after school programs also figure in the curriculum.

TIS provides bus services for students who live in the other foreign neighborhoods of Tokyo.

### Tokyo International Learning Community (TILC)

AGES: from birth to 18 years　　Founded in 1987
6–3–50 Osawa, Mitaka-shi, Tokyo　東京都三鷹市大沢 6–3–50
☎ (0422) 31–9611　🖷 (0422) 31–9648　🖳 www.tilc.org

🚌 Mitaka Station, JR Chuo, Tozai, Sobu lines (15-minute bus ride); Tamabochi-mae Station, Seibu Tamagawa Line

This is the only international school in Japan that offers full-time education in English to students with developmental delays or disabilities. Aside from the certified special education teachers, the school employs the services of an occupational therapist, a speech pathologist, a psychologist, a physical therapist, and other specially trained assistants. TILC also provides home consulting services for students attending regular international schools.

### YMCA International Open-Minded School (YIOS)

GRADES: Kindergarten to 5th      Founded in 1998
2–2–20 Toyo, Koto-ku, Tokyo    東京都江東区東陽 2–2–20
☎ (03) 3615–5632    🖷 (03) 5635–1023
🚌 Toyocho Station, Tozai Line

YIOS currently offers two classes: Kindergarten and first grade (four- to six-years-old), and grades two to five. Each class has ten to twelve students studying a U.S.–based curriculum. The school has access to complete athletic facilities and has plans to include a junior high school in the near future.

---

OUTSIDE TOKYO

### Canadian Academy

GRADES: Preschool to 12th      Founded in 1950
4 Koyo-cho Naka, Higashi Nada-ku, Kobe-shi, Hyogo
兵庫県神戸市東灘区向洋町中 4
☎ (078) 857–0100    🖷 (078) 857–3250    🖥 canacad.ac.jp

### Fukuoka International School

GRADES: 1 to 9th      Founded in 1972
3–18–50 Momochi, Sawara-ku, Fukuoka-shi, Fukuoka
福岡県福岡市早良区百道 3–18–50
☎ (092) 841–7601    🖷 (092) 841–7602    🖥 dclark@bamboo.paradigm.co.jp

### Hiroshima International School

GRADES: Kindergarten to 9th      Founded in 1962
3–49–1 Kurakake, Asakita-ku, Hiroshima-shi, Hiroshima
広島県広島市安佐北区倉掛 3–49–1
☎ (082) 843–4111    🖷 (082) 843–6399    🖥 his888@po.cisnet.or.jp

### Hokkaido International School

GRADES: 1st to 9th      Founded in 1951
19–1–55 5-jo, Hiragishi, Toyohira-ku, Sapporo-shi, Hokkaido

北海道札幌市豊平区平岸五条 19丁目 1–55
☎ (011) 816–5000　🖷 (011) 816–2500　🖳 www.his.ac.jp

### Kyoto International School

GRADES: Kindergarten to 8th　　Founded in 1957
317 Kitatawara-cho, Nakadachiuri-sagaru, Yoshiyamachi-dori, Kamigyo-ku, Kyoto
京都府京都市上京区葭屋町通中立売下ル北俵町 317
☎ (075) 451–1022　🖷 (075) 451–1023　🖳 web.kyoto-inet.or.jp/people/hellokis/

### Marist Brothers International School

GRADES: Preschool to 12th　　Founded in 1951
1–2–1 Chimori-cho, Suma-ku, Kobe-shi, Hyogo
☎ (078) 732–6266　🖷 (078) 732–6268　　兵庫県神戸市須磨区千守町 1–2–1

### Nagoya International School

GRADES: Nursery to 12th　　Founded in 1963
2686 Minamihara Nakashidami, Moriyama-ku, Nagoya-shi, Aichi
愛知県名古屋市守山区中志段味南原 2686
☎ (052) 736–2025　🖷 (052) 736–3883　🖳 nisadmin@tcp-ip.or.jp

### Osaka International School

GRADES: Kindergarten to 12th　　Founded in 1991
4–4–16 Onohara Nishi, Minoo-shi, Osaka　　大阪府箕面市小野原西 4–4–16
☎ (0727) 27–5050　🖷 (0727) 27–5055　🖳 oia-ois@sisf.mino.osaka.jp

### Saint Maur International School

GRADES: Nursery to 12th　　Founded in 1872
83 Yamate-cho, Naka-ku, Yokohama-shi, Kanagawa　　神奈川県横浜市中区山手町 83
☎ (045) 641–5751　🖷 (045) 641–6688　🖳 www.stmaur.ac.jp

### Saint Michael's International School

GRADES: Prekindergarten to 6th　　Founded in 1946
3–17–2 Nakayamate-dori, Chuo-ku, Kobe-shi, Hyogo
☎ (078) 231–8885　🖷 (078) 231–8899　　兵庫県神戸市中央区中山手通 3–17–2

### Tohoku International School

GRADES: Preschool to 12th
7–101–1 Yakata, Izumi-ku, Sendai-shi, Miyagi　　宮城県仙台市泉区館 7–101–1
☎ (022) 348–2468　🖷 (022) 348–2467　🖳 Tohokuis.webjump.com

This school separates the lower and higher grades at two different
campuses. Call Mr. Gwyn Underwood for details.

### Yokohama International School (YIS)

GRADES: Nursery to 12th　　Founded in 1924
258 Yamate-cho, Naka-ku, Yokohama-shi, Kanagawa
神奈川県横浜市中区山手町 258
☎ (045) 621–0084　🖷 (045) 621–0379　🖳 www.twics.com/-yis

# NON-ENGLISH INTERNATIONAL SCHOOLS

For foreign families who prefer to send their children to a school where their native language is taught, the following schools exist.

### Chinese School in Tokyo
14 Goban-cho, Chiyoda-ku, Tokyo　東京都千代田区五番町 14
☎ (03) 3261–5894
🚃 Yotsuya Station, JR Chuo, Marunouchi, Namboku lines; Ichigaya Station, JR Sobu, Namboku, Yurakucho, Toei Shinjuku lines

### German School Tokyo (Yokohama)
2–4–1 Chigasaki Minami, Tsuzuki-ku, Yokohama-shi, Kanagawa
☎ (045) 941–4841/4842　神奈川県横浜市都筑区茅ヶ崎南 2–4–1
🚃 Nakamachidai Station, Yokohama Subway Line

### Korean School in Tokyo
2–1 Wakamatsu-cho, Shinjuku-ku, Tokyo　東京都新宿区若松町 2–1
☎ (03) 3357–2233
🚃 Akebonobashi Station, Toei Shinjuku Line

### Lycée Franco-Japonais
1–2–43 Fujimi-cho, Chiyoda-ku, Tokyo　東京都千代田区富士見町 1–2–43
☎ (03) 3261–0137
🚃 Kudanshita Station, Tozai, Hanzomon, Toei Shinjuku lines

# JAPANESE SCHOOLS

In addition to the international private schools, you may want to consider the Japanese public schools, which are accessible to any resident of Japan. Not only are they affordable, but they also give foreign residents the opportunity to learn Japanese-language skills, experience Japanese culture, and meet Japanese people. Some foreign residents choose to send their children to Japanese private schools, which are more costly than the public ones.

Children who attend Japanese schools go to school five and a half days a week, including Saturday morning. There are three semesters in the school year, which begins in April, and vacation times are usually from July 20 to August 31, and from December 26 to January 8. There is a short (ten days or so) break in late March between the end of one school year and the beginning of the next.

## *JAPANESE PRESCHOOL AND KINDERGARTEN* (YOCHIEN)

*Yochien* are Japanese·preschool or kindergarten programs, which may be public or private. Public *yochien* start at the age of four, whereas private *yochien* offer programs from the age of three or even earlier. Public *yochien* costs are extremely reasonable. For example, in Minato-ku in Tokyo, the registration fee is ¥500, and monthly tuition is ¥4,000. Some private *yochien*, on the other hand, come close to rivaling international schools in cost, so this may help determine where you send your child.

Because the school year begins in April, the child must be of the proper age by April 1. Usually, applications for April can be picked up from the school from about November.

For young children, most Japanese *yochien* emphasize games, play, and cooperation. Academics are usually not introduced until the age of five. Many foreigners send their preschoolers to *yochien* because it provides an excellent opportunity for their children to learn the Japanese language. The programs usually run through lunch (8:30 A.M. through noon is average although programs running until 2:30 P.M. are not uncommon; on Saturdays and one other day, usually Wednesday, *yochien* end at 11:30 A.M.). Some *yochien* have lunch programs but usually each child must take his own *obento* (box lunch).

Our personal experience with *yochien* was extremely positive. The only problem we encountered was the language difference, not for the children so much as for us, the parents. We were given many information sheets in Japanese each week, and although there were a few English-speaking teachers who would translate the important information, it was still frustrating for us. On the whole, the other mothers as well as the teachers were willing to assist us when we needed help. There are many opportunities for parents—mothers in particular—to become involved at the *yochien*. Field trips, parties, and special events all require parental involvement.

For more information on the *yochien* in your area, contact the education committee of your local ward or city office. Also, be aware that each ward or city is allotted a certain amount of money to help defray preschool costs for families who send their children to private *yochien*, even if the parents are sending a child to a *yochien* outside their ward. Many foreign families are not aware that they may qualify for this stipend, so inquire at the school at the time of registration, and they will give you the required forms to fill out.

## JAPANESE ELEMENTARY SCHOOL (SHOGAKKO)

The *shogakko*, or Japanese elementary school, runs from grade one through grade six. To attend a public elementary school, a child must meet the following requirements. First, the parents must be residents of the ward where the school is located. Second, the child must be age six by March 31. Third, the parents must have proof of residence in Japan (Alien Registration Card).

If you and your child meet these requirements, you can go to the education section of your ward or city office with your proof of residency and fill out an application form. It is a good idea to take along a Japanese-speaking person because the forms must be filled out in Japanese. A school will be chosen according to where you live, and a meeting will be set up with the principal of the school. According to law, all residents of a ward or city are entitled to send their children to local public elementary schools. This means a school must automatically accept you. If you are interested in a private elementary school, you should go directly to the school to request an application form. Some of these schools have a few spaces set aside for foreign students, and so even if the school has no openings at the time for Japanese students, they may make an exception for foreigners.

Your child will then be registered in the grade appropriate to his age. If his language skills are not adequate, he will actually be placed in a lower class until he is ready to join his peers, although he will be registered in the higher grade.

Also important in the registration process is the physical examination. The checkups are given free by school-approved pediatricians and must be done in November of the year before the child is to begin school. Forms for the physical can be picked up at the ward or city office after October 1. If the November deadline is missed, a physical should be arranged with the school doctor, because no student can begin school without this completed form.

RESOURCES—BOOKS AND WEBSITES

Here are two helpful reference books for parents who are considering Japanese schools:

*Educating Andy: The Experience of a Foreign Family in the Japanese Elementary School System*, by Anne and Andy Conduit (Kodansha International, 1996)

*Japanese Lessons: A Year in a Japanese School through the Eyes of an American Anthropologist and Her Children,* by Gail R. Benjamin (New York University Press, 1997)

You may also want to check out the English homepage of the Japanese Ministry of Education (Mombusho) for some basic information: 🖳 <www.mombu.go.jp/emindex.html>. Another good resource is the ongoing Parent's Forum on Education at Tokyo with Kids, an interactive online community for English-speaking parents. Go to 🖳 <www.tokyowithkids.com/>. The Tokyo Metropolitan Government's website, Kids Web Japan, has a helpful school page, with information in seven languages. You can find their page at 🖳 <www.jinjapan.org/kidsweb/japan/about.html>.

## HOME SCHOOLING IN JAPAN

Although Japan's international schools are all first-rate and Japanese schools are a viable alternative, home schooling is an option that more and more foreign parents are choosing in order to meet their children's educational needs. The families that decide on this option are as diverse as the home-schooling approaches themselves. Some of these families are:

1. Bicultural families who don't feel comfortable in either the Japanese or a Western school system;
2. Expatriate, military, and diplomatic families who are frequently transferred;
3. Japanese families who feel that the Japanese school system is too rigid, but whose children cannot enter an international school because of the language requirements;
4. Families who find the tuition fees at the international schools too expensive;
5. Families who live too far away from any acceptable school;
6. Families whose children are not particularly happy in school;
7. Families whose religious beliefs or philosophies differ from their children's school.

Home schooling is legal in Japan. The Ministry of Education treats home schools in the same category as the international schools. To make sure that your child's education meets government standards, it is recommended that you file basic information about your child's schooling with your local ward office or city hall each year. State that you have found a suitable educational program for your child and that he or she has been "registered" for the year with whatever program you have chosen. Have all of the above information translated into Japanese and submitted to the proper authorities.

When considering home schooling, you will want to find out about the numerous accredited programs available. Often parents are overwhelmed at the thought of being totally responsible for their child's education, but with a fairly structured program a parent need not act as the sole teacher. Depending on the ages and needs of your children, you can choose either a program that includes every material you could possible need, from textbooks and maps to the pencils and paper, or a program that gives you only general guidance. Of course, a home schooler benefits from the involvement of at least one parent. We know families where each parent brings his own strong points to the program. For example, in one family the Japanese father works on language, calligraphy, and math, while the American mother uses her talents in carpentry, cooking, and music to offer her children an education in those areas.

If there are certain subjects that children cannot master at home, parents are encouraged to make use of the programs and facilities at nearby schools, if possible, or to engage a tutor. One of the biggest advantages of home schooling is the opportunity it gives children to develop their own talents and interests. A budding tennis champ or concert violinist can devote a larger proportion of time to these pursuits than enrollment in the regular school system would allow.

Socialization is a major concern of parents when they begin a home schooling program. Those who have educated their children at home for years note, however, that these fears are usually unfounded. Because the child is not in school all day, he has many opportunities to visit with people of various ages. These parents have found that by exposing their children to a wide range of activities and by opening their home to frequent visits from friends and relatives, their home-schooled children learn to communicate and socialize with all ages and types of people.

In order to foster interaction with their child's peers, home schoolers often use the morning as their "class" time and go on outings or enroll the children in music, art, or sports in the afternoons. This schedule gives children the opportunity to learn from a teacher other than the parents, as well as to meet children their own age. Other suggestions from parents who educate their children at home include joining an international school library, participating in intramural sports, and asking if your children can take part in special events at the local schools. It may be possible to make use of nearby *yochien* playgrounds and empty classrooms in the afternoons, by asking the school and explaining your intentions and goals for your child.

In the U.S. the home-schooling movement was originally associated with religious organizations, but its horizons have broadened tremendously over the past ten years. More and more parents are choosing to home school for academic excellence, and the top universities accept more home schoolers each year. Most of the overseas programs used here in Japan are from the United States. One of the best sources for information is the John Holt organization. John Holt was an American elementary school teacher who eventually became a strong advocate of home learning. He is the author of several well-known books, such as *How Children Fail* and *Teach Your Own*. These publications are available through John Holt's Music and Book Store, 2269 Massachusetts Ave., Cambridge, Massachusetts 02140, USA. Its superb catalog carries many educational materials, including books, tapes, and musical instruments. An international newsletter, *Growing Without Schooling*, was founded by John Holt in 1977. Containing pertinent and practical information, this newsletter is a valuable forum for home schoolers around the world. Be sure to check out the Holt Associates website at ⌨ <www.holtgws.com>.

A new alternative for Japanese or English speakers who want to pursue a home-school curriculum is Atmark Inter-High School, which allows students to use the Internet to study at home. The program is available for students who have graduated from junior high. Through an alliance with a high school in the United States, Atmark students can complete an independent study course and receive a U.S. diploma. For more information, see Atmark's website at ⌨ <www.at-learn.co.jp/>.

Several local websites also provide excellent material. Katherine Combs has put together a thoroughly informative webpage, Home Schooling in Japan, ⌨ <www2.gol.com/users/milkat>, with helpful articles, resources, and a support network for parents. A home-schooling newsletter is published online by Aileen Kawagoe at ⌨ <fwkk7670@mb.infoweb.ne.jp>. In addition to an ongoing forum about home schooling in Japan, the resource list is quite extensive, with numerous links to other educational sites. International School Support System (ISSS), listed earlier in this chapter, provides various programs to supplement or support home schooling.

The following is a short list of some of the most popular home-learning programs in the United States.

### The Calvert School

Dept. 2 NET, 105 Tuscany Road, Baltimore, Maryland 21210, USA
☎ (410) 243–6030   🖷 (410) 366–0674   🖳 www.calvertschool.org

The Calvert School, founded in 1897, exists as a elementary day school in addition to its Home Instruction division for kindergarten through eighth grade. The home-study curriculum is followed by hundreds of students around the world and is accredited by the Maryland State Department of Education. Their catalog is available on line.

### Clonlara

1289 Jewett, Ann Arbor, Michigan 48104, USA
☎ (313) 769–4515   🖷 (313) 769–9629   🖳 www.clonlara.org

This well-balanced program offers a flexible yet standard approach to long-distance education.

### Oak Meadow

P.O. Box 740, Putney, Vermont 05346, USA
☎ (802) 387–2021   🖷 (802) 387–5108   🖳 www.oakmeadow.com

Since 1975, this school has offered an outstanding program, with an innovative, yet academically sound curriculum. Students can be assigned their own teacher and can also participate in chat rooms with other students and teachers.

### *HOME-SCHOOLING RESOURCES*

For more international information, contact World Wide Educational Services, Strode House, 44–50 Osnaburgh Street, London NW1 3NN, England, or write John Holt's Music and Book Store and request a copy of their directory issue of *Growing Without Schooling*, which contains the names of thousands of home schoolers around the world.

Among the books for families contemplating home schooling, we can recommend *Home Schooling: Taking the First Step*, by Borg Hendrickson. Also, *Better Than School*, by Nancy Wallace; *School's Out*, by Jean Bendell; and *The Three R's at Home*, by Howard and Susan Richman, are all available from John Holt's Music and Book Store.

### HOME-SCHOOLING WEBSITES

Check out these websites for additional information and support.

**Adprima**

🖥 www.adprima.com

This site includes reviews of other home-schooling sites and chat rooms, as well as up-to-date information on curricula for home schoolers.

**Alternative Learning Exchange**

🖥 www.xs4all.nl/~altlearn/ale/

Information on alternative learning environments, including articles, links, and related news stories.

**Exploring Homeschooling**

🖥 www.outoftheboxpublishing.com

Articles and links to unique sites, books, workshops, and events.

**Family Learning Exchange**

🖥 www.FlexOnLine.Org

Useful site with resources, links, books, and a newsletter.

**National Homeschooling Association**

🖥 www.alumni.caltech.edu/-casner/nha

Advocacy services for home-schooling families, along with information on conferences, networking, and resources.

# 12

# The Care and Nurturing of Parents

TIME TO SHAPE UP

Besides the normal wear and tear of raising small children, in Japan there is the added stress of living in both a foreign culture and one of the most work-oriented countries in the world. Any parent who has successfully raised children will tell you that one very important thing to do while the children are small is to carve out a little time for yourself. This is also one of the most difficult things to do, and in Tokyo it is nearly impossible. With long work hours, business and social obligations, club or group functions, and play-group or school activities, there is very little time left for either parent to spend alone or together. For your physical as well as mental health though, it is important to make the effort to take time out.

## PHYSICAL HEALTH

If you thrive on regular exercise and plan on continuing a regime while in Japan, there are a few important things to consider. Parents with small children may not want to take the time to go to a club for exercise, but instead may want to work out at home. Because of limited space in most homes, a weight or workout room may not be possible. If you need to exercise, push back all of the furniture and go for it! Another idea is to invite some other mothers over during the day and let the kids play while you exercise together.

One of the advantages of living in Japan is the relative safety of walking or jogging alone on the streets. If you are lucky enough to live near a large park, temple, or shrine, you can walk or run in the beauty of the trees and gardens. Be aware, however, that only walking, not running, is allowed on the paths of many shrines. Check with the authorities before you start out. One man we know ran every morning for weeks in the ground of a shrine unaware that he was being told over the loudspeakers—in Japanese, of course—to stop running.

Private fitness centers and spas abound in Japan. They are popular with young Japanese, but because of work schedules, the clubs can be crowded during the evening hours and on weekends. This can work to your advantage if you have flexible hours that allow you to use the club during the day. Many clubs have a special day rate—often just a monthly fee and no registration charge. Other clubs have restricted membership and charge an annual subscription as well as outrageous registration fees. Club styles range from European-type spas, to over-decorated gyms, to clubs with state-of-the-art weight lifting equipment and personal trainers who speak three languages. The one you choose may depend more on location and cost than decor.

Most wards and cities also have a public sports center, with low entrance fees and many types of facilities. If you do not speak Japanese, you may need to take a Japanese-speaking person with you the first time you go to fill out forms and translate the various rules and regulations.

Call your local ward or city office for more information.

## MENTAL HEALTH

### Thoughts on Coping, with a Little Help . . .

How well I remember that first year in Tokyo, my emotions bouncing from bewilderment, to anger, to tears as I struggled to cope in this strange city. There were quite a few days when I took to bed, completely lethargic with depression. Normally a positive, high-energy person, I was surprised at how difficult this move was for me. I finally talked with a counselor and learned how valuable it is to seek help when you are feeling overwhelmed. A move to a foreign country can expose all sorts of weak areas in your infrastructure, whether it be a relationship or those demons of dysfunction you've been battling to some degree all your life. Fortunately, in the Tokyo area, there are a wide range of professionals who can help you to move beyond the pain, whether it is due to culture shock, mental health issues, or relationship problems.

If you find yourself singing the blues, but not seriously enough to seek assistance, you may want to try my own personal antidote for mild depression: exercise and volunteer work. I find that taking a walk or going for a run every day does wonders for my mood, not to mention my metabolism. Getting involved in any kind of volunteer work helps to avoid the isolation that makes depression even worse. By helping those less fortunate, you get a chance to see life from a different perspective, perhaps realizing that your own problems are small in comparison. (If your problems are big, don't struggle alone. Get help!)

There are numerous opportunities for volunteer work in Japan. We recommend a free book published by Foreign Executive Women (FEW) entitled *Volunteering in the Tokyo Area Directory*. Over seventy non-profit organizations are listed. The book may be ordered from Jeanne Vass, 1–12–6–202 Shoto, Shibuya-ku, Tokyo; send a fax to ☎ (03) 3481–6667 or (03) 3460–3689. The book is free, though the publisher asks that you please send money to cover the postage.

Many organizations exist throughout Japan solely for the purpose of helping foreigners cope with life. Besides providing basic information on life in Japan, these centers may offer cultural and orientation classes. The cultural classes range from Japanese flower arranging (ikebana) to basic language and cooking courses. Orientation sessions often include local tours and guest speakers.

## SURVIVAL TIPS FOR PARENTS

### *ORDER IN*

We thought of inserting this under the food section, but the mental health section seemed more appropriate! You can order take-out food from various neighborhood restaurants (ask for a menu) for those nights when you just can't deal with the kids, the weather, or the thought of cooking another meal. And if ordering in Japanese is too stressful, check out Dominoes, Pizza Hut, and Subway. All accept fax orders and are generally English-friendly. The TownPage telephone directory has listings of the ones nearest you.

### *TAKE A BREAK*

Escape for the day to a Buddhist temple for Zen meditation. This is the real thing at Sojiji Temple, founded in 1321 as the head temple of the Soto Sect of Zen Buddhism. The meditation sessions are open to public participation. The temple is located at 2–1–1 Tsurumi, Tsurumi-ku, Yokohama; ☎ (045) 581-6021. Open 10:00 A.M. to 4:30 P.M. Tuesday through Sunday. Closed on Mondays. Admission is ¥300. A 5-minute walk from Tsurumi Station on the Keihin Tohoku Line.

Many cities are now funding what they call "international associations" to run such centers, not only for foreign residents, but for Japanese citizens as well. The Nagoya International Center, 1–47–1 Nagono, Nakamura-ku, Nagoya-shi, Aichi, ☎ (052) 581–5678, was one of the first and serves as a model for the rest of the country. If you are new to an area, or simply want to learn a little more about your neighborhood and perhaps meet some new people, check out what is being offered by the groups in your area by contacting your local ward office, city hall, or community center.

In Tokyo, churches, international schools, and private clubs offer similar services and opportunities for the foreign community, so the need for government-funded community centers has not been as great as in the outlying areas.

## COMMUNITY AND INFORMATION CENTERS

KANSAI AREA

### Community House and Information Centre (CHIC)

Central Tower, 3F, 5–15 Koyo-cho Naka, Higashinada-ku, Kobe-shi, Hyogo
☎ (078) 857–6540   兵庫県神戸市東灘区向洋町中 5–15   セントラルタワー 3F
⊕ 9:30 A.M. to 4:30 P.M. Monday through Friday. Summer until 12:00 P.M. Closed in August.

This volunteer organization exists to help foreigners who live in the Kobe-Osaka area. Besides the orientation and cultural classes they offer, they publish two books that are a must for foreigners living in the area. *Living in Kobe*, a sourcebook for information and services in the area, costs ¥2,500 plus ¥310 postage from CHIC. The chapter "Kids in Kobe" has numerous listings of places of interest and services that parents need to know about. It includes information about Kyoto and Osaka, so before you travel that way make sure to get a copy.

### Kobe International Community Center

Kobe Kokusai Kaikan, 20F, 8–1–6 Goko Dori, Chuo-ku, Kobe-shi, Hyogo
☎ (078) 291–0641   兵庫県神戸市中央区御幸通 8–1–6   神戸国際会館 20F
⊕ Monday through Friday 10:00 A.M. to 8:00 P.M., Saturday 10:00 A.M. to 5:00 P.M.

Established in 1990, this center is run by Kobe International Association (a governmental body) for all residents. It offers Japanese-language and cultural classes free of charge and gives information by phone or in person. At the center there are foreign magazines and newspapers, an English typewriter and word processor available for use, as well as satellite TV and a message board.

### Kyoto International Community House

2–1 Awadaguchi Torii-cho, Sakyo-ku, Kyoto-shi, Kyoto
☎ (075) 752–3010　京都府京都市左京区粟田口鳥居町 2–1
🕐 9:00 A.M. to 9:00 P.M. Tuesday through Sunday. If Monday is a holiday, it is open that day and closed the next day.

Sponsored by the city government, Kyoto International Community House opened in September 1989 to assist the needs of the foreign community and to serve as a cultural exchange center for Japanese citizens. Among their programs are traditional Japanese culture courses (in English), a home-visit program, lectures about Asia (in Japanese), foreign movies, and classical concerts. There is a library with foreign newspapers, magazines, and books, as well as live CNN television broadcasts in the information area in the lobby.

### Osaka International House (OIH)

8–2–6 Uehommachi, Tennoji-ku, Osaka-shi, Osaka
☎ (06) 6772–5931　大阪府大阪市天王寺区上本町 8–2–6
🕐 9:00 A.M. to 9:00 P.M. daily.

OIH is a conference and international exchange center built by the city of Osaka to provide a place for cultural exchange for all residents. Besides information in English, International House provides a number of services and facilities, including cultural classes about Asia for a minimum charge, a reading corner with foreign newspapers and magazines, a library with books in English and Japanese (books must be read on-site), live CNN television in a comfortable lounge, a message board, and conference and hotel facilities for use at a reasonable cost.

## COUNSELING SERVICES

Besides the community centers, there are counseling services for foreigners that provide individual or family counseling, and others that can give assistance over the telephone, either by supplying basic information or by helping in a crisis situation. They are nonsectarian and are staffed by both trained volunteers and professional counselors.

We highly recommend the book, *The Japan Experience: Coping and Beyond*, by Tazuko Shibusawa and Joy Norton. For additional listings of counseling services, see the chapter on mental health in *Japan Health Handbook*.

## TELL Community Counseling Service (TCCS)

9–1 Hachiyama-cho, Shibuya-ku, Tokyo　東京都渋谷区鉢山町 9–1
☎ (03) 3498–0231 (English), (03) 3498–0232 (Japanese)
🕐 9:00 A.M. to 5:00 P.M. Monday through Friday.

Connected with TELL (Tokyo English Lifeline), TCCS provides individual, group, and family therapy by trained counselors. Fees are assessed on an ability-to-pay basis. It also holds workshops and employee assistance programs.

## Dr. Ana Kishida

☎ (03) 3448–1272　🖵 www.i-way1.net/Ami

A clinical psychologist with twenty years of experience in cross-cultural counseling and crisis management.

## Sasaki Educational Counseling, Shoko Sasaki

Yoyogi Terrace 211, 1–32–27 Tomigaya, Shibuya-ku, Tokyo
☎ (03) 3466–1481　東京都渋谷区富ヶ谷 1–32–27 代々木テラス 211

U.S.-trained psychologist Sasaki specializes in family therapy and relationship problems.

## Dr. Ron Shumsky

☎ (0423) 82–1263, (045) 641–6961 (Bluff Clinic)

A psychotherapist, specializing in treating children and families.

## Tokyo International Learning Community (TILC)

☎ (0422) 31–9611　🖨 (0422) 31–9648

See chapter 11 under International Schools for more information.

## Tokyo Psychotherapy Center, Dr. Masafumi Nakakuki

2–1–15–705 Takanawa, Minato-ku, Tokyo　東京都港区高輪 2–1–15–705
☎/🖨 (03) 3280–5776

Dr. Nakakuki is a bilingual psychiatrist who has practiced for over thirty years in the United States.

## Resolutions Counseling Service, Kelly Lemmon-Kishi

19–16 Uyama-cho, Hirakata-shi, Osaka　大阪府枚方市宇山町 19–16
☎ (072) 867–4437

The service's U.S.-trained social worker offers counseling for families, individuals, and couples in the areas of sexual violence, depression, and disaster response.

## SUPPORT GROUPS

Numerous support groups for people with special needs, such as Alcoholics Anonymous or Overeaters Anonymous, have English-speaking chapters throughout Japan. These groups meet regularly. To find out

---

### IMMEDIATE HELP OVER THE PHONE

**Japan Helpline**

🖳 www.jhelp.com

Run by a not-for-profit group calling itself Agape, this hotline has an online presence with basic emergency numbers and other sources of information in Japanese and English. A telephone number listed on-site will connect you with a volunteer.

**Japan Travel-Phone**

☎ Tokyo (03) 3201–3331, 0120–444–800 (toll-free)
🖳 www.jnto.go.jp (Japan Travel Updates)
🕙 9:00 A.M. to 5:00 P.M. daily.

Tourist information and assistance in English.

**Tokyo English Lifeline (TELL)**

☎ (03) 5774–0992 (phone counseling, referrals, crisis intervention)
🕙 9:00 A.M. to 4:00 P.M. and 7:00 P.M. to 11:00 P.M. daily.

TELL publishes an invaluable information/resources calendar for the foreign community. To order call ☎ (03) 3498–0261.

**TELL NET**

🖳 www.tell.gol.com

For information about volunteering and services, contact ☎ (03) 3498–0261 or fax 🖷 (03) 3498–0272.

what groups meet in your area and when, contact the organizations listed here—in particular, TELL for the Tokyo area, and the Community House and Information Centre for the Kansai area—or check the English-language newspapers and journals. (Parent support groups for special needs are listed in chapter 9.) If you cannot find a group to meet your needs, consider forming your own support group.

## INFORMATION NETWORKS

Throughout Japan, there are services that give information by phone, often in English, and perhaps in other languages as well. Keep these numbers by the phone, as these agencies can provide answers to questions on almost any subject. If they do not know the answer, they will steer you to someone who does. For a comprehensive listing of useful telephone numbers, we recommend the TELL calendar (see Immediate Help over the Phone).

The NTT TownPage is a yellow pages directory in English that you will find very handy. Pick one up for free at any NTT office or call ☎ (03) 3356–8511 to order one. You can also check them out online at ⌨ <english.itp.ne.jp/>.

An extremely useful online publication for parents in Japan is Tokyo with Kids. Through this website parents can exchange information on various topics, check out the baby-sitting and childcare network, browse the classifieds, and read all kinds of news pertinent to international families in Japan. This free site is the brainstorm (and labor of love) of Cornelia Kurz and another young mom, Emi Asada, ⌨ <www.Tokyowithkids.com>.

## NEWSPAPERS

The following newspapers are printed in Asia and can be delivered to your door at a relatively low cost. Other major newspapers from around the world can be airmailed to you in Japan, but the cost may be prohibitive. Many of these publications have websites with a limited amount of information.

### Dailies

*Asian Wall Street Journal*: ☎ (03) 3292–1458

*The Daily Yomiuri*: ☎ (03) 3242–1111
*The International Herald Tribune/Asahi Shimbun*: ☎ (03) 5541–8695
*The Japan Times*: ☎ (03) 3453–5311
*U.S.A. Today*: ☎ (03) 3270–8650

### Weeklies
*The Japan Times Weekly*: ☎ (03) 3453–4350
*The Nikkei Weekly*: ☎ (03) 3270–0251

## FREE NEWS PUBLICATIONS

A number of freebies are published in English for foreign residents and tourists. Most of them can be picked up in supermarkets, bookstores, and shops that foreigners frequent, as well as in the major hotels. Some of the publications can be subscribed to for a small fee and delivered to your door. Some are available online. All of them are full of timely and valuable information, such as phone numbers for services, articles on new businesses, and movie and concert information. Many also contain personal and classified ads, providing a good place to find used household items and appliances for sale. The listing below is by no means complete, since every six months it seems a new publication pops up and another one dies. The following are publications that have been around for a while.

> TOKYO AREA

### City Life News
Kita Bldg., 2F, 2–8–13 Shiba, Minato-ku, Tokyo
☎ (03) 3457–7541　🖷 (03) 3457–7544　東京都港区芝 2–8–13　キタビル 2F

Monthly, general interest newsletter, available around Tokyo or by subscription.

### Nippon View
2–8–6 Shiroganedai, Minato-ku, Tokyo　東京都港区白金台 2–8–6
☎ (03) 3442–0211　🖷 (03) 3442–0217

Similar to *City Life News*, this monthly publication has a full page of important phone numbers to tear out and keep by the phone. Delivered with the *Japan Times* and available around Tokyo at select locations.

### Tokyo Classified

Maison Tomoe Bldg., 3F, 3–16–1 Minami Aoyama, Minato-ku, Tokyo
東京都港区南青山 3–16–1　メゾンともえ 3F
☎ (03) 3423–6932　📠 (03) 3423–6931　🖳 www.tokyoclassified.com

A weekly magazine of classified ads, light news, and features stories, plus an extensive listing of events.

### Tokyo Notice Board

3–14–12, #603, Roppongi, Minato-ku, Tokyo　東京都港区六本木 3–14–12 #603
☎ (03) 3475–0640　📠 (03) 3475–0641　🖳 tnb@magical3.egg.or.jp

A weekly, small-format magazine with mostly classified ads, plus language exchange and personals.

### Tokyo Q (online only)

🖳 www.202.221.249.1/tokyoq

This award-winning site provides a weekly city guide of events, news, and other fun happenings around town.

### Tokyo Weekender

Tuttle Bldg., 5F, 1–2–6 Suido, Bunkyo-ku, Tokyo
☎ (03) 5689–2471　📠 (03) 5689–2474　東京都文京区水道 1–2–6　タトルビル 5F
🖳 www.weekender.co.jp

The granddaddy of them all, published since 1970, this newspaper is full of interesting tidbits and informative articles for the foreign community. Available every other Friday at major supermarkets, hotels, and restaurants; or have it delivered to your door.

---
KANSAI AREA
---

### Kinki Nippon Tourist

Nikko Bldg., 7F, 2–11–8 Sonezaki, Kita-ku, Osaka
大阪市北区曾根崎 2–11–8　日興ビル 7F
☎ (06) 6313–6868　📠 (06) 6314–1601　🖳 intlosa@tabi.knt.co.jp

A monthly paper with basic tourist information for the Kansai area. Available at major hotels, tourist locations, and from Kobe Community House and Information Centre (see Community and Information Centers above).

## MAGAZINES

Like any major city, Tokyo has a number of city magazines, full of information on what's happening around town. They fill the same void as the free publications, but are more comprehensive in the information that they give. They are full of interesting features on a potpourri of subjects. There are also some journals that are written for foreigners living in Japan, which contain cultural and regional articles. Again, the ones that have passed the test of time are listed here.

### *Eye-Ai*

Sennari Bldg., 5F, 5–6–20 Minami Aoyama, Minato-ku, Tokyo
東京都港区南青山 5–6–20　千成ビル 5F
☎ (03) 3433–8602　📠 (03) 3433–8608　🖥 www.aec.or.jp/user/river

Published monthly, full of news and information regarding the traditional culture, entertainment, and popular music and arts of Japan.

### *Hello Friends*

Kanagawa International Association, Chikyu Shimin Plaza, 1–2–1 Kosugaya, Sakae-ku, Yokohama-shi, Kanagawa
神奈川県横浜市栄区小菅ヶ谷 1–2–1 地球市民プラザ
神奈川インターナショナルアソシエーション
☎ (045) 896–2626　📠 (045) 896–2945

This is not actually a magazine, but a twice-yearly newsletter in English with helpful information for foreigners living anywhere in Japan. To receive the newsletter free of charge, call the association (closed on Mondays).

### *Kansai Time-Out*

1–1–13 Ikuta-cho, Chuo-ku, Kobe-shi, Hyogo　兵庫県神戸市中央区生田町 1–1–13
☎ (078) 232–4516　📠 (078) 232–4518　🖥 www.kto.co.jp

A monthly publication with feature articles and arts and entertainment information for the Kansai area. A must for foreigners living in the area.

### *Look Japan*

Asahi Seimei Hibiya Bldg., 1–5–1 Yurakucho, Chiyoda-ku, Tokyo
東京都千代田区有楽町 1–5–1　朝日生命日比谷ビル
☎ (03) 5511–7111　📠 (03) 5511–7110

Monthly magazine with cultural insights and general information. Sample it on their website at 🖥 <www.lookjapan.com>.

### *Tokyo Journal*

Intercontinental Marketing Corp., 1–19–8 Kakigara-cho, Nihombashi, Chuo-ku, Tokyo　東京都中央区日本橋蠣殻町 1–19–8
☎ (03) 3661–7458　📠 (03) 3667–9646　🖥 imcbooks@twics.com

Trendy and colorful, full of Tokyo film, exhibition, and festival listings, as well as a number of feature articles each month.

### Yokohama Echo

Sangyo Boeki Center Bldg., 3F, 2 Yamashita-cho, Naka-ku Yokohama-shi, Kanagawa　神奈川県横浜市中区山下町 2 産業貿易センタービル 3F
☎ (045) 671–7128　🖷 (045) 671–7187

A small monthly newsletter put out by the Yokohama Association for International Communications and Exchange (YOKE). Useful information on events, activities, sports, and exhibitions in and around Yokohama.

## PARENTING INFORMATION FROM ABROAD

Without news from your home country on a regular basis, you may begin to feel "out of it." As a parent, this problem is magnified. You need up-to-date information on current trends in health, nutrition, and education, which could have some bearing on your child's development.

We have compiled a list of popular parenting magazines from the United States, with brief descriptions and the addresses to which you can write for subscription information. Most magazines require payment before they will begin overseas delivery, and it takes six to eight weeks to process a new subscription. Unless otherwise noted, major credit cards (Visa, MasterCard, etc.,) are accepted, as are U.S. dollar checks or money orders.

### Exceptional Parent

P.O. Box 3000, Dept. EP, Denville, New Jersey 07834–9919, USA
☎ (617) 536–8961　🖷 (617) 730–8742

A magazine covering issues of concern to parents of disabled children.

### Family Life

P.O. Box 52220, Boulder, Colorado 80322–2220, USA
☎ 800–879–3661　🖷 (303) 604–7455

Fun-filled and full of interesting facts, crafts, helpful hints, and great stories by parents.

### Growing Child

P.O. Box 620, Lafayette, Indiana 47902, USA
☎ (765) 423–2624　🖷 (765) 423–4495

A monthly newsletter focusing on the issues, problems, and choices that parents face as their children grow. Most useful for first-time parents who want month-by-month information to follow the mental and physical development of their children. A great resource to compile in a notebook and pass on to other first-time parents.

### Mothering

P.O. Box 1690, Santa Fe, New Mexico 87504, USA
☎ (505) 984–8116    🖷 (505) 986–8335    🖳 www.mothering.com

Published every other month, this thought-provoking magazine deals with all aspects of parenting, from infancy through the teenage years. Of special interest is the reader's forum and the international focus of the magazine.

### New Beginnings

1400 N. Meacham Road, Schaumburg, Illinois 60173, USA
☎ (847) 519–7730    🖷 (847) 519–0035

An inexpensive bimonthly publication from La Leche League International. In addition to breastfeeding information, you will find articles on child-rearing, nutrition, and more.

### Parenting

P.O. Box 52424, Boulder, Colorado 80323–2424, USA
☎ (303) 447–9330

A magazine with a fresh layout and glossy photographs, has articles addressing parenting issues in the world today.

### Parents

P.O. Box 3055, Harlan, Iowa 51593–2119, USA
☎ (515) 247–7500

A wealth of information about every stage of development. Very mainstream, but one of the longest-running popular magazines for parents in North America.

### Twins

5350 S. Roslyn Street, Suite 400, Englewood, Colorado 80111, USA
☎ (303) 290–8500    🖷 (303) 290–9025

A magazine for parents of multiples offering support plus interesting and informative articles. Also look to the advertisements to find special equipment for twins.

### Working Mother

P.O. Box 53861, Boulder, Colorado 80322, USA
☎ (303) 447–9330

A magazine for working mothers but with information of interest to all parents on child care, health, and fashion.

## WHO'S MINDING THE KIDS?

Baby-sitters in Japan come in all shapes, sizes, and nationalities. There are many options for creative child care that are affordable. It is also possible to hire live-in help from abroad by becoming a sponsor.

If your family is interested in an *au pair* or nanny, there are two highly recommended services for European care-givers. Euromaman, a French *au pair* company, can be contacted at ▣ <maman.com>. Mr. Bertrand Roussel will handle your request in English. At the German agency Perfect Partners, ask for Sabine Hoppe, an English-speaking employee. The e-mail address is ▣ <phoppe@ metronet.de>. We know several families in Japan who have been quite happy with the nannies and *au pairs* provided by these two services.

### BABY-SITTING SERVICES

There are a number of baby-sitting services in Japan that serve both the Japanese and the foreign community. These services are numerous and competitive in the Tokyo area. To find help in your area, check the bulletin boards where foreigners post messages and exchange information. If you live elsewhere in Japan, you may have to search for a service that will meet your needs, especially if you require an English-speaking baby-sitter or maid.

The companies offering baby-sitting services are usually more expensive for a one-time job than if you have a regular, independently hired baby-sitter. Often a company will refuse to send you the same person more than once for fear that you will hire her away from the service or use her during off hours. If you want to build a relationship with one or two sitters, check with the company to see if this is possible.

Most of the services listed below have a minimum charge for a certain number of hours, then an hourly rate after that. You usually pay for transportation as well. Some of the services charge a registration fee that you pay upon joining, others charge an annual fee. Along with the names and phone numbers, we have specified below what kind of help each service offers, whether or not English is spoken, and additional comments as necessary.

## Tom Sawyer

- Osaka branch: MG Ote-dori Bldg., 3F, 2–1–6 Ote-dori, Chuo-ku, Osaka-shi, Osaka　大阪府大阪市中央区大手通 2–1–6　MG大手通ビル 3F
  ☎ Osaka (06) 6942–9227, Kobe (078) 221–6530, Kyoto (075) 371–1530, Nagoya (052) 220–3120
- Shibuya branch: Shin Taiso Maruyama Bldg., 201, 20–1 Maruyama-cho, Shibuya-ku, Tokyo　東京都渋谷区円山町 20–1　新大宗円山ビル 201
  ☎ (03) 3770–9530　🖷 (03) 3770–6889

Branches of the Tom Sawyer agency are located throughout Japan. They provide baby-sitting service twenty-four hours a day for children from birth to twelve years of age. You can become a member by paying a fee. Hourly rates for members are lower. For reservations, you must call by 8:00 P.M. the day before you require service. Generally, no English is spoken.

## Baby Life Center

37–27 Udagawa-cho, Shibuya-ku, Tokyo　東京都渋谷区宇田川町 37–27
☎ (03) 3485–0630　🖷 (03) 3469–7387

Very reasonable rates for postpartum care, babysitting, and light housework. Twenty-four-hour availability, but little English is spoken.

## Homeaid

2–1–7 Ebara, Shinagawa-ku, Tokyo　東京都品川区荏原 2–1–7
☎ (03) 3781–7536　🖷 (03) 3786–6075

Homeaid has been in business since 1989, providing both maid and baby-sitting services. It is a small agency; baby-sitters are part time in most cases and maids work only on a regular basis. You need to call a couple of days beforehand to reserve a baby-sitter. The owner, Mrs. Tajima, speaks English and only hires people with experience. Although she can provide baby-sitters who speak English, Mrs. Tajima stresses care over language, especially with infants. There is no membership fee, but there is a four-hour minimum charge for a maid and a three-hour minimum for a baby-sitter.

## Japan Baby-Sitter Service

Shuwa Jingu Residence, 505, 3–3–16 Sendagaya, Shibuya-ku, Tokyo
東京都渋谷区千駄ヶ谷 3–3–16　秀和神宮レジデンス 505
☎ (03) 3423–1251　🖷 (03) 3423–6738

This is a baby-sitting service that provides care for children up to age twelve with special needs, such as autism and Down's syndrome. Only Japanese is spoken.

### Kinder Network

B503, 1–3–18 Shibuya, Shibuya-ku, Tokyo    東京都渋谷区渋谷 1–3–18  B503
☎ (03) 3486–8278    🖷 (03) 3409–0594

Kinder Network is strictly a baby-sitting service—it does not offer to clean your house. What the baby-sitters will do, however, is play with your child, give piano lessons, help with homework, and give all of their attention to the happiness and security of your little ones. There is an annual membership fee, and then an hourly rate (three-hour minimum). Call three days in advance for a reservation, Monday to Friday from 10:00 A.M. to 6:00 P.M. The office has only Japanese-speaking personnel; some sitters may speak English.

### Nihon Baby-Sitter

3F, 7–1–29 Kishimachi, Urawa-shi, Saitama    埼玉県浦和市岸町 7–1–29  3F
☎ (03) 3822–8058    🖷 (048) 831–3626

Strictly a baby-sitting service. Sitters are available for part-time or regular sitting and can pick up children after school. Only Japanese is spoken.

### Poppins Service

TEC Hiroo, 8F, 1–10–5 Hiroo, Shibuya-ku, Tokyo
東京都渋谷区広尾 1–10–5  テック広尾 8F
☎ Tokyo (03) 3447–2100, Yokohama (045) 942–2100, Kyoto (075) 252–2100, Nagoya (052) 565–2100    🖳 www.poppins.co.jp

Poppins will provide baby-sitters for newborns to twelve-year-olds. The staff is made up of female college students with education in early childhood development, and older women who have experience as teachers or in the nursing field. They not only baby-sit, but also engage the children in activities throughout the day—they list twenty possible activities in their pamphlet. The service maintains a hot line to a doctor twenty-four hours a day from their main office. Their sitters will also clean and shop if necessary. There is a two-hour minimum charge. Only Japanese is spoken at the office, but your baby-sitter may speak some English.

### Reiyukai

1–10–4 Azabudai, Minato-ku, Tokyo    東京都港区麻布台 1–10–4
☎ (03) 3586–7852    🖷 (03) 3586–6757

This service provides experienced sitters for newborns to nine-year-olds and the elderly. Only Japanese is spoken.

## The Tokyo Area Babysitting Bulletin Board (TABBB)

This is an electronic listing of baby-sitters. Since going online in 1997, hundreds of families have subscribed to the free e-mail service which lists details and references on numerous baby-sitters in the area. TABBB is available through the Tokyo with Kids website, 🖥 <www.Tokyo withkids.com>. For more information on the site, see Information Networks in this chapter.

## Tokyo Domestic Service

#406, 2–17–65, Akasaka, Minato-ku, Tokyo　東京都港区赤坂 2–17–65　406号室
☎ (03) 3584–4769　🖨 (03) 3584–4769

The granddaddy of hired help in Tokyo, this service has been in business for thirty-five years. Bilingual maids and baby-sitters are available. There is no membership fee; help is available weekly, on a regular basis, or part time.

## *PUBLIC DAY-CARE CENTERS*

Every ward or city sponsors its own day-care centers (*hoikuen*), and as a resident of that ward or city, you are entitled to use them. These centers provide good care at a very low cost and are specifically for families with two working parents or a disabled parent. Aside from the public *hoikuen*, run by the ward or city, there are private *hoikuen* that are licensed by the ward or city. Public *hoikuen* accept children from four months of age, although some may only accept them from one year. Private *hoikuen* may accept children under four months. (See the following section.)

　The *hoikuen* schedule follows the Japanese school system in that age requirements must be met as of March 31. Your ward or city office will usually accept applications or it will direct you to your nearest welfare center (*fukushi jimusho*). A Japanese-speaking person is often useful when making your application. You will need to show proof that both parents are employed full time or that the primary care-giver is disabled or sick. After applying, you will be called in a couple of weeks for an interview with you and your child. To apply to a private *hoikuen*, go to the facility directly and ask about applications. All children must have a physical exam before entering a *hoikuen*. You should apply before the middle of January for April entrance. If you apply during the middle of the year, there may be a waiting list, and you will be accepted when there is an opening. Standard hours for *hoikuen* are 8:30 A.M. to 5:00 P.M. Monday through Friday, and at licensed centers meals are provided. The employees will most likely speak only Japanese, but these day-care centers are an economical and convenient solution for many parents throughout Japan.

## PRIVATE DAY-CARE CENTERS

In the private sector, day-care centers tend to look like international preschools. They charge large fees and have a schedule that they follow throughout the day to keep the children happy and entertained. The concept of a "nursery," to which you can take your child and leave him for a few hours, is new to Japan. As more mothers find themselves without grandparents and relatives nearby to help out with the children, the need for these services will continue to grow. There is a fine line between what should be called a nursery and what is really a day-care center that will accept drop-ins. We have listed some of both types. In Tokyo as well as out-lying areas, nursery services are often available at department stores (see chapter 2) and at churches. Also check the information bulletin boards at community centers and grocery stores to find out about day care in your area.

### Entente Child Care Room

RIC Central Tower 3F, 5–15 Koyo-cho Naka, Higashinada-ku, Kobe-shi, Hyogo
☎ (078) 858–0655   兵庫県神戸市東灘区向洋町中 5–15   RICセントラルタワー 3F

This child-care facility accepts babies from three months to children age ten. Open from 9:00 A.M. to 5:00 P.M. Monday through Friday, Entente charges both a registration and annual fee. A day's notice is preferred when dropping your child off. Japanese and English are spoken.

### EOS Social Service Club (ESSC)

1–34–6 Kita Senzoku, Ota-ku, Tokyo   東京都大田区北千束 1–34–6
☎ (03) 3723–7608   📠 (03) 3723–7766

ESSC is available for use on a regular basis only. You must become a member and pay a registration fee, then an annual fee on top of the hourly wage. All of the employees are trained, and they educate your children as well as baby-sit them. They do not come to your home; instead, the children are cared for in volunteers' homes throughout greater Tokyo. The service tries to find a home as near to your house as possible. You may use it on a regular day each week, or you may change the days and times from week to week. Only Japanese is spoken.

## Kids World

☎ 0120–00–1537 (toll-free)

This chain of child-care facilities first opened in July 1994 and has rapidly expanded throughout the Tokyo area. Each location is staffed by at least one English-speaking teacher in addition to several bilingual staff. The Creative Play day-care program, for ages one to eight, allows you to drop your child off anytime from 9:00 A.M. to 7:00 P.M. for a charge of ¥1,500 an hour. There is a registration fee of ¥2,000. Most parents we know have been very pleased with this child care, mostly because their kids love the fun activities and nurturing staff. The many convenient locations have made this especially popular among the foreigners in central Tokyo. See the Kids World Preschool description (chapter 11) as well as camp and party information (chapter 7). Price and conditions sometimes vary with the location, so call ahead for details.

## Little Mate (Keio Plaza Hotel)

Keio Plaza Hotel, 2–2 Nishi Shinjuku, Shinjuku-ku, Tokyo
東京都新宿区西新宿2丁目2 京王プラザホテル
☎ (03) 3345–1439 (direct), (03) 3344–0111 (hotel)

At the Keio Plaza Hotel nursery, reservations must be made prior to 7:00 P.M. of the previous day. Prices are ¥5,000 for two hours, after which the fee is ¥1,500 per half an hour from 9:00 A.M. to 6:00 P.M. It accepts children up to school age (about age five).

## Little Mate

Okura Hotel, 2–10–4 Toranomon, Minato-ku, Tokyo
☎ (03) 3582–0111, ext. 3838    東京都港区虎の門 2–10–4 ホテルオオクラ

This nursery is run by the same company that operates the service in the Keio Plaza Hotel, and the terms are the same (see previous entry).

## New Otani Hotel

4–1 Kioi-cho, Chiyoda-ku, Tokyo    東京都千代田区紀尾井町 4–1
☎ (03) 3265–1111, ext. 350 (baby room)

The hours at this nursery are 9:00 A.M. to 10:00 P.M. Reservations and membership are not required. There is a minimum of two hours and a charge for every thirty minutes after that. It accepts children up to school age (about five years of age).

## Potpourri

2–2–9 Eitai, Koto-ku, Tokyo    東京都江東区永代 2–2–9
☎ (03) 3630–1828 (office)    🖷 (03) 5245–7977

Potpourri is a nursery with a licensed professional staff who will take care of children under age nine. The nursery is fully equipped with food, diapers, and toys. A doctor is on call in case of emergency. The establishment is open twenty-four hours a day with overnight service. Advance reservation and prepayment is required, and you must have some proof of insurance with you before you leave your child. Only Japanese is spoken.

### St. Marian International Nursery

1–16–12 Ebisu Nishi, Shibuya-ku, Tokyo　東京都渋谷区恵比寿西 1–16–12
☎ (03) 3461–1050　🖷 (03) 3461–1021

St. Marian accepts babies as young as six weeks and children up to age six. Only Japanese is spoken.

### Tokyo Kids Club

Shigeto Bldg., 3F, 2–2–14 Moto Azabu, Minato-ku, Tokyo
☎ (03) 3440–6816　🖷 (03) 3442–5117　東京都港区元麻布 2–2–14　シゲトビル 3F

This children's language center (see chapter 13 introduction) also offers a baby-sitting service during the week at the rate of ¥1,000 an hour.

# A LITTLE ROMANCE

Many parents of young children would rather have a good night's sleep than a romantic evening out. Sleep is important, but we all know that a little romance is good for parents, too. For those times when you long for a refreshing break from parenthood, we have some ideas.

Everyone dreams of a remote island getaway with his or her spouse, but many children, especially a tiny baby, cannot go for a long period of time without Mom and Dad. Fortunately, we have found that a restaurant with the right atmosphere can create almost as much romance without the risk of sunburn.

Our first suggestion would be to find a favorite spot in the neighborhood for what we call a "quick getaway." These are the nights when you can put the kids to bed early and get the baby-sitter to stay late, or have a neighbor watch the children. No hassle with reservations, picking up an evening sitter, or traveling in rush hour. All you have to do is sneak away for a quiet dinner together. For instance, we located an inexpensive restaurant with a great house wine, just fifteen minutes from home. A couple of hours spent dining there by candlelight is just as romantic as a weekend in Kyoto—without the expense or trauma of leaving the children behind.

For foreigners, Japan is the land of earthquakes and no grandparents. This and the price of travel in Japan often make it difficult to leave the children behind for long adult vacations. If you and your spouse are desperate for some time alone, consider a trip to one of Japan's infamous "love hotels," where you can rent a room for a secluded husband and wife tryst. As outrageous as the idea may seem, the best of these hotels are clean, and they cater to married couples as well as to young lovers. In certain areas, such as Shibuya, you will find a variety of "theme" hotels. If you can stop laughing long enough to check in, you can choose between a "French chateau" or a "Scarlett and Rhett" decor, for instance. In researching this chapter, we discovered that the hourly rates are quite reasonable, and the peace and quiet make love hotels worth a visit. Try bringing a bottle of wine and some bread and cheese for a relaxing afternoon or evening. Most of the basic hotel amenities, such as robes, slippers, shampoo, and toothbrushes, are available. One word of warning: The weekends are usually quite crowded, so you may not get your first choice of room, or perhaps you will have to wait for a vacancy. To find a nearby love hotel, ask one of your good Japanese friends or just keep your eyes open for an unusual-looking building with a silly name in English. Chances are that it is a love hotel.

For another getaway option without leaving town, you can splurge on a night at one of the luxury hotels. The price for one night's stay is about the same as dinner at a fancy restaurant. We have found that room service and a night of uninterrupted sleep can do wonders to rejuvenate a relationship. Traditional Japanese inns, or *ryokan*, offer a change of pace that we find romantic. Call the Tourist Information Center (see chapter 1) for a list of *ryokan* in your area. The Japanese Inn Group, ☎ (03) 3843–2345, and the Minshuku (family-run inn) Association, ☎ (03) 3216–6556, have lots of suggestions and will also make reservations. For an elegant overnighter or weekend trip at a *ryokan*, dip into *Classic Japanese Inns* (Kodansha International, 1999), by Margaret Price. Not only does Price introduce her favorite inns, but she has a list of quick getaways from Tokyo in the first chapter. One of our favorites is Asaba Ryokan in Shuzenji, only a couple of hours out of Tokyo. Write to Asaba Ryokan, 3450–1 Shuzenji, Shuzenji-machi, Tagata-gun, Shizuoka, or call ☎ (0558) 72–7000 to make a reservation; don't forget to ask for a peaceful room overlooking the pond at the foot of the mountains. The best part is their *rotemburo*, or outdoor hot springs bath. If you visit a *ryokan* in Japan that has only segregated *rotemburo* or *ofuro* (indoor bath), do not be afraid to ask permission to bathe together. We have always been accommodated, especially if the inn is not too full or if we wait until late at night to enjoy the bath.

One drawback to staying at a *ryokan* is their policy of an early breakfast, after which they roll up your futon. Since we prefer to cuddle in our futon until a civilized hour, we try to make this clear the night before. We have even gone so far as to say that we were honeymooners in order to get special consideration. Another tactic is to skip breakfast, but again, try to discuss this the night before with your hosts since Japanese breakfasts involve a lot of preparation. The only other problems we have encountered at *ryokan* are the thin walls and no locks on the doors. We usually bring a small radio or tape player with our favorite music. We also suggest packing a bottle of your favorite beverage—do not forget an opener. Most *ryokan* food is delicious, but beer and orange juice are the standard drinks available.

When our children were very young, we were always anxious about being away from them. Fortunately, we happened to stumble upon a *ryokan* right in our neighborhood. It is not as exotic as some of the out-of-town places, but we felt relieved that we could enjoy a cheap vacation for one night (only ¥5,000) and still be within walking distance of our house. Ask around your area about local *ryokan*; you may be surprised at what you find.

As parents, we all face burnout from time to time. Taking a break from the routine is a good idea. However, when an opportunity arises to visit other parts of Japan or Asia, consider taking the kids along. Jet lag is not much of a problem, and people in this part of the world welcome children at hotels and restaurants. Children are an integral and special part of society in Asia. We have usually found it simpler and less stressful to take our kids along than to leave them behind.

# 13
# Bicultural
# Parenting
# Resources

DAD. YOU TAKE YOUR SHOES OFF
IN THIS COUNTRY.

As Japan moves toward internationalization, more respect is being shown for the advantages of bilingualism and biculturalism. An understanding of the Japanese language and Japanese customs is an advantage that you may want for your child.

Studies have shown that students of foreign languages have access to a great number of career possibilities and that language learning helps them develop a deeper understanding of their own culture as well as others. Some evidence also suggests that children who study a second language are more creative and better at complex problem solving. Besides the academic benefits, learning another language broadens a child's outlook, opening up the opportunity to communicate with many more people.

Some parents are content for their children to learn a smattering of Japanese and to enjoy bits of culture at festivals or other events. Other families make a more determined effort to see that their children absorb the Japanese culture and their own in equal amounts. This approach is especially important to the growing number of bicultural families with members of different nationalities.

Many expatriates assume that by living in a foreign country their children will automatically pick up the language. However, it is not quite that simple, especially with a language as difficult as Japanese. Commitment and extra effort on the parents' part is crucial.

While interviewing successful bilingual families for this book, it became obvious that a tried and tested formula that works for everyone does not exist. The parents' native language, the schools available, even the child's personality, all play an important part. We hope that some of our insights and suggestions will be helpful in creating a bilingual environment for your child.

Foreign families living in areas of Japan where there are no international schools or few foreign families may find that their children pick up the Japanese language fairly easily. The parents can continue to reinforce their native language, such as English, at home, in order for the child to be exposed to both languages. However, once the child becomes older and attends Japanese school and spends free time playing with Japanese friends, it then becomes more of an effort to keep up the English. Most parents in this situation mentioned several ways to reinforce the native language, such as visiting their home country at least once a year, sending the older children to summer school there, teaching English to Japanese friends from the child's class, limiting viewing of Japanese TV and watching videos in English instead, having English-speaking visitors or relatives in the house, and reading daily to the children in English.

As you can see, such solutions demand a lot of time and effort from the parents. In a few cases, parents mentioned that it was sometimes difficult to push the children to keep up with their English for two reasons: Their children were too tired after their Japanese studies at school, and they didn't like to use English because it made them stand out as "different" from their peers. We all know how important peer pressure is to kids, but especially in Japan, where "the nail that stands up gets hammered down." Being different can be painful and undesirable.

For families living among the international community, it can be a struggle for the children to learn Japanese. If the parents speak English at home and the children attend international schools, then there is very little opportunity for interaction with other Japanese children. These days, there are areas of Tokyo where one can go for days without speaking Japanese. More and more Japanese speak English well enough to hold basic conversations. One American mother who frequented her neighborhood playground in the hopes of finding Japanese playmates for her son was surprised to find that the vast majority of Japanese mothers she met spoke English. They were delighted that their children would have a chance to learn English from the American child, and English became the basic language used in their gatherings, much to the frustration of the foreigner.

If you find yourself living in a "*gaijin* gulch" in Japan, there are a few things you can do to expose your children to the Japanese language. First, it is a good idea to study the language yourself and practice using basic expressions with the children. If your children are preschool age, then you may want to get involved in a neighborhood playground or preschool (*yochien*). There are some Japanese preschools that accept children as young as eighteen months of age, but the average *yochien* accepts children from the age of three or four.

For Tokyoites, an ideal balance in language may be achieved by sending a child to a Japanese *yochien* five days a week until age five or six, and then on to an international school with a strong dual language program, such as Nishimachi International. This school emphasizes Japanese in its curriculum, although the basic instruction is in English. By attending a *yochien*, a child's Japanese-language skills may be advanced enough to participate in the "F" program at Nishimachi. These are students who are studying Japanese as a first language in a very intense program, similar to the Japanese school system, in addition to their international education. Of the expatriates we interviewed, quite a few claimed that their children were completely bilingual thanks to this system.

In an English-speaking family environment, another option is to send a child to Japanese school from *yochien* on through high school. There is no doubt that the Japanese school system offers a thorough education, and more and more foreign families are taking this route. However, depending on the child's personality, this can be a stressful and demanding choice. Mothers play an important supporting role in the Japanese educational system, and a foreigner should be aware of the time and commitment involved. One British mother said the hardest part of having a child in the Japanese school system was the reams of paper sent home with her child each day. Because she couldn't read *kanji*, she had to depend on a neighbor or her husband's secretary to translate some of the information. This is a problem in the lower grades, but fortunately the older students can read the material themselves.

If you are concerned that your child is not hearing enough Japanese, try limiting English videos in favor of Japanese TV shows. You could enroll your child in a tutoring program, such as Kumon, where he or she can get extra help in a variety of subjects, from *hiragana* to math, usually with Japanese students. Take advantage of extracurricular activities or summer camps where your child can meet other Japanese children. One family invited a Japanese college student to stay with them for the summer. She was asked to speak Japanese to the children in exchange for English lessons with the mother.

In central Tokyo, Seiko Wakabayashi's Tokyo Kids Club is a

children's language center where foreign children are taught Japanese through games, songs, and arts and crafts. The school offers an introduction, a beginners' course, and an advanced course, all taught by bilingual instructors. Students are accepted from age three to twelve, and there is a baby-sitting service during the week. Classes are held from 10:00 A.M. to 5:30 P.M. Monday through Friday. Japanese conversation lessons for parents are also available. For more information, see Tokyo Kids Club (chapter 12).

The Association of Foreign Wives of Japanese (AFWJ) is an organization familiar with the challenges of bilingual and bicultural development in children. Although membership is open only to foreigners married to Japanese men, the journal published by this group contains many interesting articles and resources about bilingualism. For contact numbers and information about groups in your area, phone Beverly Nakamura in Yokohama at ☎ (045) 742–6979, 🖷 (045) 721–1315, or Rose Iwata in Tokyo at ☎ (03) 3397–1007. The AFWJ website is 🖳 <www.bekkoame.ne.jp/~ycishikawa/AFWJ.html>.

The Association for Multicultural Families, which was formed as a support group for Japanese women married to foreign men, offers a wealth of information and advice on all matters pertaining to bilingualism and biculturalism. Whether you need information on dual nationality or just somebody to share your problems with, the association is an important source of information. For more information about groups in your area write to Yoshiko Delehouze, 1–15–9 Inokashira, Mitaka-shi, Tokyo.

The International Children's Bunko Association (ICBA) was formed in 1980 by a British educator living in Tokyo to address the needs of Japanese returnee children who had acquired fluency in other languages. There are branches of ICBA all over Japan and in some foreign countries as well.

The founder of ICBA, Opal Dunn, believed that reading was the key to retaining proficiency in a second language. Therefore, each ICBA branch maintains a library of children's books, as well as cassette tapes and videotapes. In addition, at each branch, volunteer native speakers read to the children and conduct games and activities in English.

Not only overseas returnees but all English-speaking children are welcome to join ICBA. This program enables foreign children whose stronger language is Japanese to interact in English. Several foreign mothers volunteer their time at ICBA so that their children can have access to the educational services there. To find out about the ICBA branch nearest you, call ☎ (03) 3496–8688.

Children's English Circles, run by volunteers with the College Women's Association of Japan, ☎ (03) 3444–2167 and 🖷 (03) 3444–2204, aim to keep up the English skills of elementary school children returning from abroad.

For information and support regarding early language programs, contact either of the following organizations in the United States.

### Advocates for Language Learning

P.O. Box 4962, Culver City, California 90231, USA
☎ (310) 313–3333   🖳 senortom@aol.com

### The National FLES Institute

University of Maryland at Baltimore, Department of Modern Languages and Linguistics, Baltimore, Maryland 21228, USA
☎ (410) 455–2336

A newsletter on bilingualism in general is *The Bilingual Family Newsletter*, published by Multilingual Matters. For further information, write Multilingual Matters Ltd., Bank House, 8a Hill Rd., Clevedon, Avon BS21 7HH, England, or call ☎ (01275) 876519.

For families who are attempting to maintain proficiency in a Romance language, the Early Advantage Programs for Children offers help. This company sells the BBC course for children wishing to study French, Spanish, or Italian. Using a character called Muzzy, the programs consist of fun-filled videos with songs and animation. For more information, contact Early Advantage Programs for Children, 47 Richards Avenue, Norwalk, Connecticut 06857, USA.

Teach Me Tapes is the name of a company that carries instructional cassette tapes and books for young children in several foreign languages, including Japanese. For more information, write to Teach Me Tapes, 10500 Bren Road E., Minneapolis, Minnesota 55343, USA.

The Intercultural Press is a book shop in the United States that specializes in books and videos relating to intercultural issues and experiences. They carry several of the books on our suggested reading list. For further information, write to The Intercultural Press Inc., P.O. Box 700, Yarmouth, Maine 04096, USA, or call ☎ (207) 846–5168, 🖷 (207) 846–5181, or visit 🖳 <interculturalpress.com>.

Suggested titles in English for parents who are interested in a bilingual education for their children include:

*The Bilingual Family: A Handbook for Parents*, by Edith Harding and Philip Riley (Cambridge University Press, 1986).

*Educating Andy: The Experience of a Foreign Family in the Japanese Elementary School System*, by Anne and Andy Conduit (Kodansha International, 1996).

*Language Acquisition of a Bilingual Child: A Sociolinguisttic Perspective*, by Alvino E. Fantini (Multilingual Matters, 1985).

*Languages and Children: Making the Match*, by Helena Curtain and Carol Ann Bjornstad Pesola (Longman, 1994).

*A Parent and Teacher's Guide to Bilingualism*, by Colin Baker (Multilingual Matters, 2000).

Recommended books in Japanese on the same subject include:

*Bilingual*, by Masayo Yamamoto (Taishukan, 1991).

*Nihon ni Okeru Bilingualism*, by Yamamoto, Maher, Yashiro, and Kim (Kenkyusha, 1991).

## WEBSITES

### ERIC Clearinghouse on Languages and Linguistics

1118 22nd St. NW, Washington, D.C. 20037, USA
☎ 800–276–9834   💻 www.cal.org/ericcll

This organization has a database of research and other information on bilingualism.

### Intercultural Press

💻 www.interculturalpress.com

(See discussion earlier in this section for more information.)

### Master Communications / Asia For Kids

P.O. Box 9096, Cincinnati, Ohio 45209, USA
☎ (513) 563–3100, phone orders 800–765–5885   📠 (513) 563–3105
💻 www.afk.com

Asia for Kids offers an educational catalog for students of Asian languages and culture. Its collection includes books, videos, cassettes, software, dolls, games, posters, crafts, and resource material for parents and teachers. Most countries in Asia are covered, and the material is offered in different languages.

# 14
# Tips for Residents-to-be

JAPAN......

So you are off to Japan! Whether you are planning a brief vacation or are about to leave on a new overseas posting, your entire family is very lucky. There are many positive aspects about life in Japan with children. Incredibly low crime rates and subways safe enough for first-graders mean a lot to parents. Perhaps the most endearing aspect of Japan is the nature of the Japanese themselves. Children are greatly respected, and they play an integral part in Japanese society. To the parent, that can mean anything from feeling welcome with your children at any restaurant or concert to knowing that the whole neighborhood will help keep an eye on your children.

We have lived in Japan a combined total of twenty years. It may be interesting to note that one of us was dragged to this country kicking and screaming while the other embarked upon the adventure with great enthusiasm. Anyway, after having babies and educating children here, we both agree that Japan is one of the best places in the world for parents and their kids to live.

## SOME THOUGHTS ON MOVING: VITAL TIPS FOR AN EASY TRANSITION

For almost everyone, moving is an emotional experience. For many of us, a major move is downright traumatic, right up there with death and divorce in the feelings of loss and confusion. When you add the pressures of worrying about how your children will adjust to a new situation and all the changes involved, anxiety levels can run sky high.

It helps to be as prepared as possible for the transition, both in terms of the time you need to get organized and the time your family will need to adjust to the idea emotionally. Some moves are easier than others due to these factors. A smooth or rocky transition may also depend on your children's ages, temperaments, and whether your family falls into the "have to move" category as opposed to the "want to move" group. Even if your family is enthusiastic about the move, leaving close friends and familiar surroundings for the unknown is often hard to do.

Perhaps your family is fortunate to have a support system within the company; many corporations understand the value of providing families with orientation and relocation programs. A good program can further prepare you for the move by giving you advice on what to bring, where to live, and even what school may be the best fit for your child.

Another plus is being able to choose the timing of the move. Moving in the middle of the school year makes it more difficult for some children to have a sense of closure about leaving. For others, moving during the school year gives them the benefit of having extra attention as a new student in a new school. Most families end up moving during summer vacation when there is time to get settled before school starts, although the children may find it harder to meet new friends when school isn't in session.

There are some people who handle moving incredibly well. Many friends in the foreign service, for example, think nothing of picking up and moving to a new country every two years. These families are often well-organized and, for the most part, have mastered the logistical challenges of moving. Of course, even for seasoned veterans, some moves are more stressful than others but, most importantly, they anticipate their next assignment and whatever new adventures await them.

A positive attitude really does seem to make a difference. Even if you don't have all the criteria for a perfect move, your whole family can still survive and even benefit from the experience. Perhaps you can't control all of the external factors about moving (or life for that matter!), but you can control the way you look at it. And whether we like it or not, parents are the emotional barometer for the family. If our children sense that we are frightened or depressed about moving, they will start to feel the same way.

But what if you are feeling frightened and depressed? How do you cope? Start by writing down all of your fears and then make another list of possible good things that could come out of the move. Gradually add to both lists—pros and cons. As soon as you have had time to adjust to the idea (i.e., when you can talk about moving without bursting into tears), call a family conference to break the news.

Try to convey a sense of excitement about the move. At the same time, listen to your children's reactions and validate their feelings as much as possible. Depending on the age of the child, this does not mean that you have to "fix" things, just listen and commiserate, initially. After the shock has worn off, you can hold another conference where each family member makes his or her own list of pros and cons. Then you can venture to ask each child: "How can I make this easier for you?"

One idea is to research the new city or country and make a list of interesting things to see and do. Then the whole family can sit down and make a wish list of long- and short-term dreams and goals for the new life: that red convertible that Dad would love to own one day or a chance to travel to exotic locales. Perhaps this move will open the door for the pursuit of some of those dreams.

If you don't already have a pet, the promise of one is enough to cheer up most kids. Our family discovered, for instance, that walking the dog was an easy way to meet the neighbors and make new friends. It also forced us to get out, have a bit of exercise, and breathe in the fresh air, even on days when we might have been feeling down in the dumps.

Another way to make a move easier for kids is to make sure that they can stay in touch with old friends. Setting up e-mail is helpful. Several friends may even decide to get a newsletter going. Our son did that one year when his best friends moved away to Singapore, Canada, the United States, and Australia. It took some time for these newsletters to circle the globe, but each edition was treasured.

Arranging for summer or holiday visits with friends will give the children something to look forward to. Ask your kids what would help to assuage their fears and you may get some good suggestions. We allowed our son to place a long-distance call for advice to a friend who had recently moved away. Their conversation eliminated a lot of his anxiety about what to expect.

Children, like adults, feel more comfortable when they have some control over their lives. For younger children this may take the form of daily routines they can depend on or favorite toys that they keep nearby. Because a preschooler's predictable environment gives him a sense of security, moving is likely to be a stressful experience.

Keeping this in mind, try not to be impatient with regressions in weaning, toilet training, sleeping through the night, or separation anxiety. As you make your way to your new destination, try to stick with familiar food, toys, and bedtime routines as much as possible.

When moving with an infant, your best bet is to breastfeed for as long as possible. Not only will antibodies in the breast milk protect against germs in the new surroundings, nursing provides the ultimate feeling of security for a baby. Moving is definitely not the time to consider weaning.

If you are dealing with elementary-school-age kids, one of the most important things is to help them set up a new social life. Children are always pained at leaving friends, and often fear that they won't make any new ones. It is wonderful if you can live near their school or at least in a neighborhood full of kids attending the same school. If this isn't feasible, then encourage your child to invite friends over for a playdate as soon as possible.

When it comes to getting settled in a new school, school counselors report that there are fewer adjustment problems among children who move directly into their new home. Living in temporary quarters is more stressful on everyone so, if possible, try to travel ahead and set up housing before you actually move to the new area.

Some of the easiest transitions are where at least one parent gets involved in their children's new school right away, volunteering to chaperone field trips, providing baked goods for a class party, and so on. In addition to being a source of comfort and support for your child, your presence will also allow you to observe the situation at school firsthand.

Parents who have interesting experiences to share should offer to speak to their child's class. After moving back to the United States, one father spoke to his daughter's fifth grade about living in Japan, much to her delight. She felt very special that day, especially when he brought enough Japanese sweets for her to share with the whole class.

Education can vary greatly, depending on where you live. Keep a close watch on your child's progress in the first few months at his or her new school. There may be a need for tutoring in a subject or counseling to help smooth the way. It's much better to catch any problem in the beginning. In Tokyo, there is an organization called International School Support Services (ISSS), run by Patrick Newell, which offers tutoring and other forms of support (see chapter 11).

When moving to another country or to a new neighborhood, one newcomer's tip is to take frequent photographs of the kids with their new friends and to then give the friends and their parents copies. Whether it is the school play, or an afternoon of sledding in the backyard, most of the parents appreciate the pictures and it helps them remember who you are.

It is a good idea in any case to keep a collection of cute pictures of your children at all ages. Classrooms everywhere eventually do projects that require childhood pictures, whether it's VIP day or something for the yearbook. Rather than frantically digging through boxes the night before, keep an assortment of photos in a large envelope and, as the years go by, get in the habit of making several copies of the best pictures to have on hand.

Wherever we move, we have a large collection of family photos in cheap plastic box frames which immediately gets arranged on the largest wall in the family room. My children derive much pleasure from seeing themselves at various stages, posing with special friends or beloved relatives. It somehow helps them to see where they have been and maybe even give them an idea of where they are going.

In a strange city it is especially important to make your new home a place of comfort and refuge. Some children feel more secure if their old room with all its familiar furniture and treasures is moved intact. If this isn't possible, try to order a special set of cozy bed linens for each child's room before you move. The kids will enjoy helping to select a new bedroom theme or color scheme and you will avoid the stress of trying to run out and buy it all upon arrival.

Even if you have adequately prepared for the move, endlessly validated and supported your child's feelings, and done all you could to make things work, some children will just have more difficulty coping than others and their adjustment will take longer. With these children you have to continue to be patient, take their complaints seriously, and let them have as much choice as possible in looking at alternatives in their education and extracurricular activities.

During the period of adjustment you will find a unique opportunity for your family to grow closer and stick together as a team. And remember, after a year or maybe less, the odds are that every member of the family will be thriving in the new surroundings.

The nicest aspect of moving for our family has been the never-ending element of serendipity, those pleasant surprises and coincidences which occur when you least expect them. Remind your children to expect the unexpected and encourage them to wake up every morning wondering what new adventures the day will bring. This is not always easy to do, but by setting this example, you are teaching your children a powerful lesson about how to cope with life.

When a move comes up, the most difficult part is letting go. It is so much easier to stay in one cozy place living our safe little lives. It is hard to stop seeing change as a loss. The bonuses are often hidden down the road and you have to trust that they will be there. Our family is so much closer and our lives much richer for having made the big move (several times) and survived. We'll never forget how it feels to be the outsider or the new kid on the block and, as a result, we have all become more compassionate and stronger people.

## BEFORE YOU MOVE

Try not to be daunted by the sheer logistics of transporting your family and household goods to Japan in one piece. Moving to Japan and settling in is not to difficult if you know what to expect and make plans before you go.

If you live in the United Sates, you may want to obtain a copy of *The Summary of Information for Shippers of Household Goods*, published by the Interstate Commerce Commission, Washington, D.C. 20423, USA. This booklet gives a step-by-step plan for moving, including definitions of terms and helpful suggestions for packing and hiring a moving company. You can order a copy by writing to the above address.

### SETTING UP A SUPPORT NETWORK

There are many details to attend to before moving overseas. One of the most important is setting up bank accounts, post office boxes, or other means of taking care of bills and mail that will come to your home address. One of the easiest ways to do this is to recruit a close friend or relative to receive mail and even pay small bills on your behalf. We call this person our "contact." There will also be times when you will need something from home or want flowers or gifts sent to someone in your home country.

To make this easy for your contact to do, you may want to give them access to a small amount of money for this type of gift and for postage. If you will need things sent to you overseas, leave your contact person with a supply of address labels and envelopes. We have one friend who asks her contact to videotape television programs for her children. Each year when she is on home leave, she buys a supply of videotapes and envelopes, which she stamps with the correct postage. All her contact has to do is tape the show and drop it in the mail.

By all means set up an e-mail account as soon as you arrive in Japan. Staying in touch with friends and family back home will be much easier and less expensive. Also, the Internet has just about everything you could possibly need or want to know, no matter where you live.

### DON'T LEAVE HOME WITHOUT . . .

You may find that many products that you can buy regularly in your home country are not available in Japan. Stock up on these! It is especially important to buy products for babies and children in large quantities before moving, not just to save money, but to save time and energy as well.

There are many listings throughout the book of mail-order sources in the United States for children's items that are not available in Japan. There are also a number of co-ops in Japan that sell imported goods and cater to foreigners (see the listing in chapter 10). Of course, you can always ask your contact to send "care packages," but if you have the chance before you move—buy the store out!

What to stock up on? Seasonal costumes and decorations for the kids and the house; vitamins; books, videos, and games in English; Western-size bedding; indoor shoes and slippers for the entire family; and all of the special food and toiletry items you cannot live without! There are also some medicines you will need to buy abroad if you have young children in the house. For this information, as well as mail-order sources that will ship these items overseas, see chapters 3, 4, 8, 9, and 10.

Before leaving home, you may also want to buy a large supply of Western-size envelopes, address labels, airmail stationery, and any other personalized stationery you may want with your new address on it. Not only are these items difficult to find in Japan, but they are also expensive.

## MAIL ORDER FROM ABROAD

Shopping by mail-order catalog and the Internet has become a way of life for many parents in the United States and other countries. Not only do we save the time and anxiety involved in dragging our children through the stores but we also find that the financial savings can be quite substantial.

In Japan we are faced with the unusually high cost of outfitting our babies and children, plus the unavailability of certain products that we know and trust. Fortunately, many catalog companies now ship overseas, and throughout the book we have compiled some of the best.

Before you leave home, you may want to e-mail or call these mail-order companies and ask them for a copy of their latest catalog and overseas shipping instructions. By doing this, you will have the catalogs as a resource as soon as you step off the plane, instead of waiting weeks for the company to send you one.

To receive a copy of any of the catalogs listed in this book, contact the company by mail, telephone, fax, or e-mail. Many companies will send you a catalog free of charge; others may charge a small fee to cover mailing costs. Payment may be made by U.S. check or money order and most major credit cards are accepted, although there is often a minimum purchase for credit card orders. The four major U.S. credit cards accepted are Visa, MasterCard, American Express, and Discover Card. A few companies now accept Japanese credit cards. When placing an order with a credit card by fax, be sure to include the expiration date, shipping address, and item number or description along with your signature. For overseas shipments, there is either a set rate or a charge based on the weight of the package. Many companies use Federal Express or United Postal Service for delivery within a week. If you are not in a hurry, sea-mail orders are much cheaper. Remember that Japanese tax and duty may be owed when the package arrives, and the catalog companies have no estimates as to what that cost will be.

These catalogs are also handy for ordering gifts for friends and relatives in other countries. The company will usually gift-wrap and mail the package directly to the recipient. We have contacted all the catalog companies listed in this book and have ourselves ordered from most of them and found them committed to offering you the best available clothes, books, tapes, games, toys, and baby equipment on the market.

## ORIENTATION PROGRAMS

It is helpful if your family can attend a orientation program, if possible, prior to your departure. Even if you are not able to take part in one of these seminars, the company or institution that runs them may be willing to send you orientation information through the mail.

If you live in a major city, you can contact the local Japan Society for information on lectures, language studies, or orientation programs. Learning the Japanese language is a real challenge, so you may want to take either a crash course or a few basic lessons before you leave for Japan. As in any country, a basic vocabulary will make life much easier. The Berlitz School offers some excellent programs, from a traveler's guide complete with phrase book and cassette, to intensive private language courses. We have found that cassette language tapes played in the car and around the house get the children excited about the move and help them to feel comfortable trying out a new language.

## ORIENTATIONS AT HOME

### Lloyd, Thomas and Ball

P.O. Box 39236, Washington, D.C., USA
☎ (202) 244–9445   ☏ (202) 244–9446

Lloyd, Thomas and Ball, one of the most comprehensive U.S. orientation programs, is run by Gary Lloyd, Carol Thomas, and Linda Ball, all formerly with Business Council for International Understanding Institute. They train families and businessmen for life in 147 countries and their programs on Japan are excellent. In exploring the role and function of families overseas, Lloyd, Thomas and Ball offers learning sessions for the whole family, from four-year-olds to teenagers to parents. An intensive language program is often incorporated in the workshops.

### Prudential Relocation International

2 Corporate Drive, Shelton, Connecticut 06484, USA
☎ 800–243–5537  or  800–622–6722

Formerly Moran, Stahl, and Boyer, Prudential Relocation International's intercultural division has training facilities in Chicago, Houston, Atlanta, and Los Angeles. One of the top cross-cultural training and consulting firms in the United States, it has been conducting training seminars and workshops covering over one hundred countries for more than twenty-seven years.

Among the services Prudential offers are cross-cultural training for executives, repatriation training, and seminars on working with the Japanese. In conjunction with family or group orientations, there is a program for teenagers and children who are making an overseas move with their family.

## ORIENTATIONS IN JAPAN

If you did not have time to take part in an orientation program back home, there are some services in Tokyo that can help you adapt to life in Japan. The following companies have been established to help foreigners cope with the adjustments. They can assist you in every detail of settling in Japan, from getting a driver's license to finding the right school for your children. Elsewhere in Japan, the various government and community centers (see chapter 12) sometimes offer orientation classes for foreign residents.

### Oak Associates and Welcome Furoshiki

- Tokyo branch: Aoki Bldg., 3F, 4–1–10 Toranomon, Minato-ku, Tokyo
  東京都港区虎の門 4–1–10 アオキビル 3F
  ☎ (03) 5472–7077   🖷 (03) 5472–7076   🖳 oakassoc@gol.com
- Osaka branch: Nishii Bldg., 7F, 1–15–14 Utsubo Hommachi, Nishi-ku, Osaka-shi, Osaka　大阪府大阪市西区靭本町 1–15–14　西井ビル 7F
  ☎ (06) 6441–2581   🖷 (06) 6441–2560   🖳 oakosaka@gol.com

Oak Associates is a company that has been assisting newly arrived expatriates in Japan since 1980. The company offers a variety of orientation programs, from a one-time orientation on business practices for the executive to a complete lifestyle orientation for the whole family. The services can be customized to meet your individual needs. Oak Associates' personnel can help with all the practicalities of setting up house in Japan, and they remain available for consultation anytime during the client's stay.

Welcome Furoshiki is a division of Oak Associates and serves as a sort of welcome wagon for foreigners. This service is sponsored by businesses and is free of charge. A Welcome Furoshiki representative will come and visit your hotel or home and give you an information packet about life in Tokyo, all wrapped in a *furoshiki* (a traditional Japanese cloth used for carrying things). The representative can also assist you with any other questions you may have. To set up an appointment for a visit or for more information, call ☎ (03) 5472–7074 (for Tokyo and Yokohama). For Osaka, Kyoto, and Kobe, call ☎ (06) 6441–2584. For the Nagoya area, call ☎ (052) 836–9261.

## Tokyo General Agency (TGA)

Prime Square City, 2F, 1–1–7 Hiroo, Shibuya-ku, Tokyo
東京都渋谷区広尾 1–1–7　プライムスクエアシティ 2F
☎ (03) 3409–2031　🖷 (03) 3409–2033　🖳 familysupport@tga.co.jp

TGA provides a complete range of services for business people and their families moving to Japan from overseas. TGA has three types of services. For both overseas companies opening offices in Japan and for companies already established here, TGA offers a complete range of one-time and on-going services tailored to the specific needs of each particular company. TGA also offers the Family Support Service, which is designed to facilitate a quick and easy transition to life in Japan for the entire family. Through the TGA Club, foreign residents are invited to take part in activities that can help them understand and relate to Japanese society.

Membership fees are quite reasonable and include an excellent monthly newsletter as well as opportunities to take trips and participate in Japanese cultural activities.

## HRS

IBM Japan Headquarters Bldg., 3–2–12 Roppongi, Minato-ku, Tokyo
東京都港区六本木 3–2–12　日本IBM本社ビル
☎ (03) 5563–3880　🖷 (03) 3587–2818

HRS offers personalized orientations for people upon their arrival in Japan. They will customize a neighborhood tour, design your *meishi* (business card), and track down any resources you and your family need.

## Tokyo Orientations

1–12–6 Higashi Azabu, Minato-ku, Tokyo　東京都港区東麻布 1–12–6
☎ (03) 3746–0566　🖳 orientok@twics.com

Tokyo Orientations, a relocation company serving Tokyo and Yokohama, provides newly arrived expatriates with practical information to enable them to function in their new home as quickly and smoothly as possible. Cultural insights supplement topics pertinent to everyday household operations. Staff members assist clients in obtaining the necessary documents and becoming familiar with their neighborhood. They also address the individual needs and concerns of each family. Follow-up telephone assistance is available throughout the client's stay in Tokyo.

# REFERENCE BOOKS, MATERIALS, AND WEBSITES

There are number of useful and comprehensive books and websites that you should read or consult about living in Japan. They will help you to understand the insurance system, emergency procedures at hospitals, what to do in case of a major earthquake, and just about everything you may need to know while living as a foreigner in Japan. There are also books and sites that will give you information on food, shopping, and cultural attractions. Most books are available at the major English-language bookstores listed in chapter 4 or through the foreign-resident service organizations throughout the country. The following is a short list of books to which you should have access during you stay in Japan (medical books are listed in chapter 10).

*Japan Health Handbook*, by Meredith Maruyama, Louise Shimizu, and Nancy Tsurumaki (Kodansha International, 1998). An amazingly comprehensive book about all aspects of health care here; parents will appreciate the informative chapters on pregnancy and childbirth, and on children's health.

*Kids Trips in Tokyo*, by Ivy Maeda, Kitty Kobe, Cynthia Ozeki, and Lyn Sato (Kodansha International, 1998). A wonderful collection of outings for kids of all ages, with excellent maps and other helpful information.

*Living in Japan* (American Chamber of Commerce in Japan, 1997, 12th ed). Tips on coping with the everyday aspects of life in Japan, from arriving here, to immigration, to your departure. The chapter on legal matters is especially helpful. To order, write to the American Chamber of Commerce, 7F, Fukide Bldg., No. 2, 4–1–21 Toranomon, Minato-ku, Tokyo, or call ☎ (03) 3433–5381. In Kansai, write c/o Searle, Osaka Higashi, P.O. Box 698, Osaka, or call ☎ (06) 6222–6251.

*Living in Kobe* (Community House Information Service, 1999, 6th ed). See chapter 12 for listing under Community House and Information Centre.

*Tokyo City Atlas: A Bilingual Guide* (Kodansha International, 1998). You will need a good map while you are living in Tokyo, and this is one of the best. Printed in book form, the roads and landmarks of the guide are in both English and Japanese.

*Tokyo City Guide*, by Mayumi Barakin and Judith Greer (Charles E. Tuttle, 1996). This guidebook—easy to read and full of helpful tips—is popular with tourists and residents alike.

*Tokyo for Free*, by Susan Pompian (Kodansha International, 1998). You'll find plenty of unique ideas here for family outings even for the tightest budget! The book includes area maps and detailed directions listing landmarks and station exit numbers to every one of its more than three hundred entries.

### CD-ROMs

### How to Survive in Japan (SHC Co. Ltd.)
2–29–4 Hakusan, Bunkyo-ku, Tokyo　東京都文京区白山 2–29–4
☎ (03) 3815–7911　🖷 (03) 5803–2087　🖳 www.shc.co.jp

### WEBSITES
See the back of the book for an up-to-date list of sites covering everything from travel and relocation to Japanese culture and giving birth in Tokyo.

# INDEX

## A

adoption  282–85
Advocates for Language Learning  376
After the Stork  80
Aiiku Baby (equip. rental)  89
aikido  190
Aioi Baby (equip. rental)  89
airplane, travel by  24–28
Akachan Hompo (baby equip.)  86
*Aki Matsuri* (Autumn Festival)  257
Akihabara, shopping at  66
All Saints' Eve  244
Allegretto (clothing rental)  72
allergy clinics  295
alternative learning experiences  228
Amazon.com (books, toys)  104
American Club, garage sale at  71
American Library Association (posters)  95
American Pharmacy  296
American School in Japan (ASIJ)  328
*American-Japanese Coloring and Talking Books*  99
amusement parks  158–72
Amway, in Japan (vitamins, etc.)  297
Anna Miller's  54
antique mart  71
Antique Toy Museum  220
Aqua Birth House Underwater Birth Group  265
aquariums  172–175
Aristoplay (educational games)  118
Ark (clothing rental)  72
art museum, children's  228
Art.com  95
arts and crafts, Japanese  181
Asakusabashi Shopping District
    party favors at  252
    shopping at  66
Association of Foreign Wives of Japanese
    (AFWJ)  276, 375
*au pair*  361
Autumn Festival  257
Azabu Juban, shopping at  50–51

## B

Baby Center (clothing)  79
baby equipment  85–90
    rental  89–90
Baby Futabado (equip. rental)  90
Baby Healthy (childbirth)  265
Baby Lease (equip. rental)  89
baby-sitting services  361–64

Back to Basics Toys  118
Baker Books Puffin Book Club  105
ballet  185–88
    supplies  186,188
baseball  205
Bean-throwing Festival  237
bedding, Bena  58
Bena (bedding)  58
Benten Supermarket  298
Beverly Hills Collar Company (I.D. tags)  16
bicycle helmets  23
bicycling  195–98
    lodge/tour  195
    theme park  195, 196
Big Kids (costume rental)  252
Bike Shop Nukaya  23
*Bilingual Family Newsletter*  376
bilingualism  372–77
    books on  376–77
    websites  377
Bingoya (traditional toys)  114
birth
    after care  275–76
    at home  280–81
    premature  279–80
    stories  277–81
birth announcements  285–87
Birth Education Services in Tokyo (BEST)  263
birthday parties  247–48
Blue and White (gifts, crafts)  51, 76
books
    guides  391–92
    mail order  117–20
    reference  391–92
bookstores  99–105, 117–18
boy scouts  205–6
breastfeeding  274–75
British School in Japan  329
bus  18

## C

calling an ambulance, procedure  305–6
Canadian Academy  337
CD-roms  392
cesarean  277–79
cherry-blossom viewing  238
childbirth
    choosing location  262
    clinics and hospitals  267–74
    education classes  263–65
    hospitals  269–71
    midwives  265–66
    ob-gyn clinics  272–74
Childbirth Education Center (CEC)  264
Childbirth School  265

Children's Better Health Institute (magazine publisher) 108
Children's Castle 216, 228–30
children's clothing 68–75, 79–82. See also *baby equipment.*
    in department stores 39–50
    Familiar 68
    Jumpin' Kiki 55
    mail order 79–82
    Miki House 53
    Shinryudo 58
    Total Fashion Seikado 58
    used 70, 73–75
Children's Day 240
children's museum 225, 231
    Children's Museum 54
children's room, decorating 91–96
    furniture for 95–96
    posters for 95–96
Children's Wear Digest 80
Chinese School in Tokyo 339
Chinzanso Garden and Restaurant 139
Christian Academy in Japan (CAJ) 330
Christmas 245
    cards 246
    decorations 67
    in Japan 241
Christmas Depot, holiday supplies at 251
Christmas Store, party favors at 252
circumcision 269
*City Life News* 356
clothing 68–75, 79–82. See also *children's clothing, maternity clothing, sportswear,* and *used clothing.*
    Gap 55, 69
    L. L. Bean 55, 69, 81
    Land's End 69, 81
    Laura Ashley 54, 61, 69, 77
    Marie Foret 87
    Pocket Town 57
    Storybook Heirlooms 81
    Tenyodo 58
    Wooden Soldier 82
clothing sizes 38
community centers 351–52
computer goods 66
costume rentals 252–53
counseling services 352–54
CPR 305
craft stores 67
crafts 51, 114
Crayon House (books) 99

**D**

Daiei 63

Daimaru Peacock (supermarket) 51, 60
dance supplies 186, 188
day-care centers
    private 365–67
    public 364–65
decorating. See also *interior.*
    children's room 91–96
dental health 310–12
department stores 36–50
*Dezome Shiki* (New Year Parade of Firemen) 255
diaper services 90–91
diner 60
discount stores 63–66
    ¥100 shops 65
    Naka Okachimachi 67
disease. See *vaccinations.*
Disney store 47
Disneyland 160
dogs, theme park 172
Doll Festival 238
dolls 110–11, 117
    doll museum 225
    doll-making 181
driver's license, Japan 20

**E**

earthquakes 306
Easter 243
Ebisu Garden Place 51–52
educational books and toys 117–20
    Nature Company 55
educational games 118–20
Educational Toy Library 115
electronic goods 66
elementary school, Japanese 341–42
emergency
    calling an ambulance 288, 305–6
    general vocabulary, in Japanese 288–91
    kits 307
    medical treatment 304–5
    preparation for 306–8
    telephone numbers 305–6
entertainment, websites on Japan. See endpapers.
extracurricular activities 181–82
*Eye-Ai* (magazine) 358

**F**

fabric
    Hobbyra Hobbyre 61
    shops 75–79
Fabrications 76
Familiar 68
family outings 194
family planning 281–82

family portraits 249
Family Travel Guides Catalog 28
feeding
    baby formula 295–97
    breastfeeding 274–75
Fiona (books) 100
Fire Museum (Shobo Hakubutsukan) 220
fireworks 255
fish market, Tsukiji 164
fishing 203–5
Foreign Buyer's Club (import groceries, etc.) 299
    bookstore 100
free publications 356–57
furniture 87, 96

**G**

Gap (clothing) 55, 69
garage sale 71
gardens 139–55
    zoological 175–178
getaways, ideas for 367–69
gift shops 249–51
    Blue and White 51
    Nature Company 55
Ginza Festival (Ginza *Matsuri*) 257
girl scouts 205–6
Girls' Day 238
Golden Week 239
*Good Birth, A Safe Birth* 274
Good Day Books 100
guide books 391–92
gymnastics 185
    summer programs 218

**H**

haircuts, Zusso 56
Halloween 244
Hama Detached Palace Garden 141
*Hanabi Taikai* (fireworks) 255
Hankyu Department Store 49
Happoen Gardens 144
Harajuku, shopping at 52–54
Harmonyland (amusement park) 170
health
    children's 294–314
    of parents 348–55
help agency 276
helplines 354
Herbs for Kids 297
Hibiya Koen 140
*Hina Matsuri* (Girls' Day) 238
Hiroshima City Culture and Science Museum 226
Hiroshima International School 337
hobbies 61
    Tokyu Hands 64, 251

*hoikuen* (day care center) 364–37
Hokkaido International School 337
holidays
    Japanese 234–42
    supplies 249–51
    Western 242–46
home birth 280–81
home schooling 342–46
horseback riding 192–94
hospitals, childbirth 269–71
hotlines 354
*How My Parents Learned to Eat* 99
*How to Survive in Japan* 391
¥100 Shops 65

**I**

"I" Club 39
ice hockey 199
ice-skating 198–202
IMAX theater 219
Independence Day 244
infertility 282–83
information centers 351–52
information networks 355
Inokashira Koen 151
Intercultural Press 376
interior 58. See also *decorating*.
    Interior Station Hoshinoya 58
    Palms Resale and Import Shop 55
    Pier 1 Imports 55, 95
    Uhn Good 61
International School of the Sacred Heart 330
International School Support Services (ISSS) 331
international schools 326–39
    non-English 339
Isetan Department Store 39, 56
    "I" Club 39
    toy hospital at 116
Itoya (stationery) 61
    holiday supplies at 249

**J**

J. C. Penney Company 262
Japan, moving to 380–86
Japan Allergy Clinic 295
Japan Automobile Federation 20
Japan Council of International Schools (JCIS)
    326–27
Japan Foundation Library 122
*Japan Health Handbook* 274, 304, 391
Japan Helpline 354
Japan International School (JIS) 331–32
Japan-Europe Trading Company (imported
    foods) 299

Japanese, medical vocabulary 288–91, 314
*Japanese Children's Favorite Stories* 99
Japanese holidays 234–42
Japanese schools 339–42
    books on 341–42
Jena Co. (books) 101
Joypolis, Yokohama 165
JR Infoline Service 17
judo 191

**K**

*Kansai Time-Out* (magazine) 358
Kappabashi, shopping at 67
karate 191
Kawai Music Schools 206
kendo 191
Kichijoji, shopping at 55
Kiddyland (toys) 52, 113
    holiday supplies at 250
*Kids Trips in Tokyo* 391
kimono 67
*Kinki Nippon Tourist* 357
Kinko's 65
Kinokuniya Bookstore 101
*Kinro Kansha No Hi* (Labor Thanksgiving Day) 245
kitchen supplies (wholesale) 67
Kite Museum 221
Kobe International Community Center 351
Kobe Joba Club (horseback riding) 192
Kobe Maritime Museum 227
Kobe Municipal Suma Aqualife Park 174
Kobe Portopialand (amusement park) 170
*Kodomo No Hi* (Children's Day) 240
koen. See parks.
Koganei Koen 152
    cycling course at 197
Komazawa Olympic Koen 149
    bicycling course at 197
    tennis courts at 189
Korakuen Amusement Park 161
Korean School in Tokyo 339
Kumon Institute of Education 182
Kyoto International Community House 352
Kyoto International School 338
Kyoto Monkey Park (amusement park) 170
Kyoto Municipal Zoo 178

**L**

L. L. Bean 55, 69, 81
La Leche League International 105, 262
Labor Thanksgiving Day 245
LaForet 53
Lake Sagami Picnic Land 161
Land's End 69, 81
Laura Ashley 54, 61, 69, 77

libraries 120–23
    magazine 123
    toy 115–16
Little America Bookstore 102
*Living in Japan* 391
*Living in Kobe* 391
Loft, Seibu 250
Lonlon Department Store 56
*Look Japan* (magazine) 358
Lycée Franco-Japonais 339

**M**

magazines
    for kids 106–9
    local 357–59
    parenting 359–61
mail order 386–87
    baby products (abroad) 88–89
    baby products (Japan) 87–88
    birth announcements 286–87
    children's clothing 79–82
    children's room decoration (abroad) 95–96
    children's vitamins 297
    holiday goods (abroad) 253–54
    maternity clothing 261–62
    posters/art (abroad) 95–96
    toys (abroad) 117–20
Marineland 172
Marist Brothers International School 338
maritime museum 227
martial arts 190–92
Maruzen (books) 102
maternity clothing 261–62
    in department stores 39–49
Matsuya Department Store 40
medical advice, online 305
medical emergency 305–6
medical vocabulary 288–91, 314
Meiji Shrine (Meiji Jingu) 52
    skating rink at 202
    tennis courts at 189
mental health 349–51
midwives 265–66
Miki House (children's clothing) 53
Minato-ku Sports Center Pool 184
Ministry of Education 342
Mitsukoshi Department Store 42, 51
modeling 208–15
Mombusho (Ministry of Education) 342
money, museum 223
Mont Blanc (bakery) 55
moving to Japan 380–86
Musashi Koyama Shopping Area 57
museums 219–28
    children's 225, 231

music   119
   museums   222, 223
music box museum   223
music contest   208
Music for Little People   119
Music for Youth   207
music schools   206–8
music scores (Skysoft)   104

**N**

Nagoya International Center   351
Nagoya International School   338
Naka Okachimachi, shopping at   67
nannies   361
National Azabu Bookstore   103
   holiday supplies at   251
National Children's Castle   216, 228–30
Nature Company (gifts, etc.)   55
*Nengajo* (New Year's cards)   247
New Year cards   247
New Year Holiday   236
New Year Parade of Firemen   255
newspapers   355–56
Nezu Art Museum and Park   145
*Nighttime Parenting*   105
Nikko Edomura (old Japan theme park)   162
*Nippon View*   356
Nishimachi International School   333
*Noryo Taikai* (festival)   256
NTT TownPage   355
nursery schools. See *preschools*, 316–26

**O**

ob-gyn clinics, private   272–74
*obento*
   making of   301
   *obento* boxes   110
*obi* fabric   67
Office Depot   65
   holiday supplies at   250
*Ohanami* (cherry-blossom viewing)   238
Okachimachi, shopping at   67
Omotesando, shopping at   52–54
Oriental Bazaar   52
Oriental Trading Company (holiday supplies, mail order)   253
orientation programs   387–90
Osaka Aquarium (Kaiyukan)   175
Osaka Baby Center (equip. rental)   90
Osaka International House (OIH)   352
Osaka International School   338
Osaki New City (shopping mall)   59
*osembei* shops   51
*Oshogatsu* (New Year's)   236

**P**

paper products   66, 67
parent
   getaways   367–69
   support groups   276
parenting
   information, from abroad   359–61
   magazines   359–61
   websites. See endpapers.
parks
   amusement   158–72
   large   138–55
   neighborhood   126–39
   *shinsui* (water attractions)   127
party entertainment   254
party favors   251–52
pediatric care   308–10
petting zoos. See *zoos*,   175–78
pharmacy   57, 295, 296
photography studios   248–49
physical health   348–49
Pier 1 Imports   55, 95
plane, travel by   24–28
Planetariums   219–28
plastic food samples   67
playgrounds. See *parks*.
poison   306
police emergency   305
Pony Land   163
pony rides   192–99. See *horseback riding*.
posters   95–96
premature birth   279–80
preschools   316–26
   Japanese   340
psychotherapy   352–54

**R**

railway museums   222, 223, 224
rainy-day activities   218–31
Rand McNally and Co.   96
Rascals in Paradise (family travel)   28
recycle shops   70–71, 73–75
reference books, on Japan   391–92
relocation
   to Japan   380–86, endpapers
   orientation programs   387–90
rental
   clothes   72–73
   costume   252–53
   kimono   72
   rental services   72–73
restaurant supplies (wholesale)   67
Rock 'n' Roll Diner   60
roller-skating   202

*Rules of the Road*  20

**S**

Safety Superstore  88
Safety Zone  88
Saint Mary's International School  334
Saint Maur International School  338
Saint Michael's International School  338
Salvation Army, bazaar  70
Sanrio  42, 45, 51, 58, 59, 110
    Puroland (amusement park)  163
    Theme Parks  165
Santa Maria School  335
*Sayonara, Mrs. Kackleman*  98
science museums  220–27
Sega Amusement Theme Park  165
Seibu Department Store  43
Seibu Loft, holiday supplies at  250
Seibu-en (amusement park)  165
Seisen International School  335
Sesame Place (amusement park)  166
Sesame Street  166
*Sesame Street Magazine*  107
*Setsubun* (Bean-Throwing Festival)  237
Seven-five-three Day  241
Shiba Koen  146
Shiba Pool  184
*Shichi-go-san* (Seven-five-three Day)  241
Shimokitazawa, shopping at  60
Shinagawa Aquarium  174
Shinjuku Gyoen  151
Shinkansen Museum  223
shoes, Thom McAn  55
*shogakko* (Japanese elementary school)  341–42
*Shogatsu* (New Year's)  236
shopping districts  50–63
Showa Memorial Park  154
    bicycling course at  197
singing, professionally  215
skiing, indoors  198
skin clinic  295
Snow Festival in Sapporo  255
soba, Sarashina  50
Sogo Department Store  44
Sony Plaza  61
Space World (amusement park)  171
special events  255–57
speciality stores  63–66
    shopping districts  66–68
sports  182–85, 188–205
Sports Day  240
sports equipment, rental 201
sportswear  55, 80
Star Festival (*Tanabata*)  234, 240

stationery
    Itoya  61, 249
    Seibu Loft  250
Subway Museum  224
summer camps  215–18
summer festival  256
summer programs  215–18
Sumo Museum  224
Sunshine City Planetarium  224
Sunshine Kokusai Aquarium  174
supermarket
    Chujitsuya  60
    Daimaru Peacock  60
    imported foods  297–300
support groups  354
support network, setting up  385–86
Suzuki Method (music lessons)  206
Sweden Center, party favors at  252
swimming  183–85
    water theme parks  168, 171

**T**

t'ai chi chuan  191–92
*Taiiku No Hi* (Sports Day)  240
Takashimaya Department Store  46, 219
talent agencies. See *modeling.*
Tama-tech (amusement park)  166
Tama Zoo  177
Tamagawa Cycling Course  197
Tamagawa Takashimaya Shopping Center  60
*Tanabata* (Star Festival)  234, 240
taxi  18–19
    taxi coupons  19
    van-size  34
*Teach Me Japanese*  99
Teletourist  31
television programs  231–32
TELL. See *Tokyo English Life Line.*
tennis  188–190
    summer programs  218
TEPCO Electric Energy Museum  224
Thanksgiving  245
Theater for Children  208
theme park
    amusement parks  158–72
    bicycling  195, 196
    high-tech theme space  160
THERE (shopping center)  68
"Tire Park"  147
Togo Jinja, antique mart at  71
Tohoku International School  338
Tokyo American Club, garage sale at  71
*Tokyo City Atlas: A Bilingual Guide*  391
*Tokyo City Guide*  391

Tokyo Classified 357
Tokyo Disneyland 160
Tokyo English Life Line (TELL) 275, 276
Tokyo for Free 391
Tokyo International School (TIS) 336
Tokyo Journal (magazine) 358
Tokyo Metropolitan Central Library 123
Tokyo Metropolitan Children's Museum 231
Tokyo Notice Board 357
Tokyo Q 357
Tokyo Sea Life Park 173
Tokyo Summerland (amusement park) 167
Tokyo Swimming Center 184
Tokyo Tower 224
Tokyo Tower Aquarium 174
Tokyo Weekender 357
Tokyu Department Store 48, 56
Tokyu Hands (hobby, home improvement) 64
    holiday supplies at 251
Tourist Information 33–34
Tower Records (books, etc.) 103
toy hospitals 116–117
toy libraries 115–16
toy museums 220, 221, 227
toys 109–20
    Amazon.com 104
    in department stores 40–50
    discount 67
    DoBe 58
    Grab Bag 56
    Kiddyland 52, 113
    Kobayashi 50
    mail order 117–20
    Mandarake 102
    Sanrio 42, 45, 51, 58, 59, 110
    Takeya 67
    Toys R' Us 114
    Toys to Grow On 120
    traditional Japanese 110–11, 114–15
    Ultraman Shop 56
train 16–18
train museums 222, 223, 224
transportation, museums 225, 227
travel. See also endpapers.
    Japan Travel Updates 34
Tsukiji Fish Market 164
Tuttle Bookshop 104

U

Ueno Park
    bicycling course 198
    zoo 177
Ultraman Shop 56
UNICEF Japan 246
United Rent All 73, 201

Universal Studios (amusement park) 171
Universal Taxi 34
used goods and clothing 70, 73–75. See also
    recycle shops.
    Chicago 53
    Grab Bag 56

V

vaccinations 302–4
Valentine's Day 243
Vintage Clothes (used clothing) 70
vitamins, children's 297
voice-overs 214–15
Volunteering in the Tokyo Area Directory 350

W

washi paper 67
water theme parks 168, 171
websites. See endpapers.
western holidays, celebration of 242–46
Whole Foods for the Whole Family 105
Wild Blue (water theme park) 168
Womanly Art of Breastfeeding, The 105

Y

Yamaha Music Center 208
Yamaha school 181
YMCA International Open-Minded School
    (YIOS) 337
YMCA Japan, summer programs and 217
yochien (Japanese preschool) 340
Yokohama Children's Allergy Center 295
Yokohama Children's Museum 225
Yokohama Cosmo World (amusement park) 168
Yokohama Doll Museum 225
Yokohama Dreamland (amusement park) 168
Yokohama Echo (magazine) 359
Yokohama International School (YIS) 338
Yokohama Science Center 226
Yokohama Zoological Gardens (Zoorasia) 177
Yomiuriland (amusement park) 168
Yoyogi Koen 150
    cycling center at 198
Yuki matsuri (Snow Sapporo) 255

Z

Zen meditation 350
Zoobooks (magazine) 108
zoological gardens 175–78
zoos 175–78

The authors, Diane and Jeanne, at a local playground in Tokyo with their "research assistants," Kennedy, Kane, Michelena, Nathan, and Gabriella. After living in Japan for a combined total of seventeen years, Diane and Jeanne returned to the United States with their families. Jeanne is now an attorney in Dallas, Texas, specializing in corporate law. Diane, columnist for the *Tokyo Weekender* and author of *Design with Japanese Obi*, frequently travels to Japan from her home on the East Coast.

かいていばん・にほんこそだてべんりちょう
改訂版・日本子育て便利帳
JAPAN FOR KIDS: REVISED EDITION

2000 年 4 月21日　第 1 刷発行
2001 年 4 月20日　第 2 刷発行

著　者　　ジーン・ヒューイ／ダイアン・ウィルチャー
発行者　　野間佐和子
発行所　　講談社インターナショナル株式会社
　　　　　〒112-8652 東京都文京区音羽 1-17-14
　　　　　電話　03-3944-6493（編集部）
　　　　　　　　03-3944-6492（営業部・業務部）
　　　　　ホームページ　http://www.kodansha-intl.co.jp
印刷所　　株式会社 平河工業社
製本所　　株式会社 堅省堂

落丁本・乱丁本は、小社業務部宛にお送りください。送料小社負担にてお取替えします。なお、この本についてのお問い合わせは、編集部宛にお願いいたします。
本書の無断複写（コピー）、転載は著作権法の例外を除き、禁じられています。

定価はカバーに表示してあります。

**Websites**

*One of the most important things to have while living in Japan is information, not only information about the world, but about those things that are of special concern to parents.*

*The Internet is a great resource for parents. Just turn on your computer and tap into the Information Superhighway for a wealth of data on family development, medical issues, or anything else you need to know. Below are a few general websites to get you started.*

## GENERAL

- **Family Internet—Directory Online (FIDO)** 🖥 <www.clark.net/pub/soh/fido> provides links to more than five hundred family-friendly sites. Free online newsletter.

- **International Schools in Japan** 🖥 <www.jmarket.com/isij> provides a directory of schools from elementary through high school, with links.

- **J Guide** 🖥 <fuji.stanford.edu/jguide> is a very informative site with great links to hundreds of Japan-related sites.

- **Japan Travel Updates** 🖥 <www.jnto.go.jp> provides maps, city guides, hotel information, and photos, all in English, to help you explore Japan.

- **NTT TownPage** 🖥 <english.itp.ne.jp> is a handy electronic telephone directory in English.

- **Rob's Japan FAQ** 🖥 <homepages.go.com/~tenjin97/iriguchi.html> offers helpful, practical tips for people moving or traveling to Japan.

- **Virtual Relocation** 🖥 <www.virtualrelocation.com/International/Asia/Japan> is the most comprehensive website we have found, with tons of information on moving, education, culture, and anything else you need to know.

## PARENTING & FAMILY LIFE

- **The Cybermom** 🖥 <www.thecybermom.com> includes helpful tips, articles on parenting, and bulletin boards, where mothers from all over the world weigh in on parenting issues.

- **Moms Online** 🖥 <www.momsonline.com> puts out a free weekly newsletter that covers a variety of topics, from kids' crafts to toilet training. There is also a list of helpful hints by moms for moms.

- **The Nature of Nurturing** 🖥 <seldomfar.com/nurturing/> provides well-selected articles, a parents' forum, and other links that give support and encouragement to parents.

- **Parent Soup** 🖥 <www.parentsoup.com> is a large site with chats, message boards, articles, and advice on many parenting topics.